# THE
# SPITFIRE
## STORY

# THE
# SPITFIRE
## STORY

## ALFRED PRICE
*Foreword by*
*JEFFREY QUILL*

## ARMS AND ARMOUR PRESS
LONDON   NEW YORK   SYDNEY

First published in 1982
by Jane's Publishing Company Limited, London.
This edition published 1986 by Arms and Armour Press Limited,
2–6 Hampstead High Street, London NW3 1QQ.

Distributed in the USA by Sterling Publishing Co. Inc.,
2 Park Avenue, New York, N.Y. 10016.

Distributed in Australia by
Capricorn Link (Australia) Pty. Ltd., P.O. Box 665,
Lane Cove, New South Wales 2066, Australia.

Designed by Michael Carter.

ISBN 0-85368-861-3

Printed and bound in Great Britain.

**1.** PS 925, a late production Spitfire PR 19, pictured after the war wearing the 6C code markings of the Photographic Reconnaissance Development Unit. *(RAF Museum)*

**2.** Spitfire VBs of No 92 Squadron, photographed early in 1941. *(Charles Brown, copyright RAF Museum)*

# CONTENTS

# FOREWORD

Alfred Price has produced an extensively researched and very readable book about the Spitfire. The treatment and the general lay-out is such that it provides a coherent narrative if read from beginning to end, or if required primarily for reference purposes the particular point of interest to the reader can be identified very easily.

The Spitfire was an extraordinary aeroplane which was designed and produced and reached its peak of activity at an extraordinary period in the history of our country and of the world. Its full history is therefore highly complex and inevitably means different things to different people. Moreover, the Spitfire became an international legend within its own service lifetime and so its history has been susceptible to some distortions by the impact of legend.

It has also generated a substantial literature during the past 40 years or so, written at different times and from many differing points of view. It is certain that no single book can tell the whole story in all its many ramifications, nor reflect all its manifold facets but Alfred Price, an experienced aviation historian and researcher, has traced the main history of the aeroplane and its developments from first inception to the final fulfilment of its military potential in a clear, logical and well documented way. Thus it is a valuable historical work, as befits a Fellow of the Royal Historical Society.

Jeffrey Quill

# PREFACE

Many books have been written about my father's creation, the Spitfire. So, when Alfred Price invited me to write a contribution to this book my first reaction was 'Oh Hell, not another Spitfire saga!' However, on reading the manuscript it soon became apparent that here was something different and rather special. This work tells the story of the Spitfire in far greater detail and depth than anything previously attempted. The narrative runs from the conception of the new fighter by my father and his brilliant design team, then through her birth, production, and the uniquely far-reaching development of the basic design carried out under my father's successor, Joe Smith.

Much material never before in print, and previously not considered to exist, is included thanks to the author's known reputation for unearthing long-hidden documents. For me a particularly interesting example of this were the memoranda on the Spitfire exchanged between my father and his Chief Assistant, Harold Payn, in 1935. I had no idea that they had survived. I feel that they illustrate so well my father's technical capabilities and his complete grasp and understanding of every aspect of the design of the embryo Spitfire; they also illustrate his readiness to listen to sound comment and criticism and his great urge to seek the simple solution to problems. Thus, from the memoranda we learn that, had the Air Ministry insisted on the Spitfire having an improved view for the pilot, his first approach would have been to examine the possibility of simply raising the pilot up a little in his seat rather than to immediately initiate complex design changes.

Although I was only 16 when my father died (at the age of 42) in 1937, I can still well remember the importance he placed on another quality, namely 'common sense'. He used frequently to impress upon me how vital he considered this attribute to be. Good technical know-how but without common sense usually only resulted in mediocrity — that was his theme, which I soon learnt by heart!

In the wartime film about my father, 'The First of the Few', he was portrayed as something of a dreamy romantic, who, for example, gained inspiration for his high speed designs from watching seagulls in flight. I had always been rather dubious about this as it was out of character with the man I remembered. One day recently, therefore, I asked Jeffrey Quill, who came to know my father very well during the last 18 months of his life, if there was any truth in this portrayal. 'Look', he replied, 'your father was a hard-headed, highly practical man. In my opinion, the last thing he would have done when he had some design problem would have been to hang around watching bloody seagulls!' So much for that story!

All who wish to learn more about the little fighter aircraft that has, in her country of birth, such a unique and special place in public esteem and has in fact become a legend, must not fail to read *The Spitfire Story*, the latest of Alfred Price's many aviation books.

Dr Gordon Mitchell

*For Noni*

# INTRODUCTION

My aim in writing this book has been to tell the story of the evolution and development of the Spitfire as fully as possible. No single book could cover every last minute detail of that story, but this one will take the reader much more deeply into it than anything previously written. To cover the story within a book of reasonable length, however, I have had to stick rigidly to my theme and omit related subjects not strictly part of this story. I have, therefore, not tried to cover the development of the Seafire naval fighter, nor the Spiteful and Seafang designs which were intended to succeed, respectively, the Spitfire and Seafire in production. Similarly, I have not attempted any detailed analysis of the serial numbers of production aircraft. The story runs from the lead-in designs to the prototype Spitfire, then through its various versions from the Mark I to the Mark 24; the sole omissions are the Marks 15 and 17, which were allocated to the Seafire.

Throughout this book I have depended almost entirely on figures from Royal Air Force trials reports, which relate to individual Spitfires whose modification state and take-off weights were specified. Unless otherwise stated the aircraft were carrying their full service equipment, guns and ammunition (or cameras in the case of unarmed reconnaissance versions), and had all internal fuel tanks full. Unless otherwise stated all speeds are given in miles per hour (true)—as distinct from miles per hour (indicated)—tankages are in Imperial gallons and distances in statute miles.

Previously published figures on the performance of the Spitfire have usually been given without any clear indication of the modification state of the aircraft at the time they were taken. As a result these are often misleading. Take one example: the figures usually quoted for the performance of the Spitfire I at the time of the Battle of Britain state its maximum speed was 362 mph at 18,500 feet and it had a service ceiling of 31,900 feet. Now these figures do indeed refer to a Mark I Spitfire: the first production aircraft K9787, recorded during its service trials at Martlesham Heath in August 1938. At that time the aircraft carried no armour, laminated glass windscreen, IFF equipment or gun heating ducting and it was fitted with a simple wooden two-bladed propeller; fully loaded its take-off weight was 5,819 pounds. In fact the fully equipped Spitfire Is being delivered at the time of the Battle of Britain had a loaded weight of about 6,155 pounds, their maximum speed was about 350 mph and the service ceiling with the more efficient constant speed propeller was over 33,000 feet. Similarly misleading figures

have been published previously about almost every other version of the Spitfire, and it is hoped that those given in this volume will at last set the record straight.

In putting together this story I am particularly grateful for the help and kindness I received from Jeffrey Quill, Ernie Mansbridge and the late Beverley Shenstone, on whose reminiscences and documents I have leaned heavily. Mrs H. Payn, Mrs G. Pickering and Mrs W. Scales kindly gave me access to their late husbands' papers. Air Marshal Sir Humphrey Edwardes Jones, Air Commodore George Heycock, Group Captain Hugh Wilson and Group Captain Samuel Wroath all flew the prototype Spitfire at various times and contributed valuable information. Amongst others who provided considerable assistance with other aspects of the Spitfire story were Sir Stanley Hooker, Air Chief Marshal Sir Neil Wheeler, Air Marshal Sir Geoffrey Tuttle, Lord Thomas, Air Commodore Henry Cozens, Gordon Green, Hugh Scrope, Jack Davis and Hugh Murland. I am also grateful to the following for the use of photographs and other material: Group Captain Allan Wright, Jim Oughton, Charles Cain, David Birch, Peter Arnold, Captain Keith Sissons, Air Commodore G. Cairns, Fred Jones, Wing Commander Innes Westmacott, Dick Forder, Paul Lambermont, Jerzry Cynk, Alex Vanags-Baginskis, W. B. Klepacki, J. Horsfall, C. F. Geust, Roberto Gentilli, Mrs E. Cave-Brown-Cave, Peter Arnold and John Batchelor. Several museums and libraries gave invaluable help, including the R. J. Mitchell Museum at Southampton, the Royal Air Force Museum at Hendon, the Smithsonian Institution in Washington DC, the US National Archives, the Public Archives of Canada, the Public Record Office at Kew, the Imperial War Museum, and the library of the Royal Aircraft Establishment at Farnborough.

Peter Endsleigh Castle did the art work, and he and Harry Robinson did the line drawings. As always, Alec Lumsden made a fine job of copying the photographs. Peter Arnold and Michael Stevens checked the manuscript and suggested many improvements.

Until the end of 1942 all Royal Air Force aircraft mark numbers were given in roman numerals. From 1943 until 1948 the new aircraft entering service carried arabic mark numbers while the older types retained their roman numerals. From 1948 all aircraft carried arabic mark numbers. As a convention in this book, Spitfire marks up to XVI are given in roman numerals and those of later versions are given in arabic numerals.

3

**3.** Supermarine S.6 being prepared at Calshot for the 1929 Schneider Trophy contest, by RAF and works mechanics. Reginald Mitchell is seen standing on the far right.

**4.** Ground running of the S.6B S 1595, the aircraft which won the Schneider Trophy outright for Britain in 1931 and later captured the world absolute speed record at 407 mph. On the far right, with his back to the camera, may be seen Mitchell; standing just in front of the starboard wing can be seen Trevor Westbrook, the General Manager of Vickers Supermarine.

4

# 1.

# A WEAPON IS FORGED

Reginald Joseph Mitchell was born on 20 May 1895 in the village of Talke near Stoke-on-Trent, the first of five children of schoolmaster Herbert Mitchell. Very early on he became interested in the new field of aviation and during his teens he spent much of his spare time building and flying model aircraft. In 1911, at the age of 16, he left school and was apprenticed to the Stoke engineering firm of Kerr Stuart & Co which built steam locomotives. Mitchell completed his apprenticeship there and began working in the drawing office. But his heart was in aviation and in 1916, when he was 21, he moved to a new job with the aircraft firm of Pemberton Billing Ltd at Woolston near Southampton. The company's main work was with the repair of aircraft for the Admiralty, although it did build a few to its own designs which were noted more for their originality than the length of their production runs. Shortly before the war ended the company was renamed the Supermarine Aviation Works.

Reginald Mitchell advanced rapidly in the company and in

1919, when he was 24, his talents were recognised with his appointment to the post of Chief Designer. During the years that followed Supermarine concentrated on the design and production of seaplanes and first achieved prominence in 1922 when its Sea Lion biplane flying boat won the Schneider Trophy contest by completing the circuit at an average speed of 145 mph. Three years later, in 1925, the Supermarine S.4 monoplane floatplane, an exceptionally clean design for its day, gained the World Speed Record for floatplanes at 226 mph; but during the run-up to the Schneider Trophy contest it developed wing flutter and crashed, although the pilot escaped with his life. In the same year the company's first design to gain a substantial production order appeared, the twin-engined Southampton reconnaissance flying boat; eventually 79 were built for the Royal Air Force and foreign governments.

Supermarine's small racing seaplanes still continued their run of successes. In 1927 the S.5 won the Schneider Trophy at a speed of 281 mph. During the next contest, in 1929, the new S.6 floatplane won the contest and shortly afterwards gained the World Air Speed record at 357 mph. In 1931 an S.6B won the Schneider Trophy outright for Britain, and later in the year a slightly modified aircraft of the same type took the World Air Speed record to 407 mph.

This series of racing successes brought considerable fame to

**5.** Photograph of the wind tunnel model of the Supermarine Type 224 fighter, taken in 1932. This design differed in several respects from the aircraft as it finally flew: the model had a fin extension under the fuselage, greater anhedral at the wing root than the final aircraft, a carburettor air intake above the engine and a four-bladed propeller. *(Mansbridge)*

the Supermarine company, but few orders. In the nature of things, the market for high speed racing seaplanes was extremely limited: total production of the S.4, S.5, S.6 and S.6B designs amounted to only eight aircraft. Throughout this period it was the contracts for the construction and overhaul of the Southampton flying boats that provided the company with most of its work. In 1928 Vickers (Aviation) acquired a majority shareholding in the company, though initially the take-over resulted in few changes.

This was the position in the autumn of 1931, when the Air Ministry issued Specification F.7/30 for a new fighter to replace the ageing Bristol Bulldog in the Royal Air Force squadrons. This document is important to the Spitfire story, and is reproduced in full as Appendix A. As laid down in the initial paragraph, the new fighter was to have:

i Highest possible rate of climb
ii Highest possible speed above 15,000 feet
iii Fighting view
iv Manoeuvrability
v Capability of easy and rapid production in quantity
vi Ease of maintenance.

It was to be armed with four machine guns and be able to carry four 20 pound bombs. Any approved engine of British manufacture could be used to power the new fighter.

When F.7/30 was issued the nation was in the middle of a slump and times were hard for the British aircraft industry. There was intense competition amongst companies to produce a fighter to secure what promised to be lucrative orders from the Royal Air Force and (hopefully) foreign governments. It is a measure of the degree of latitude permitted by the specification that, during the next three years, no fewer than eight

**6.** The Supermarine Type 224 pictured on the hard standing on the River Itchen side of the factory at Woolston early in 1934, during engine running trials prior to the first flight. The corrugated leading edge of the wing, covering the steam condenser, is clearly seen. *(Shenstone)*

designs of widely differing configurations were built to F.7/30. Five were biplanes: the Bristol 123, the Hawker PV 3, the Westland PV 4, the Blackburn F.7/30 and the Gloster SS 37. The other three were monoplanes: the Bristol 133, the Vickers Jockey and the Supermarine Type 224.

Supermarine's entry to the competition, the Type 224, was a low-winged monoplane of all-metal construction—a considerable novelty at that time. Like the Bristol 123, the Hawker PV 3, the Westland PV 4 and the Blackburn submissions, the Type 224 was to be powered by the 660 horsepower Rolls-Royce Goshawk engine which was the most powerful available for the purpose. The Goshawk was designed to work with the newly developed evaporative cooling system, which promised a much cleaner aerodynamic design than was possible with the older system of external radiators to dissipate the heat from the engine coolant. With evaporative cooling the water coolant was pumped through the water jacket around the engine under pressure, so that although the coolant temperature was higher than the normal boiling point of water steam did not form. As the water emerged from the engine it was depressurised and steam immediately formed. This steam was then piped through to a condenser fitted in the leading edge of the wing, where it condensed back into water and ran to a collector tank before being pumped back to the engine.

The Supermarine design was the only monoplane to use the evaporatively cooled Goshawk. In its case the steam condenser ran along almost the entire leading edge of the wing; and when the steam condensed the water trickled down into collector tanks fitted at the top of the fairings of the fixed undercarriage. To increase the rate of heat dissipation, the outer skinning of the leading edge of the wing was corrugated.

Compared with what was to follow, the Type 224 was not a very refined design, either structurally or aerodynamically. Ernie Mansbridge was one of those who worked with Mitchell in designing the fighter; he told the author: 'We were a bit over-cautious with the wing and made it thicker than it need have been. We were still very concerned about possible flutter,

**7.** Front view of the Type 224, running its engine at Eastleigh at about the time of its maiden flight, showing the exhaust ducting which carried the fumes forwards into a Y-shaped pipe under the nose, then down to an outlet under the forward fuselage. The wheel fairings housed the collector tanks for the condensed coolant liquid and also, at the top of the insides of the legs, two of the four machine guns; the other two machine guns were mounted along the sides of the fuselage. *(Shenstone)*

**8.** Close up of the nose of the Type 224, after the early-type exhaust ducting had been removed and individual exhaust ducts fitted. Now air for the oil cooler entered via the intake just below and behind the propeller, and exhausted through louvres on each side of the fuselage just above the leading edge of the wing. The cuffs at the wing leading edge near the wing root carried ram air to the engine carburettor. Initially it was planned that the new fighter to Specification F.37/34 would have similar carburettor air intakes and oil cooling. *(Shenstone)*

having encountered that with the S.4 seaplane. With the S.5 and S.6 we had braced wings, which made things easier. But the Type 224 was to be an unbraced monoplane, and there were not many of those about at the time.'

The Type 224 made its first flight in February 1934 and soon revealed a fundamental problem in using evaporative cooling in a low-winged monoplane design. All the other aircraft fitted with the Goshawk had been biplanes, with the steam condenser fitted into the upper wing; in this case gravity carried the water from the condenser to the collector tank and from there to the engine. But in the case of a low-winged monoplane such as the Type 224, the condensed steam was collected in tanks at the top of the undercarriage 'trousers'; from there it had to be pumped up to the header tank at the front of the engine. Since the water temperature was just below boiling point any slight decrease in pressure—as for example at the low-pressure side of a pump—could cause it to turn back into steam. If this happened the pump would cease working and the engine would overheat. And that was what began to happen with disconcerting frequency during the flights of the Type 224.

The pilots who flew the Type 224 all remember clearly the problem with engine overheating. Flight Lieutenant (later Group Captain) Hugh Wilson told the author: 'The engine used to overheat almost all the time. We were told that when the red

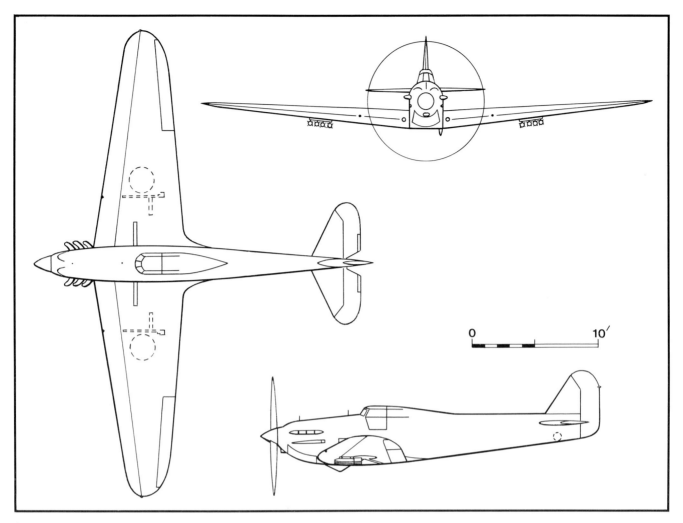

Supermarine Drawing No 300000 Sheet 2 depicted the improved Type 224 described in the firm's Specification No 425 issued in July 1934. The small triangular fairing beneath and to port of the rear of the engine housed the collector tank for the engine coolant water after it had condensed from steam. As in the case of the Type 224, the carburettor air intakes were positioned in the wing leading edges and the oil cooler intake was immediately below and behind the propeller boss.

light came on in the cockpit the engine was overheating. But the trouble was that just about every time you took off the red light did come on—it seemed it was always overheating!' Jeffrey Quill tried out the Type 224 later in its career but the problem still remained: 'The evaporative cooling system was a real pain in the backside, with those red lights flashing on all the time. I once made a jocular remark to Mitchell about the system. I said that with the red lights flashing on all over the place, one had to be a plumber to understand what was going on. He didn't say anything, he just looked very sour. He was rather sensitive about that aeroplane and obviously I had trodden on his toes.'

Even if there was no steam blockage at the pump the Type 224's Goshawk was liable to overheat during a rapid climb to altitude—an important function for an interceptor fighter. Ernie Mansbridge recalls watching the test flights Mutt Summers made in the new fighter from Eastleigh: 'We always knew when he got to 15,000 feet because a couple of bursts of steam would emerge from the wing tips. The climb was made at full power and relatively low airspeed, and when it reached that altitude the condenser was full and steam would start to trail back from the relief valves in the wing tips. Once that happened the pilot had to level off to give the engine time to cool down a

little, before resuming the climb.' And on the ground the Type 224 also made enemies, as many a mechanic learned the folly of leaning against the leading edge of the wing before it had cooled down after a flight.

All of these failings might just have been acceptable, had the Type 224 had a performance greatly superior to that of its competitors. But it did not. The fighter had a top speed of only 238 mph and took eight minutes to climb to 15,000 feet. The winner of the F.7/30 competition was the far more robust and nimble Gloster SS37, a radial-engined biplane of conventional design developed from the Gauntlet, which was to go into service with the Royal Air Force as the Gladiator. The SS 37 had a maximum speed of 242 mph, which was greater than that of any of the competing monoplanes except the Bristol 133. In the rate-of-climb the Gloster fighter was able to demonstrate the clear superiority of the biplane in this respect: it reached 15,000 feet in 6½ minutes, 1½ minutes earlier than the Type 224.

From the logbook of George Pickering, one of the test pilots at Supermarine who flew it, we know the Type 224 was given the name 'Spitfire' some time before July 1935. After the service trials at Martlesham Heath the sole prototype went to Farnborough where several pilots tried their hand with it; it ended its days in mid-1937 as a ground firing target on the range at Orfordness. In the meantime, however, the Supermarine design team was to show that it could produce something far better to go with the evocative name.

In the summer of 1934, even as the Type 224 was undergoing its trials at Martlesham, Supermarine had opened discussions with the Air Ministry regarding an improved design with a

Some of the men responsible for the Spitfire:
**9.** From left to right: Captain J. 'Mutt' Summers, who took the prototype on her maiden flight; Major Harold Payn, Assistant Chief Designer; Reginald Mitchell, Chief Designer; S. Scott-Hall, Air Ministry Resident Technical Officer; Jeffrey Quill, who later became the firm's Chief Test Pilot. *(Flight)*

**10.** Joseph Smith, the Chief Draughtsman during the design of the Spitfire, led the design team during the development phase of the aircraft after Mitchell's death.

**11.** Alan Clifton, head of the Technical Office. *(Shenstone)*

**12.** Beverley Shenstone worked on the aerodynamics of the new fighter. *(Shenstone)*

10, 11

12

better performance. The new aircraft, designated the Type 300, was to be based on the Type 224. But by cleaning up the design a little, fitting a retractable undercarriage, getting rid of the draggy corrugated wing leading edge and lopping more than 6 feet off the wing span, it was estimated that the fighter's speed could be increased by 30 mph to 265 mph using the same Goshawk engine. Towards the end of July 1934 this proposal was submitted to the Air Ministry as the Supermarine Specification 425a*.

At this time aircraft design depended largely on what the chief designer and his team thought 'looked right'. On Mitchell's way of doing things his Chief Draughtsman, Joe Smith, later wrote:

> He was an inveterate drawer on drawings, particularly general arrangements. He would modify the lines of an aircraft with the softest pencil he could find, and then re-modify over the top with progressively thicker lines, until one would finally be faced with a new outline of lines about three-sixteenths of an inch thick. But the results were always worth while, and the centre of the line was usually accepted when the thing was re-drawn.

The Air Ministry was lukewarm towards the new proposal, which offered a performance little better than other fighter
*Given in full in Appendix B.

This projected development, depicted on Supermarine Drawing No 300000 Sheet 11 issued in the autumn of 1934, shows the final derivative powered by the Goshawk engine but with a fully faired cockpit and thinner wing.

designs then on offer. Mitchell was not put off by this rejection, however, and he and his team continued work on further refinement of the Type 300 design. By the early autumn this was being offered as a fighter smaller still with a wing span of 37 ft 1 in, a somewhat thinner wing, a faired cockpit and stressed skin construction. Still the engine was to be an evaporatively cooled Goshawk but the top speed would be around the 280 mph mark. With a better engine the maximum speed would be higher still and there was a suggestion that the fighter should be fitted with a Napier Dagger then developing 700 horsepower, with the prospect of more than 800 later. During a meeting of the board of Vickers (Aviation) Ltd on 6 November 1934 this idea was turned down in favour of an even better engine now in the offing: the Rolls-Royce PV XII, later to be named the Merlin. At this time the PV XII was suffering its share of teething troubles and was not yet ready for production. But during the previous July it had passed its 100 hour type test, developing 625 horsepower for take-off and 790 horsepower at 12,000 feet. The target output for the new 27 litre engine was 1,000 horsepower.

During November 1934 Mitchell received permission to proceed with the design of a PV XII-powered Type 300 fighter. The man behind the decision was Sir Robert McLean, the managing director of Vickers (Aviation) Ltd. At his instigation the board of the company provided the finance for Mitchell to begin detailed design work as a private venture, pending an Air Ministry contract. Thus for a short while design work—but not metal cutting—proceeded under private funding.

The decision to combine the revised Type 300 airframe with the PV XII engine drew immediate interest from the Air Minis-

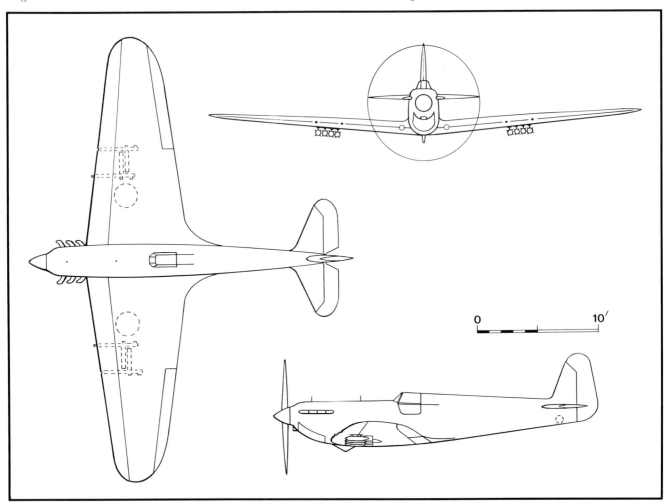

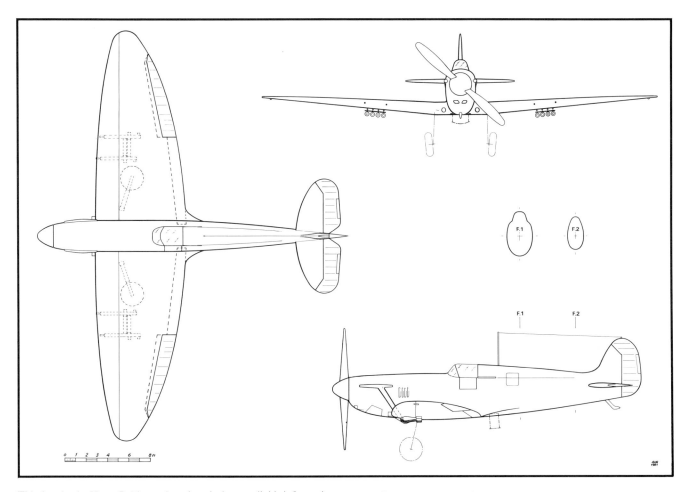

This drawing by Harry Robinson, based on the best available information from contemporary drawings and descriptions, and interviews with some of those involved with the design of the aircraft, shows the shape of Mitchell's new fighter in January 1935 at the time Air Ministry Specification F.37/34 was issued. Although in most respects it was the same as the prototype in the form it later flew, there were some significant differences: the Rolls-Royce PV XII engine (later named 'Merlin') featured evaporative cooling using the wing leading edge as a condenser and was to have a triangular sump behind and beneath the engine and a retractable auxiliary radiator behind the cockpit; the carburettor air intakes were to be in the wing leading edges; the engine exhaust gasses were to be ducted down the side of the fuselage and vented below the wing leading edge; the oil cooler air was to be drawn in through ducts in front of the engine, and vented through four louvres on either side of the fuselage behind the engine; the canopy was to be fitted more closely around the pilot and there was to be no glazing aft of the cockpit; the fuselage was to have been shorter, the tailplane lower, the dihedral angle less and the ailerons of different shape than on the final aircraft, and it was to have been armed with only four machine guns but able to carry eight 20-pound bombs.

try, however. On 1 December 1934 contract AM 361140/34 was issued, providing £10,000 for the construction of a prototype fighter to Mitchell's 'improved F.7/30' design. The new aircraft was to be ready in October 1935.

Several previous accounts have suggested that the new fighter was throughout a private venture. This is not borne out by the evidence of documents written at the time. In fact the Type 300 with the PV XII engine was a private venture for less than a month, ending with the issue of the Air Ministry contract on 1 December. Whether a particular venture was private or government depended, essentially, on whose money was at risk: if the firm's capital was at stake it was a private venture; if the government put up the risk capital it was a government venture. The aircraft in Specification 425, and the early improvements on it, had indeed been drawn up at the com-

pany's expense; but the expense was not large and no constructional work had yet been started on the new fighter.

The contract for the new Supermarine Type 300 fighter was formalised on 3 January 1935 and a new Air Ministry specification, F.37/34, was written around Mitchell's improved design. The specification* was in fact a short addendum to F.7/30 and permitted little the former did not. Contrary to what some accounts have stated, F.37/34 set no performance targets for the new fighter. The latter was to be armed with four machine guns and, in spite of the problems it raised for the Type 224, the system of evaporative cooling for the engine was to be retained.

The larger PV XII engine weighed about one-third more than the Goshawk. So to compensate for the forward shift of the centre of gravity the sweep-back of the leading edge of the wing was reduced. From there it was a short step to embody the elliptical wing which would be the most distinctive recognition feature of the new fighter. On the selection of this shape the late Beverley Shenstone, the aerodynamicist on Mitchell's team, told the author:

The elliptical wing was decided upon quite early on. Aerodynamically it was the best for our purpose because the induced drag, that caused in producing lift, was lowest when this shape was used: the ellipse was an ideal shape, theoretically a perfection. There were other advantages so far as we were concerned. To reduce drag we wanted the lowest possible wing thickness-to-chord ratio, consistent with the necessary strength. But near the root the wing had to be thick enough to accommodate the retracted undercarriage

*Reproduced in full at Appendix C

**13.** The Heinkel 70 transport, an extremely clean design which first flew in 1932, was used as the criterion for aerodynamic smoothness for the Spitfire. But the German aircraft's eliptical wing and tail shapes did not, as some accounts have stated, influence the choice of this shape for the wings and tail of the British fighter. *(Flight)*

and the guns; so to achieve a good thickness-to-chord ratio we wanted the wing to have a wide chord near the root. A straight-tapered wing starts to reduce in chord from the moment it leaves the root; an elliptical wing, on the other hand, tapers only very slowly at first then progressively more rapidly towards the tip. Mitchell was an intensely practical man and he liked practical solutions to problems. I remember once discussing the wing shape with him and he said joking-ly: 'I don't give a bugger whether it's elliptical or not, so long as it covers the guns!' The ellipse was simply the shape that allowed us the thinnest possible wing with sufficient room inside to carry the necessary structure and the things we wanted to cram in. And it looked nice.

The Type 224 had had a thick wing section and we wanted to improve on that. The NACA 2200 series aerofoil section was just right and we varied the thickness-to-chord ratio to fit our own requirements: we ended up with 13 per cent at the chord and 6 per cent at the tip, the thinnest we thought we could get away with. Joe Smith, in charge of structural design, deserves all credit for producing a wing that was both strong enough and stiff enough within the severe volumetric constraints.

It has been suggested that we at Supermarine had cribbed the elliptical wing shape from that of the German Heinkel 70 transport. That was not so. The elliptical wing shape had been used on other aircraft and its advantages were well known. Our wing was much thinner than that of the Heinkel and had a quite different section. In any case, it would have been simply asking for trouble to have copied a wing shape from an aircraft designed for an entirely different purpose. The Heinkel 70 did have an influence on the Spitfire, but in a rather different way. I had seen the German aircraft at the Paris Aero Show and been greatly impressed by the smooth-ness of its skin. There was not a rivet head to be seen. I ran my hand over the surface and it was so smooth that I thought it might be constructed of wood. I was so impressed that I wrote to Ernst Heinkel, without Mitchell's knowledge, and asked how he had done it; was the aircraft skin made of metal or wood? I received a very nice letter back from the German firm, saying that the skinning was of metal with the rivets countersunk and very carefully filled before the applica-tion of several layers of paint. When we got down to the detailed design of the F.37/34 I referred to the Heinkel 70 quite a lot during our discussions. I used it as a criterion for aerodynamic smoothness and said that if the Germans could do it, so, with a little more effort, could we. Of course, the Heinkel's several layers of paint added greatly to the weight; we had to do the best we could without resorting to that. As in the case of any aircraft, Mitchell's design team was faced with a mass of conflicting requirements which had somehow to be reconciled to produce the most effective compromise. The structure, for example, had to be as light as possible yet be strong and rigid enough for the aircraft to be able to manoeuvre to set limits without breaking up. For the F.37/34 Mitchell and his team brought considerable ingenuity to bear on this problem and its solution had a major bearing on the efficiency of the resultant fighter. The most critical part of the structure was the thin wing, which had to be very stiff if flutter problems were to be avoided at high speeds. To give the neccessary strength, each of the main spars was built up from two square-section tubular booms each constructed from five concentric sections, mounted one above the other and connected by a thick spar web. Stiffened by ribs at regular intervals, the thickly skinned leading edge of the wing combined with the main spar to form a very strong and rigid D-shaped torsion box that ran the full length of the wing. This torsion box was to carry most of the wing loads and, at the same time, serve as the steam condenser for the evaporative cooling system. The four machine guns were to be installed in the wing at mid-span and fire forwards through tubes passing through the steam condenser. The clever use of the D-shaped torsion box made it possible to build a very thin and light wing of great strength. That wing—thinner and lighter than that of any contemporary fighter—was to be one of the secrets of the success of the F.37/34.

A further significant design feature of the wing of the new fighter was that it featured 'washout', unusual at that time. In the flying attitude the incidence was to be +2° at the root and −½° at the tip, giving a twist along the length of the wing of 2½°. This feature, not evident to the casual observer, was to remain with the aircraft throughout its long development life and contributed to its success as a fighter. It meant that during tight turns in combat close to the aircraft's limits the wing root would stall before the tip, causing a judder which gave ample warning of the approach of a full stall while still allowing the pilot adequate aileron control. Many famous pilots have singled out this feature of Mitchell's fighter for particular praise.

The undercarriage legs were attached to the rear of the main spar and retracted outwards and slightly backwards, to fold into recesses cut in the non-load-carrying part of the wing behind the torsion box. The narrow track for the undercarriage was accepted because it reduced the bending loads on the main spar during landings, compared with those if the track were wider.

To overcome some of the problems of the evaporative cooling system, the F.37/34 fighter was to have a retractable auxiliary radiator fitted behind the cockpit; this could be lowered for take-off and in the climb, and raised in cruising or high speed flight when it was hoped the evaporative cooling would be sufficient.

Apart from the retractable radiator, the new fighter was to have no air intakes on the underside of the fuselage or wings. Like the earlier Supermarine fighter designs the carburettor air intakes were to be in the wing roots; and the oil cooler intake was to be half way down the nose with outlets on either side of the fuselage immediately behind the engine. Because the specification called for an aircraft that would be suitable for night fighting, the hot exhaust gases were to be ducted to the underside of the fuselage and vented from there.

One frequently repeated myth has it that the airframe of the F.37/34 fighter was 'developed' from Mitchell's line of racing seaplanes. This is simply not true. Certainly Mitchell learned a great deal about high speed flight from his work designing seaplanes for the Schneider Trophy; but it is quite a different thing to say that the new fighter was developed from these. In

Method of construction of the wing spar booms of the F.37/34, each made up of five square concentric tubes which fitted into each other. Two such booms, joined by a web, formed the main spar of each wing. The main spar, with the thickly skinned leading edge of the wing forward of it, combined to form a D-shaped torsion box of considerable strength which bore the main loads on the wing. Initially this torsion box was to have also served as the steam condenser for the evaporative cooling system.

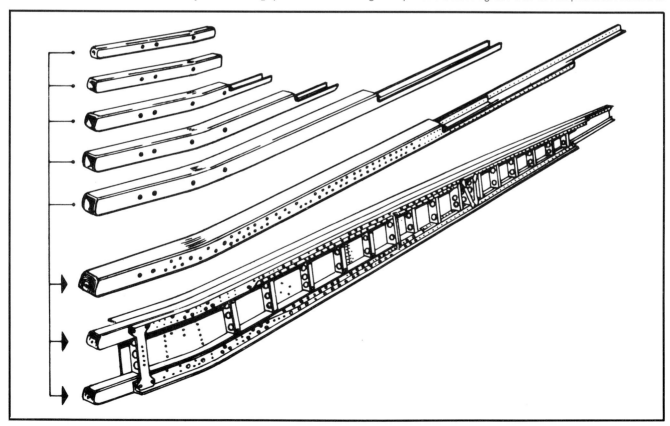

fact there was not a single component of any significance in the new fighter that bore any close resemblance with its counterpart in a racing seaplane.

Probably the work for the Schneider Trophy had a greater direct effect on the engine of the new fighter than its airframe. The sodium cooled valves and sparking plugs able to operate under high boost conditions, both fitted to the Merlin, were the outcome of work done at Rolls-Royce for the contest. Also the contest produced many useful lessons in the design of propellers for high speed aircraft.

During the early months of 1935 the detailed design of the F.37/34 advanced rapidly. Amongst the few documents which have survived from this important period in the fighter's evolution are two memoranda written in March 1935 concerning its shape; one was from Mitchell's Chief Assistant, Major Harold Payn, to Mitchell; the other was Mitchell's reply. Payn was concerned that the new fighter might not be manoeuvrable enough:

> The high C.G. position in relation to the equivalent mean chord is, in my opinion, a very serious adverse feature indeed of this machine which will have to compete in aerobatics as a fighter. I feel sure that in normal flight the rolling moments produced by the present amount of dihedral, and by the disposition of the present finnage will be insufficient to counter the anti-pendulum effect of the relatively high C.G. It is anticipated that with the present dihedral the machine will be laterally unstable. For ordinary conditions of flight below the stall, a further increase of at least 2 degrees dihedral is believed to be necessary.

Payn went on to say that he felt certain the additional dihedral (in addition to the 4½ degrees then being considered) would also moderate the flatness of the aircraft in the spin and so make recovery easier. He then commented on the new fighter's ailerons:

> The manoeuvrability of any monoplane can never reach the high order attainable in a biplane having the same landing speed if both types are fitted with normal ailerons. In this machine the ailerons are still considered too small, and the rate of roll (which entirely limits the manoeuvrability in ordinary flight) will be anything but snappy. I am not at all certain that a high order of manoeuvrability is absolutely essential for this class, but I do fear that this feature will be criticised. The ailerons are certain to be fairly heavy at top speed chiefly due to the effect of 'washout' of the wings, whereby the ailerons derive practically no balance effect from the shielded 'Frise' noses.

The view over the nose of the new fighter was a further cause for concern:

> The view is fair and quite good enough for ordinary flying, but for a fighter with fixed guns at the present incidence a portion of the important conical zone whose axis lies in the line of flight through the line of sight, is blanked by the high engine and the top run of the fuselage to the cockpit. I am of the opinion that at least three more degrees clear view downwards iş necessary over the nose as an absolute minimum.

In his reply, written a week later, Mitchell went through Payn's comments in turn. Concerning the position of the centre of gravity he said:

> The C.G. position is always over the chord in low wing monoplanes, and even though this is agreed to be an undesirable feature, it is very difficult to see how it can be avoided in this type of aircraft without seriously impairing other features. An increase of 1½ degrees in the dihedral angle of the machine has already been carried out as a result of discussion and comparison of statistics from Weybridge machines. There is no evidence to shew that the machine as at present laid down with increased dihedral will not be perfectly satisfactory on lateral control and stability.

The 1½ degree increase in dihedral angle mentioned by Mitchell, which appears to have been incorporated in the design after Payn wrote his letter, brought the total dihedral angle up to 6 degrees. This was to be the dihedral on the first prototype and subsequent production aircraft. Mitchell then went on to discuss the question of altering the ailerons:

> It is agreed that the manoeuvrability of a monoplane is likely to be worse than its equivalent biplane, but we hope in this design to get it very nearly as good, as the span of the aircraft is very little more than that of a biplane conforming to the same specification. I entirely disagree with the suggestion that the ailerons are too small. It is stated that the ailerons are certain to be fairly heavy at top speed, and yet it is suggested that they should be increased in size, which is obviously the easiest way to make them heavier still. We have been through the experience of large chord ailerons too many times to be caught again. Even on our present fighter [the Type 224] we found that by practically halving the chord of the ailerons we got a very much lighter control which is as, if not more, effective. With very high speed aircraft it is obviously essential that the aileron controls must be particularly light. The only way of attaining this is to have them with a very narrow chord and well balanced. To attain very light operating loads on large chord ailerons is very dangerous, as a very high degree of balance has to be obtained, and this leads to the possibility of over-balance being obtained in the dive due to small deflections. I believe this is the cause of several accidents involving ailerons. Furthermore, the general manoeuvrability of the machine is not affected by the size of the ailerons, but rather by the ease with which aileron is applied. This is obviously the case since full aileron movement is never used in ordinary manoeuvring. The aileron volume on this machine is only a little less than that on the present F.7/30 fighter, and is very considerably higher than that used on the Heinkel machine which is considered to be an efficient aircraft of the same type. If the ailerons are too small, I consider it is likely to shew up at very low speeds near the stall. This condition has not been criticised. It is considered that there is no evidence to warrant any modification of the aileron design.

Mitchell's reference to the 'Heinkel machine', the He 70, is interesting and illustrates once again the influence of this design on the new British fighter (though not on the selection of the elliptical wing). He then went on to answer the criticism of the poor visibility forwards and downwards from the new fighter:

> It is agreed that the view can be improved, but only with the sacrifice of performance by increasing the size of the body. In the design of this aircraft the performance has been considered of paramount importance, and various sacrifices of other requirements have been made to obtain this object. It is considered desirable not to depart from this policy. If at a later date it is thought necessary to improve the view at the nose, this is best done by merely raising the pilot, and can easily be done at a later date if considered essential.

The relatively poor view over the engine was one which Spitfire pilots would have to live with throughout its long career; and few of those who took it into action would have wished to sacrifice performance to improve the view. One important conclusion that can be drawn from the reply is that Reginald Mitchell was certainly no 'figure-head' leader of the design team; he had a firm grasp of every detail of the design of the new fighter and was fluent with the problems to be solved.

The overwhelming credit for the world-beating fighter now taking detailed shape in the drawing office at Woolston must of course go to Mitchell and his small design team, and the Rolls-Royce engineers at Derby struggling to perfect their new engine. But there were others, working for the government, who deserve a share of the credit also.

Specification F.37/34 had called for a fighter armed with four machine guns, but it was becoming clear that this was insufficient fire power to destroy the fast all-metal bombers then going into service in several air forces. Squadron Leader Ralph Sorley was in charge of the Operational Requirements section at the Air Ministry at the time the F.37/34 was taking shape. Later he wrote:

Like so many others, I had spent many years trying to hit targets with one, two or even four machine guns with, I confess, singularly poor results. Others were so much better but I estimated that, if one could hold the sight on for longer than two seconds, that was better than average. We were now going to have to hold it on at appreciably higher speeds so the average might even be less than two seconds. The two- or four-gunned biplanes had been equipped with Vickers guns in general, the residue of vast stocks left over from the 1914-18 war. By 1934 a new Browning gun was at last being tested in Britain which offered a higher rate of fire. After much arithmetic and burning of midnight oil, I reached the answer of eight guns as being the number required to give a lethal dose in two seconds of fire. I reckoned that the bomber's speed would probably be such as to allow the pursuing fighter only one chance of attack, so it must be destroyed in that vital two-second burst.

Sorley's arguments convinced the Deputy Chief of the Air Staff, Air Vice Marshal Edgar Ludlow-Hewit, and as a result the main 1934 fighter specification, F.5/34, called for an aircraft armed with eight machine guns. Some accounts have linked this

**14.** Squadron Leader Ralph Sorley pressed for the new Supermarine fighter to be fitted with the eight-gun armament. *(IWM)*

specification with the aircraft Mitchell was working on, but in fact there was no formal link between the two.

The specification that *did* affect the new Supermarine fighter was F.10/35*, which asked for a fighter with at least six guns though eight were desirable. Towards the end of April 1935 Sorley paid a visit to the Supermarine works to discuss with Mitchell both his new fighter and the latest Air Ministry specification. When he returned to London Sorley reported:

On Friday, 26th April 1935, I saw at Supermarines a mock-up of a fighter which they are building to Specification F.37/34. This is one got out by A.M.R.D. [the Air Member for Research and Development—Air Marshal Sir Hugh Dowding] to cover the redesign of the Supermarine F.7/30.
2. According to the 37/34 Specification it is to comply generally with the requirements of the F.7/30 Specification subject to certain concessions. As designed, it has every feature required by our latest specification 10/35 with the following differences:

|  | 37/34 | 10/35 |
|---|---|---|
| (i) Guns | 4 in wings | 6 or 8 in wings |
| (ii) Bombs | 4×20 | Nil |
| (iii) Fuel | 94 gallons = ½ hr maximum plus nearly 2 hrs at normal rpm | 66 gallons = ¼ hr maximum plus 1 hr at normal rpm |

3. Mitchell received the Air Staff requirements for the 10/35 while I was there and is naturally desirous of bringing the aircraft now building into line with this specification. He says he can include 4 additional guns without trouble or delay. (ii) and (iii) are, of course, deletions which he welcomes. The saving in fuel amounts to 273 lbs (Mitchell's estimate is 59 gallons); thus there is a big saving in weight (180 lbs even after adding the additional 4 guns).
4. [In this paragraph Sorley talked about the new Hawker fighter which later became the Hurricane.]
5. Both aircraft look to be excellent in the hands of Mitchell and Camm and I suggest that they are likely to be successes. I say this because I foresee in these two aircraft the equipment we should aim at obtaining for new squadrons and re-equipping Bulldog squadrons in 1936 *if* we commence action *now* to make this possible.

Sorley then went on to suggest that either or both of the new monoplane fighters should be ordered into production 'off the drawing board' even at the expense of the Gloster F.7/30 (which later became the Gladiator): 'I am aware that this is an unorthodox method but with the political situation as it is and the possibility of increased expansion close upon us we should take steps to produce the latest design in the shortest possible time.'

At this time Sorley's rank was only that of Squadron Leader; his position in charge of Operational Requirements meant that although he had access to the Air Staff he had little power of his own to influence events. Only by gaining the support of those who held the real power could he achieve his aims.

On 5 May Air Commodore R. H. Verney, the Director of Technical Development, commented on Sorley's letter:

1. As a matter of principle I am against asking firms to make alterations on prototypes once the decision to place the order has been given and I have had my design conference with the designer. But I realise that there are special circumstances which may make the cases of these monoplanes an exception to the rule.

*Reproduced in full in Appendix D

**15.** Believed to be the only one to survive showing the wooden mock-up of the F.37/34, this photograph was taken in 1936 in the Supermarine hangar at Hythe where Stranraer flying boats were being assembled. The mock-up, less wings, had been hoisted out of the way prior to disposal. Note the transport joint mid-way along the fuselage and the downwards ducting for the exhaust pipe as originally considered for this aircraft. *(via C. F. Andrews)*

2. As regards the Supermarine F.37/34 I agree that there should be no great difficulty in adding the four additional guns. Deleting the bombs would be a help, but I should not be in favour of reducing the tankage, as this could be done in production models if required; it is always much easier to decrease than to increase, and experience shows that as the engine power goes up we often wish to add extra tankage. Nor need the aeroplanes be flown with full tanks.

3. [This paragraph dealt with the Hawker monoplane fighter.]

4. We must realise that we have very little experience of monoplanes of this type, and difficulties in developing them are certain to have to be faced. I should be very opposed to holding back on the Gloster F.7/30 with the Perseus engine, and feel that we should press this forward as quickly as possible, as a reserve.

5. The question as to how much should be risked to save delay in putting either or both of these two monoplanes into production, if they should prove satisfactory, is a matter of policy rather beyond me. It should be realised that if the design and construction of jigs, etc, were begun there would

be a risk of serious alteration, and possibly wholesale scrapping, if changes have to be made. I would rather say that directly the aeroplanes have been flown and we know the best or the worst, as the case may be, that then would be the time for a production gamble if circumstances necessitate.

Air Marshal Dowding agreed with Verney's comments and the matter was referred to the Chief of the Air Staff, Air Chief Marshal Sir Edward Ellington. Towards the end of May Ellington's deputy, Air Vice-Marshal Christopher Courtney, wrote to Dowding conveying the official edict on the changes to be made to the new Supermarine and Hawker fighters:

In the first place I quite agree that nothing should be allowed to delay the construction and flying tests of these aeroplanes. But I think we could possibly bring these aircraft into line with the F.10/35 Specification without necessarily imposing delays.

2. Guns

As regards the Supermarine, since D.T.D. says there should be no great difficulty in adding the four additional guns, I should certainly like this done. [Then he went on to discuss the new Hawker fighter.]

3. Bombs

I imagine that the deletion of the bomb requirement from the specification will please everyone and should make things easier for the firms.

4. Petrol

I agree with you that the tankage should be left unaltered, unless it has to be cut down in order to fit in the extra guns.

5. Jigging and Tooling

I raised the question with the C.A.S. recently and the ruling was that no steps should be taken in this direction until the aircraft had actually been flight tested.

So it was that the new Supermarine fighter was brought into line with F.10/35, the armament to be '8 Vickers Mark V or Browning guns with 300 rounds of ammunition per gun.' The revised contract permitted 'Reduction of fuel to 75 gallons, though the actual tankage need not be reduced unless it is necessary to do so to provide space for the guns.' To Reginald Mitchell this was an opportunity to shed 1·6 cubic feet of volume from the engine area and he grasped at it; the prototype of the new fighter was fitted with tanks for only 75 gallons of fuel.

Jack Davis, one of the draughtsmen at Supermarine, was given the task of deciding how to fit the extra four guns into the new fighter. He told the author:

It did not take me long to work out where the guns had to go. The rib positions had all been decided so it was just a question of fitting the guns in between them. But as one went further out the wing became thinner, and the ammunition boxes had to be longer to accommodate the same 300 rounds for each gun. This meant the outer guns had to be quite a long way out. In fact, to get them into the wing, I had to design very shallow blisters to fit around them. The aerodynamics people did not like the idea but they accepted it: there was no alternative if we were to get the eight guns in without redesigning the entire wing.

In June 1935 a 1/24th scale model of the F.37/34 fighter (it was never referred to as the F.10/35, even after it had been altered to conform with this specification) underwent wind tunnel tests at Farnborough to determine its spinning characteristics. The model tested was representative of a full-scale aircraft with a span of 37 ft 1½ in, a length of 29 ft 2 in, a wing with 4½ degrees dihedral and an all up weight of 4,900 pounds. In their report on the tests Messrs R. Alston and H. Stone wrote:

In common with other modern low-wing monoplanes having a single long engine of high horse-power, the wing loading is high (22.3 lb/sq ft) and the fuselage load is widely distributed. . . . Past experience coupled with theory leads to the conclusion that such a design is fundamentally bad from a spinning point of view and requires a really good tail unit if trouble is to be avoided.

Tests with the original model, which had the tailplane set midway up the fuselage, showed it was liable to go into a fairly flat type of spin from which recovery was very slow. Tests with a revised fin and rudder of 40 per cent greater area gave only a negligible improvement, indicating that in the spin the rudder was being shielded by the tailplane. The next step was to raise the tailplane by the equivalent of 1 foot on the full sized aircraft, and this brought about a marked improvement. Mitchell was unwilling to raise the tailplane by this amount, however, so a compromise was reached: the height of the tailplane was to be 7 inches higher than the original and the fuselage was extended by 9 inches.

At the middle of 1935 the design of the F.37/34 fighter was still unsound in one important aspect: its PV XII engine was still to have evaporative cooling and this, as we have seen, could not be made to work properly on a low winged monoplane. Mitchell was reluctant to resort to the more normal forms of

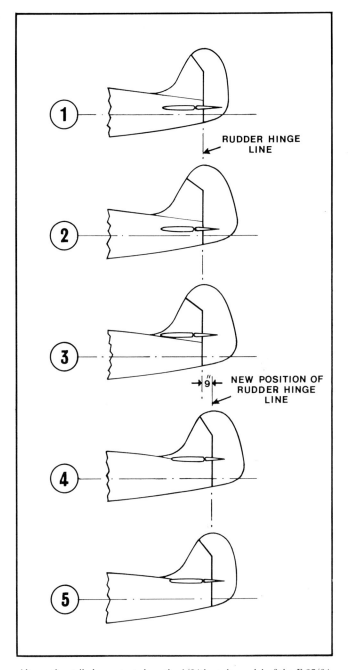

Alternative tail shapes tested on the 1/24th scale model of the F.37/34, during spinning trials in the Farnborough wind tunnel in the late spring and early summer of 1935:

1 Original shape of tail, which gave poor spin recovery characteristics.
2 Rudder area increased by 40 per cent, but gave little improvement.
3 Raising the tailplane by the equivalent of 1 foot, plus the larger rudder, gave a marked improvement to the spin recovery characteristics but Mitchell was unwilling to alter his design by so much.
4 Fuselage lengthened so that the rudder hinge line was the equivalent of 9 inches further back, the tailplane raised by the equivalent of 9 inches above the original and the enlarged rudder retained.
5 The final compromise: fuselage lengthened by the equivalent of 9 inches, tailplane raised by the equivalent of 7 inches, original rudder used.

external radiator, which would have considerably increased the drag of the new fighter. In retrospect the problem of engine cooling might seem only a trivial part of the story, but as things stood it could have led to the downfall of the fighter.

When the Merlin (as the PV XII was now named) was running at full power it produced about 12,500 centigrade heat units of excess heat each minute, the equivalent of 400 one-kilowatt electric fires running simultaneously. About 90 per cent of this heat had to be removed by the liquid cooling system, the remainder by the oil cooler.

Fortunately, at this time Fred Meredith at Farnborough had conducted some experiments which showed that a new type of ducted radiator might solve the problem. In Meredith's radiator the air entered from the front through a duct whose cross-sectional area was progressively widened, to reduce its velocity and therefore increase the pressure. The slightly compressed air then passed through the matrix of the radiator where it was heated and so expanded; then it was passed through a divergent duct at the rear which caused an increase in the velocity of the airflow. Thus the ducted radiator acted rather like a ram jet: the ram air was compressed, heated, and then expelled from the rear with increased velocity to produce thrust. The amount of thrust produced by the ducted radiator was small and only under optimum conditions would it exceed the drag. But compared with the alternative cooling systems Meredith's design was greatly superior.

**16.** Frederick Meredith, who worked at the Royal Aircraft Establishment at Farnborough, pioneered the system of ducted radiator cooling employed on the F.37/34.

The Supermarine Type 305, turret fighter version of the F.37/34, submitted to Air Ministry Specification F.9/35 in August 1935. It is interesting to note that this aircraft was to have carried its proposed armament of four Lewis or Browning guns in a streamlined barbette above the rear fuselage, remotely controlled by the gunner from his position immediately behind the pilot; had it been built, this would have been one of the first aircraft to have carried this type of armament. In the event, however, this proposal was rejected in favour of the Boulton Paul design which later became the Defiant.

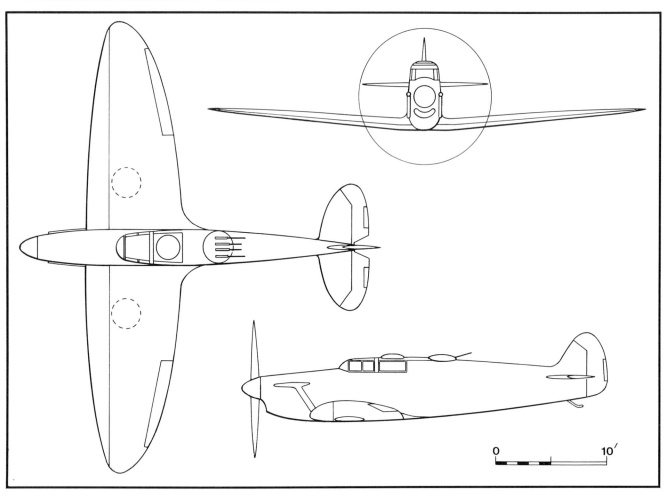

0                    10′

The efficiency of the cooling system was further improved by the use of ethylene glycol as the coolant. This had a boiling point considerably higher than that of water, which meant the radiator could be run much hotter and so the necessary heat dissipation could be accomplished with a smaller and lighter radiator holding less coolant. It was found that an ethylene glycol system could be built for between a third and a half the weight of an equivalent water cooling system.

Reginald Mitchell knew good ideas when he saw them, and enthusiastically embodied the new cooling system into his fighter. By August 1935 the design had altered in several important aspects from the F.37/34 submission at the beginning of the year, though the external appearance of the aircraft had changed relatively little. The revised design now carried eight guns instead of four, no bombs, tankage for 75 gallons of fuel instead of 94, it had a slightly longer fuselage and a raised tailplane, a wing of increased dihedral and ducted radiator in place of evaporative cooling. Work had begun to cut the metal that would transform the nice-looking design into what was hoped would be a successful aircraft.

Also during the summer of 1935 an interesting variation of the F.37/34 design issued from the Project Office at Supermarine: the Type 305 fighter, a two seater with its moveable four-gun armament controlled by a gunner, submitted to Specification F.9/35. This aircraft was to have its wings and tail almost exactly like those of the single seater, though the chin radiator and much longer cabin made it look quite different from the side. For the two-seater the armament was to be housed in a streamlined barbette, remotely controlled by the gunner from a separate sighting blister. Harold Payn worked out a scheme for the remote control of the guns of the Type 305; but the work was not taken very far before the Supermarine design was rejected in favour of one by Boulton and Paul which later became the Defiant. In retrospect it is clear that the failure to gain the F.9/35 contract was no great loss; war would show that the turret fighter was not a viable concept and Mitchell and his team were well out of it.

During the late summer and autumn the F.37/34 fighter began to take shape slowly in one of the erecting shops at Woolston. At this time a few minor alterations were made to the aircraft: the span of the wings was reduced slightly, to 37 feet; and the fuselage aft of the cockpit was altered to an oval section and the cockpit widened to conform with this, with a small additional glazed area aft of the sliding canopy to allow better vision rearwards.

On 26 November Air Commodore Verney inspected the work in progress on the aircraft and afterwards wrote:

1. The fuselage is nearly completed, and the engine installed. The wings are being plated, and some parts of the undercarriage still have to be finished. I like the simple design of the undercarriage very much. Also the flush riveting of the surfaces of the fuselage and wings. The glycol radiator is in the starboard wing, with controlled inlet cooling. Tubular honeycomb oil coolers (of American manufacture) are set forward under the engine.
2. As far as I can see it cannot be flying this year, but it should be early in January. It is in many ways a much more advanced design than the Hawker, and should be a great deal lighter.

Verney's reference to the 'tubular honeycomb oil coolers . . . set forward under the engine' indicates that even at this late stage the oil cooler air intake was still situated immediately under the propeller boss and the air was to vent from louvres on the sides of the fuselage just aft of the engine. The decision to move the oil cooler away from the engine to a position under the port wing must have been taken shortly after the visit.

Early in January 1936 Jeffrey Quill, who had just left the R.A.F. and begun working for Vickers as a test pilot, was taken to Woolston by Mutt Summers to see the work in progress there. Already it was understood that Quill would be responsible for much of the testing of Mitchell's new fighter. He was taken into the experimental shop to see it; but the wings were off (probably for the installation of the oil cooler in the port wing) and it seemed far from complete. The aircraft's small size and clean lines impressed Quill and he looked forward to getting his hands on it.

On 6 February the F.37/34 was discussed before the Secretary of State for Air, Viscount Swinton, during a meeting held at the Air Ministry. Those present were informed that under the new Programme F the Royal Air Force was to receive a total of 900 monoplane fighters of advanced design. At least 600 of these were to be the new Hawker fighter, the remainder the Supermarine F.37/34. Asked when the latter was likely to begin flying, Dowding replied that the firm had said it would be flying by 20 February; but he thought it could hardly do so before April. He continued 'The firm has a good designer in Mitchell, but they are very slow'.

Later that day Sir Robert McLean visited the Air Minstry and gave it as his view that the new fighter would make its maiden flight on the 18th. He considered it would have a maximum speed of between 340 and 370 mph.

On the 18th, however, the F.37/34 had just been completed and was undergoing engine runs on the hardstanding on the River Itchen side of the works at Woolston. Once these were done the wings were removed and the aircraft was loaded on to a lorry, which took it to the works airfield at Eastleigh for re-assembly prior to the maiden flight.

Although there had been some delays in getting the prototype into the air, Vickers saw no difficulty in getting the F.37/34 into production if an order was placed in good time. On 21 February the company informed the Air Ministry:

Provided the contractor's trials are completed by the end of March 1936, Martlesham trials by the end of April 1936 and a production order is placed by 1st May 1936, the firm should be able to start production of the single seat fighter in 15 months, ie September 1937, at a rate of 5 a week. In this event it should be possible to turn out a total of between 360 and 380 by 31st March 1939.

It was to prove a grossly over-optimistic forecast.

After re-assembly at Eastleigh the prototype F.37/34 underwent further engine runs. Then it was subjected to a minute inspection by officials of the Aeronautical Inspection Directorate and pronounced fit to fly.

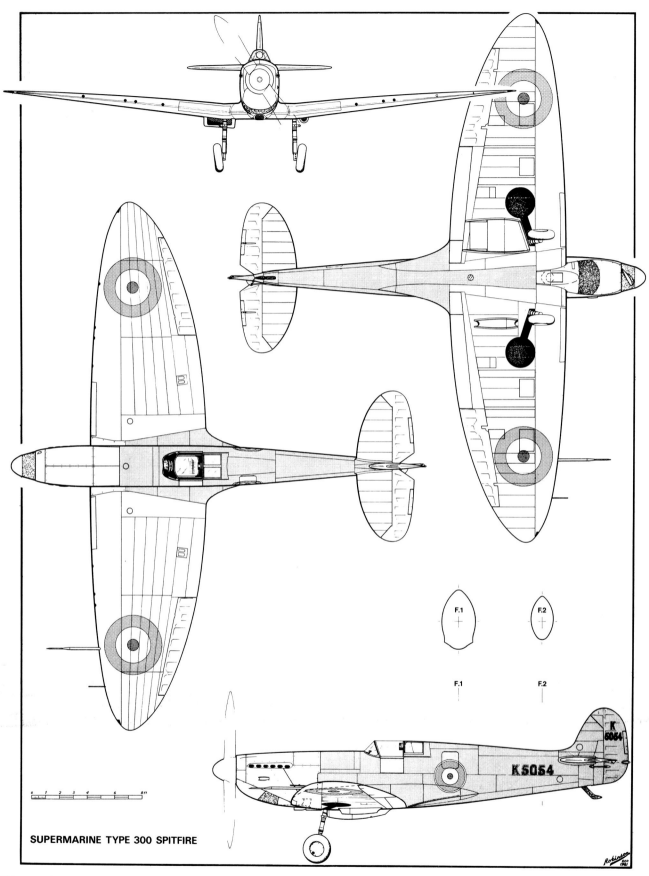

**SUPERMARINE TYPE 300 SPITFIRE**

This very detailed drawing by Harry Robinson depicts the prototype F.37/34, K 5054, at the time of her maiden flight in March 1936 before she had been painted. The method of plating the wings of the prototype, which can be clearly seen, differed considerably from that of subsequent production aircraft. For her first flight K 5054 was fitted with a fine pitch propeller and the undercarriage was locked down.

# Appendix A

## SPECIFICATION No F. 7/30
## 1st October 1931

### Single Seater Day and Night Fighter

**1. General Requirements**

(a) The aircraft is to fulfil the duties of 'Single Seater Fighter' for day and night flying. A satisfactory fighting view is essential and designers should consider the advantages offered in this respect by low wing monoplane or pusher.

The main requirements for the aircraft are:
  (i) Highest possible rate of climb
  (ii) Highest possible speed at 15,000 feet
  (iii) Fighting view
  (iv) Manoeuvrability
  (v) Capability of easy and rapid production in quantity
  (vi) Ease of maintenance.

(b) The aircraft must have a good degree of positive stability about all axes in flight and trimming gear must be fitted so that the tail incidence can be adjusted in flight to ensure that the aircraft will fly horizontally at all speeds within the flying range, without requiring attention from the pilot.

(c) When carrying the total load specified in paragraph 3, the aircraft must be fully controllable at all flying speeds, especially near the stall and during a steep dive, when there must be no tendency for the aircraft to hunt.

(d) The aircraft must have a high degree of manoeuvrability. It must answer all controls quickly and must not be tiring to fly. The control must be adequate to stop an incipient spin when the aircraft is stalled.

An approved type of slot control, or other means which will ensure adequate lateral control and stability, at and below stalling speed, is to be embodied.

The design of the aileron control is to be such that operation of the ailerons in flight will produce the minimum of adverse yawing effect on the aircraft.

(e) The aircraft is to be designed to accommodate the equipment listed in paragraph 6 and scheduled in detail in the Appendix 'A' [not included] to this Specification.

(f) The crew, armament and equipment are to be arranged as specified in paragraph 7 of this Specification.

(g) The arrangements for alighting and taking off must be as specified in paragraph 8 of this Specification.

(h) The aircraft and all parts thereof are to be designed and constructed in conformity with the requirements of the Director of Technical Development, Air Ministry.

A 'Type Record' for the aircraft, including all drawings and a complete set of strength calculations and weight estimates must be submitted to the Director of Technical Development or his authorised representative for acceptance. The contractor, pending acceptance, may proceed with construction if he so desires, but the Director of Technical Development reserves the right to reject any part or parts so made if subsequently found to be under strength or otherwise unsuitable for H.M. Service.

Two copies of fully-dimensioned General Arrangement drawing to the aircraft as actually built, together with a General Arrangement drawing showing the layout of the complete equipment, are to be supplied to the Director of Technical Development (R.D.A3) immediately on the completion of the first aircraft. Similarly in the case of any subsequent aircraft if differing from the first.

(i) The aircraft is to be constructed throughout in metal and is to be constructed and protected as to adequately withstand sudden changes in temperature and humidity such as are experienced in semi-tropical climates. Streamline wires, tie-rods and other parts not of stainless steel are to be coated with cadmium or zinc by an approved process. Aluminium and aluminium alloy parts are to be anodically treated.

(j) As soon as possible after the mock-up conference the contractor is to supply to the Director of Technical Development (R.D.4.) a General Arrangement Drawing of the engine installation (including fuel, oil and water systems, tankage and engine controls). (See also paragraph 10).

(k) On the completion of the first aircraft off the contract the contractor shall supply to the Director of Technical Development such details of the equipment and its accessories and the detail weights, length and quantities thereof as will enable the Appendix 'A' Schedule of Equipment to be completed.

This information is to be supplied by amending a copy of the current Appendix 'A' to agree with the approved aircraft, in conformity with the current master schedule.

Similarly, on the delivery of the last aircraft off the contract, if alterations have been made to the equipment, a suitably amended copy of the current Appendix 'A' is to be supplied to the Director of Technical Development.

(l) All materials used must, where possible, be to B.E.S.A. or other standard Specifications as approved by the Director of Technical Development.

All materials quoted under approved Specifications are to be to the latest issue of the Specification. A list of approved Specifications showing the latest issue numbers may be obtained on application in writing to the Director of Technical Development.

Similarly, all A.G.S parts incorporated in the aircraft are to be to the latest approved issue of the appropriate drawings but the issue number should not be quoted on the aircraft drawing. Where the contractor proposes to use materials for which standard approved Specifications are not available, the contractor is required to notify the Director of Technical Development, in writing, of his intention, and to supply such information and test pieces of the materials proposed as the Director of Technical Development may deem necessary, to enable adequate tests of the materials to be carried out.

(m) Two copies of rigging and maintenance notes are to be supplied to the Director of Technical Development (R.T.P.) not later than the date on which the first aircraft is delivered to the experimental establishment.

In order to facilitate further reproduction of any diagrams contained in the notes, tracings thereof are to be supplied also.

The note should anticipate any difficulty likely to be encountered by the Service Unit during the development of a new type and are to include:-
  (i) leading particulars, principal dimensions, and the capacities of fuel and oil tanks in tabular form;
  (ii) complete and detailed instructions for rigging the aircraft;
  (iii) any unusual features (including non-standard equipment) from the point of view of maintenance;
  (iv) lubrication instructions;
  (v) description of the engine mounting and installation in so far as they are peculiar to the particular aircraft;
  (vi) three-view general arrangement drawings (showing the horizontal datum line on the side view) and diagrams of the petrol and oil systems;

(vii) the approved equipment layout drawings as called for in paragraph 10 (d).

It is to be observed that these notes are required only for a preliminary guide for those who will be responsible for maintaining the aircraft in its early stages and it will suffice if they are written on the lines of a works instruction.

In the event of the aircraft being adopted for use in the Royal Air Force the contractor will be required to prepare notes and drawings covering the repair of the aircraft by Service Units.

## 2. Power Unit

(a) Any approved British engine may be used. It is to be noted that, when an engine is in process of development, provision is to be made in the aircraft design for a possible increase in engine weight.

(b) The installation of the engine is to be so arranged that the engine is capable of being rapidly and easily removed from the aircraft.

Supports and footholds are to be provided to facilitate minor repairs and adjustments to the engine installation.

(c) The whole of the cowling is to be designed to facilitate rapid and easy removal and replacement and is to be sufficiently robust to withstand frequent removal and constant handling; wire skewers are not to be used.

(d) The cowling is to be finished in an approved manner so as to give adequate protection against corrosion and to prevent the reflection of light which might betray the presence of the aircraft or dazzle the crew.

(e) Before drawings relative to the engine installation can be accepted the engine, fuel, oil and water systems, and the accessories and piping therefore, must be fitted in the first experimental aircraft and put in proper running order, so that the installation as a whole may be examined and, if satisfactory, approved by the Director of Technical Development, or his authorised representative.

(f) The airscrew is preferably to be of metal construction, and is to be designed in accordance with the required performance of the aircraft as specified in paragraph 4 of this Specification, but no airscrew will be accepted which allows the maximum permissible r.p.m. to be exceeded in full throttle horizontal flight at the supercharged altitude of the engine, or the normal r.p.m. to be exceeded in full throttle climbing flight at the best rate of climb above this altitude.

A standard engine instruction plate is to be fitted in a position where it will be clearly visible to the pilot.

## 2. (A) Tankage including gravity tanks to be provided for the endurance specified in paragraph 3.

(a) Adequate air space is to be provided in the oil tank: at least 1 gallon for air-cooled engines and 2 gallons for water-cooled engines.

(b) A gravity fuel tank is to be provided sufficient for at least 20 minutes at full throttle at ground level.

(c) The fuel tanks are to be adequately protected from deterioration in a manner approved by the Director of Technical Development and may be either:-
(i) Carried inside the fuselage
or
(ii) Carried inside the main planes. In this case the construction of the portions of the main planes containing the fuel tanks and the installation of the fuel tanks therein must be such that there can be no possibility of escaping fuel or fuel vapour from a damaged tank spreading to any inflammable portions of the aircraft structure
or
(iii) Carried externally in such a position that if damaged the escaping fuel will be blown clear of all parts of the aircraft structure when in flight.

(d) All tanks are to be provided with readily removable sumps or with approved means of removing all dirt and foreign matter from the interior of the tank.

(e) The delivery from the tank to the piping system is to be so arranged as to prevent as far as is practicable the passage of foreign matter from the tank into the piping system.

Means are to be provided, under the control of a member of the crew, for stopping and restarting the flow from any of the fuel tanks at each outlet from which the fuel would otherwise escape if the pipe line or balance pipe connected therewith were to break.

(f) Arrangements are to be made for the rapid and easy draining of the tanks, and rapid and easy filling with standard filler nozzles.

(g) All tanks are to be designed to be readily removable from and replaceable in position in the aircraft, with a minimum of disturbance to the aircraft structure and to other installations.

## 2. (B) Fuel and Oil Systems

(a) The fuel and oil systems shall be in general accordance with the requirements of Specification No 18 (Misc)

(b) All pipe joints are to be of approved metallic type, and together with all cocks, plugs, etc., are to be locked in accordance with A.G.S. Mod 157.

(c) The bore of the main fuel pipes must be such that the flow of fuel sufficient to maintain full power on the ground is exceeded by 100 per cent when the carburettor unions are uncoupled and the supply is in the condition of minimum head with the aircraft set at the appropriate angle so defined hereunder in clause (d) (i).

The last section of the delivery pipe to the carburettor is to be of the approved flexible type.

(d) The fuel feed may be either:-
(i) By approved fuel pumps from the main tanks direct to the carburettors with a by-pass to a gravity tank, so situated that, when the aircraft is flying at its maximum climbing angle, or when the aircraft is tail down on the ground, whichever condition gives the greatest inclination of the aircraft axis to the horizontal, the minimum effective head above the jet level of the highest carburettor when the gravity tank is practically empty is not less than the minimum specified for the type of carburettor used.

In calculating the minimum effective head due allowance must be made for any effect due to acceleration when the aircraft is in motion.

The delivery from the pumps to the carburettor must be via an approved release or reducing valve to a distributor cock or cocks so arranged that the following selections can be made.
(1) Pumps to carburettors and gravity tanks
(2) Pumps to carburettors direct
(3) Gravity tanks to carburettors
(4) Off
Wind driven pumps are not to be used.

An overflow pipe of sufficient bore to deal with all excess fuel must be provided from the gravity tank to the main tank or to some other approved point in the fuel system.

A prismatic flow indicator visible to the pilot is to be fitted in the overflow pipe
or
(ii) By gravity tanks alone feeding direct to the carburettor. Such gravity tanks must conform to the requirements laid down in (i) above.

(e) A diagram of the fuel system is to be affixed in an approved position in the aircraft.

(f) An approved type of petrol filter is to be fitted so that the whole of the fuel passes through it before reaching the carburettor. The filter must be disposed so that it will be accessible for cleaning.

## 2. (C) Cooling Systems

(a) Provision is to be made for adequate oil cooling and a thermometer registering in a position visible to the pilot is to be fitted in such a position as to indicate the temperature of the oil supplied to the engine.

In addition, on the first aircraft, an oil thermometer registering in a position visible to the pilot, is to be fitted in the return pipe from the engine between the scavenger pump and the oil cooler.

(b) If a water or evaporating engine is used, the cooling system, which is to be installed in accordance with the requirements of D.T.D., is to be designed to fulfil English summer requirements, with provision for changing to a system fulfilling Tropical summer requirements, with a minimum of alteration. If water indicators are used they are to be fitted with shutters or other approved means of temperature control.

(c) In addition to the thermometer fittings and thermometers normally required on radiators for production aircraft, the experimental aircraft is to be provided with approved thermometer fittings in the outlet header tanks or each radiator or auxiliary radiator.

## 2. (D) Engine Starting and Silencing

(a) The exhaust manifold of approved type supplied with the engine is to be fitted in such a manner as to provide adequately for silencing, and for flame-damping during night flying.

(b) Provision is to be made on the aircraft by the installation of the requisite approved fittings for the installation of an R.A.E. Mark II Starter and for the rapid and easy attachment of a compressor type engine starter carried on a separate trolley.

(c) Provision is to be made for rapidly warming the engine oil. It must be possible to take off within 2½ minutes from a cold start.

## 3. Load to be carried

In addition to any stowages and mountings necessitated by the requirements of paragraphs 6 and 7 and by alternative loads, the following load is to be carried during the acceptance flights:-

|  | Removable | Fixed | Total |
|---|---|---|---|
| *Crew (1)* | 180 | — | 180 lb |
| Oxygen | 15 | 8 | 23 |
| Instruments | 1 | 25 | 26 |
| R/T Apparatus | 46 | 6 | 52 |
| Electrical Equipment | 41 | 17 | 58 |
| Parachute and belt | 20 | 3 | 23 |
| *Armament* |  |  |  |
| 4 guns and C.C. gear* | 120 | 20 | 140 |
| Gun sights | — | 5 | 5 |
| 200 rounds S.A.A. | 145 | — | 145 |
| Signal Pistol & Cartridges | 7 | 1 | 8 |
| Military Load; | 575 | 85 | 660 lb |

*This item will be adjusted to the actual gun installation adopted

| Fuel | For ½ hour at full throttle at |
|---|---|
| Oil | ground level, plus 2.0 hours at full |
| Water (if required). | throttle at 15,000'. |
|  | Oil—ditto plus 50% excess. |
|  | Water—ditto. |

## 4. Contract Performance

The performance of the aircraft, as ascertained during the official type trials when carrying the total load specified in paragraph 3 and with an airscrew satisfying the requirements of paragraph 2 (e) shall be:-

Horizontal speed at 15,000 ft not less than 195 mph
Alighting speed not to exceed 60 mph
Service ceiling not less than 28,000 ft
Time to 15,000 ft not more than 8½ mins

The specified alighting speed must not be exceeded, but may be obtained by variable camber or equivalent devices provided that control and manoeuvrability are not adversely affected.

## 5. Structural Strength

(a) The strength of the main structure when carrying the load specified in paragraph 3, plus 100 lb shall not be less than as defined hereunder:-

Load factor throughout the structure with the centre of pressure in the most forward position: 9.0
Load factor for wing structure with the centre of pressure in its most backward position in horizontal flight: 6.0
Load factor in a terminal nose dive: 1.75
Inverted Flight
(1) Load factor at incidence corresponding to the inverted stall and with C.P. at 1/3 of the chord: 4.5
(2) Load factor at incidence appropriate to steady horizontal inverted flight and at the maximum speed of horizontal normal flight: 4.5

(b) The alighting gear must be able to withstand an impact at a vertical velocity of 10 feet per second and at this velocity the load on the alighting gear must not exceed three times the fully loaded weight of the aircraft.

(c) When subject to the impact forces on alighting, as specified above, the load factor for the alighting gear must not be less than 1-1/3, and for the remainder of the structure not less than 1-1/2. The load factor for the structure and the attachment fittings of the alighting gear must always be greater than that for the alighting gear itself by the margin indicated above.

(d) The maximum weight per wheel of the aircraft in pounds must not exceed 12 times the product of the wheel and tyre diameters in inches with the aircraft carrying the full load specified above.

(e) The above factors are to be determined by the approved official methods as published by the Directorate of Technical Development and the detail requirements given in A.P. 970 are also to be satisfied. With a view to minimising the risk of flutter, attention should be given to the recommendations of R. & M. 1177, particularly as regards the static balance of ailerons.

(f) The wing is to be sufficiently rigid to withstand satisfactorily any torsional or other loads which may be encountered during service operations.

(g) Ribs (both main plane and tail unit) are required to develop, on test, factors 20 per cent greater than those specified for the aircraft as a whole.

## 6. Equipment

The equipment as listed hereunder and as scheduled in detail in the Appendix 'A' to this Specification is to be provided for and the contractor will be required to supply and fit all parts necessary for its installation; in the case of R/T panels, etc., the position for all instruments and the identities of plugs and leads must be indicated by fixed labels.

It is to be noted that the weights of various items of fixed equipment listed hereunder and scheduled in detail in the Appendix 'A', but not quoted in paragraph 3, are to be allowed for in design.

Diagrams of the wiring and piping for all equipment installations are to be provided, for carrying in a canvas bag fitted in an approved position on the aircraft.

All equipment is to be installed in accordance with the requirements of the Director of Technical Development.

(a) Armament
| Reflector sight | (To be installed |
| Ring and Bead Sight | in accordance with |
| Signal Pistol and 8 cartridges | Specification |
| 4 × 20 lb bombs | No G.E. 126) |

2 × .303'' Vickers guns installed
in the cockpit under the control
of the pilot with
C.C. gear as necessary.
and either:-

(i) 2 × .303'' Vickers guns installed in the cockpit or wings. If in the cockpit and synchronised an additional C.C. gear reservoir is to be fitted for them. If in the wings adequate locating arrangements are essential.

or:-

(ii) 2 × .303'' Lewis guns installed so that synchronisation is unnecessary. These guns do not require heating. 2000 rounds of ammunition for the above guns with links or drums as necessary. The minimum supply to be forwarded for any gun is 400 rounds. 400 round drums will be available for Lewis guns.

(b) Electrical Equipment

| Services are to be provided for: | (To be installed in |
| Navigation and Identification Lights | accordance with |
| Gun Heaters | Specification |
| (as necessary for outboard guns) | No G.E. 164) |
| Wing tip flares | |
| (on concealed brackets) | |
| Instrument Lighting | |

(c) Instruments and General Equipment

The following instruments (of luminous pattern, where available) are to be fitted in the cockpit in accordance with the requirements of the Director of Technical Development:-

1 Air Speed Indicator
1 Altimeter
1 Revolution Indicator
1 Oil Pressure Gauge
Fuel Contents Gauge (1 per main tank)
1 Oil Thermometer (An extra oil thermometer is required on the first aircraft).
1 Radiator Thermometer (if required). An extra water thermometer is required on the first aircraft.
Boost Gauge (if required)
1 Watch and Holder
1 Compass
1 Pilot's Fighting Harness (Sutton Type)
Oxygen Apparatus
1 Map Case
1 Turn Indicator
(d) Wireless Equipment
Earth System, Bonding and Screening in accordance with Specification G.E. 125.
R/T Apparatus (Two-way)
R/T Box
Fixed Aerial.
(e) Parachute Equipment
1 Irving type Parachute

## 7. Disposition of Crew. Armament and Equipment

(a) The Pilot's view is to conform as closely as possible to that obtainable in 'pusher' aircraft. The following requirements indicate the ideal view which is considered to be necessary, and the aircraft should be designed to conform as closely to them as is possible in practice.

(b) The pilot must have a clear view forward and upward for formation work and manoeuvring, and particular care is needed to prevent his view of hostile aircraft being blanked out by top planes and centre sections when manoeuvring to attack. Planes should be so disposed as not to obstruct the pilot's view of other aircraft, when his own is pointing within 60° of their direction.

The direction in which obstruction by planes is least serious is in the backward and downward directions.

(c) For landing a good view forward and downward is necessary, and the pilot must be able to see within 17° from the vertical over the side when wearing the Sutton harness.

The point on the ground on which the pilot desires to land should not be obstructed by planes during the gliding approach. This applies especially to normal landing manoeuvres such as banked turns and side slips.

The windscreen should be sufficiently high to enable the pilot to have a clear view forward through the screen. When taxying with the tail down the pilot, with minimum movement of his head, should be able to see directly in front of his aircraft, while with tail up for taking off he should be able to see the ground 50 feet ahead over the centre line of the aircraft, with his seat in the normal flying position. The top fuselage coaming, on either side of the windscreen, should be as narrow and tapered as possible consistent with adequate protection from the slipstream.

(d) For gun aiming purposes the pilot should have an unobstructed view forward over as wide a cone as possible, the sight being the axis of that cone with his eye the apex.

(e) The pilot is to be provided with 4 guns, and stowage for 2000 rounds of ammunition as detailed in paragraph 6(a).

Provision is to be made for fitting of a G.3 camera gun complete with firing and cocking controls. The mounting and controls must be quickly removable and must not interfere with the guns and sights in any way. This provision is secondary and must not influence the design of the aircraft in any way.

(f) The pilot is to be provided with a map case, and stowage for knee-type writing pad mounted in a convenient position.

(g) The relative positions of the pilot's seat and rudder bar are to be designed to be adjustable both vertically and horizontally to suit pilots of different trunk length and leg reach.

(h) The design of the cockpit must be such as to provide the comfort necessary for the pilot to fulfil his various duties efficiently, and must allow complete freedom of movement, particularly in an emergency that obliges the pilot to take to his parachute.

The cockpit is to be adequately screened from the wind but the windscreen must not interfere with the satisfactory use of sights, one of which should be on the centre line of the aircraft, the sights being interchangeable in position.

The cockpit is to be painted internally with an approved grey-green paint. This instruction does not apply to the instrument board.

The cockpit padding and other upholstery is to be rendered fireproof to the satisfaction of the Director of Technical Development.

(i) Standard clips are to be provided under the wings for the carrying of one standard bomb rack for 4 × 20 lb bombs.

Room is to be provided to enable the bomb release gear for these bombs to be fitted inside on the port side of the cockpit.

The arrangement of the bomb carrier installation must be such that sufficient clearance is provided to enable the bombs to be released even when the aircraft is in a very steep dive.

(j) Arrangements are to be made to provide adequate cockpit heating without resort to electrical appliances.

(k) The dynamo for the electrical equipment is to be stowed internally and driven from the engine. The aircraft designer must agree the details of the drive with the engine designer.

## 8. Arrangements for alighting and taking off

(a) The aircraft is to be designed to pull up quickly on alighting and wheel brakes of an approved type are to be fitted.

The brake controls shall be such that the brakes can be applied together or independently. It is essential that the pilot shall not be obliged to abandon the aircraft or engine controls when applying the brakes. Means are to be provided for locking the brakes in the 'on' position so that wheel chocks may be dispensed with if so desired. The whole of the braking system is to be capable of rapid and easy removal when not required.

(b) The aircraft is to be suitable for operation from small, rough-surfaced and enclosed aerodromes.

(c) The alighting gear is to be of oleo or equivalent type in which the use of rubber in tension is eliminated.

(d) The wheel track of the alighting gear must be such as to provide stable taxying conditions in any direction in a wind of 20 mph without any tendency for the aircraft to capsize.

(e) The wheels of the alighting gear are to be provided with approved means for lubricating the wheel bearings, which are to be designed so that no wear takes place on the axle.

(f) The design and disposition of the alighting gear are to be such as to allow of the aircraft being readily and securely supported without the use of elaborate jacking, trestling or slinging during and subsequent to the removal of the alighting gear or the wheels of the alighting gear. If necessary, special arrangements are to be made in the design of the aircraft structure to permit of such support being readily given and the points of support so specially provided must be clearly marked on the aircraft.

## 9. Miscellaneous

(a) The aircraft is to be constructed in quickly detachable units for ease of transport and storage.

(b) Means are to be provided for locking the slats in the closed position and maintaining the controls in a central position when the aircraft is left unattended on the ground. The means so provided must preclude the possibility of the pilot attempting to take-off with the slats and/or the controls locked.

(c) Suitable holding-down rings are to be provided under the bottom planes.

(d) The aircraft is to be provided with all necessary handgrips and other facilities for ease of handling on the ground.

(e) Provision is to be made in the design for the protection of all moving parts against the destructive effects of sand and, as far as may be possible, for their lubrication by grease gun from a central point.

(f) Detachable covers of approved type are to be supplied for the engine and cockpit as a protection against deterioration when the aircraft is pegged down in the open.

(g) The attachment points for the pilot's fighting harness together with those parts of the aircraft to which the belt loads are transmitted are to be capable of withstanding the failing load of the belt or harness.

(h) The design of the structure in the vicinity of the cockpit is to be such as to afford the pilot as much protection as possible in the event of a heavy landing, or crash or overturning.

Such structure should be appreciably stronger than the adjacent parts so that these latter may absorb some of the shock by deformation before the former yields.

(i) The design of the aircraft is to be such that standard Service equipment can be used for ground operations such as fuelling, rigging, manhandling, etc. Particulars of service ground equipment can be obtained on application in writing to the Director of Technical Development (R.D.A.5.).

(j) The design and layout of the aircraft is to be such as to offer every facility for rapid and easy inspection and maintenance in service and, in general, is to permit of maintenance operations being performed with standard Service equipment. Special equipment (including tools) shall be provided with the aircraft if an essential supply, but the introduction of non-standard articles is to be avoided whenever possible.

(k) Parts that require to be frequently replaced or inspected are to be easily accessible, and fully visible to a mechanic working on them.

(l) Control cables are to be arranged so that the deterioration due to wear is a minimum. Means are to be provided to facilitate the fitting of new cable and its rapid threading through fairleads. The splicing of cable in place is prohibited.

(m) Positive-locking devices shall be provided for all joints and fastenings; such devices are to be rapidly and easily adjustable.

(n) Adequate facilities are to be provided for inspecting the fuselage interior and working parts, particularly those of the tail skid and tail plane adjusting gear.

(o) Arrangements are to be made for defining the position of the centre of gravity in accordance with Aircraft Design Memorandum No 205.

## 10. Provision of Mock-up

(a) In order that the proposed disposition of the crew, armament etc., may be properly examined and approved by the Director of Technical Development before construction is commenced the contractor is required to provide a suitable 'mock-up' of the aircraft at his works. The 'mock-up' so provided must include all parts and components which are likely to interfere with the all-round view from the cockpit and must shew the internal arrangements of the cockpit and such details of the engine installation as the arrangements for engine-starting and the positions of cocks, pumps, etc.

(b) The 'mock-up' must be erected full size and must be constructed true to scale and all instruments and equipment must be represented full size.

(c) The 'mock-up' must be capable of being inclined at angles corresponding to the cruising and alighting attitudes of the aircraft and to this end must be constructed to the correct height from the ground.

(d) Within 10 days of the mock-up conference the contractor is to submit to the Director of Technical Development (R.D.A.4.) two copies of provisional drawings of the layout as decided at the mock-up.

Four copies of the layout drawings as finally approved are to be supplied to the Director of Technical Development (R.D.A.4).

These equipment layout drawings are to be a 1/8th scale and are to consist of skeleton views of the fuselage and other pertinent structure shewing views of all equipment:

(1) positioned on the starboard side of the aircraft, viewed from the inside;
(2) positioned on the port side, viewed from inside;
(3) positioned in plan, together with
(4) full views of instrument boards, W/T panels, etc. and
(5) a schedule of equipment indexed to correspond to 'balloon' pointers (a spare column is to be provided for notes or alterations).

Each of the drawings is to shew also seats, tanks, controls, etc. appropriate to each view.

In accordance with the procedure laid down in Aircraft Design Memorandum No 135 the contractor is to supply a bare W/T panel as and when required.

## 11. Test Specimens

(a) The Contractor will be required to supply and ordinarily test (see clause (d)) such specimens of parts of the aircraft as the Director of Technical Development may consider should be tested in order to ensure that the design and construction of the aircraft will be satisfactory.

(b) Tenders for the supply of aircraft in accordance with this specification are to include a Schedule of the specimens and tests considered sufficient to meet the requirements of clause (a) and are to cover the cost of supplying and testing the specimens. Any schedule that is considered by the Director of Technical Development to be inadequate will be returned to the firm concerned for amendment.

(c) The specimens and tests that will generally be essential are indicated hereunder:

| | |
|---|---|
| Complete ribs. | The specimens are to be tested under the conditions of normal flight and, when appropriate, inverted flight. Metal ribs will be required to undergo, in addition, a vibration test. |
| Metal spars. | The specimens will be submitted to the standard test, if applicable, and otherwise to such test as the Director of Technical Development may require. |

(d) Except as provided for hereafter, the testing shall be done by the Contractor, or he shall arrange for it to be done at some approved Testing Establishment; in either case, due notice of the time and place of the tests shall be given to the Director of Technical Development so that he may arrange for a representative to witness them; the conditions governing the tests are to be in accordance with the requirements of the Director of Technical Development and the tests are to be performed to his satisfaction; reports on the tests are to be supplied to the Director of Technical Development in duplicate. If neither of the aforementioned arrangements is possible, the tests will be done at the Royal Aircraft Establishment, at the Contractor's expense.

(e) The Director of Technical Development reserves the right to call for specimens and tests additional to those referred to in the Contractor's Schedule, should he at any time after the placing of the contract consider them to be necessary.

(f) No specimen of any part of the aircraft shall be submitted for testing without it being previously certified by the Inspector-in-Charge at the Contractor's works, that the specimen is typical, as regards materials, dimensions, limits and workmanship of the actual part.

(g) A thin coat of oil or vaseline may be applied to metal specimens to prevent corrosion. Varnish, enamel or similar substances must not be used for this purpose.

## 12. Provision of Drawings for a Model

If at any time the Director of Technical Development shall so desire, the contractor shall supply the drawings and data necessary for the construction of a true-to-scale model of the complete aircraft suitable for aerodynamic trials in a wind tunnel; such drawings, if required, would form the subject of an amendment to contract.

## 13. Publication of Test Results

The Director of Technical Development reserves the right to publish data contained in reports of any wind tunnel or other tests relating to the design of the aircraft which may be undertaken on his behalf.

## 14. Pre-acceptance Test Flights

(a) Prior to the delivery of the aircraft to the Departmental Establishment at which the Type Trials are to take place it shall have been certified to the Director of Technical Development:

(i) That the aircraft has been subjected by the contractor's pilot to the flight tests referred to in the 'Statement of Special Contract Conditions' accompanying the contract and

(ii) that these tests have shewn that the aircraft is safe to be flown by pilots of the Royal Air Force.

(b) The tests referred to in (a) shall include:-

(i) A demonstration that the aircraft may be spun, both to the right and to the left, without undue risk when loaded in accordance with paragraph (3) of the Specification, and with the Centre of Gravity at the aft authorised limit. For this purpose it is required that the aircraft, after being put into a spin, shall be allowed to complete not less than eight turns before the pilot sets his controls for recovery. The aircraft will be deemed satisfactory as regards its behaviour in a spin if the height loss in recovery does not exceed 1500 feet. This height loss is to be reckoned from when the pilot sets his controls for recovery until the aircraft 'flattens out' from the landing dive.

(ii) A dive to the terminal velocity.

(iii) A demonstration of satisfactory behaviour during normal aerobatics such as the loop, roll, stalled turns, etc.

AIR MINISTRY
Directorate of Technical Development

# Appendix B

## SUPERMARINE SPECIFICATION
## No 425a
## 26th July 1934

### Supermarine Day and Night Fighter to Air Ministry
### Specification F.7/30
### Proposed Modifications

### Arrangement

It is proposed to modify the existing aeroplane by building a new pair of wings incorporating a retracting chassis. The new wings are of reduced area, the present inner sections of negative dihedral being dispensed with. Split trailing-edge flaps are provided to increase the lift and thus retain the same landing speed. The existing aircraft is shown on Drawing No 22400, Sheet 1 and the proposed arrangement on Drawing No 30000, Sheet 2.

### Construction

Construction is greatly simplified by making each wing in one piece. Other features which simplify construction are the substitution of lattice for a plate web, enabling the riveting of the nose to be more easily carried out, and the provision of smooth in place of corrugated covering.

### Pilot's View

As a result of eliminating the downward-sloping wing roots, the view for a pilot is not quite so good close in to the fuselage, but is improved further out by the reduction of span.

### Main Particulars and Dimensions

|  | Existing Machine | Modified Machine |
|---|---|---|
| Span | 45 ft 10 ins | 39 ft 4 ins |
| Length Overall | 29 ft 10 ins | 29 ft 4 ins |
| Wing Area (gross) | 295 sq ft | 255 sq ft |
| Wing Loading | 16.8 lb sq ft | 18.4 lb sq ft |
| Power Loading | 8.25 lb/bhp | 7.85 lb/bhp |

### Weight and Performance

It is estimated that the proposed modifications will result in a saving of 250 pounds weight, and an improvement in top speed of 30 mph, the climb remaining practically unaltered. The following features giving the comparisons between the existing and the modified aeroplanes, are estimated. Performance tests so far carried out are incomplete, but present indications are that the estimates are reasonably correct.

|  | Existing Machine | Modified Machine |
|---|---|---|
| Weight | 4,950 pounds | 4,700 pounds |
| Max. Speed | 235 mph | 265 mph |
| Climb to 15,000 ft | 8 mins | 8¼ mins |

# Appendix C.

## SPECIFICATION F.37/34
## 3rd January 1935

### Experimental High Speed Single Seat Fighter
### (Supermarine Aviation Works)

### 1. General

This specification is intended to cover the design and construction of an experimental high speed single seat fighter substantially as described in the Supermarine Specification No 425a and drawing No 30000 Sheet 13, except that an improvement in the pilot's view is desirable. The aircraft shall conform to all the requirements stated in Specification F.7/30 and all corrigenda thereto, except as stated hereunder.

### 2. Power Unit

(a) The engine to be installed shall be the Rolls Royce P.V.XII

(b) The airscrew shall be of wooden construction. The Provisions of Para 2(f) of Specification F.7/30 as regards the provision for the effect of a metal airscrew on weight and C. of G. movement can be ignored.

(c) The fuel system shall be in accordance with DTD Specification No DTD 1004. A duplicate engine-driven system may be used.

(d) A cooling system is to be of the evaporative cooling type, using wing condensers in association with an auxiliary radiator.

(e) Hand starting gear only is provided for engine starting.

### 3. Load to be Carried

The service load shall be as defined in Specification F.7/30, except for departures which may subsequently be agreed between the contractor and the Director of Technical Development. The fuel load to be carried is to be 94 gallons with oil appropriate to the endurance implied by this fuel.

### 4. Equipment and Miscellaneous

(a) Non-standard navigation lights of the type approved by DTD may be fitted, and will be supplied by the contractor.

(b) The requirement for Para 8(a) of Specification F.7/30 that the braking system is to be capable of rapid and easy removal is to be deleted.

(c) The reference to the hand holds or other aids to the handling at the wing tips of Para 9(d) of Specification F.7/30 is to be altered to read: 'Internal provision is to be made for taking holding-down guys at the wing tips. Hand holds or grips will not be necessary.'

(d) The requirement for Para 6 as regards gun installation is modified. All four guns may be installed outside the airscrew disc.

(e) Tail wheel is to be fitted if practicable.

### 5. Structural Strength

(a) Para 5(d) of Specification F.7/30 is to be altered to read: 'The alighting gear must be able to withstand an impact at a vertical velocity of 10 feet per second, and at this velocity the load on the alighting gear must not exceed 4½ times the fully-loaded weight of the aircraft.'

(b) Wheels not conforming with Para 5(d) of Specification F.7/30 will be accepted, but the actual size and type proposed must be approved by the Director of Technical Development.

# Appendix D

## REQUIREMENTS FOR
## SINGLE-ENGINE SINGLE-SEATER DAY
## AND
## NIGHT FIGHTER (F.10/35)
## April 1935

### 1. General

The Air Staff require a single-engine single-seater day and night fighter which can fulfil the following conditions:-

(a) Have a speed in excess of the contemporary bomber of at least 40 mph at 15,000 ft.

(b) Have a number of forward firing machine guns that can produce the maximum hitting power possible in the short space of time available for one attack. To attain this object it is proposed to mount as many guns as possible and it is considered that eight guns should be provided. The requirements are given in more detail below.

### 2. Performance

(a) Speed. The maximum possible and not less than 310 mph at 15,000 ft at maximum power with the highest speed possible between 5,000 and 15,000 ft.

(b) Climb. The best possible to 20,000 ft but secondary to speed and hitting power.

(c) Service Ceiling. Not less than 30,000 ft is desirable.

(d) Endurance. ¼ hour at maximum power at sea level plus 1 hour at maximum power at which engine can be run continuously at 15,000 ft. This should provide ½ hour at maximum power at which engine can be run continuously (for climb etc.), plus 1 hour at most economic speed at 15,000 ft (for patrol), plus ¼ hour at maximum power at 15,000 ft (for attack). To allow for possible increase in engine power during the life of this aircraft, tankage is to be provided to cover ¼ hour at maximum power at sea level plus 1¼ hours at maximum power at which engine can be run continuously at 15,000 ft.

(e) Take off and landing. The aircraft to be capable of taking off and landing over a 50 ft barrier in a distance of 500 yards.

### 3. Armament

Not less than 6 guns, but 8 guns are desirable. These should be located outside the airscrew disc. Re-loading in the air is not required and the guns should be fired by electrical or means other than Bowden wire.

It is contemplated that some or all of these guns should be mounted to permit of a degree of elevation and traverse with some form of control from the pilot's seat. Though it is not at present possible to give details, it is desirable that designers should be aware of the possibility of this development, which should not, however, be allowed to delay matters at this stage.

### 4. Ammunition

300 rounds per gun if eight guns are provided and 400 rounds per gun if only six guns are installed.

### 5. View

(a) The upper hemisphere must be, so far as possible, unobstructed to the view of the pilot to facilitate search and attack. A good view for formation flying is required, both for formation leader and flank aircraft and for night landing.

(b) A field of view of about 10° downwards from the horizontal line of sight over the nose is required for locating the target.

### 6. Handling

(a) A high degree of manoeuvrability at high speeds is not required but good control at low speeds is essential.

(b) A minimum alteration of tail trim with variations of throttle settings is required.

(c) The aircraft must be a steady firing platform.

### 7. Special Features and Equipment

(a) Enclosed cockpit

(b) Cockpit heating

(c) Night flying equipment.

(d) R/T.

(e) Oxygen for 2½ hours.

(f) Guns to be easily accessible on the ground for loading and maintenance.

(g) Retractable undercarriage and tailwheel permissible.

(h) Wheel brakes.

(j) Engine starting. If an electric starter is provided a ground accumulator will be used with a plug-in point on the aircraft—an accumulator for this purpose is not required to be carried in the aircraft. The actual starting must be under control of the pilot. In addition hand turning gear is required.

| Date and Hour | Aeroplane Type and No. | Pilot | Passenger(s) | Time | Height | Course | REMARKS |
|---|---|---|---|---|---|---|---|
| | | | Time carried forward :— | 124 | 85. | | |
| 1. 2. 36. | Valentia K.4605 | Self | - | | 10 | | Full load Tests |
| " | " | " | - | | 10 | | " |
| 5. 2. 36 | " | " | Handasyde & Quill. | | 30 | | " |
| " | " | " | " | | 10 | | " |
| " | " | " | " | | 10 | | " |
| 7. 2. 36. | G4/31 K.4556 | " | Mr Quill. | | 10 | | Contractors Tests |
| " | " | " | R Handasyde | | 30 | | " |
| 8. 2. 36 | Falcon. | " | - | | 70 | | Local |
| 29. 2. 36. | " | " | - | | 15 | | Contractors Tests |
| 25. 2. 36 | G4/31. 4556 | " | K Quill | | 25 | | " |
| " | " | " | - | | 45. | | " |
| " | Valentia K.4605 | " | K Quill | | 70 | | Brooklands to Martlesham |
| 5. 3. 36 | G4/31 K.4556 | " | - | | 30 | | |
| 5. 3. 36 22.10.36 | Supermarine Spitfire | Self | X | 20 | 0 | X | Experimental flying at Southampton X |
| 7. 3. 36 | Falcon. | Self | - | | 25 | | Brooklands to Eastleigh. |
| 14. 3. 36 | " | " | - | | 25 | | " |
| " | " | " | - | | 38 | | Eastleigh to Brooklands |
| 19. 3. 36 | Hart T. K.5782 | " | - | | 20 | | Local Test |
| 20. 3. 36 | Falcon | " | - | | 70. | | Brooklands to Eastleigh |
| " | Hart K.5784 | " | - | | 10 | | Local. |
| " | " | " | - | | 70 | | " |
| " | Falcon | " | - | | 70 | | Eastleigh to Brooklands |
| | | | TOTAL TIME :— | 1455 | 15 | | |

Reproduction of the pages of Mutt Summer's logbook for February and March 1936. These show that he flew the G.4/31 Martlesham Heath on 5.3.36. After that comes the entry mentioning '20 hours experimental flying' in the 'Supermarine Spitfire' between 5.3.36 and 22.10.36, which was undoubtedly inserted some months later.

17

18

19

20

# 2.

# K 5054: THE FIRST OF
# THE MANY

Near the end of the first week in March 1936 K 5054, the prototype F.37/34, was ready to begin flight trials. In accordance with Vickers' policy it was arranged for Captain J. 'Mutt' Summers, the parent company's Chief Test Pilot, to journey to Eastleigh to conduct the maiden flight. The date of the all-important first flight is far from clear, however; certainly there is reason to doubt that it was on 5 March as most accounts have stated.

At first sight it might seem a simple matter to establish when K 5054 first flew: 'Mutt' Summers's flying logbook still exists. But for 5 March 1936 it stated:

    5.3.36  G.4/31  K 7556  Self  30 [mins]  Brooklands to
                                              Martlesham

Then, on the next line:

    5.3.36 to 22.10.36    Supermarine Spitfire    20 [hours]
                          Experimental flying at Southampton

The entries raise as many questions as they answer. It is known that on the 5th Summers delivered the G.4/31, the prototype of the monoplane bomber later named the Wellesley, for its initial service trials at the RAF test establishment at Martlesham Heath. The delivery of a prototype aircraft to the RAF for the first time was an important event for the company, and much more than a simple delivery flight. Summers would have shown service officers over the G.4/31, emphasizing its good features to the RAF pilots upon whose opinions of it in the air would depend confirmation of an order already placed for 79 of these aircraft. So 5 March would have been quite a full day for 'Mutt' Summers. It is unlikely in the extreme that he would have agreed later the same day to rush over to Eastleigh to conduct the maiden flight of an important new fighter.

We do know that Summers's logbook was written not by him but by his secretary. And from the wording, there is no doubt that the second entry for 5 March was written in several months after the first flight of K 5054; probably it was written on 22 October (why else should she have chosen to mention

that particular date, when the new fighter would be in pieces in the hangar at Eastleigh two months into a modification programme?). Moreover, the new fighter was not to receive the name 'Spitfire' until May 1936. Because it was written so long after the event, the second entry for 5 March in Summers's logbook must be treated with caution.

We can see why 5 March has come to be taken as the date of the maiden flight of the F.37/34; but if it was not on that day, when was it? 'Mutt' Summers's logbook provides no further clues. Nor does Reginald Mitchell's diary though it too exists for 1936; he used his diary as a forward engagement calendar and made no mention of the maiden flight of the new fighter. Indeed, in spite of an intensive search, this author has found no document written at the time which gives a specific date for the maiden flight of K 5054.

Jeffrey Quill remembers the day on which K 5054 first flew with considerable clarity, however. He had been told to take the firm's Miles Falcon from Brooklands to Martlesham that morning, to pick up Summers and fly him to Eastleigh for the maiden flight of the new fighter. Quill and Summers landed at Eastleigh on the morning of that day (which is another pointer that the G.4/31 delivery flight did not take place on the same day as the first flight of K 5054). And the flight in the Falcon is noted in Quill's logbook for 6 March 1936; he admits he might have made a slip of the pen and put in the wrong date but he made the entry shortly afterwards and considers it unlikely. So, on balance, the surprisingly meagre evidence would seem to point to K 5054 having made her maiden flight on the 6th, rather than 5th March 1936 as has so often been said in the past.

Late on the morning prior to her first flight K 5054 was wheeled out of the hangar at Eastleigh and comprehensively photographed—at least 12 pictures were taken from various angles and these have been widely published, though never with any suggestion that they were taken a few hours before the maiden flight. In these photographs K 5054 was unpainted but carried service markings; the undercarriage legs lacked fairing doors and the aircraft was fitted with a fine-pitch propeller. Less obviously, the undercarriage legs were locked down for the first flight.

It was well into the afternoon before K 5054 was ready to get airborne. From Meteorological Office records it is known that in the Southampton area the weather was practically identical on 5 and 6 March 1936: clear skies, visibility moderate to good, a light wind from the west or southwest. Summers climbed into the cockpit and strapped in, then started the engine. When he was satisfied all was as it should be he waved away the chocks, then with a burst of power the little fighter surged forward over the grass.

**17, 18, 19** and **20.** Four photographs, out of a series of at least a dozen, depicting the F.37/34 a few hours before her maiden flight. At this time the aircraft was unpainted, the unfaired main undercarriage legs were locked down and the aircraft was fitted with a fine pitch propeller. Between the two hangars in the background, in the head-on and tail-on shots, can be seen the Miles Falcon aircraft in which Jeffrey Quill flew Mutt Summers from Martlesham Heath for the maiden flight. Behind the Hawk can be seen the airport cafe where during the testing of F.37/34 many of the pre-flight and post-flight discussions took place. *(Vickers, Wood)*

Jeffrey Quill was one of those who, with Mitchell and most of his design team, observed the scene:

Mutt taxied around for a bit then, without too much in the way of preliminaries, went over to the far side of the airfield, turned into wind and took off. With the fine pitch prop the new fighter fairly leapt off the ground and climbed away. It then passed out of our sight but I know what Mutt would have been doing. First he would have needed to confirm that the technical people had worked out the stalling speed correctly, so that he could get back on the ground safely. To that end he would have taken it to a safe altitude, about 5,000 feet, and tried a dummy landing to find the best approach speed and make sure that when it stalled the aircraft did not flick on to its back or do anything unpleasant like that. Probably Mutt did a few steep turns to try out the controls. Then, having checked that everything really important was all right, he landed and taxied in. That first flight took about 20 minutes.

When the aircraft came to a stop everyone gathered round and he shut down the engine. Then, still in the cockpit, he said 'I don't want anything touched.' Some of those present misunderstood his meaning and thought he had said that the aircraft was absolutely right as it then stood. As I know well, that was not the case. Mutt simply meant that he had found no major snag, the thing was functioning all right as a piece of machinery and he didn't want the controls or anything else altered before the next flight. Mutt was far too experienced and wily a pilot to say that nothing would be needed to be done, on the basis of a single flight; he knew that the real testing had not even begun. Nevertheless everyone was elated by his comment: there are plenty of aeroplanes that made their first flight and then had to stay on the ground for a long time because something major did have to be altered. But Mutt's comment became widely reported and equally widely misinterpreted.

During the three days following the maiden flight the fine pitch propeller was replaced by one of coarse pitch designed to take the fighter to its maximum speed; undercarriage doors were fitted, the legs unlocked and the mechanism tested. Summers made the second flight on the 10th, during which he retracted the undercarriage in the air. On the following day he made the third flight.

At the Secretary of State for Air's meeting at the Air Ministry, on 17 March, Air Marshal Dowding spoke of his visit to Eastleigh two days earlier to see the new fighter. The minutes of the meeting recorded:

He was glad to be able to report that it was flying remarkably well and the firm, who were very pleased with it, said that it would probably be very much faster (350 to 360 mph) than the Hawker fighter. Its only drawback was that it had a very poor downward and forward view. He had tried the retractable undercarriage, the flaps and other gadgets, and they seemed to be very efficient.

Later the meeting was informed that problems with starting the engine were causing some delays to the test programme. A new engine of the same type was on its way to Eastleigh for installation in the F.37/34.

Probably Summers made two or three more flights in K 5054 before she went into the hangar for the first engine change. The prototype was ready again on the 24th and George Pickering, the resident Test Pilot of Supermarine, made his first flight in the new fighter. Mitchell mentioned it in his diary though he referred to the aircraft erroneously, on this occasion and on others, as the 'F.37/35'. On the following day Pickering took the aircraft up again and noted in his logbook: 'SS Fighter K 5054, 50 mins, Climb to 17,000', level speeds, diving to 430 mph, testing chassis'. Without doubt the '430 mph' mentioned was the true airspeed attained (equivalent to an indicated airspeed of about 350 mph at 15,000 feet) and not the indicated airspeed. As we shall observe shortly, had the prototype been taken to 430 mph indicated (as some accounts have stated) she would probably have broken up in the air.

On 26 March Jeffrey Quill made his first flight in the new fighter. Beforehand Summers briefed him on the points to watch:

He stressed the need to make a careful approach during the landing. The flaps could be lowered only to 57 degrees on the prototype. With the wooden prop ticking over there was very little drag during the landing approach and she came in very flat. If one approached too fast one could use up all of the airfield in no time at all.

Then it was my turn, and off I went. Of course, at that time I had no idea of the eventual significance of the aeroplane. To me it was just the firm's latest product, running in competition with Hawkers and a highly important venture. And if I bent it I would probably be out on my neck!

I made my first flight, getting the feel of the aircraft, and landed normally. Then I decided to taxi back to the take-off point and do another take-off. That second time did not feel quite right, and only when I was airborne did I realise I had left the flaps down. I retracted the flaps, flew around for a bit, then went back and landed. Of course, everyone had noticed my *faux pas*. But Mitchell was very kind about it. He just grinned and said 'Well, now we know she will take off with the flaps down.' And that was the end of the matter.

During the week that followed Quill and Pickering took K 5054 up six times. One of the first things that had to be done was to establish the error in the airspeed indicator readings due to 'position error'. Position errors were those due to the position of the pitot head relative to the wing; they varied throughout the speed range and could be measured only in the air. Jeffrey Quill described the method used to measure the discrepancies in the system:

These trials had to be flown early in the morning, because we had to have completely still air. We needed a straight measured course, so we used a section of the Portsmouth to Eastleigh railway line between two bridges. On each we stationed a man with a stopwatch and they were connected by field telephone. Then I had to fly the aeroplane along the course very accurately, first at 100 mph indicated, then back at 120, and so on up to the maximum speed of the aircraft. From the readings taken by the men on the ground, we could work out the position errors and correct for them in our other test work.

During the ensuing months Quill came to know Reginald Mitchell well. The latter was still active, though he was suffering from cancer in an advanced stage. Quill later recounted:

Whenever the new fighter was flying Mitchell would get into his car and drive from his office to Eastleigh. As I was coming in to land I would see his yellow Rolls-Royce parked and know he was there. He kept a close eye on things. After the flight I would often go over to the airport café with Ernie Mansbridge and a few others, and sit down for the debrief over a cup of coffee. Mitchell would usually sit in. He was a great listener, he would not do much talking. It was known that he was not in good health, though at that time I had no idea just how ill he was. He was basically a very nice, kind-hearted, man. But he didn't suffer fools gladly and he used to get bloody angry sometimes—I now realise this was probably a symptom of his illness.

If there was a bit of time between flights he would sometimes invite me into his car and we would sit there and discuss things. He wanted to know all about how the aircraft handled. And sometimes I could get him talking, which was a wonderful experience. He was a man of enormous common sense, a great technician who could take all the mystery out of a subject when he explained it. At that time I was only 23 and had not trained as an engineer, so I had something of an inferiority complex when it came to dealing with the aerodynamics and structures experts at Woolston with slide rules sticking out of their pockets. But Mitchell put me right about this one day, in his usual very direct way. He said 'Look, I'll give you a bit of advice Jeffrey. If anybody ever tells you anything about an aeroplane which is so bloody complicated you can't understand it, take it from me its all balls!' I have never forgotten what he said, and in fact it's absolutely true. The really great engineers—and Mitchell was one of them—have the ability to take a really complex issue and give a crystal clear explanation of the problem and its solution.

In the course of the initial flight testing the only real fault found on the new fighter was that the rudder horn balance was too large and as a result the control was unacceptably light; at high speed the aircraft became directionally unstable. Otherwise there was little to complain about, except that K 5054's maximum speed was well below the 350 mph that had been predicted. It was hoped that this would be increased with the

incorporation of certain planned minor modifications, and after testing with a selection of different propellers.

Early in April the initial test programme was complete and K 5054 had to undergo ground resonance tests. There was no rig to run these at Eastleigh so on the 6th George Pickering flew the aircraft to Farnborough. During the tests it was found that wing flutter was liable to occur at speeds somewhat lower than expected. As a result the never-to-be-exceeded maximum airspeed for the prototype was set at 380 mph indicated. After the tests Pickering collected the aircraft on 9 April and returned it to Eastleigh.

On the following day, 10 April, K 5054 went back into the hangar at Eastleigh for initial modifications. Of these the main ones were that the size of the rudder horn balance was reduced and the top of the fin squared off, the carburettor air intake was lowered slightly to increase the ram air pressure and the engine cowling was strengthened—there had been some problems with it rattling in flight. Also the prototype was painted for the first time, with a very smooth light blue-grey finish. Ernie Mansbridge recalled how this was done:

> The finish was put on by the same people at Derby who did the Rolls-Royce cars. We asked Rolls what they did to get such a fine finish on their cars. They put us in touch with the firm that did it for them, and some of the firm's people came down to Eastleigh and they had the prototype for three or four days. They put filling in the various joints and rubbed it all down, put more filling on and rubbed it down again. Then they applied the paint, they really did a very nice job.

To raise the maximum limiting speed of the aircraft would require a major structural redesign of the wing; K 5054 was to continue with the wing she had.

**21.** The F.37/34 photographed in the hangar at Eastleigh early in May 1936, following initial modifications and painting. *(Shenstone)*

**22.** Ernie Mansbridge, left, who directed the flight testing of the new fighter, pictured with Jeffrey Quill. *(Mansbridge)*

Also at about this time the Vickers parent company suggested and the Air Ministry accepted a name for the new fighter: Spitfire. By all accounts Mitchell himself was not pleased with the choice and was heard to say 'Its the sort of bloody silly name they would give it!' During a recent BBC Television documentary on the Spitfire, great play was made on the alleged inspired selection of the name by Sir Robert McLean. If inspiration there was in picking the name it must have come much earlier: the same name had been given to the unsuccessful Type 224. Indeed, it is of interest to note that on occasions in 1936 K 5054 was sometimes referred to as the 'Spitfire II', the 'Spitfire I' being the Type 224.

Resplendent in the new finish K 5054 recommenced flying on 11 May. That morning Jeffrey Quill took her up for just over an hour for level speed and handling trials and found that with the re-balanced rudder she was much more pleasant to handle. That afternoon Mutt Summers flew the fighter for the benefit of

John Yoxall, *Flight*'s photographer, for the first air-to-air photographs. Jeffrey Quill flew the Falcon carrying Yoxall, and Reginald Mitchell went along for the ride.

Quill flew K 5054 again on the 13th, then on the 14th he conducted high speed dives to take her to the maximum permissible speed. During the first he reached 360 mph indicated and found that the aircraft handled perfectly and there were no problems. Quill pulled out, then climbed back to 20,000 feet for the second dive. Again the speed built up rapidly and as it reached 380 mph, the maximum allowed and equivalent to a true airspeed of 465 mph, there was a loud bang. Gently the pilot eased the aircraft out of the dive and took her back to Eastleigh. After landing it was found that the lower fairing on the port undercarriage leg had broken away and struck and damaged the underside of the fuselage.

The damage was not serious, however, and by the following day it had been repaired and the prototype was able to resume trials. At this time there was considerable pressure to get the new fighter to the Royal Air Force trials establishment at Martlesham Heath as soon as possible. The Hawker fighter, which later became the Hurricane, was already there and if the Spitfire did not begin service trials soon it might fail to get an order by default. But at this stage the Spitfire was still not yet fit to be delivered. Ernie Mansbridge explained why:

Even with the new finish and the lowered carburettor air intake, the best we could then get out of the Spitfire was 335 mph. From our 'spies' we heard that the new Hawker fighter was doing nearly 330, and 5 mph was not very much to justify production of the Spitfire which was obviously more complicated to build. Fortunately, our propeller people discovered that the tips of the propeller were running into Mach problems. So they designed and built a new one which paid special attention to that, with a thin section and a very fine

**23, 24, 25.** Part of a series of photographs taken on 11 May 1936, on the afternoon following the first flight of the newly named Spitfire, after initial modifications and painting. Mutt Summers flew the fighter, Jeffrey Quill flew the Miles Hawk from which *Flight* magazine's photographer John Yoxall took the pictures; Reginald Mitchell went along in the Hawk to see his new design from the air for the first time. The two small doors at the top of the undercarriage legs gave a lot of trouble and one is seen hanging open in view below; later in the test programme they were removed. *(Flight)*

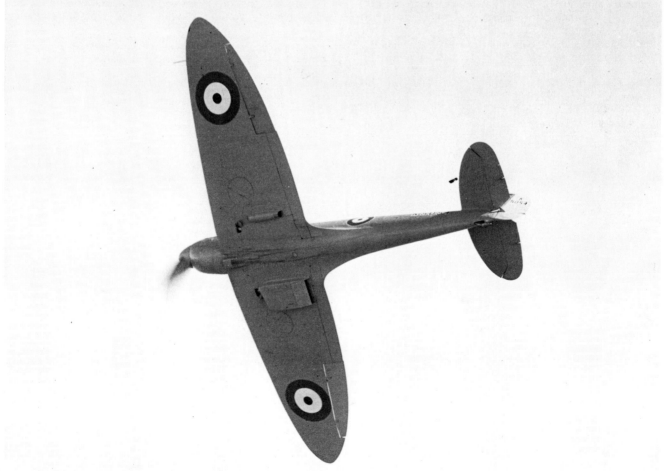

incidence. The new propeller was fitted on 15 May and Jeffrey went off and did a set of level speeds with it. When he came down he handed me the test card with a big grin and said 'I think we've got something there!' And we had, we'd got 13 mph. After correcting the figures we made the maximum speed 348 mph, which we were very pleased with.

After one further flight, on the 16th when Quill took the Spitfire up to 30,000 feet, the aircraft went back into the hangar for final preparations before she was delivered to Martlesham. Ideally she should have had her armament fitted for the Service tests, but at this time there were not enough Browning guns available. During the Air Staff meeting on 22 May the question of the Spitfire's armament was raised but, the minutes recorded, 'It is not possible to let both this aircraft and the Hawker F.36/34 have Browning guns and therefore on this aircraft ballast is fitted in lieu.'

On 26 May everything was ready and Mutt Summers delivered the Spitfire to Martlesham. Even at this early stage the new fighter received special treatment. Flight Lieutenant (later Air Marshal Sir) Humphrey Edwardes-Jones commanded A Flight at Martlesham at that time; he told the author:

Normally a firm's test pilot would bring in a prototype aircraft for service testing, and it would be first handed over to the boffins who would weigh it very carefully and check that the structure was as it should be. It was usually about 10 days before it came out for its first flight with us. With the Spitfire protype it was quite different. Mutt Summers brought her over, and orders came from the Air Ministry that I was to fly the aircraft that same day and report my impressions.

After the new fighter had been refuelled and Summers had shown Edwardes-Jones around the cockpit, the latter was ready for his first flight:

Usually the first flight of a new aircraft did not mean a thing at Martlesham, they were happening all the time. But on this occasion the buzz got around that the Spitfire was something special and everybody turned out to watch—I can remember seeing the cooks in their white hats lining the road. I took off, retracted the undercarriage and flew around for about 20 minutes. I found that she handled very well. Then I went back to the airfield.

There was no air traffic control in those days and I had no radio. As I made my approach I could make out a Super Fury some way in front of me doing S turns to lose height before it landed. I thought it was going to get in my way but then I saw it swing out to one side and land, so I knew I was all right. But it had distracted my attention at a very important time. As I was coming in to land I had a funny feeling that something was wrong. Then it suddenly occurred to me: I had forgotten to lower the undercarriage! The klaxon horn, which had come on when I throttled back with the wheels still up, was barely audible with the hood open and the engine running. I lowered the undercarriage and it came down and locked with a reassuring 'clunk'. Then I continued down and landed. Afterwards people said to me 'You've got a nerve, leaving it so late before you put the wheels down.' But I just grinned and shrugged my shoulders. In the months that followed I would go quite cold just thinking about it: supposing I had landed the first Spitfire wheels-up! I kept the story to myself for many years afterwards.

Once down I rang the number at Air Ministry I had been given, as ordered. The officer on the other end said 'I don't want to know everything, and obviously you can't tell me. All I want to know now is whether you think the young pilot

officers and others we are getting in the Air Force will be able to cope with the aircraft.' I took a deep breath—I was supposed to be the expert, having jolly nearly landed with the undercarriage up! Then I realised that it was just a silly mistake on my part and I told him that if there were proper indications of the undercarriage position in the cockpit, there should be no difficulty. On the strength of that brief conversation the Air Ministry signed a contract for the first 310 Spitfires on 3 June, eight days later.

On the following day K 5054 had her fuel and oil tanks drained and she was sent off for weighing. On the very accurate Martlesham weighbridge her tare weight was found to be 4,082 pounds; and the all-up weight (including the full fuel load of 75 gallons, 7 gallons of oil, 200 pounds allowed for the pilot and parachute and 436 pounds for service equipment—mainly ballast weights in lieu of guns, ammunition and the radio set) came to 5,359 pounds. There followed a careful series of checks to establish the centre of gravity of the aircraft under differing load conditions. The aft limit was established at 9.9 inches aft of the datum point (the vertical datum line ran immediately in front of the fuel tank), achieved when the aircraft was normally loaded but ballast weighing 150 pounds representing 2,400 rounds of ammunition had been removed (as though the ammunition had been fired off). The forward limit of the centre of gravity, at 8.4 inches aft of the datum, was established by removing 54 pounds of ballast representing the radio installation and 60 gallons of fuel weighing 462 pounds which left only the normal reserve for half an hour's flying time.

When the prototype Spitfire went to Martlesham two technical representatives from Supermarine went with her, Ernie Mansbridge and Ken Scales. The author is indebted to the former both for his reminiscences and for the use of documents he wrote at the time. Almost every day Mansbridge wrote a report to the firm describing the progress of the Spitfire's trials sometimes in great detail; and fortunately for history he kept carbon copies of these, 95 pages of them.

On 4 June the Spitfire was ready to fly again and both Edwardes-Jones and Flight Lieutenant Simmonds made short flights to test handling. Mansbridge noted 'After these flights it was found that the elevator fabric had been damaged and the elevator flap operating rod and its fairing bent, apparently by a stone or something thrown back during taxying.'

This minor damage was put right and on the following day Edwardes-Jones carried out the speed runs in the new fighter during which he noted that the oil temperatures were on the high side. Then, in Mansbridge's words:

The aircraft was refuelled and Sdn Ldr Anderson took off to repeat the test. On reaching 11,000 ft however he found petrol coming back into the cockpit. By opening the hood and turning on his oxygen supply he managed to get down safely. The leak is apparently a pinhole through the centre of one of the deBergne rivets attaching the flange for the contents gauge on the lower tank. This is being replaced by a bolt and the tank will be pressure tested first thing in the morning.

Further speed trials were flown on the 6th and the 8th, on the latter day watched by Reginald Mitchell who was visiting Martlesham to see how his new fighter was progressing. During these trials the maximum speed of the prototype was measured at 349 mph at 16,800 feet, 1 mph more than Jeffrey Quill had recorded three weeks earlier. Some time before Bill Lappin of Rolls-Royce had made a friendly £5 bet with Mitchell that the Spitfire would not be able to reach 350 mph on the 990 horsepower of the Merlin Type C with which it was fitted. On hearing how close the fighter had come to that target figure Lappin sportingly paid up.*

*The report of the initial trials at Martlesham is given at Appendix B.

**26.** The prototype Spitfire pictured at Martlesham Heath, shortly after delivery to the test establishment on 26 May 1936. For these initial service trials only the long pitot head was fitted. *(RAF Museum)*

In the course of these flights there had been a few minor problems with the aircraft. On 8 June Mansbridge wrote 'The starboard wheel flap has developed slack in the trunnion and some of the rivets are pulling slightly. This is being closely watched and will be removed if it gets any worse. Pilots have been asked to raise and lower the chassis at as low a speed as they can.' He went on to report:

There have been no serious criticisms, but the following points have been suggested as worth consideration:
1. Windscreen. The present windscreen is not satisfactory for 'following' an aircraft which is being attacked. For ordinary handling the pilots have got used to the screen and do not complain.
2. Klaxon. The chassis horn is not loud enough and cannot be heard above the general roar of the aircraft. This would be even more so with headphones on. Suggest trying a high-frequency horn mounted nearer the pilot—better still, an intermittent signal.
3. After Flt Lt Skelton's landing with the skid on the ground and the aircraft at about 45° to the ground, it is thought that there is too much elevator. The best way of countering this is not decided, but it is suggested that (subject to tests with the C of G forward), the upward movement should be reduced to 2/3 and the gearing altered to give more movement to the stick.
4. Elevator trimmer. This requires gearing down to give less sensitive movement.
5. Rudder. This is considered too heavy in dives but this point will be further considered during diving tests.
6. Radiator flap. Difficult to close at high speeds (but less so than on the Hawker).
7. Oil filler. The door in the cowling is not large enough to take the standard RAF Bowser nozzle. It should be enlarged 1'' all round.
8. W/T [radio installation] door. The sergeant considers that

the W/T people will criticise accessibility of the W/T unless another door is put on the other side of the fuselage.

The trials at Martlesham continued until 16 June, when Jeffrey Quill arrived to collect K 5054 and take her back to Eastleigh for the press day planned for two days later. When Quill landed it was found that the engine had lost quite a lot of oil, but an extensive examination failed to reveal the cause. The Vickers press day on the 18th was an important occasion and as well as the Spitfire it was intended to demonstrate the firm's other new products: the prototypes of what were to become the Wellesley and Wellington bombers, the Walrus amphibian and the Stranraer and Scapa flying boats. The question was, should the Spitfire be allowed to take part in the air display with the oil leak? Quill later recalled:

There was quite a discussion as to whether she should fly or be taken out of the display. Of course, we did not want to pull her out unless it was absolutely necessary. So I said 'OK, we've got an oil leak. But she carries 7 gallons and I'm going to be up for only 5 minutes. So what the Hell, we'll just lose a bit of oil.' Bill Lappin of Rolls-Royce was against it, but Mitchell gave the go-ahead and we flew her against Lappin's advice.

The decision nearly proved disastrous for K 5054. Quill started up and taxied out for the demonstration, somewhat embarrassed by over-enthusiastic press photographers who crowded in too close for comfort when he began his take off. But the Spitfire built up speed rapidly and soon left them behind. Then, just as Quill was committed to the take-off, he noticed the needle of the oil pressure gauge suddenly drop to zero. He was in a difficult position: there was no room to stop, the engine might suffer a seizure or bearing failure at any moment and if it did he would have to choose between crashing in the town of Eastleigh or on the sprawling Southern Railway locomotive works. I pulled up and took her round on minimum throttle in a wide circuit, trying to get her back on the ground as soon as possible without risking spinning in. During the landing

approach Quill found himself a little too low and had to demand one last burst of power from the Merlin. The redoubtable engine kept going and he was able to get the Spitfire back on to the airfield. Afterwards it was found that an oil pipe had come adrift and drained the lubrication system. The Merlin engine had suffered surprisingly little as a result, but had to be changed.

The Spitfire was ready to fly again with the new engine on 23 June and Quill took her up for a quick test flight. Now K 5054 was ready for her first public demonstration. Hugh Edwardes-Jones went to Eastleigh to pick her up and fly to Hendon, and on the 27th he showed the Spitfire off in front of a large crowd at the Royal Air Force Pageant there. Two days later Mutt Summers demonstrated the Spitfire at the SBAC display at Hatfield. Public interest in the new fighter was immediate and *Flight* magazine waxed lyrical about the display Summers had given at Hatfield:

It is claimed—and the claim seems indisputable—that the Spitfire is the fastest military aeroplane in the world. It is surprisingly small and light for a machine of its calibre (the structural weight is said to have been brought down to a level never before attained in the single seat fighter class), and its speed and manoeuvrability are something to marvel at.

**27** and **28.** Jeffrey Quill pictured getting airborne in the prototype on 18 June 1936, during the first demonstration of the aircraft before the general press. As the pilot was committed to his take-off, at about the time the second photo was taken, the Merlin engine suffered a complete oil failure. With considerable skill Quill took the aircraft round on a wide circuit on minimum throttle and put her back on the ground as soon as he could. In the background of the second photograph can be seen the Southern Railway locomotive works at Eastleigh, where the valuable aircraft nearly finished up. *(Flight, Smithsonian)*

**29.** Mutt Summers landing the prototype at Hatfield, during the Society of British Aircraft Constructors' display on 29 June 1936. The limited 57° travel of the flaps is clearly visible on this photograph. During this display and the Royal Air Force Pageant two days earlier, the aircraft carried the number '2' in black on each side of the fuselage forward of the roundel.

Tight turns were made at high speed after dives, and the control at low speeds was amply demonstrated. The demonstration was cramped by low clouds, but after the main flying display the machine was taken up again and gave one of the smoothest displays of high-speed aerobatics ever seen in this country.

By 1 July the prototype was back at Martlesham and being prepared to resume the service trials. Hugh Edwardes-Jones took her up on the 4th and tested the operation of the automatic boost control at various speeds and altitudes. On the 8th King Edward VIII inspected the establishment at Martlesham and was shown over several of the latest aircraft, including K 5054 which was highly polished for the occasion. Squadron Leader David Anderson flew her during the flying display in the King's honour that afternoon.

On 11 July Edwardes-Jones took the prototype Spitfire up to the greatest altitude yet, 34,700 feet. It took him 37 minutes to get there.

The undercarriage legs on K 5054 had hinged flaps at both the top and the bottom, so that when the wheels were retracted the undersurface of the wing was completely clean. These flaps gave considerable trouble, however, and often failed to close properly. It was decided to remove them in turn and see what difference, if any, they made to performance. On the 18th the top flaps were removed and Flight Lieutenant Simmonds flew a series of accurate level speed tests. 'The observed figures,' Mansbridge noted, 'within the accuracy of observation, do not appear different from those previously obtained.'

On the 24th Flight Lieutenant Simmonds flew speed runs with the lower wheel flaps removed and found that these, too, had no observable effect on performance. From then on, the top and bottom flaps were left off the aircraft.

By that time the Spitfire had accumulated several relatively minor snags. It was planned to return her to Eastleigh early in August for modifications and Mansbridge wrote:

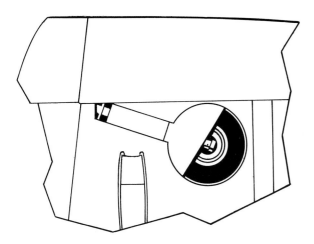

Detail of the retracted main undercarriage leg of K 5054, after the top and bottom fairing doors had been removed in July 1936.

I would suggest the following points for consideration while the aircraft is back:
1. Repair radiator leak.
2. Locate short circuit in Klaxon wiring.
3. Remount Klaxon immediately behind pilot's head.
4. Touch up or remove paint.
5. Increase oil cooling.
6. Enlarge door in cowling giving access to oil filler.
7. Provide hinged flap in undersurface for access to glycol pipes in wing root.
8. Increase wing flap movement to 90°.

With regard to (4), the paint is now getting in a rather poor condition having cracked along all seams. In addition some large patches have come right off. With regard to (5) as mentioned above, the Chief Engineer requires more cooling and until that is provided any engine trouble will probably be attributed to overheating of the oil. With regard to (7), considerable time was spent removing screwed fairings in order to tighten up a Jubilee clip to stop a glycol leak.

During a conversation with the author Ernie Mansbridge went into greater detail on the problems he was now finding with the external finish of K 5054: 'In flight the wings of an aircraft flex, a car body does not. Because of this flexing we soon had cracking of the finish. And this became more serious during the high altitude trials, when the filling would shrink with the cold. After a bit the wing surface on the prototype took on an appearance rather like crazy paving. It became a continual problem for us, to try and patch up the paintwork as best we could.'

Towards the end of this series of trials K 5054 was fitted with a Fairey-Reed three-bladed metal airscrew. On 29 July Jeffrey Quill journeyed to Martlesham to test it. He found that with the three-blader the take-off was similar to that with the wooden two-bladed airscrew, but climbing performance and top speed were slightly worse. The two-bladed airscrew was refitted and on 1 August Quill returned K 5054 to Eastleigh. The initial service trials were now complete*, and the prototype was now to be fitted with the 8-gun armament and receive several minor modifications.

Initially it had been hoped that this modification work would take only a few weeks. But, as we can see from the references to the Spitfire in the minutes of the Secretary of State for Air's meetings during the summer and autumn of 1936, the process dragged out rather:

*The report on these trials is given in full at Appendix C.

15 September
The gun mountings are now completing and the work of providing access to the guns from the upper surface is in hand. It is estimated that the aircraft will be ready for gun trials in a month's time.
23 September
The installation of the reflector sight is completed and that of the wireless is very nearly completed. Work on the gun installation is going ahead. It is anticipated that the aircraft will be ready for gunnery trials about the third week of October.
29 September
The gun installation work is nearly finished and it is anticipated that the aircraft be ready for flight by mid-October. But if a Merlin F is delivered early its installation will take priority. The tail parachute installation, essential for spinning tests, is now being hastened and spinning tests are not likely therefore to be held up until the new engine is fitted.
6 October
The Merlin F has arrived at Woolston and installation is in progress. A small amount of other miscellaneous work is also in hand. Flying is anticipated about the end of October. Work on the tail parachute installation is still lagging and hastening action has been taken.
13 October
K 5054 is at the firm's works. Gun access doors in the top surface of the wings are nearing completion. Installation of the Merlin F engine is proceeding and will be followed by the introduction of the new Serck oil cooler and undercarriage jacks. Arrangements are in hand to forward the Browning guns ex-Hurricane for installation in this aircraft during the week. It is not anticipated that the aircraft will be flying for the next four weeks.
27 October
The Browning guns have arrived at the firm's works and installation work is in hand. Alteration to the ammunition box necks is necessary and it will probably take about two weeks to complete the gun installation. The engine installation is nearly completed but awaits the arrival of the oil cooler. The tail parachute installation details are made up and are being embodied. Flying is anticipated in three weeks time.
23 November
The Browning gun installation is nearly finished. Work on the installation of the Merlin F is finished except for the [oil cooler] air intake which is now being fitted. The tail parachute installation is nearly finished. Flying is anticipated by December 1st.

In the event K 5054 did not fly again until 3 December, on the power of the slightly different Merlin F engine which developed 1,050 horsepower at 16,000 feet. On that day and the next Jeffrey Quill flew the aircraft four times, paying particular attention to the oil temperature readings at various airspeeds and power settings. At the end of the last of these he ran short of fuel and landed at the RAF airfield at Tangmere. By now the Spitfire was the subject of great interest wherever she went, and everyone came out to see the aircraft. Then, in Quill's words:

I taxied to a standstill and shut down, and could hear a tapping sound rather like raindrops hitting the aircraft. But it was a clear day. I checked I had shut everything down but the tapping sound continued. Then as I climbed out I saw the reason. Several mechanics were standing around the rear fuselage, tapping it with their knuckles disbelievingly. 'My God', one of them exclaimed, 'its made of tin!'

For the RAF, the Spitfire possessed several features that were entirely novel.

30, 31, 32

**30, 31, 32.** The prototype on or about 3 December 1936, when she resumed flying following the installation of the eight Browning guns and a manifold over the exhausts to reduce glare for night flying. At the time the photographs were taken the markings had not been repainted on. The aircraft was now fitted with the Merlin F engine and had a strengthening strip along the top of the cowling immediately above the exhausts. On the rear fuselage, just in front of the fin, can be seen the shackle for the spin-recovery parachute; a horn balance guard had been fitted at the top of the fin, to prevent the parachute cable snagging there. The man about to climb the steps was Ken Scales, the foreman in charge of maintenance work on the prototype. *(Shenstone)*

After his diversion, on the 5th Quill returned the Spitfire to Eastleigh, and flew a second time that day to investigate further the efficiency of the new oil cooler. During this period he tried out one or more new features during almost every flight. On the 6th, 7th and 10th December he tested the prototype with a four-bladed wooden airscrew; this gave no improvement in performance over the previously used two-blader, and the latter was refitted.

On 7 December Quill spun the Spitfire for the first time and found that with the centre of gravity at its forward permissible

position, she came out in the normal way. The next step was to show she would do the same thing when spun with the centre of gravity as far back as it might become in normal service use (ie with all the ammunition fired). In this case there was always a risk that the aircraft might spin at so flat an angle that it would not come out using the normal stick-forwards-and-opposite rudder technique. To get the aircraft out of the spin in this case, K 5054 was fitted with a spin recovery parachute; Jeffrey Quill described the system and its operation:

It was all a bit of a lash-up. The small parachute, about 3 feet in diameter, was folded and housed in a box about 9″ by 6″ by 2″, fitted in the cockpit on the right side. From the parachute a steel cable ran out between the front of the canopy and the windscreen, then to the base of the fin where it was attached to a ring bolt. To stop it flapping about in the airflow, the cable was held down at regular intervals with sticky tape. If the aircraft got into a flat spin and would not come out using the normal recovery procedure, the idea was that I should slide back the canopy, grab the folded parachute

**33.** The prototype seen at Tangmere, on 4 or 5 December 1936, after Jeffrey Quill had landed there after running short of fuel during a test flight. *(RAF Museum)*

**34.** The cockpit of the prototype, photographed late in 1936 or early in 1937, after the fitting of guns but before the application of camouflage. Note the unusual gun firing button in the centre of the control column grip, and the random positioning of instruments. *(R. J. Mitchell Museum)*

and toss it out on the side opposite to the direction of the spin (taking care not to let the cable pass across my neck if the parachute had to be tossed to the left!). The parachute would then stream out behind the tail and as it opened yank the aircraft straight, thereby providing what was in effect a much more powerful rudder.

Once the parachute had pulled the aircraft straight it could be jettisoned, and by pushing down the nose a normal spin recovery should then be possible. Quill tested the parachute and jettison system on the 11th and found it functioned as expected. Then on the 13th, 15th and 16th he flew K 5054 seven times with the centre of gravity moved progressively further aft and put her into spins both to the left and the right. On each occasion he found that the aircraft recovered normally, without recourse to the parachute.

After the spinning trials were successfully completed K 5054 was tested with other different types of propeller. On 19 and 20 December she was flown with a de Havilland three-blade two-pitch airscrew with various pitch settings.

Following the Christmas break, K 5054 resumed flying early in 1937. This next series of trials would have been worthy of

Heath Robinson himself. On the prototype the external skinning had been attached with flush riveting throughout. But this process was complicated and expensive. Could the simpler and cheaper dome-headed rivets be substituted in some places on the production aircraft, without too great a loss in performance? On 5 and 7 January Jeffrey Quill took the prototype up seven times to find out. The trial called for extremely accurate flying. Ernie Mansbridge described how the 'split pea' trials were conducted, in his lucid report:

Method of Test
    The rivet heads were represented by split peas attached to the wing surface by Seccotine in the positions which would be used on production aircraft. The split peas were removed in stages in order to ascertain the effect of applying snap rivetting to different parts of the aircraft.
    The pilot carried out a set of level speed runs in each condition and these were analysed.
    It should be noted that the split peas were the same diameter as the proposed rivets but the average height of the peas was .11'', compared with .085'' for the proposed rivets.

Results of Tests
    The loss of speed due to fixing split peas all over the aircraft is 22 mph
    This is made up as follows:

| | | |
|---|---|---|
| | Leading edge aft to spar at .25 chord | 8 mph |
| Aft of spar on wing | Transverse rows on wing, fuselage and tail | 4.5 mph |
| | Fore and aft rows on top surface of wing | 5.5 mph |
| | Fore and aft rows on under surface of wing | 3 mph |
| | Fore and aft on fuselage | 1 mph |

Rudimentary though they may have been, the split-pea trials did establish the important fact that while dome-headed rivets were not acceptable on the wings, they could be used in fore and aft rows on the fuselage with only a minimal reduction in performance. And they would be used in this way on production Spitfires.

From 22 December, the Spitfire had been fitted with its radio mast and aerial. And on 8 January it was fitted and flown with a tail wheel for the first time, a split-type with two small wheels and a central axle. The next day, K 5054 was flown with the single-wheel Dunlop tailwheel. Mitchell had objected strongly to the fitting of a tail wheel at all, because this gave more drag than the streamlined skid previously fitted. But the Air Ministry were adamant; what they knew, and what Mitchell could not be told, was that the decision had been taken to build hard all-weather runways at the RAF's main front line airfields. And a streamlined tail skid would not have lasted long during operations off such a surface.

Altogether, from 3 December 1936 to 21 January 1937, K 5054 spent a total of 25 hours 57 minutes airborne in the course of 48 flights by Jeffrey Quill which embraced spinning, split-pea, airscrew, oil cooling, tail wheel and general handling tests.

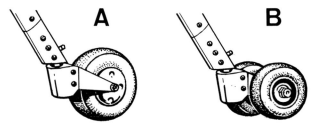

Tail wheels tested on K 5054 in January 1937: A, the Dunlop single wheel type which later became standard; B, the split-type tail wheel which was rejected.

The testing continued much of the way through February, until the 23rd when George Pickering flew the Spitfire back to Martlesham. Once again Ernie Mansbridge went with her, to keep an eye on the service trials and report any problems found with the aircraft. On the 26th he informed the works:

When the tanks were being filled it was noticed that the slowest rate of supply from the standard RAF petrol lorry is too fast for the tanks, as only 10 gallons had run through into the bottom tank before the top tank completely filled and the petrol overflowed.

As a result of this comment the pipe connecting the two tanks would be made wider on production aircraft.

The main feature of the new series of trials at Martlesham was to be the firing of the Spitfire's guns (there were no facilities for this at Eastleigh). On 26 February the four port guns were tested on the butts and fired perfectly; on 1 March the four starboard guns were similarly tested. On 6 March the fighter was taken up to 4,000 feet with a full load of ammunition and the guns fired again; all functioned perfectly. Also for this flight the aircraft was re-fitted with the split-type tail wheel and Mansbridge afterwards reported:

The split tail wheel has been fitted for today's flights. The pilots noted the lack of the bouncing tendency, but on the second flight the wheels were completely locked by mud and could not be revolved until the mud had been dug out from between the wheels.

This type of tail wheel was not fitted again, and from then on the single-wheel Dunlop type was used.

On 10 March Flight Lieutenant Dewar took off from Martlesham for what was intended to be the final one in the series of armament tests: the firing of all guns at 32,000 feet. On this occasion the trial did not go quite according to plan, however. The official report stated:

Only three of the eight guns fired, the number of rounds fired from these guns being as follows:

| | |
|---|---|
| No 4 Port gun | 171 |
| No 2 Starboard | 4 |
| No 3 Starboard | 8 |

The cause of the stoppages in Nos 2 and 3 guns, and the failure of the remaining 5 to fire at all, was the low air temperature (−53°C) [−63°F], coupled with the fact that the guns being mounted in the wings must have their breeches open until firing takes place.

That was bad enough, but when Dewar touched down at Martlesham after the flight the shock of landing released the breech blocks of three of the guns that had not fired, and each loosed off a round in the general direction of Felixstowe! Pending an investigation the firing trials were halted. Mansbridge informed the company: 'It has been decided that there is to be no more air firing of Browning guns until some positive form of fire and safe mechanism is fitted. Captain Adams is dealing with this matter.'

Testing of other aspects of the Spitfire continued, however, and during a flight on 16 March the radio mast broke due to side whip and had to be removed.

Then, on 22 March, K 5054 suffered her first major accident. Flying Officer Sam McKenna was testing the Spitfire with revised gearing between the stick and the elevators, following complaints of elevator buffeting when pulling out of loops and tight turns. McKenna made a series of loops, pulling steadily increasing accelerations up to 4 G. Then he dived the aircraft to 350 mph indicated and made tight turns at up to 4 G. When the trial was complete however, and he throttled back to 1,600 rpm

to return to Martlesham, the oil pressure suddenly fell to zero and the engine began to run roughly and noisily. This condition got steadily worse so McKenna switched off the engine and decided to make a forced landing. He selected a strip of heathland near Sutton beside the Woodbridge—Bawdsey road, and glided the Spitfire in with flaps lowered and undercarriage up; fortunately the propeller had come to rest in the horizontal position. The tail wheel touched first and ran along the ground for about 100 yards, then the fuselage dropped and the aircraft slithered across the ground for a further 50 yards before she came to rest just ten yards short of a hole eight feet deep.

The official RAF report on the accident listed the damage suffered by K 5054:

> The intake chutes of the radiator and the oil cooler were badly torn, but the oil cooler was undamaged and the radiator appeared to be sound except for slight superficial damage to the casing. There is a wrinkle in the bulkhead in front of the main spar, but unless there is further damage behind it (which seems unlikely), this is of no consequence.

> The engine bearer was badly dented, presumably by a connecting rod coming through the crankcase, but in other respects the airframe appeared to be airworthy: it was lifted by crane and the undercarriage lowered in a perfectly normal manner.

Four holes were found in the engine crankcase, and several of the big-ends and connecting rods had failed. The basic cause was found to be excessive heating due to an oil failure within the engine, which was taken to Rolls-Royce for detailed investigation.

The damaged Spitfire was driven back to Supermarine for repair and work began on fitting a system for heating the aircraft guns during flight. The troublesome external finish was removed and the prototype was repainted with a drab brown

**35, 36.** K 5054 photographed on 22 March 1937, after Flying Officer Sam McKenna made a belly landing beside the Woodbridge to Bawdsey Road following engine failure during a test flight from Martlesham Heath. The two flap indicator doors above the starboard wing, hinged from the rear, were a feature unique to the prototype; on subsequent aircraft a single door hinged from the side was fitted. *(Crown Copyright)*

**37.** The prototype on the ground at Eastleigh, some time after September 1937 after she had been camouflaged and had ejector exhausts fitted. Note the revised outline of the top of the engine cowling, following repairs after the belly landing earlier in the year. The shackle for the spin recovery parachute remained in place, but the rudder horn balance guard had been removed. From left to right, Messrs Fry, Ken Scales (in cockpit), A. Preskett and G. Scruby.

and green camouflage top-coat and silver undersides. Several accounts have stated that K 5054 emerged from these repairs 'modified to full production standard', but this was not so. As will be seen in the next chapter, there were important differences between the prototype and production Spitfires which went far beyond the application of a new coat of paint.

In the meantime Reginald Mitchell's health had deteriorated steadily and from the beginning of 1937 he was able to spend less and less time at Supermarine. An operation in March to arrest the cancer proved unsuccessful and his condition was found to be incurable. Reginald Mitchell died on 11 June at the age of 42, a great loss to all who knew him. But by then his legacy to the nation, the fastest and potentially the most effective fighter aircraft in the world, had proved its capabilities beyond any reasonable doubt.

During Mitchell's last months Harold Payn, who held the post of Assistant to the Chief Designer, was put in charge of the day-to-day running of the Supermarine design team, responsible to Rex Pierson the Chief Designer at Vickers plant at Weybridge. Then, shortly after Mitchell's death, Joe Smith was promoted from Chief Draughtsman to Chief Designer at Supermarine.

Jeffrey Quill flew the repaired prototype for the first time on 9 September, and during the six weeks that followed he and George Pickering tested the aircraft with no fewer than eight different types of airscrew, including the Schwarz fixed pitch wooden three-blader.

On 19 September the Spitfire was flown for the first time with ejector exhausts. This system had been developed for the Merlin engine by Messrs R. N. Dorey and H. Pearson at Rolls-Royce. Each minute that it ran at full power, the Merlin gulped in through the carburettor air intake a volume of air about as great as a single-decker bus; after combustion, this air was squirted out of the exhausts at about 1,300 mph. By carefully canting the exhaust pipes rearwards, Rolls-Royce engineers found they could get 70 pounds of thrust—the equivalent of 70 horsepower at 300 mph—almost for nothing. It was a useful addition, which would increase the speed of the prototype to about 360 mph.

On 25 October Flight Lieutenant Isherwood took K 5054 back to Martlesham for trials with the new gun heating system. Remote reading thermometers were fitted to the outboard guns, to measure the temperatures there at high altitude and give an indication of the effectiveness of the heaters. During this period electrical heating shoes and various types of hot air ducting from the radiator and oil cooler were tried. For each

**38, 39.** Jeffrey Quill about to take-off from Eastleigh on the evening of 20 January 1938. during the initial series of night flying tests of K 5054. Note the revised inlet to the oil cooler since the repairs after the belly landing the previous year, the fairing over the rear of the oil cooler to duct hot air to warm the machine guns on the port side (the starboard guns drew their hot air from the rear of the coolant radiator), and the gun heating air exhaust duct under the outer section of the port wing. In the close-up photograph additional test instrumentation can be seen fitted to a bracket just below the windscreen. *(Flight)*

major modification the Spitfire had to return to Eastleigh. At about this time a streamlined fairing was fitted over the rear of the oil cooler and the whole of the heated air emerging from it was ducted into the wing, past the guns on the port side and exhausted from a streamlined outlet under the wing just out-board of the port outer gun. The aircraft was flown with this system in January 1938 but it would appear not to have been satisfactory.

Also in January 1938 Jeffrey Quill conducted the first night flying trials with K 5054, with four flights from Eastleigh. He reported that in his opinion the glare from the exhaust flames was too bright to be acceptable for general service use; he felt that unless some type of exhaust shielding was fitted, the aircraft would not be suitable as a night fighter.

By the end of February the system of gun heating had been revised yet again, this time with a couple of hot air ducts each 3½ inches in diameter, carrying air from the rear of the radiator in the starboard wing to the guns in either wing. This method gave the best results so far and in this condition Jeffrey Quill flew the Spitfire back to Martlesham on 4 March.

The new series of firing trials went off better than before, but still the problem was not quite solved. On 14 March Mansbridge wrote in his report to the company:

The starboard guns appear satisfactory and have fired throughout the tests without a hitch. The port guns nos 1 and 2 [the inboard weapons] also appear satisfactory. The port guns nos 3 and 4 are not satisfactory.

Clearly the system of ducting hot air from the back of the radiator could be the answer to the gun-heating problem, pro-vided the inside of the wing was modified to make the best use of the available hot air. The Air Ministry report following this latest series of firing trials stated:

It was decided to insert a bulkhead in the port wing out-board of the wheel-bay and to lead the hot air duct from the fuselage to this bulkhead. The hot air duct is to be coated with non-conducting material, and all available openings are to be blanked off in the wing structure. The introduction of this bulkhead will reduce the area required to be heated by approximately one-half, and it is hoped that this will materi-ally increase the wing heating.

While these changes were being decided, trials with other aspects of handling the Spitfire continued. On 14 March Flight Lieutenant Hyde conducted the first service night flying trials with the aircraft. He reported that he did not find the flames streaming back from the ejector exhausts particularly trouble-some, though this was probably because it was a bright moonlit night.

On the next evening, the 15th, the Spitfire was again flown at night but suffered damage in a landing accident. Ernie Mans-bridge reported what had happened to his company.

While night flying last night the aircraft stood up on her nose at the end of the 3rd landing. The pilot (Sgt Wareham) had made 2 excellent landings. On the 3rd he came in faster than usual, touched down about half way across the aero-drome and then ran over the 'fire-belt' at the edge on to some

soft stuff and nosed over when almost at a standstill. He said subsequently that the flaps did not come down and when he eventually got down the brakes would not work. When inspected about 15 mins after landing the gauge shewed 5 lbs so the trouble was evidently lack of air pressure due to carrying out landings and taxiing down wind (using rudder and thus losing air*) without giving the compressor time to restore the supply. This is a point that will want watching in the squadrons as the rpm are so low with the fixed pitch airscrew that the compressor doesn't do its job under these conditions. The damage consists of :

1. Broken airscrew
2. Flattened spinner
3. Front cowling panel under engine buckled
4. Port oleo leg fairing twisted

In a follow-up letter Mansbridge wrote that the root cause of the accident was that the air compressor fitted to the Spitfire was of the same type as that designed originally to top up the air bottles of aircraft like the Heyford bomber, which flew for 4 or 5 hours on each flight and used the compressed air only for the brakes. On the Spitfire, which used compressed air for both flaps and brakes and which flew much shorter sorties, this compressor was not powerful enough; a stronger one would be needed on production aircraft.

The damage incurred by the night flying accident was not serious and by the 19th, three days later, it had been repaired and the aircraft was ready to fly again. During the next four days there were several further climbs to altitude to measure gun temperatures, but until the internal bulkhead had been fitted inside the wing these were still not satisfactory.

Then, during renewed night flying trials on 23 March, the Spitfire suffered more serious damage in another accident. Ernie Mansbridge noted:

The night flying test has again resulted in damage to the aircraft. The pilot bounced rather heavily and everyone expected to see him open up and go round but he elected to continue the landing. It was of course dark and therefore diffficult to see what happened. The machine touched down and the noise was much greater than usual. It ran on and then suddenly swerved around and stopped.

On examination it was found that the port oleo leg had torn away from the spar by the failure of the bolts. The stub axle is bent, but which happened first is doubtful. The machine settled down on the port wing tip and the starboard leg. The

*While taxiing down wind the pilot would have had to use differential braking to steer the aircraft.

**40.** Modified blister-type exhausts fitted to K 5054 during night flying trials on 23 March 1938, to reduce glare. That evening the aircraft was badly damaged in a landing accident.

40

port leg and wheel were pushed up into the wing, fortunately missing the main structure. The plating at the tip is slightly buckled on the top surface, and the new pitot head has collapsed.

The official report issued later suggested that metal fatigue of the port undercarriage leg could have been a major contributary cause of the accident and noted that by that time K 5054 had done some 400 landings.

For this trial the Spitfire had been fitted with modified blister exhausts in place of the ejector type; the former were supposed to give less glare. The modified blister exhausts were not found to give any improvement over the ejector type and were not used again.

Once again K 5054 was returned to Eastleigh by lorry. The repair work, and modifications to the gun heating system, lasted into the middle of July and it was the 19th before Jeffrey Quill took her up for the next flight. In the meantime however the importance of the prototype had been eclipsed by the maiden flight of the first production Spitfire, K 9787, on 15 May. Now the main task of the prototype was to prove the effectiveness of modifications considered for production aircraft—of which the most important were those to solve the nagging

**41** and **42.** K 5054 photographed at Eastleigh in September 1938, shortly before she left her home airfield for the last time. *(R. J. Mitchell Museum)*

**43** and **44.** K 5054 pictured after the fatal accident on 4 September 1939, showing damage to the cockpit area. In the right hand photograph the base of the aerial mast can be seen, with its mounting, forced hard against the top of the forward flare chute with the cable to the pilot's Sutton Harness between. *(RAE)*

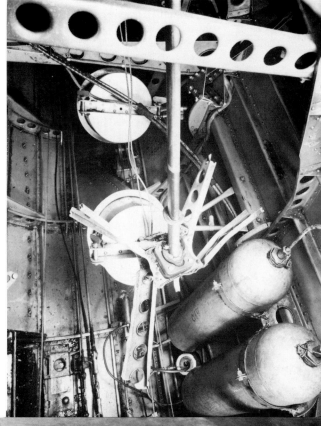

44

problem of providing sufficient gun heating at high altitude. On 27 July George Pickering took K 5054 back to Martlesham to try out the effectiveness of the heating with the additional bulkhead in the port wing. But still there was insufficient warm air at the two outer guns and in September the prototype was back at Eastleigh for yet more modifications. On 4 October Jeffrey Quill returned the aircraft to Martlesham yet again and during the final series of trials there, between the 6th and the 14th, the gun heating system was at last shown to work as it should.

With the successful completion of the gun heating tests K 5054 ended her part in the development story of the Spitfire. By then she had flown about 160 hours over a period of 31 months; by modern standards the number of hours and the intensity of the flying would be considered low, but they were about normal for that time. By the end of October 1938 twenty production Spitfires had flown and new modifications would be tested out on these.

At this time K 5054 was still one of the fastest aircraft in the world, however, and could serve usefully as a 'high speed hack'. Accordingly on 7 November Squadron Leader Bruin Purvis collected the prototype from Martlesham and flew her to Farnborough, where she was to spend the rest of her days. During the next three months she was flown mainly by Purvis and Flying Officer Pebody in work associated with the planned attempt on the World Air Speed Record by the so-called Speed Spitfire*. Initially this work occupied most of the prototype's flying time at Farnborough, though after February 1939 the aircraft was also used for other trials. For example, Squadron Leader George Heycock and other pilots used the prototype during trials to test various combinations of fuel octane values, spark plugs and carburettor settings, to get the best performance out of a Merlin engine on a high performance fighter. On 20 May 1939 K 5054 appeared in public for the last time, when Flight Lieutenant Hall flew her during the Empire Air Day display at Odiham. Altogether eleven RAF pilots flew the prototype during her time at Farnborough and they clocked a total of 98 hours' flying time.

The flying career of K 5054 came to an end on 4 September 1939, the day after Britain entered the war. Flight Lieutenant 'Spinner' White had been testing some new spark plugs that afternoon and afterwards returned to Farnborough. George Heycock saw what happened next:

White was an experienced pilot but he misjudged his landing. He held off a bit too high, the aircraft stalled out and bounced. And as was often the case with a tailwheel aircraft, the bouncing got worse and worse. After two bounces and two leaps into the air, it finally tipped over on to its nose. There was an appalling pause during which it seemed to stand almost perpendicular on its nose; then, unfortunately, it fell onto its back and trapped poor 'Spinner' upside down in the cockpit. We all ran out to try to help, but we couldn't lift the aircraft by ourselves. Then someone brought up a crane which lifted the tail so that we could get the unconscious pilot out. But 'Spinner' White had suffered serious neck injuries and he died in hospital four days later.*

K 5054 was never repaired after the accident. Parts of the aircraft went to the Photographic Department at Farnborough, where they were used to build prototype installations for the fitting of cameras in the wings and fuselage of reconnaissance Spitfires.

Some accounts have stated that K 5054 ended her life having flown only 151 hours 30 minutes; and this figure does indeed appear on her service record card. However, examination of Jeffrey Quill's and George Pickering's logbooks reveals a total of 89 hours 20 minutes flying in K 5054; and it is clear there were several other flights they made which for one reason or another they did not log. In spite of the blanket entry of '20 hours experimental flying' in Mutt Summers's logbook, it is highly unlikely his total flying time in the prototype exceeded half that. So the total flying time by the firm's test pilots in K 5054 probably amounted to about 110 hours. Since Farnborough records account for 98 hours' flying by the prototype during her nine months there, it is clear that the figure of 151 hours 30 minutes refers only to her *service* flying time. The true total flying time for the first Spitfire was probably about 260 hours.

K 5054 cost the British taxpayer £15,776. Rarely has government money been better spent.

*See Chapter 5.

*Part of the official report on the accident is given at Appendix D

# Appendix A

## SPITFIRE PROTOTYPE K 5054

General particulars of aircraft on 26 May 1936, at the time of delivery to Royal Air Force Martlesham Heath for trials.

**Dimensions:** Wing span 37 ft (according to Vickers figures) Length 29 ft 11 ins, Height (over tip of airscrew) 12 ft 8 in, Gross wing area 242 square ft

**Weights:** Tare weight 4,082 pounds
Fully loaded weight 5,359 pounds (tare weight plus the fuel load of 75 gallons, 7 gallons of oil, 200 pounds for pilot and parachute, 436 pounds for service equipment and ballast in lieu of guns, ammunition and radio set). During the flight trials in June 1936 the weight was 5,332 pounds
Wing loading when fully loaded 22 pounds per square foot

**Armament:** none fitted originally. From December 1936 eight .303-in Browning guns with 300 rounds per gun

**Power plant:** initially a 990 horsepower Rolls-Royce Merlin Type C. After December 1936 a 1,045 horsepower Merlin Type F fitted

**Propeller:** initially a two-bladed fixed pitch wooden airscrew, diameter 10 ft 8 in. Various other types were tested on the prototype later, including the Fairey-Reed three-bladed fixed pitch metal type; the de Havilland three-bladed two-pitch metal type; the Schwarz three-bladed fixed pitch wooden type and a four-bladed fixed pitch wooden type.

**Other dimensions:** Flap travel 57°
Dihedral angle 6°. Aspect ratio 5.67
Wing incidence +2° at root, −½° at tip (2½° twist along span)

**Performance:** Maximum limiting speed 380 mph (indicated). Other performance figures given in Appendix B.

# Appendix B

## AEROPLANE AND ARMAMENT EXPERIMENTAL ESTABLISHMENT MARTLESHAM HEATH July 1936

### Interim Performance Report

A.M. Ref:- 431708/35/R.D.A.1
A.&A.E.E. Ref:-M/4493/20—A.S. 56

**Aircraft:** Spitfire I K 5054
**Weight:** 5332 lb (Ballast in lieu of guns, carried in wing)
**Engine:** Merlin C
Normal R.P.M. 2600. Max. Perm. R.P.M. 3000
Rated Boost 6 lb/sq. in. Take-off Boost 6 lb/sq. in.
**Airscrew:** Drg No 300700/C (sheathed) Serial No C 3614

**Level speeds:**

| Height | True Air Speed, m.p.h. | R.P.M. | Boost lb/sq. in |
|---|---|---|---|
| 10,000 | 330 | 2785 | +6 |
| 13,000 | 341 | 2890 | +6 |
| *16,800 | 349 | 3025 | +6 |
| 20,000 | 345 | 3015 | +3⅛ |
| 25,000 | 337 | 2915 | 0 |
| 30,000 | 324 | 2760 | — |

*Full throttle height

**Climb:**

| Height ft | Time mins | Rate of Climb ft/min | A.S.I. m.p.h. | R.P.M. | Boost lb/sq. in |
|---|---|---|---|---|---|
| S.L. | 0 | 2400 | 175 | 2070 | +6 |
| 5,000 | 2 m | 2680 | 175 | 2250 | +6 |
| 9,400 | 3 m 33 s | 2920 | 175 | 2400 | +6 |
| 15,000 | 5 m 52 s | 2300 | 158 | 2360 | +1¾ |
| 20,000 | 8 m 12 s | 1770 | 143 | 2320 | +1¼ |
| 25,000 | 11 m 36 s | 1220 | 128 | 2270 | — |
| 30,000 | 17 m | 680 | 113 | 2200 | — |

| | |
|---|---|
| Service ceiling | 35,400 ft |
| Take-off (in 5 mph wind) | |
| Take-off run | 235 yds |
| Distance from rest to clear 50 ft screen | 480 yds |
| Landing (in 5 mph wind) | |
| Landing run (with brakes) | 220 yds |
| Landing run (without brakes) | 480 yds |
| Distance from 50 ft screen to rest (with brakes) | 525 yds |

The following results have been obtained during tests with airscrews of other designs:
Design Drawing No 3001000 Serial No C 5003
Level speed 15,600 ft 345 mph T.A.S. 2840 r.p.m. +6 lb/sq. in
Climb
8,600 ft, 2,750 ft/min 2250 r.p.m. +6 lb/sq. in, 175 mph A.S.I.
Fairey Reed 3 Blade, Design Drawing No 61640A

From the scanty information obtained under level flight conditions, the full throttle height is at about 16,800 ft, the r.p.m. approximately 3,000 and the true air speed slightly less than that obtained with the airscrew to Design Drawing No 300700/C.

Similarly for climbing flight, the full throttle height is approximately at 8,600 ft with an A.S.I. of 175 mph and r.p.m. 2400.

Take-off was not measured with this airscrew but the pilot's impression was that the take-off was about the same as with No 300700/C.

Suitability

Taken all round, the airscrew to Drg No 300700/C appears the most suitable.

# Appendix C

## AEROPLANE AND ARMAMENT EXPERIMENTAL ESTABLISHMENT MARTLESHAM HEATH
### September 1936

**Handling trials of the Spitfire K-5054**

A.M. Ref:-431708/35/R.D.A.1.
A.&A.E.E. Ref:-M/4493/20—A.S.56

Handling trials were done at a total weight of 5332 lb, the centre of gravity was 9.7 inches aft of the datum point.

Limits 8.25''-9.9'' aft—extended by .01 chord to 10.8 inches aft.

## CONTROLS

### Ailerons
On the ground the aileron control works freely and without play. Full movement of the control column can be obtained when the pilot is in the cockpit.

In the air the ailerons are light to handle when climbing and on the glide they become heavier with increase in speed, but by no more than is required to impart good 'feel'.

The aeroplane was dived to 380 mph A.S.I. and up to that speed the ailerons were not unduly heavy, and gave adequate response.

The ailerons are effective down to the stall and give adequate control when landing and taking off. The response is quick under all conditions of flight, and during all manoeuvres required from a fighting aeroplane.

There was no snatch or aileron vibration at any speed, and in general the aileron control is excellent for a high speed fighting aeroplane.

### Rudder
On the ground the rudder control operates freely and without play. There is an excellent adjustment for the position of the rudder bar. In the air it is moderately light and extremely effective. The rudder becomes heavier with increase of speed, but by no more than is necessary in a high speed aeroplane, and at the highest speeds it is still effective.

The aeroplane responds easily and quickly to the rudder under all conditions of flight.

Although the rudder is heavier than the ailerons, it should not be made lighter as with a very light rudder the pilot might overload the aeroplane at high speeds.

### Rudder Bias Gear
The rudder bias control was quick and easy to operate, it is effective and gives adequate range.

### Elevators
On the ground full movement of the elevators can be obtained. Operation is light and there is no play.

In the air the elevator control is light and very effective down to the stall.

Heaviness increases with speed, but by no more than is necessary. In the dive the aeroplane is steady. The elevators give rapid response with a small movement of the control column. When landing the control column need not be fully back.

The control is satisfactory as regards 'feel' and response, but would be improved if the movement of the control column for a given movement of the elevators was slightly greater. A small movement of the control column produces so large an effect that an unskilled pilot might pull the nose of the aeroplane up too much when landing; however, a change to alter the gearing between control column and elevator is not considered advisable until spinning trials show it to be safe.

### Tail Trimming Gear
The tail trimming gear, which is of the trimmer tab type, is easy to operate and very effective. A very small movement of the lever has a powerful effect, and a lower gearing would be an advantage. There is adequate range for trim for all conditions of flight, in fact, only half the available movement of the lever is required.

### Engine Controls
Engine controls are well placed in the cockpit. They work easily and without play and do not slip.

### Flaps
The flaps are operated pneumatically and move down through an angle of 60°C [in fact 57°]. Control is by a switch moved one way for 'down' and the other way for 'up'. The system worked well and gave no trouble in maintenance.

When the flaps are down they reduce the stalling speed by about 12 mph A.S.I. (uncorrected) and the aileron control is better at the stall with the flaps down than with them up. Putting the flaps down caused a noticeable change in trim, which can easily be taken up on the trimming gear or on the elevators. Although these flaps appreciably reduce the flatness of glide, yet this aeroplane would be easier to bring in if the flaps were made more effective either by putting the angle up to 90° or increasing their area.

Since this aeroplane was first flown at this Establishment the pilots have had experience of very high drag flaps on several aeroplanes, and they are unanimous in their opinion that higher drag flaps on the Spitfire would improve its characteristics in the approach, and make it easier for the unskilled pilot to get into a small aerodrome.

If the flaps are modified to give higher drag, two 'down' positions should be provided (say 60° and 90°) because a very high drag flap, although suitable for use in daytime, involves too sudden a change of attitude when flattening out during a landing at night.

The ideal system of operation is a smaller lever by which the flaps can be set to any position as required, but failing this, a system of operation to allow of two settings for the flaps at 60° and 90° is essential.

### Brakes
The brakes are hand operated with differential control on the rudder. They are smooth, progressive, easy to operate and effective. They do not tend to tip the aeroplane up at the end of the landing-run.

## FLYING CONTROLS

### Stability
Laterally the aeroplane is stable. If one wing is depressed and the control column released the aeroplane will return to a level keel in a reasonable time. Directionally the aeroplane is stable under all conditions of flight, engine on or off. Longitudinally the aeroplane is neutrally stable with engine on and stable in the glide. The aeroplane is unstable in the glide with flaps and undercarriage down.

In general the stability characteristics are satisfactory for a fighting aeroplane and give a reasonable compromise between controllability and steadiness as a gun platform.

## Characteristics at the stall

As the elevator control is very powerful the aeroplane will stall long before the control column is moved right back. The stall is normal. There is no vice nor snatch on the controls. In tight turns, giving approximately 3g as registered on the accelerometer, at speeds from 140 mph A.S.I. downwards there was a distinct juddering on the whole aeroplane. Under these conditions the aeroplane is probably in a semi-stalled condition and this juddering effect may be due to slight buffeting on the tail. This can be stopped at once if the control column is eased forward.

Tests according to A.D.M. [aircraft design memorandum] 293 were done with the following results:-

On No 1 test with the undercarriage and flaps up it is difficult to keep the aeroplane steady when the control column is right back. It wallows from side to side and there is snatch on the control column from the elevators. With the undercarriage and flaps down the aeroplane is steadier in the stalled glide and there is no snatch.

In Test No 2 with the undercarriage and flaps down it was possible to pull the wing up when ailerons were applied to unbank, but in turns both to the left and to the right, the aeroplane tends to take charge at the stall and cannot be said to comply with these tests when the control column is pulled right back.

In the third test with the undercarriage and flaps up, the wing can be pulled up, but in this test again the aeroplane takes charge to such an extent that the pilot found it almost impossible to make sure of centralising the rudder. With the undercarriage and flaps down the aeroplane's behaviour was much the same.

In tests Nos 2 and 3 the movements of the aeroplane are more violent to the right than to the left after applying the controls. No spin resulted in either of these two tests.

This aeroplane, in common with other fighters tested at this Establishment, cannot be said to comply fully with tests Nos 2 and 3, as its behaviour depends so much on the way the pilot uses his controls. Its behaviour in test No 1 indicates that there is sufficient lateral control at the stall for a heavily loaded high speed aeroplane of this type.

### Aerobatics

Loops, half rolls off loops, slow rolls and stall turns have been done. The aeroplane is very easy and pleasant to handle in all aerobatics.

### Landing and take-off

The aeroplane is easy and normal to take-off. There is a slight tendency to swing, but this is not so pronounced as on a Fury and is automatically and easily corrected by the pilot. The aeroplane is simple and easy to land, but requires very little movement of the control column as the elevator control is so powerful, and it is not necessary to have the control column fully back.

If the engine is opened up with the flaps and undercarriage down, the aeroplane can be easily held by the control column. The aeroplane does not swing when landing.

### Sideslipping

The aeroplane does not sideslip readily.

### Ground handling

The ground handling is exceptionally good. The aeroplane is easy to turn and taxi in fairly strong winds. It is a more satisfactory aeroplane for operating in high winds than the normal biplane fighter.

## UNDERCARRIAGE

The undercarriage has excellent shock absorbing qualities, and good rebound damping.

The controls for the hydraulically retracting mechanism are simple and well arranged. The undercarriage can be raised in about 10 seconds and lowered in about 15 seconds, without undue effort. The indicators were satisfactory. The wheels cannot be seen, but when the undercarriage is lowered two small rods project through the wings to show its position.

When the undercarriage is fully up or down, the hand lever of the oil pump can no longer be moved, and this is a useful additional indication that the undercarriage is in the required position.

A Klaxon to warn the pilot that the undercarriage is up works when the throttle is pulled back beyond two thirds, but is not loud enough to be heard by him with the cockpit open and the engine on.

## FLYING VIEW

View forwards is fair and upwards is good. View to the rear is fair for a covered cockpit.

The present windscreen gives great distortion. If a curved windscreen of this shape cannot be made in either moulded glass or in suitable material to give no distortion, it is considered that it should be replaced by a flat-sided type, even though this might involve a slight reduction in performance.

With the cover open, the cockpit is remarkably free from draught, and it is possible to land and take-off with the cockpit cover open without using goggles.

## COCKPIT COMFORT

The cockpit is comfortable and there is plenty of room, even for a big pilot. The head room is somewhat cramped for a tall pilot. It is not unduly noisy and the instruments and controls are well arranged. The cockpit is easy to enter and leave when the aeroplane is on the ground and foot steps on the wing are not considered necessary.

At speeds over 300 mph A.S.I. the cockpit cover is very difficult to open, although it has been opened at 320 mph A.S.I., and will stay open. Attention should be given to this question, as it is most important that the pilot should be able to get out of the aeroplane at the very highest speeds without difficulty. A small air flap operated by the handles on the sliding cover might make it easier to open at high speeds.

Although no heating is provided the cockpit was kept warm by heat from the engine and exhaust at 25,000 ft. Gloves were not necessary.

## INSTRUMENTS

All instruments are well arranged and are clearly visible to the pilot. The compass is steady at all speeds.

## SUMMARY OF FLYING QUALITIES

The aeroplane is simple and easy to fly and has no vices. All controls are entirely satisfactory for this type and no modification to them is required, except that the elevator control might be improved by reducing the gear ratio between the control column and elevator. The controls are well harmonised and appear to give an excellent compromise between manoeuvrability and steadiness for shooting. Take-off and landing are straightforward and easy.

The aeroplane has rather a flat glide, even when the undercarriage and flaps are down and has a considerable float if the approach is made a little too fast. This defect could be remedied by fitting higher drag flaps.

In general the handling of this aeroplane is such that it can be flown without risk by the average fully trained service fighter pilot, but there can be no doubt that it would be improved by having flaps giving a higher drag.

# Appendix D

## FATAL ACCIDENT OF K 5054
## 4 September 1939

The account which follows is taken from the official report on the accident of K 5054, at Farnborough on 4 September 1940.

*     *     *

The accident occurred at 1530 hours on the 4th September 1939 on Farnborough aerodrome, during a landing run after an experimental test flight of 45 minutes. The aeroplane was observed to make a normal approach and touch down [sic]; the tail then began to lift slowly until the airscrew touched the ground; the aeroplane was then moving at a comparatively low speed, the tail rose sharply and the aeroplane turned over on to its back.

The pilot, Flight Lieutenant G. S. White, suffered injuries which subsequently proved fatal.

After the accident a preliminary examination revealed that the wheels were free, i.e. there was no binding of the brakes; the undercarriage was locked down and the indicators signalled 'down'; the elevator trimmer tab was set .62 ins down (measured from T.E. of tab to T.E. of elevator); the cockpit ventilator was fully open; the Sutton harness was locked back, and the pilot's seat was fully raised.

The fuselage bulkheads forward of the W/T compartment, the cockpit hood and windscreen, the tail unit and the airscrew were damaged beyond repair. The wireless mast was telescoped into the fuselage until the base of the mast jammed against the top of the forward flare chute.

Subsequent examination of the structure showed that the anchorage cable of the Sutton harness passes through two guides on the under surface of the wireless mast bearer. Thus when the mast was forced into the fuselage it carried the cable attachment to it and shortened its effective length. This had the effect of pulling the pilot hard back into the seat, probably violently, with sufficient force to distort the seat back. The strong point at the head rest had partly collapsed under the side load due to failure of the longitudinal member fitted to carry that load. This allowed the head rest to move forward, and the pilot's injuries were consistent with this movement combined with the jerk on the Sutton harness.

# 3.

# A PROBLEM OF PRODUCTION

On 3 June 1936, before the service trials of the prototype Spitfire had really begun at Martlesham, the Air Ministry had placed an order for 310 examples of the new fighter. The agreed cost of the entire order was £1,395,000, or £4,500 per airframe excluding engine, guns, instruments, radios and other items paid for by the service. Eight weeks later, at the end of July, the Air Ministry issued Specification F.16/36* which set out the respects in which production Spitfires were to differ from the prototype. Of these, by far the most important concerned the revision of the wing structure to make it stiffer and raise the maximum limiting speed to 450 mph (indicated), 70 mph higher than that of the prototype. To achieve this the web connecting the upper and lower booms of the main spar was to be moved from the front to the rear of the booms and thicker gauge light alloy used to cover the leading edge of the wing. These would give the D-shaped torsion box running the length of the wing the necessary extra stiffness. Other important changes to the airframe were that the fuel tankage was to be increased from 75 gallons on the prototype to 84 gallons on production Spitfires, and the flap travel was increased from 57 degrees to 85 degrees.

Quite apart from the changes demanded by the Air Ministry, there were those incorporated by the company to ease the complex task of mass production. In the production aircraft several parts were to be forged or cast rather than built up from separate pieces, and much more extensive use was to be made of pressings and extruded sections. To incorporate these changes work began on an almost complete internal redesign of the Spitfire. Jack Davis, one of the draughtsmen involved, recalled: 'The task of redoing the drawings took about a year. One couldn't conveniently use prototype drawings for the production aircraft, there were so many changes. Though some of the production drawings might have looked the same as those for the prototype, it was much better to redraw and renumber the whole lot. I don't think a single one of the prototype drawings was used for the production aircraft.'

In February 1936, shortly before the prototype made her first flight, Sir Robert McLean had said his firm would be able to begin production of the new fighter 15 months after the placing of the order, at a rate of five aircraft per week. The Air Ministry placed its order in June, so the first production aircraft should have become available in October 1937. Soon after the order was placed, however, it became clear that this date had little chance of being achieved.

In 1936, when it received the order for 310 Spitfires, the Supermarine company employed about 500 people and was engaged in fulfilling orders for 48 Walrus amphibians and 17 Stranraer flying boats for the Royal Air Force. Its production facilities comprised small factories at Hythe and Woolston close together astride Southampton Water, and an assembly hangar at the nearby airfield at Eastleigh. The simple fact was that the small company had nothing like enough capacity to be able to fulfil the large order it had landed. And Vickers (Aviation) Ltd, the parent company, now had no spare capacity either because it had just received an order for 180 Wellington bombers.

The answer was to sub-contract part of the work and in November 1936 General Aircraft Ltd at Feltham received an order to build Spitfire tails. But Sir Robert McLean was not keen to sub-contract out too much of the hard-won Spitfire order. Early in 1937 the problems of mass producing the new fighter began to surface, as can be seen from the minutes of the Secretary of State for Air's meetings:

2 February

Lord Weir [adviser on aircraft production matters] referred to DAP's [Director of Aeronautical Production] report on his visit to the Supermarine works on 25th January and observed that the trouble which had always been anticipated over production of the Spitfire has now come to a head. He wondered whether General Aircraft who were already working on complete tail units for the Spitfire could not assist still further and so ease the production position.

10 February

Lord Weir inquired how serious the setback in the Spitfire production programme would probably be. AMSO [Air Member for Supply and Organisation, Air Chief Marshal Sir Cyril Newall] replied that it would be extremely serious and the firm frankly admitted that they had entirely miscalculated the magnitude of the task. Suggestions had been made to them of the steps to put things right and we are now awaiting their reply.

16 February

Lord Weir asked whether AMSO had anything further to report on the Spitfire programme. AMSO replied that certain suggestions had been made by DAP to Sir Robert McLean for improving the situation at Southampton, eg that Supermarine should make use of General Aircraft and other firms which had capacity to spare, as sub-contractors. Sir Robert McLean had, however, rejected this suggestion and had offered instead to increase the monthly output of Spitfires to 18 by reducing the Walrus monthly output to a quite unacceptable figure. What he was obviously trying to do was to keep the whole of the Spitfire production under his own control and he had, for instance, said that it would be impossible to get fuselages made outside without a great deal of confusion and difficulty. AMSO had told Sir Robert McLean

**45** and **46.** K 9787, the first production Spitfire, photographed in May 1938 shortly after her first flight, with Jeffrey Quill at the controls. *(Charles Brown, copyright RAF Museum)*

that this proposal was totally unacceptable, and he must accept further proposals. S of S [the Secretary of State for Air, Viscount Swinton] said that he had been under the impression that Sir Robert McLean had promised to send a representative to General Aircraft to discuss ways and means and he was extremely disturbed by what AMSO had said. It really was a disgraceful state of affairs, and he felt that if this sort of thing went on it might be necessary for the Air Council to see the whole of the Vickers board of directors and tell them that they must take immediate and practical measures to put an end to what could only be described as an intolerable situation. Lord Weir remarked that he had always understood that the Spitfire would be built mainly outside the Supermarine factory at Southampton, because the latter had nothing like enough floor space. It seemed clear that the only hope of getting satisfactory deliveries of Spitfires was for Supermarine to make use of General Aircraft . . . Lord Weir went on to say that he would be seeing the DAP the following day and would take the opportunity of discussing Spitfire production with him. He suggested that after he had done so he might perhaps take an early opportunity of discussing the whole matter with Sir Charles Craven of Vickers, before there was any question of collective Air Council action.

In the face of this pressure Sir Robert McLean backed down and agreed to farm out a lot more of the work on the Spitfire

order. Eventually it was agreed that four-fifths of the work would go to sub-contractors. The production programme was revised and it was now planned to build four Spitfires in December 1937, 6 each in January and February 1938, eight in March and ten each in April and May.

It was not long before even this less-ambitious programme began to fall apart at the seams. At this time the technical office at Woolston had a staff of only some 15 technicians and 70 draughtsmen and they were swamped with the task of trying to produce the necessary production drawings for the Spitfire as well as design drawings for the S.7/38 amphibian (which became the Sea Otter) and the B.12/36 heavy bomber. Again the minutes of the Secretary of State for Air's meetings reveal the depressing state of affairs, now in mid-1937:

8 June

S of S said that he had noted with regret the statement made in Mr Clegg's [an official at the Air Ministry] report of 29th May that in his opinion the first Spitfire would not be delivered in December, as promised by Sir Robert McLean, owing to the fact that a good deal of material due to be supplied by Supermarine had not been delivered [with the result that the assembly of sub-contractive parts was being held up] and that in addition General Aircraft were unable to supply components in accordance with arrangements already made, owing to their not yet having received certain information and drawings. Mr Clegg replied that Supermarine were very badly behind with deliveries of raw material but while it was impossible, for the reasons stated in his report, to give any definite date for the probable start of production, a slight setback was, he feared, inevitable.

**14 September**
S of S said that he was very disturbed to see from a report from Mr Clegg dated 4th September that Spitfire deliveries were not likely to start before February 1938, that we should probably not get more than 28 by the end of June instead of the firm's estimated total of 74, and that the firm themselves admitted that the Spitfire deliveries they had promised were incapable of achievement. He would like to hear DAP's views on this matter, since he felt that if the position was as stated the situation in fighter squadrons early in 1938 would be exremely serious, as they would have practically no really up-to-date aircraft. CAS [Chief of the Air Staff, by then Marshal of the Royal Air Force Sir Cyril Newall] agreed. DAP replied that he agreed with Mr Clegg's view, he believed that he himself had stated on more than one occasion in the past that it would be well not to count on any Spitfires from this factory before 1938.

At about this time there was a reorganisation of Vickers aircraft production interests. Vickers (Aviation) Ltd and Supermarine Aviation (Vickers) Ltd were now placed under Vickers-Armstrongs Ltd; and the Chairman of the new umbrella company was Sir Charles Craven, who was determined to curtail the previous independence of the managing director Sir Robert McLean.

For his part Sir Robert McLean placed the blame for the delays to the Spitfire programme squarely with the sub-contractors, and was unwilling to admit responsibility for any of the failings to his chairman. In his quarterly report to the board of Vickers Ltd, for the period ending 31 December 1937, he wrote:

On the Spitfire the erection of the fuselages which are being made complete at these works has proceeded in accordance with programme, and at the end of December six fuselages were delivered to Eastleigh for final assembly. At the end of December six sets of spars and leading edges for wings had been completed and delivered to sub-contractors for completion. The detailed production and the delivery of other components to sub-contractors is proceeding satisfactorily. Owing to delays which have occurred in the progress of work at sub-contractors on wings, primarily due to their inexperience of this class of work, the delivery of wings is about 3 months behind programme and the first complete aircraft will not be delivered until the end of March.

It is difficult to reconcile this statement with those being made at the Secretary of State for Air's meetings at this time:

**18 January 1938**
AMSO made a statement on sub-contracting difficulties which had arisen in connection with the Spitfire and explained that the main source of trouble appeared to be the failure of the parent firm to supply accurate drawings to the various sub-contracting firms. The position was, however, gradually improving. AMRD [Air Member for Research and Development, Air Marshal Sir Wilfrid Freeman] said that he too had heard bitter complaints from sub-contractors about the poor quality of the drawings they had received from the Supermarine company. Mr Self [a deputy Under Secretary of State for Air] remarked that this was borne out by the fact that General Aircraft had recently preferred a claim for £40,000 on the grounds that there had been a serious hold up in the production of Spitfire components, owing to delays in the supply of accurate drawings from Supermarine. Mr Self also mentioned that the Supermarine company were now

quoting a price of £7,000 per aircraft for the whole of the contract for 310, which was greatly in excess of what we had expected. He did not, of course, propose to accept this quotation, and the matter would be argued in detail with the firm. In reply to a question from CAS, he added that he would be very disappointed if the Hurricane when in full production came out to more than £4,000, and he thought the price of the Spitfire ought to be the same. CAS observed that some difference would appear to be justified by comparison of the relative sizes of the two orders.

**3 February**
S of S referred to the delays which have occurred in the Spitfire programme and asked whether Sir Charles Craven was satisfied that the sub-contractors, who were being so extensively employed, could meet the demands made on them. The DAP in reply said he was himself much more satisfied with the ability of the sub-contractors than that of Supermarine themselves. He added that he expected the first Spitfire to be delivered this month or in March.

**8 February**
The S of S inquired if there was any further information about the production prospects of the Spitfire. AMRD replied that he had nothing to report beyond the fact that when DDTD [Deputy Director of Technical Development] had been at the Supermarine erecting shop at Eastleigh recently he had asked if he could see how the Spitfire was getting on, and on going into the erecting shop he had seen only one Spitfire there in the course of erection. AMSO said that in his opinion

**47.** The cockpit of an early production Spitfire, showing the standard blind flying panel introduced into RAF aircraft during the late 1930s. *(Vickers)*

47

**48.** Early production Spitfires undergoing final assembly in the hangar at Eastleigh. *(Flight)*

the firm themselves were almost entirely to blame for the present unsatisfactory state of this contract in not having cleared the drawings for production more promptly and for their failure to keep a proper eye on their sub-contractors.

5 April

AMRD said that the real trouble appeared to lie in the chaotic state of the firm's sub-contracting arrangements. Several of the sub-contractors were becoming exasperated by delays by Vickers in providing them with the parts without which they could not complete their sub-contracting work. For example, there were 60 or 70 tail planes lying at Shorts works awaiting details, and in several instances when the necessary parts had been received from the parent firm it was found that they would not fit . . . .

Not until 15 May was the first production Spitfire, K 9787, ready to fly. Jeffrey Quill took it up on that day and found it was all that had been expected, and with the extra 28 degrees of flap travel it came in steeper than the prototype and was easier to land. Subsequent flutter tests at Farnborough revealed that the aircraft could be taken up to 470 mph indicated airspeed, 20 mph more than the Air Ministry had demanded.

Now the Spitfire could be dived faster than ever before, Jeffrey Quill discovered a new problem: at speeds above 400 mph indicated, the aircraft's ailerons became almost immovable. At the time, however, the significance of this was not appreciated. He told the author:

When we flew the first production Spitfire and dived it to 470 mph indicated and found the ailerons so heavy, this was considered at the time to be quite a good thing. The technical people were rather afraid of things like aileron reversal and they felt that if the ailerons became rock solid at very high speeds so much the better—it would stop the young buggers from throwing the fighter around too much and perhaps pulling the wings off. With many others, I felt that in a war most combats—whether against bombers or fighters—would take place well below 400 mph indicated; and there the situation was manageable, even if it was sometimes hard work. We knew there was a problem, but before the war nobody complained—the Spitfire had not yet been in a dogfight. Perhaps I should have shouted louder at the time. But I did not appreciate—and neither did anyone else at the time—that this might become a serious tactical limitation.

Even after the first production aircraft began flying, and others reached the final stages of assembly, the minutes of the Secretary of State for Air's meetings continued to present a gloomy picture on the Spitfire:

5 July

AMDP [a new post, Air Member for Development and Production, Air Chief Marshal Sir Wilfrid Freeman] said that the General Manager of Supermarines had promised some time ago that four Spitfires would be delivered during June. In fact none were delivered. Three might be delivered by the end of July. He had visited Supermarines with DGP [another new post, Director General for Production, Mr Ernest Lemon] and

found that production was seriously out of balance. There were 78 fuselages but only three sets of wings. He had ordered Supermarine to make additional jigs with all possible speed, and General Aircraft were also ordered to duplicate their jigs. DGP said that the position was pitiful. Material was coming off the factory very badly, and men were being taken off the fuselages owing to the lack of wings.

Jeffrey Quill has written some interesting remarks on the problem of getting the Spitfire into production, which have been included in full at Appendix B.

Not until 19 July did the RAF receive its first production Spitfire, K 9788 the second in the batch, which was delivered to Martlesham for trials. It was followed by the first production aircraft K 9787, on the 27th. On 4 August No 19 Squadron at Duxford, which was to be the first unit to receive the new fighter, received its first Spitfire K 9789; K 9790 arrived on the 11th and K 9792 on the 16th (K 9791 was to remain with Supermarine for trials work). The formation of the first Spitfire squadron will be described in the next chapter.

Only two Spitfires were delivered to the RAF in September 1938, but in October there were 13 and production continued at this rate until the end of the year. By the beginning of 1939 a total of 49 Spitfires had been delivered to the RAF. Although the new fighter was now coming off the production lines in useful numbers, it must be remembered that the aircraft was still deficient in one important respect: the early production Spitfires lacked gun heating, which meant their guns could not be relied upon to fire at high altitude. The weakness was a considerable worry to those privy to the facts. The Chief of the Air Staff, Marshal of the Royal Air Force Sir Cyril Newall, pungently summed up the position in September 1938 when he stated 'If the guns will not fire at heights at which the Spitfires are likely

**49.** K 9842, the 56th production aircraft, being pushed out of the assembly hangar at Eastleigh in January 1939 prior to a test flight. In the foreground, left to right, are Arthur Nelson the foreman of the Eastleigh erection shop, Mr Richardson the Chief Inspector at Eastleigh, Mr Fox from the Aeronautical Inspection Directorate and Jeffrey Quill. *(Flight)*

**50.** K 9845 undergoing a compass swing at Eastleigh prior to her maiden flight. The absence of a hot air outlet under the outer section of the port wing reveals that this aircraft was not fitted with gun heating. *(Flight)*

**51.** K 9846, the 60th production aircraft, being readied for a flight. Just visible under the marking on the port wing is the streamlined hot air outlet indicating that this aircraft was fitted with gun heating; it was probably the first production aircraft to have it. *(Flight)*

**52.** Revised exhausts fitted to K 9787, the first production Spitfire, in a partially successful attempt to reduce glare for night flying.

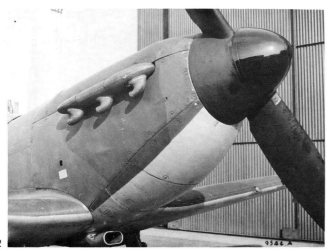

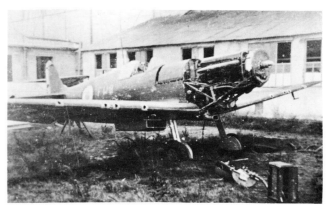

**53.** Taken in France during the winter of 1940-1941, this photograph is believed to depict the 208th production Spitfire which had been sold to the French Air Force and delivered for evaluation in June 1939. *(Gentilli)*

to encounter enemy bombers, the Spitfires will be useless as fighting aircraft . . . .'

Not until the following month was the revised gun heating system fitted to the prototype Spitfire and shown to work efficiently. And not until early 1939, when 60 of the new fighters had been delivered, was gun heating built into production aircraft.

It would be some months before the financial implications of the delays and the increased cost of the programme were sorted out. The final cost of the first 310 Spitfire airframes was £1,870,242, an average of about £6,033 each or about £1,533 more than had originally been estimated. During 1937 a follow-on order for 200 Spitfires had been placed and airframes under this contract would cost £5,696 each.

At this time there was considerable foreign interest in acquiring Spitfires. One of the first such expressions, early in 1937, had come from the Mitsubishi company in Japan which sought to purchase a single example of the new fighter; it is interesting to speculate on the effect on the Pacific War had that deal gone through! Belgium, Turkey, Holland, Yugoslavia, Switzerland, Lithuania and Estonia all inquired after placing orders or receiving licenses to build the Spitfire. The prices of Spitfires quoted to foreign governments were for complete aircraft, and varied according to the equipment specified. The first foreign contract, for 12 Spitfires for the Estonian Air Force at £12,604 each, was signed in February 1939. Due to the shortage of Spitfires for the RAF, however, the first two of these were not to be delivered until the end of August. Greece placed an order for 12 Spitfires, Portugal for 15. Also early in 1939 the French government asked to buy a single Spitfire and, as the most important friendly government interested in the aircraft, it was allowed to jump the queue; its aircraft was flown to France in June 1939 and apart from its markings was a completely standard production Spitfire, the 208th built, even with its instruments calibrated in British markings and units. In the event this was to be the only Spitfire sold overseas before the outbreak of war in September 1939, when the British government suspended all further sales abroad.

One further aspect of Spitfire production needs to be mentioned at this stage. With the war clouds gathering over Europe it was clear that far more Spitfires were going to be needed than could be built at the Supermarine plants around Southampton. Accordingly the government financed the construction of a large factory at Castle Bromwich near Birmingham for the production of Spitfire fighters and Wellington bombers (in the event the latter were never built there), to be managed and equipped by Morris Motors Ltd. Work on building the new plant began in July 1938; it would play an important part in the Spitfire story, but later.

# Appendix A

## SPECIFICATION No F.16/36
## 28th July 1936

### Spitfire I Development and Production

*This Specification covered the 310 Spitfires of the first production contract, which was signed on June 3rd 1936. The first paragraph stated:-*

The aircraft are to be constructed in strict accordance with the drawings and schedules covering the design, construction, etc., of the experimental aircraft built to Specification No F.37/34 in the form in which that aircraft is finally accepted by the Director of Technical Development as the prototype of the production aircraft, except as modified by other requirements of this Specification or by alterations accepted by the Director of Technical Development to facilitate production.

*The document then went into contractural details not important to the Spitfire story, before listing in paragraph 10 the changes to the prototype aircraft which were required or permitted:*

(i) Provision is to be made in the structure for such extra weight as will be entailed, should a Fairey Reed three-blade metal airscrew be fitted in place of a wooden two-blade airscrew.

(ii) Two chutes, each 30 inches long × 5¾ inches in diameter, are to be provided to enable the pilot to drop forced landing flares.

(iii) The capacity of the lower fuel tank is to be increased by 9 gallons, and space shall be reserved in one of the wings for an extra tank of 9 to 12 gallons capacity. Should the extra tank be required, a hand pump will be necessary for feeding its contents to the upper tank, on which a suitable connecting point is to be provided.

(iv) Arrangements are to be made for the safe disposal of any petrol which may leak from the tanks.

(v) The lower fuel tank is to be provided with a detachable sump.

(vi) The stiffness of the wings is to be increased so as to ensure freedom from flutter up to an indicated airspeed of 450 mph. In particular, the spar web is to be moved from front to rear of the flange and thicker leading edge sheeting is to be provided.

(vii) A tube through which the Very pistol may be fired is to be provided.

(viii) Hot and cold air intake pipes of Rolls-Royce type are to be fitted if found suitable.

(ix) A locker of dimensions not less than 14″×10″×4″ is to be provided to hold the pilot's personal belongings.

(x) A tail wheel with an electrically conducting tyre is to be fitted.

(xi) A curved windscreen is to be fitted in lieu of flat panels if a satisfactory type can be obtained sufficiently early.

(xii) The cockpit hood shall be easy to open at all speeds of which the aeroplane is capable.

(xiii) A means of regulating the temperature of the cockpit by the admission of cold air thereto is to be provided.

(xiv) At those parts of the mainplane or tailplane where riveting of the covering would be particularly difficult to do, the ribs may be made with their lower booms of wood and the covering attached by stainless steel wood screws.

(xv) The undercarriage horn is to be modified so as to give a more audible warning.

(xvi) The wing tip navigation lamps are to be of standard pattern.

(xvii) The gun firing control is to be of Dunlop pneumatic type.

(xviii) The pump which actuates the undercarriage retracting mechanism shall be modified so as to increase the speed of raising and lowering the undercarriage.

(xix) The mechanical control for rotating the undercarriage lock is to be made specially robust.

(xx) If possible, R.A.E. Type G landing lamps shall be fitted.

(xxi) Provided no reduction in the performance will be entailed, the hinged flaps on the wheels may be replaced by fixed flaps which, when retracted, will not cover the wing apertures completely.

(xxii) The wing tips and the end bay of the fuselage are to be made easily detachable. These components, together with each wing as a whole, shall comply with current interchangeability requirements.

(xxiii) The plating for the wings and fuselage may be made of Alclad, which shall be protected by varnish in accordance with the relevant A.D.M.

(xxiv) The spar tubes may be made of Hiduminium, provided all relevant requirements as regards their strength are met.

(xxv) Forgings may be of non-stainless steel, protected in accordance with current requirements.

(xxvi) The aeroplanes shall be 'camouflaged'. Further instructions in connection with this requirement will be issued at a later date.

(xxvii) A simple type of jack, suitable for raising the aeroplane when the undercarriage retracting mechanism has to be tested, is to be provided to 'special order only'.

(xxviii) The pilot's instrument board is to be arranged to take the new flying instrument panel.

(xxix) The gearing of the elevator trimming tabs is to be reduced, and back-lash at the tabs on both elevator and rudder is to be eliminated, or minimised as far as possible.

(xxx) The pipe-lines in the braking system are to be secured to the oleo legs.

(xxxi) The fairing over joints in the wing covering is to be such that cracks will not develop therein.

(xxxii) The clearance above the pilot's head is to be increased.

(xxxiii) The oil cooling is to be improved so that it will be satisfactory for English summer conditions.

# Appendix B

## COMMENTS BY JEFFREY QUILL
## ON PUTTING THE SPITFIRE
## INTO PRODUCTION

The extracts from the minutes of the Air Ministry meetings, about the early problems of Spitfire production, tend to put the whole blame for the early production delays upon Supermarine and Sir Robert McLean. They should be read bearing in mind certain considerations.

Of course it was right that Supermarine, as prime contractor, should carry the main burden of responsibility for the delays. But since the main cause of delay was the lateness of the wings, it was obviously unrealistic to absolve from all blame the sub-contractors responsible for wing production.

It should also be remembered that technologically the Spitfire had a much more advanced structure than the Hurricane and other contemporary types, and was therefore much more difficult to put into production. The problem of forecasting production accurately was correspondingly more difficult than for other types.

The Air Ministry, who were on bad terms with McLean at that time anyway, were naturally highly critical of him for having made over-optimistic forecasts of production dates. But if, in June 1936, McLean and Supermarine had made coldly pessimistic forecasts, emphasising the difficulties of producing this very advanced aircraft, the Air Ministry might well not have ordered the Spitfire into production at all. There were plenty of people in official positions in 1936 who were saying that the Spitfire would be far too difficult to produce and maintain in service, and that its margin in performance over the Hurricane was not worth the extra effort. Clearly the firm was not keen to add fuel to that particular fire. Although in hindsight the company's initial forecasts can be seen to have been optimistic they were not irresponsibly so, because the difficulties were all overcome in time. Although McLean's initially optimistic stance may have had an element of commercial tactics about it, events proved that it was just as well for us all that he adopted it.

The root cause of the problems of getting the Spitfire into mass production really lay in the years of neglect of the aircraft industry, by successive governments up to 1936. At the last possible moment they initiated the re-armament programme and expected an industry starved of orders since 1919 suddenly to increase production capacity by four or five times, and change over to building far more complex types of aircraft, all within a space of just two or three years. Of course there were going to be enormous problems and with the best will in the world mistakes were going to be made. It was all very well for the Air Ministry to say to Supermarine 'What you can't do yourselves you must sub-contract'. But where were sub-contractors to be found with the necessary experience, on the fringes of an industry which hitherto had hardly sufficient orders to keep itself alive?

# 4.

# THE MARK I IN SERVICE

On 19 July 1938 the first Spitfire to be delivered to the Royal Air Force, serial K 9788, arrived at Martlesham Heath for trials. Eight days later it was followed by the first production aircraft, K 9787.

No 19 Squadron at Duxford was chosen to introduce the new fighter into service and its first aircraft, K 9789, arrived on 4 August. Squadron Leader Henry Cozens commanded the unit and he made his first flight in the Spitfire on the 11th. He later told the author:

At that time there were no pilots' notes on the Spitfire, no conversion courses and, of course, no dual control aircraft. I was shown round the cockpit, given a cheerful reminder to remember to extend the undercarriage before I landed, wished 'Good Luck', and off I went.

Cozens found the Spitfire a delightful aircraft to fly, much faster than the Gauntlet the unit had operated until then.

Two further Spitfires were delivered in August and No 19

**54.** K 9789, the first Spitfire to be delivered to No 19 Squadron, pictured at Duxford soon after its arrival on 4 August 1938.

Squadron and No 66, a sister squadron at Duxford earmarked to receive the new fighter, were ordered to undertake intensive flying trials with a couple of Spitfires. The purpose of these trials was to discover any bugs that had not been ironed out of the aircraft. Cozens and the other pilots at Duxford were greatly impressed with the Spitfire and considered it a major improvement over the Gauntlet biplanes they had flown before. But, as Cozens later recounted, there was room for improvement:

For one thing the engines of these first Spitfires were difficult to start: the low-geared electric starter rotated the propeller blades so slowly that when a cylinder fired there was usually insufficient push to flick the engine round to fire the next; there would be a 'puff' noise, then the propeller would resume turning on the starter. Also, the early Merlin engines leaked oil terribly; it would run from the engine, down the fuselage and finally got blown away somewhere near the tail wheel. Yet another problem was what we called 'Spitfire Knuckle': when pumping up the undercarriage it was all too easy to rasp our knuckles on the side of the cockpit. There was a further problem for the taller pilots, who were always hitting their heads on the inside of the low cockpit canopy.

54

**55.** Squadron Leader Henry Cozens commanded No 19 Squadron in August 1938, the first unit to receive Spitfires. *(Cozens)*

All of these problems had been pointed out by the Supermarine test pilots, and modifications were in hand to cure them. A higher speed starter motor cured the engine starting problem. A new bulged canopy provided the necessary extra headroom for the taller pilots. An engine driven hydraulic system to raise and lower the undercarriage did away with the need to hand pump, and the resultant 'Spitfire Knuckle'. These improvements were all introduced on the production line early on. The improved oil seals for the Merlin took longer to bring in, and indeed leaking oil was to remain a problem throughout the engine's long career.

New Spitfires arrived at Duxford from the makers one at a time at irregular intervals. Not until 31 October was Cozens able to put up a formation of six aircraft for the first official air-to-air photographs of the new fighter in RAF service. And it was December 1938 before No 19 Squadron had its full complement of sixteen Spitfires.

During the early months of 1939 the rate at which Spitfires left the assembly hangar at Eastleigh increased steadily; in May there were 41. The first 77 production Spitfires were delivered with the two-bladed wooden airscrew. From the 78th aircraft

**56.** First Spitfire write-off: as Pilot Officer G. Sinclair was landing after his first flight in the new fighter, on 3 November 1938, the stub axle of the port main wheel sheared and the aircraft flipped on to its back. Sinclair was not hurt.

**57.** Squadron Leader Cozens leading a formation of six of his brand new Spitfires on 31 October 1938, for an official photographer in a Blenheim. The squadron numbers on the tails of the fighters were painted on shortly before this flight and removed soon afterwards. *(IWM)*

**58.** Spitfire I of No 19 Squadron pictured early in 1939, bearing the newly introduced WZ code letters and a red-blue fuselage marking. *(RAF Museum)*

the de Havilland three-bladed metal airscrew was fitted as standard. By then all new aircraft had the bulged cockpit canopy; and production Spitfires were being delivered with the hot air ducting in the wings to keep the guns warm at high altitude (the existence of this ducting was betrayed by a small rearwards-pointing air outlet under each wing just outboard of the outer guns; these outlets are omitted from almost all published general arrangement drawings of the Spitfire).

By the late 1930s, bombers were beginning to appear carrying armour protection for the crew and vital parts of their structure. Something heavier than the .303-in Browning gun would be necessary to penetrate steel armour of any thickness. The weapon selected by the Royal Air Force for its fighters was the French Hispano 20 mm cannon, which had the best armour

**59.** K 9791, the fifth production Spitfire which was retained by Supermarine for trials, pictured with a mock-up installation for fixed underwing fuel tanks. Jeffrey Quill tested the aircraft in this configuration on 9 January 1940.

penetration capability of any weapon of that calibre then available. In July 1939 a Spitfire, L 1007, was tested at Martlesham fitted with two 20 mm Hispano guns each with 60 rounds, in place of the eight Brownings. The two-cannon Spitfire was found to be 10 pounds lighter than its equivalent with eight machine guns, but due to the additional drag from the cannon barrels and the bulges covering the ammunition magazines it was 3 mph slower; in all other respects the modified Spitfire had performance and general handling characteristics little different from those of a standard aircraft. During the initial firing trials by the cannon Spitfire over the range at Orfordness, the Hispano guns developed frequent stoppages; and a stoppage became a near certainty if the fighter was pulling 'G' at the time of firing. The reason was that the Hispano gun had originally been designed to be mounted on the top of the fighter's engine and fire through the airscrew hub, so that the weight and rigidity of the engine could absorb the recoil forces. The weapon did not take kindly to being installed in a less-rigid mounting in the wing, the only place where there was room for it in the Spitfire. The early service career of the Hispano gun in the Spitfire was a sad tale of frequent stoppages and failures, as the cannon tried to shake apart itself and the feed system during firing.

**60.** Close-up of L 1007, fitted with the prototype 20 mm Hispano cannon installation in June 1939.

When war came, in September 1939, a total of 306 Spitfires had been delivered to the Royal Air Force. Nos 19, 41, 54, 65, 66, 72, 74, 602, 603 and 611 Squadrons were all fully equipped with the type and No 609 Squadron was in the process of re-equipping. A further 71 Spitfires were held by maintenance units, either for fitting of operational equipment or awaiting delivery to operational squadrons to replace losses; 11 of these fighters were being employed for trials work and one was being flown at the Central Flying School. The remaining 36 Spitfires delivered before the war had all been written off in accidents.

The Spitfire fired its guns in anger for the first time on 6 September 1939, when No 74 Squadron was one of several fighter units scrambled to intercept an enemy force reported on radar moving up the Thames Estuary. Anti-aircraft guns at Clacton reported engaging a formation of enemy twin-engined aircraft then, soon afterwards, No 74 Squadron sighted a force of fighters below and dived to attack. It was nearly an hour before the air situation over the Thames estuary was finally resolved. And when it was, it became clear that the Luftwaffe

**61.** Trans-Atlantic Spitfire: soon after the outbreak of war L 1090 was sent to Canada and in May 1940 it was flown in a comparative trial against a US Army Air Corps XP-40 fighter (seen on the left) at the RCAF base at Uplands. The Spitfire carried the small (15-inch diameter) red and blue fuselage roundels applied to production aircraft during the spring and summer of 1939; note also the unusual position of the serial number, stencilled in small characters mid-way up the fin. *(Smithsonian)*

was nowhere in the area. By the time the so-called 'Battle of Barking Creek' reached its inglorious conclusion, Fighter Command had lost three aircraft destroyed and one pilot killed. The 'enemy twin-engined aircraft' engaged by the AA gunners had been the Blenheims of No 64 Squadron, one of which was shot down. The fighters attacked by the Spitfires of No 74 Squadron proved to be Hurricanes of No 56 Squadron, two of which were shot down. The root cause of the 'battle' had been a technical fault at the Chain Home radar station at Canewdon near Southend. As a result radar echoes coming from aircraft to the west of the station were not filtered out and instead appeared on the screen looking exactly like those from aircraft approaching *from the east*. As more and more British fighters had taken off to engage, their echoes were added to the phantom raiding force which became progressively larger. Once the existence of a large 'raiding force' was firmly established in everyone's mind, the misidentification and subsequent shooting down of aircraft was only to be expected from a defensive system inexperienced in war and over-quick on the trigger. Following a court of inquiry into the incident, the production of radar Identification Friend or Foe (IFF) equipment for Royal Air Force aircraft was given the highest priority.

The Spitfire first saw action against the Luftwaffe on the afternoon of 16 October 1939, when two 3-aircraft sections from Nos 602 and 603 Squadrons engaged nine Junkers 88 bombers of Kampfgeschwader 30 trying to attack Royal Navy warships in the Firth of Forth. The Spitfires broke up the attack, claimed at the time to have been made by 'Heinkel 111s'. Squadron Leader Ernest Stevens, commanding No 603 Squadron, shot down one of the bombers into the sea off Port Seton and the section from No 602 Squadron got another off Crail. At least one other Junkers 88 was damaged, without loss to the Spitfires.*

For the rest of 1939 and the early part of 1940 Spitfires saw infrequent action during the rare occasions when German bombers and reconnaissance aircraft came within range of their bases in England (as yet no Spitfire fighter squadrons had been sent abroad).

On 13 January 1940 Pilot Officer George Proudman took off in the prototype cannon Spitfire from Drem, and joined Hurricanes of No 111 Squadron in the interception of an enemy aircraft reported off the coast by radar. Proudman later reported:

*A detailed first-hand account of the action, as seen from the German side, appears in *Spitfire At War* by Alfred Price, Ian Allan Ltd.

At 20,000 feet, 5 miles east of Fifeness, a Heinkel 111 aircraft appeared followed by three Spitfires of No 602 Squadron who were carrying out a No 1 attack. The Heinkel commenced to dive and No 2 of the Spitfire section received a bullet in his windscreen, causing him to break away prematurely and leaving a gap before No 3 could carry on the attack. I then filled in the gap and carried out an attack. At about 12,000 feet I was in range at 300 yards and I opened fire. Almost immediately a piece of shining metal dropped from the Heinkel's fuselage and is believed to be one of the undercarriage wheels. Only one round of H.E. ammunition was fired as the starboard gun stopped. The port gun stopped after 30 rounds of ball ammunition had been fired.

The Heinkel was finished off by conventionally armed Spitfires and Hurricanes and crashed into the sea.

The action showed that the Hispano was a very effective weapon, when it worked. The trouble was that it was still nowhere near reliable enough. Quite apart from fact that the mounting was not sufficiently rigid, the cannons were canted on their sides in the Spitfire and this gave rise to problems with ejecting the belt links and cartridge cases. And if one of the cannon developed a stoppage in action, the unbalanced recoil forces from the remaining gun when it was fired caused the aircraft to yaw and this made accurate fire impossible. All in all it was clear that more work would be needed before the cannon-Spitfire would be ready for large-scale service.

The Spitfire first encountered its German equivalent, the Messerschmitt 109E, over northern France, Belgium and Holland in May and early June 1940, in the period leading up to and during the Dunkirk evacuation. Still no Spitfire fighter squadrons had been based outside Britain and the fighters had to operate near to the limit of their radius of action from airfields in southern England. Nevertheless the fighter acquitted itself well and its appearance came as a nasty surprise for some of the Luftwaffe units operating in the area.

Following the end of the Dunkirk evacuation, early in June 1940, there was a period of relative quiet as both sides prepared for the action that was to become known as the Battle of Britain. From the outbreak of war until the end of July 1940, eight squadrons had re-equipped with Spitfires to join the original eleven: Nos 64, 92, 152, 222, 234, 266, 610 and 616 Squadrons.

By this time the Spitfire Is being delivered to the Royal Air Force differed in several respects from those at the beginning of the war. Externally the main difference was the larger boss covering the pitch control mechanism of the Rotol or de Havilland constant speed airscrews now being fitted, and the thick slab of laminated glass in front of the windscreen. An IFF radar transponder was installed in the rear fuselage with aerials running from the fuselage aft of the cockpit to the tips of the tailplane, on each side. Internally there was 73 pounds of steel armour plating, behind and beneath the pilot and in front of the fuel and glycol header tanks; and covering the upper fuel tank was a thicker sheet of dural.

A further significant move was the change, in the Royal Air Force's front line fighter squadrons, from 87 octane to 100 octane petrol in the spring of 1940. Although this gave no improvement at or above the 16,500-foot full throttle height of the Merlin II and III engines fitted to the Spitfires, below that altitude the maximum boost pressure could be raised from 6¼ pounds to 12 pounds without causing detonation in the cylinders; the resultant extra power increased the maximum speed by a useful 25 mph at sea level and 34 mph at 10,000 feet.

The new features incorporated in the Spitfire since production began added about 335 pounds and brought the all up weight to about 6,155 pounds. Moreover, some of the changes increased drag and so reduced the aircraft's top speed: for

**62.** The first operational Spitfire fighters to land in France: three aircraft of No 92 Squadron pictured at Le Bourget near Paris on 16 May 1940, when they escorted the Flamingo airliner in which Prime Minister Mr Churchill visited his French opposite number. In the foreground are Flying Officer Robert Stanford-Tuck and Pilot Officer Alan Wright. *(Wright)*

62

Spitfires of No 66 Squadron pictured at Gravesend, early in September 1940. **(63)** One of the unit's aircraft comes in to land, past others dispersed around the airfield perimeter and a Hurricane of No 501 Squadron. In the background ships moving up the Thames can be seen. **(64)** Armourers removing depleted ammunition boxes and replacing them with full ones. **(65)** While one man refills the tanks from a Crossley refueller, the other prepares to plug in the electrical starter trolley. *(The Times)*

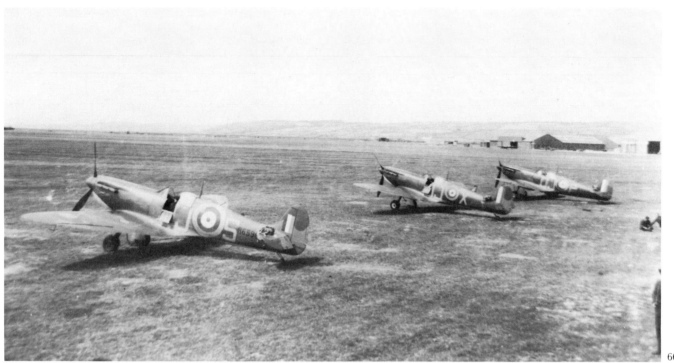

example the toughened glass mounted in front of the windscreen cost 6 mph, the IFF wire aerials reduced speed by a further 2 mph. The maximum speed usually quoted for the Spitfire I is 362 mph at 18,500 feet; but this figure referred to the first production aircraft K 9787 at an all up weight of 5,819 pounds. By the summer of 1940 the maximum speed of a fully equipped production Mark I was somewhat lower, about 350 mph at the same altitude.

By the late spring of 1940 the Hispano cannon was judged to be working well enough for an operational unit, No 19 Squadron, to be issued with two-cannon Spitfires. Before this installation was placed into large scale production Air Chief Marshal Dowding had to be certain it was working properly. On 24 July he wrote to the Secretary of State for Air, Sir Archibald Sinclair:

The present situation is that the guns of about six Spitfires in No 19 Squadron are working satisfactorily, and the defects in the others will probably be rectified in about a week or ten days.
I quite realise that information concerning the fighting qualities of the cannon Spitfire is required as early as possible,

and I will take the first opportunity of getting it into action; but I am not at all keen on sending it up against German fighters since it will be extremely badly equipped for that task . . . . I say the cannon Spitfire is badly equipped to meet German fighters because it has only two guns and even the Me 109 has two cannon and two machine guns. Furthermore, it has fired off all its ammunition in five seconds.

So you will see that the existing cannon Spitfire is not an attractive type, but it has been necessary to produce it as an insurance against the Germans armouring the backs of their engines. They have not done this yet, their engines are still vulnerable to rifle-calibre machine gun fire and, therefore, the eight gun fighter is a better general fighting machine than one equipped with two cannons only.

To differentiate the eight-gun Spitfire from those fitted with the two-cannon armament, the former was designated the Mark IA and the latter the IB.

This is not the place for a detailed description of the Battle of Britain. However this author has conducted an extremely detailed survey of both sides' air operations on the day when the greatest number of aircraft was destroyed, 18 August 1940*, and this has revealed several points of interest concerning the Spitfire. On the evening of the 17th Fighter Command's squadrons had available a total of 1,171 fighters: 675 Hurricanes, 348 Spitfires, 95 Blenheims, 39 Defiants, 9 Gladiators and 5 Whirlwinds. Thus the Spitfires comprised about a third of the Command's strength in modern single-engined fighters at that time. Of the 348 Spitfires, 276—a little over 79 per cent—were serviceable; just under 81 per cent of the Hurricanes were serviceable. It has often been said that the Hurricane was a much more rugged and easily maintainable aircraft

**66.** Spitfires of No 92 Squadron dispersed in the open at Pembrey during the Battle of Britain. The light square on the port wing of the aircraft nearest the camera was in gas detection paint; this aircraft was the personal machine of Pilot Officer Alan Wright. *(Wright)*

**67.** The Messerschmitt 109E, the Luftwaffe equivalent to the Spitfire during the Battle of Britain. The two aircraft were very evenly matched as regards performance, each having advantages over the other.

**68.** Pilot Officer David Glaser of No 65 Squadron, pictured in his Spitfire during the Battle of Britain. The photograph is of particular interest because it is one of the few to show the often-fitted blinkers immediately in front of the cockpit, to shield the pilot's eyes from exhaust glare during night flying. *(Glaser)*

*See *Battle of Britain: The Hardest Day* by Alfred Price, Jane's Ltd

than the Spitfire, but it is clear from these figures that the margin between the two was not great.

To meet the three major attacks mounted by the Luftwaffe on 18 August Fighter Command put up a total of 110 Spitfire and 210 Hurricane sorties. This was in almost direct proportion to the number of each type available, and they engaged the enemy in about this proportion also. What was the relative effectiveness of the Spitfire and the Hurricane in combat? British fighters probably destroyed or damaged beyond repair 59 German aircraft on that day; of these 29 can be allocated to Spitfires or Hurricanes acting alone, 10 to the former and 19 to the latter. From this admittedly small sample the number of victories scored by the Spitfires and Hurricanes was almost directly proportional to the number of each type which engaged the enemy. In other words, in spite of its lower performance, on this day the Hurricane was as likely to score a 'kill' as was a Spitfire. During the action 5 Spitfires and 26 Hurricanes were destroyed or damaged beyond repair in the air. Allowing for the difference in the numbers present, it can be seen that the Spitfire's better performance meant that it was almost three times more likely to survive contact with the enemy than the Hurricane.

Compared with the Messerschmitt 109E, its main dogfighting rival during the Battle of Britain, the Spitfire I was marginally faster in level speed below 15,000 feet and marginally slower above 20,000 feet. The Spitfire could out-turn the Messerschmitt at almost any altitude or speed, but the latter was the superior aircraft in the climb. In truth the differences between the Spitfire and the Me 109 in performance and handling were only marginal, and in a combat they were almost always surmounted by tactical considerations: which side had seen the other first, had the advantage of sun, altitude, numbers, pilot ability, tactical situation, tactical co-ordination, amount of fuel remaining, etc.

When chased by an Me 109, a Spitfire would try to shake off the pursuit by using its better turning performance. If a Messerschmitt was chased by a Spitfire, the German pilot would often push down the nose and bunt the fighter. Under this condition of negative-G the Daimler Benz engine, with its system of direct fuel injection, would continue running. The Merlin engine, with its float-type carburettor, would cease delivering fuel and cut out. If he was quick and able enough the Spitfire pilot could roll his fighter on to its back, pull into the dive, then do an aileron turn to get back the right way up to follow the Messerschmitt down; it was a far from satisfactory solution to the problem. Questioned on how this disadvantage came about, and why Rolls-Royce had not inroduced fuel injection for the Merlin even when the problem was known, Sir Stanley Hooker told the author:

Before the war, when the Merlin was designed, I don't think anyone even considered the possibility that fighter pilots would ever want to bunt their aircraft across the sky. The first thing we heard about the problem was from a whole lot of complaining fighter pilots at the time of the Battle of Britain. Now the fact is that if we had fitted fuel injection to the early Merlins we should have lost power. The evaporation of the fuel squirted into the supercharger reduced the temperature of the fuel-air mixture by about 25 degrees C, giving an increase of the order of 60 horsepower—which meant 6 or 7 mph more on the top speed of a Spitfire. It may not sound much, but for many a pilot it made the difference between life and death. Quite apart from that, the fitting of fuel injection to the Merlin simply was not on as a short-term measure: it would have taken a year or so to get such a re-designed engine into service because the balance of the engine, carburettor and supercharger was critical and one could not alter one part alone without reducing the efficiency of the whole.

Engineers at Farnborough and Rolls-Royce began a crash programme to produce a new type of carburettor that would continue functioning under negative-G conditions, but it would be some time before this was in service.

During the Battle of Britain No 19 Squadron's cannon-Spitfires had little success. During the combat on 16 August both cannon functioned properly on only one of the seven Spitfires which engaged; on the 19th it was none out of three; on the 24th it was two out of eight and on the 31st it was three out of six. The unit's commander, Squadron Leader R. Pinkham, bitterly complained:

In all the engagements so far occurring it is considered that had the unit been equipped with 8-gun fighters it would have inflicted far more severe losses on the enemy . . . . It is most strongly urged that until the stoppages at present experienced have been eliminated this Squadron should be re-equipped with Browning gun Spitfires. It is suggested that a way of doing this would be to allot the present cannon Spitfires to an Operational Training unit, and withdraw Browning gun Spitfires from there for use in this Squadron.

Air Chief Marshal Dowding accepted this suggestion and ordered that the exchange should take place immediately. On 4 September the Squadron delivered its aircraft to the Operational Training Unit at Hawarden and in exchange received the latter's elderly but machine gun fitted 'hacks'. Afterwards the No 19 Squadron diarist noted: 'First day with the eight-gun machines, and what wrecks. At least the guns will fire . . . .'

In order to gain operational experience with the Spitfire Jeffrey Quill was allowed to re-join the Royal Air Force for a short period in August and September 1940, and he flew with No 65 Squadron from Hornchurch during the Battle of Britain. Quill was credited with the destruction of a Messerschmitt 109 on 16 August and he shared in the shooting down of a Heinkel 111 on the 18th. When the test pilot returned to Supermarine he had some clear ideas on what was needed to improve the effectiveness of the fighter. The most important change needed was something to give better aileron control during a high speed dive—at speeds above 400 mph (indicated) the ailerons seemed to lock solid and the pilot had to apply all his strength with both hands to get any movement (the Me 109 had similar problems). Quill's complaints reinforced those reaching the company from Fighter Command, and Joe Smith began working immediately to improve matters.

The cause of the immovable ailerons at high speed was soon isolated. Under these conditions it was found that the airflow caused the fabric covering of the ailerons to balloon out and so make the trailing edge of the control surface much thicker; and this in turn greatly increased the stick force needed to move the ailerons. The answer was to replace the fabric covering of the ailerons with light alloy, which was much stiffer and would not balloon out at high speeds. Jeffrey Quill tried out a Spitfire fitted with the metal-covered ailerons in November 1940 and at high speed found them delightfully light compared with the fabric covered ones. He then took the modified Spitfire to Tangmere where it was flown by the commander of No 602 Squadron, Squadron Leader 'Sandy' Johnstone. In his official report on the modified Spitfire Johnstone afterwards wrote: 'The effectiveness of the new ailerons is so great that one has to fly the aircraft to believe it . . . .' Almost immediately afterwards a crash programme was initiated to fit all Spitfires in front-line units with the metal-covered ailerons.

On his return Quill also pointed out the vital importance of improving rearwards visibility from the Spitfire: many pilots

**69** and **70.** Cannon-armed Spitfire IBs of No 92 Squadron, which received this version in November 1940 after the main faults which had dogged the new weapon had been cleared. *(Wright)*

69

70

**71.** Mark I P 9565 fitted with the prototype installation of a fixed 30 gallon extra fuel tank under the port wing. The handling characteristics of this aircraft were reported as poor, however; during dives at indicated airspeeds greater than 350 mph the ailerons became very heavy and 'considerable force' was required to hold up the port wing.

shot down had never seen what hit them. He proposed two solutions, one interim and one for the long term. His interim solution was that the hood should be bulged out at the sides, so that the pilot had greater sideways movement to look backwards; this hood was introduced some months later. For the long term Quill wanted a major redesign of the rear fuselage and a 'tear drop' canopy fitted; this too would come, but much later. Quill saw that vision forwards required improvement also. On the Mark I the side panels of the windscreen were made of curved pieces of plexiglas which were very bad optically and caused considerable distortion; a new windscreen was designed with optically flat side panels which greatly improved visibility in the vitally important forward hemisphere, and this was fitted to later marks. In action it was found that during a sustained high speed dive the windscreen would often frost up suddenly, with the result that the pilot was unable to see properly and so became extremely vulnerable to enemy attack; a simple louvre ducting air on the inside of the windscreen would prevent this phenomenon on later aircraft. And to lessen the chances of pilots being trapped in their aircraft work began on a revised, jettisonable, canopy so that the pilot could get rid of it quickly in an emergency.

After the detachment Quill was able to put over the views of the fighter pilots with great force. 'I remember emphasising that, whatever previous thinking on the matter may have been, nobody should delude himself that the day of the 'dogfight' was over. It was very much with us and likely to remain with us,' he recalled. 'And, like all fighter pilots, I was hollering that the Spitfire needed more speed, faster climb, more fire power, etc, etc!'

After further modifications some cannon Spitfire IBs were issued to No 92 Squadron in November 1940. The revised mountings and feed systems were at last made to work properly; but by then the Battle of Britain had ground to a virtual halt and the cannon Spitfire Is were able to achieve few successes. The best compromise armament was found to be two 20 mm Hispano cannon and four .303-in Browning machine guns, and this was tested out on X 4257 in the summer and autumn; in the years to come this armament would equip the vast majority of Spitfires built.

A few specialised variants were built based on the design of the Mark I: the so-called 'Speed Spitfire', intended for an attempt on the world landplane speed record; and a whole family of high speed photographic reconnaissance versions. Both of these will be dealt with in detail in subsequent chapters. Also there was a host of one-off modifications to individual aircraft, including: the modification of R 6722 as a floatplane, though it never flew in this form; a series of modifications to the trials aircraft K 9791 which was flown at various times with several different airscrews, a wooden mock-up of the cannon installation, and a mock-up installation of a fixed blister-type fuel tank under each wing; and P 9565 fitted with a single 40-gallon long range fuel tank under the port wing only.

Production of the Spitfire I continued at the Supermarine plants until March 1941, when it was phased out in favour of the Mark V. Westland Aircraft Ltd at Yeovil built 50 more between July and September 1941, to a contract signed the previous year. Altogether, 1,556 Mark Is were built.

# Appendix A

## FIRST PRODUCTION SPITFIRE K 9787

Figures taken from the trials report of this aircraft, tested at Martlesham Heath in August 1938. In each case figures are given only when they differ from those of the prototype K 5054.

**Dimensions:** Wing span 36 ft 10 in. Length 29 ft 11 in. Flap travel 85°

**Weights:** Tare weight 4,482 pounds
Fully loaded weight 5,819 pounds (tare weight plus a fuel load of 84 gallons, 6 gallons of oil, 200 pounds for pilot and parachute, 458 pounds for guns, ammunition, radio and other items of service equipment).
Wing loading when fully loaded, 24 pounds per square foot

**Power plant:** Rolls-Royce Merlin II
Rated power 990 BHP at 2,600 rpm, 12,250 ft at 6¼ lbs boost
Maximum power
1,030 BHP at 3,000 rpm, 16,250 ft at 6¼ lbs boost

**Propeller:** Airscrew Company two-bladed fixed pitch wooden, 10 ft 8 ins diameter.

**Performance:** Maximum limiting speed 470 mph (indicated)

| Height feet | Top Speed mph | Time to Climb mins | Rate of Climb ft/min |
|---|---|---|---|
| 2,000 | 295 | 1 m 0 s | 2,195 |
| 5,000 | 307 | 2 m 18 s | 2,295 |
| 10,000 | 328 | 4 m 18 s | 2,490 |
| 15,000 | 348 | 6 m 30 s | 2,065 |
| 18,500 | 362 | 8 m 25 s | 1,700 |
| 20,000 | 360 | 9 m 25 s | 1,480 |
| 25,000 | 349 | 13 m 36 s | 900 |
| 30,000 | 315 | 22 m 25 s | 325 |

Service ceiling (height at which rate of climb was 100 ft/min): 31,900 ft
Take-off run (zero wind) 420 yds
Take-off speed 86 mph
Distance to clear 50 ft screen 720 yds
Landing speed 60 mph
Landing run (with brakes) 380 yds

### Author's Comments

The first production Spitfire was 13 mph faster than the first prototype as tested in May 1936, due almost entirely to the additional thrust from the ejector exhausts. It was also 460 pounds heavier than the prototype, however, and this difference was reflected in the lower climbing performance. The main respects in which K 9787 differed from the prototype in its final form were as follows:

Revised wing internal structure, to raise maximum limiting speed from 380 to 470 mph.
Lower fuel tank enlarged, to increase total tankage from 75 to 84 gallons.
Fitted with landing lights and standard Royal Air Force blind flying instrument panel.
Flap travel increased to 85 degrees.
Pitot head moved to position below port wing.
Shape of front of radiator altered so that it ran perpendicular to the airflow.
Slightly altered shape of lower portion of wheel leg fairings.
Wing tips made detachable.
More powerful air compressor fitted.

The Spitfire I had an effective operational radius of action of about 130 miles, allowing for 15 minutes at full power for combat and an operational fuel reserve sufficient for half an hour's flying. If the aircraft made a maximum-rate climb to combat altitude, and was flying in formation with others, the operational radius of action fell to below 100 miles.

# Appendix B

## SPITFIRE I K 9793

Figures taken from the short trials report of this aircraft, tested at Martlesham Heath in June 1939. This was the seventh production Spitfire which had been fitted with the de Havilland three-bladed two-pitch metal airscrew which became standard on the 78th and subsequent production aircraft. The new metal airscrew was considerably heavier than the earlier wooden one (345 pounds compared with 83 pounds) and to compensate for this 135 pounds of lead ballast was removed from the nose and 40 pounds of it was repositioned in the rear fuselage. The figures below are given only when they differ from those of Spitfire K 9787 described in Appendix A.

**Weights:** Tare weight 4,598 pounds
Fully loaded weight 5,935 pounds
Wing loading when fully loaded, 24.5 pounds per square foot

**Propeller:** de Havilland three-bladed two-pitch metal, 9 ft 1¼ in diameter.

**Performance:**

| Height feet | Top Speed mph | Time to Climb mins | Rate of Climb ft/min |
|---|---|---|---|
| 2,000 | | 1 m 17 s | 1,625 |
| 5,000 | | 3 m 0 s | 1,845 |
| 10,000 | | 5 m 30 s | 2,150 |
| 15,000 | | 8 m 6 s | 1,725 |
| 18,600 | 367 | | |
| 20,000 | 366 | 11 m 24 s | 1,305 |
| 25,000 | | 16 m 0 s | 875 |
| 30,000 | | 23 m 48 s | 470 |

Service ceiling (estimated) 34,400 ft
Take-off run (zero wind) 320 yds
Distance to clear 50 ft screen 490 yds
Landing speed 72 mph
Landing run (with brakes) 235 yds

### Author's Comments

This aircraft had a maximum speed 5 mph higher than the first production aircraft and its take-off and high altitude performance were greatly improved, due to the two pitch propeller. Due to the greater weight of the latter, however, climbing performance below 20,000 feet was somewhat worse.

# Appendix C

## SPITFIRE I   N 3171

Figures taken from the trials report of this aircraft, tested at Boscombe Down in March 1940. This Spitfire was fitted with a Rotol constant speed propeller, laminated glass windscreen (which knocked about 6 mph off the maximum speed), thickened alloy sheeting over the upper fuel tank and had a domed-top canopy. Compared with the Spitfires being delivered in the Battle of Britain, later in the year, it lacked armour plating and IFF equipment, and it was tested on 87 octane instead of 100 octane fuel; later aircraft would, therefore, have had a slightly lower maximum speed at full throttle height but have had a substantially higher maximum speed at lower altitudes. The higher engine power at low altitudes would probably have just about cancelled out the extra weight of the armour and IFF set, in the climb, Figures are given only when they differ from those of Spitfire K 9793 described in Appendix B.

**Weights:** Tare weight 4,713 pounds
Fully loaded weight 6,050 pounds
Wing loading when fully loaded, 25 pounds per square foot

**Power plant:** Rolls-Royce Merlin III
Rated power 990 BHP at 2,600 rpm at 12,250 ft at +6¼ lbs boost

**Propeller:** Rotol three-bladed constant speed wooden, 10 ft 9 in diameter.

**Performance:**

| Height feet | Top Speed mph | Time to Climb mins | Rate of Climb ft/min |
|---|---|---|---|
| 2,000 | | 42 s | 2,820 |
| 5,000 | | 1 m 48 s | 2,850 |
| 10,000 | 320 | 3 m 30 s | 2,895 |
| 15,000 | 339 | 5 m 18 s | 2,430 |
| 20,000 | 353 | 7 m 42 s | 1,840 |
| 25,000 | 345 | 10 m 54 s | 1,250 |
| 30,000 | 319 | 16 m 24 s | 660 |

| | |
|---|---|
| Service ceiling | 34,700 ft |
| Take-off run | 225 yds |
| Distance to clear 50 ft screen | 370 yds |
| Landing speed | 66 mph |
| Landing run (with brakes) | 310 yds |

**Author's Comments**

The increase in tare weight of 115 pounds compared with K 9793 was due almost entirely to the extra weight of the constant speed propeller, plus the lead ballast which had to be carried in the rear fuselage to balance the additional weight on the extreme nose. The report mentioned that the Merlin III installed in this Spitfire was slightly down on power and this could have reduced its top speed by about 2 mph. In spite of this and the extra weight and drag, however, which reduced the top speed by 14 mph compared with K 9793, the trial demonstrated that the constant speed airscrew was well worth having: the rate of climb was increased by about a half and take-off distance was reduced by about a third.

# 5.

# THE SAGA OF THE SPEED SPITFIRE

During the summer of 1937 ideas began to crystallize on the possibility of modifying a Spitfire for an attempt on the world landplane speed record*. At that time the record was held by the American millionaire Howard Hughes in a Hughes H-1 racer and stood at 352 mph. This was tantalizingly close to the maximum speed of the prototype Spitfire; but it has to be remembered that in the latter case the speed was measured at its full throttle height of 16,800 feet. The regulations for the world speed record demanded that the aircraft fly the 3 kilometre (1.86 mile) course at an altitude not greater than 75 metres (245 feet); it was to fly the course twice in each direction and the speed recorded was the average measured during those four runs. The prototype Spitfire (the only one flying at that time) was capable of only about 290 mph at ground level.

Obviously the Spitfire would require extensive alteration for the record attempt, but 352 mph—plus the 5 mph margin necessary to exceed the previous record—was considered well within the reach of the aircraft. At Rolls-Royce work began on a special sprint version of the Merlin and on 7 August a more-or-less standard Merlin II, running at 18 pounds boost on a special fuel mix of straight run gasoline, benzol and methanol with a dash of tetraethyl lead, achieved an output of 1,536 horsepower at 2,850 rpm over a four minute run; it was more than one-third more power than a similar engine running on normal 87 octane fuel.

In November the British plans for a record attempt received a jolt when on the 11th Hermann Wurster flying a modified Messerschmitt 109 captured the world landplane record for Germany with a speed of 379 mph. At a high level meeting at the Air Ministry in London on the 25th, however, it was felt that a modified Spitfire could do somewhat better than this: Rolls-Royce were predicting 2,000 horsepower from the sprint Merlin and on this it was estimated that a suitably cleaned-up Spitfire would be able to reach 385 mph at low altitude. On the strength of this the Air Ministry issued a contract to fund work for the record attempt.

The 48th production Spitfire K 9834, then in a very early stage of construction at Woolston, was selected for modification into what became known as the 'Speed Spitfire'. It was fitted with a stronger engine mounting to accommodate the increased torque from the sprint engine. To cool the more powerful engine a pressurized water system was to be used, with a deeper radiator inside a lengthened duct which extended to the trailing edge of the wing; to make room for the longer duct the inboard section of the starboard flap was removed (because the

*The absolute speed record, held by the Italian Macchi-Castoldi MC.72 floatplane, stood at 440 mph which was obviously beyond the reach of the Spitfire.

removed section was close to the aircraft centre line, no serious rolling problem was expected when the flaps were lowered). Under the port wing a larger diameter oil cooler was fitted. The gun mountings, radio fittings and flare chutes were omitted and their doors replaced by attached panels. The aircraft was flush riveted over all external surfaces, a streamlined skid was fitted in place of the tail wheel and the aircraft had a longer, more streamlined windscreen and flat canopy. The wing span was reduced to 33 feet 8 inches, and the tips rounded. To absorb the extra power the Speed Spitfire had a coarse pitch four bladed wooden airscrew 10 feet in diameter, 8 inches less than that of the prototype; the reduced diameter gave lower tip speeds at maximum revolutions and so reduced the problem of Mach effects. With a carefully applied filling in all cracks and a finely polished finish, it was estimated that the airframe drag of the Speed Spitfire would be about 53.3 pounds at 100 feet per second compared with 60.2 pounds for the standard fighter aircraft. The weight of the modified aircraft was to be 5,490 pounds, just over 300 pounds more than that of the standard aircraft.

By January 1938 Rolls-Royce had the sprint Merlin running at 1,796 horsepower at 3,200 rpm, with +21 pounds boost. By May it had reached 2,122 horsepower at 3,200 rpm with +28 pounds boost and in June it developed 2,100 horsepower during a 15 minute-type test.

In the meantime, however, the Germans had not been resting on their laurels. On 6 June a Heinkel 100 established a new 100 kilometre closed circuit record at 394 mph. That was close to or possibly better than the best the Speed Spitfire was likely to achieve, and the latter was still far from ready.

It was November before the Speed Spitfire, as yet unpainted, was ready to fly and Mutt Summers took it up for the first time on the 11th. Then all joints in the airframe were carefully filled and the aircraft was given a high gloss finish with royal blue top surfaces and silver undersides. Jeffrey Quill flew it for the first time on 14 December and described some of its operating problems to the author:

One of the peculiarities of the engine was that for running at its maximum boost of 27½ pounds it had to have special spark plugs fitted but it could not be run cold on these. So it had to be started and warmed up using normal plugs, then the mechanics had the difficult task of doing a full plug change on the hot engine. The cowling was then replaced and the engine could be re-started on the racing plugs and run at full boost.

The Speed Spitfire had a special streamlined perspex windscreen which was extremely bad optically. But one had to put up with such things in the interests of speed—think

**72, 73, 74.** The Speed Spitfire photographed at Eastleigh, late in 1938 or early in 1939, during running trials of the sprint Merlin fitted to this aircraft. *(Flight)*

what it was like for the pilots in the Schneider Trophy contest.

With the coarse pitch four bladed propeller there was tremendous torque and one could not use full power for take-off, one just used as much as was necessary. In the air at full power, torque could still be a problem and the aeroplane would tend to track sideways unless one flew it carefully and trimmed it out on the rudder.

For the world speed record attempt the aircraft had to have a barograph fitted in the rear fuselage, and if it showed that during the flight the aircraft had gone above 400 metres (1,300 feet)—for example during the turns between runs—one was disqualified. It took quite a bit of time to wind an aircraft like that up to its maximum speed, about a couple of minutes. The initial acceleration was good, but at the very top of the speed range the speed crept up only very slowly. So the trick was to get the aircraft flying flat out at just under 1,300 feet, then ease down the nose to get a little more speed and cross the starting line at just under 245 feet going as fast as one possibly could.

The Speed Spitfire was built to an Air Ministry contract and early on, much to Quill's chagrin, it was decided that if there was to be an attempt on the world record an RAF pilot should make it. The pilot chosen was Flight Lieutenant Harry 'Bruin' Purvis, an experienced test pilot at Farnborough.

In the meantime, however, doubts were growing that the Speed Spitfire would be able to secure the landplane speed record at all, especially if the Heinkel 100 managed to get in its attempt first. The Air Member for Development and Production, Air Marshal Sir Wilfrid Freeman, was understandably reluctant to launch a full-scale attempt at the record—with all the attendant publicity—unless there was a good chance of it succeeding. On 23 December his views were conveyed to the Director at Farnborough:

> . . . the High Speed Spitfire and the question of tests over a speed course are to be kept carefully apart from one another excepting only if, as a result of A.S.I. observations in the natural course of your flying, you come to the view that the High Speed Spitfire is likely to pick up a ground speed of the order of 450. If you come to this conclusion, then we shall be asking that you let us know and then the question of putting it over a speed course will be reviewed.
>
> To put the matter bluntly, we are very anxious not to give the firm any ammunition for raising any awkward questions if the speed is on the border line but not definitely such as to justify a wholehearted attempt to put up a really good show.

Unless there was such evidence, the purpose of the trials with the Speed Spitfire was to be stated as 'high speed research and development'. In the meantime, in case the Speed Spitfire was shown to be fast enough to justify a record attempt, the speed course at Gosport was to be brought to readiness and its instrumentation calibrated. The aircraft used for this calibration 'should be one which cannot be claimed to be a record-breaker and which is, nevertheless, of sufficient performance to give a real proof of the installation.' The prototype Spitfire K 5054, which was by then at Farnborough, was assigned to this task.

Purvis made his first flight in the Speed Spitfire on 24 February 1939 from Eastleigh and he took it up several times during the weeks that followed. The maximum speed reached was 408 mph at 3,000 feet, equivalent to about 400 mph at 200 feet. It was imperative to squeeze the speed of the aircraft up further and the decision was taken to dispense with the large radiator entirely; it was calculated that this would raise the maximum speed to about 425 mph at 200 feet. Still the engine would have to be cooled, of course, and for this a so-called 'boiling tank' was to be fitted: the upper fuel tank would be removed and a combined condenser and water tank fitted in its place; when the engine was running the water was to be fed through the engine and back to the tank, where as much as possible was condensed and the rest was to be ejected from the base of the engine in a jet which would trail behind the aircraft. The aircraft had to be back on the ground before the water ran out, but since the fuel capacity was much reduced the Speed Spitfire was expected to run out of both fuel and water at about the same time.

Yet again, however, the project was overtaken by events in Germany. On 30 March Hans Dieterle flew four runs in the Heinkel 100 at an average of 463 mph to take both the land-plane record and the world absolute speed record, and place these far beyond the reach of the Speed Spitfire. And less than a month later Fritz Wendel in a Messerschmitt 209 broke even that record with a blistering 469 mph over the course*.

*Wendel's record for a piston-engined aircraft was to survive for 30 years, until a much-modified Grumman F8F Bearcat achieved 482 mph in 1969.

**75, 76, 77.** The Speed Spitfire photographed at Farnborough in March 1939. These views show well the altered line of the wings and the enlarged radiator and oil cooler. *(RAF Museum)*

**78.** The aircraft on the ground at Eastleigh early in 1939, with a ground towing dolly in place under the tail and the fairing removed to reveal the radiator matrix.

Early in June the Speed Spitfire went into the hangar at Eastleigh for the installation of the boiling tank. But the German successes had stripped the project of its urgency and the aircraft was crated and taken to Belgium the following month where it was shown in the exhibition at the International Aeronautical Salon in Brussels. At this time the radiator and fairing under the starboard wing had been removed and the wing underside faired over, but the boiling tank had not been fitted.

During the final month of peace the Speed Spitfire returned to Southampton, but with the increasing urgency to provide Spitfire fighters for the RAF the work of fitting the boiling tank went on at only a low priority. It was almost the end of April 1940 before the aircraft was ready for tests with the revised cooling system and on the 30th Jeffrey Quill prepared to fly it:

I was taxi-ing out at Eastleigh for the take-off and suddenly the whole engine and cockpit became enveloped in steam; it got everywhere. Obviously something had burst. I shut down the engine and climbed out, and the aircraft was towed back into the hangar.

The cause of the leak of steam was a split in the boiling tank. And before it could be repaired the German offensive had begun in the west and the Allied war position had taken a grave turn for the worse. The RAF launched a ruthless 'trawl' for Spitfires from the various trials establishments, to get as many as possible for the front-line squadrons. Supermarine were ordered to bring the Speed Spitfire to a usable service condition and to this end a standard Merlin XII engine, three bladed airscrew and radiator, were fitted. With its reduced-span wing and exceptionally clean airframe the Speed Spitfire was still one of the fastest aircraft in the world at low altitude; but it would have required a disproportionately large number of man hours to re-convert it back into a fighter. So in November 1940 the

**79.** The Speed Spitfire on exhibition at the International Aeronautical Salon in Brussels in July 1939. At this time the aircraft was fitted with a Hamilton three-bladed two-pitch metal airscrew; the coolant radiator had been removed and the wing faired over, but the boiling tank had not yet been fitted. Contrary to what some accounts have said, the oil cooler was still in place underneath the port wing.

aircraft, still in its blue and silver high speed finish but bearing RAF markings, was delivered to the Photographic Reconnaissance Unit at Heston. Soon after its arrival an oblique camera was fitted into the rear fuselage on the port side just behind the cockpit and it was intended to use the aircraft for high speed low altitude reconnaissance. But the problem remained that because of the previous alterations to accommodate the boiling tank, there was now room for only some 60 gallons of fuel in the aircraft. Wing Commander (later Air Marshal Sir) Geoffrey Tuttle commanded the PRU at the time and he told the author what happened when he tried to use the Speed Spitfire for this intended purpose:

The range was ridiculously low—if you tried to photograph Brest from St Eval you would have run out of fuel about 20 miles short of the English coast on the way back. I took the aircraft out once to photograph a simple target in the Calais area, to see how it worked. And I had an absolutely absurd thing happen. As I was running in on the target at low altitude over the Channel I popped out of cloud to find myself in formation with a Heinkel 111. He must have been frightened to death but he needn't have worried, I didn't have any guns! I peeled away to get out of his fire in case he opened up, and had to re-align on the target. But even that small devia-

tion depleted my fuel to such an extent that I was unable to photograph my target and had to abandon the mission. After that we used the Speed Spitfire solely as a run-about aircraft.

Unfortunately Tuttle did not record in his logbook the date of the single unsuccessful operational mission by the aircraft. Another of those who flew it at this time was Flight Lieutenant (later Air Chief Marshal Sir) Neil Wheeler who recalled:

It was a fascinating aircraft to fly. You could formate on a Hurricane, then open up and pull away right across his nose accelerating the whole time. The first time I flew it I put it into a shallow descent and got up to 430 mph indicated. But there was too much distortion from the curved windscreen, it had no guns, limited fuel and shortened wings. It was a magnificent toy, but no use at all for photo reconnaissance missions.

The Speed Spitfire was used throughout the war as a 'high speed hack', and survived until June 1946 when it was scrapped.

**80.** The Speed Spitfire, now K 9834, photographed in November 1940 shortly after delivery to the Photographic Reconnaissance Unit, with Flight Lieutenant Neil Wheeler in the cockpit. The aircraft had retained its blue and silver colour scheme and high speed windscreen, but was fitted with a Merlin XII engine and standard radiator; it carried standard RAF roundels on the sides of the fuselage and under the wings (but not on top), and a small fin flash. *(Wheeler)*

**81.** Though mutilated, this photograph shows interesting underside detail of the aircraft and the oblique camera port just behind the cockpit. K 9834 is seen soon after arrival at the PRU with the commander, Wing Commander Geoffrey Tuttle, standing in front. *(Tuttle)*

**82.** K 9834 photographed in March 1942, by which time she had been fitted with a normal **PR** windscreen and was established in use as the unit hack. *(Tuttle)*

# Appendix A

## THE 'SPEED SPITFIRE' K 9834

In each case the structural features and performance figures are given only when they differ from those of the first production Spitfire K 9787. Unless otherwise stated, all figures refer to the Speed Spitfire in the form in which it flew late in 1938 and early in 1939.

Changes made to this aircraft:

Strengthened engine mounting and front bay of fuselage, to accommodate more powerful engine.

Special Merlin II engine fitted

Pressurized water cooling system and enlarged radiator, in place of glycol cooling system.

Enlarged oil cooler

Four-bladed wooden airscrew

Detachable wing tips removed and remaining outer portions of wings rounded off. All removable doors replaced by attached panels.

Tail wheel replaced by a streamlined tail skid

Radio installation and landing flares omitted, replaced by attached panels.

Low drag windscreen and flat canopy fitted

Starboard flap shortened, to allow the lengthened fairing of the radiator to extend to the trailing edge of the wing.

Low drag pitot head, fitted to leading edge of port wing.

Dome headed rivets on the fuselage replaced by flush rivets.

All joints filled and high speed finish applied to airframe.

**Dimensions:** Wing span 33 ft 8 in
Gross wing area 231 square ft

**Weights:** Tare weight 4,520 pounds
Fully loaded weight 5,490 pounds (tare weight plus fuel load of 84 gallons, 6 gallons of oil, 200 pounds for pilot and parachute, 86 pounds for other items of equipment).
Wing loading when fully loaded, 23 pounds per square foot.

**Power plant:** Rolls-Royce Merlin II Special, 2,100 BHP at 3,200 rpm at sea level at +28 pounds boost, running on a special fuel mixture of 60 per cent benzol, 20 per cent straight run gasoline, 20 per cent methanol and 4 cc of lead per Imperial gallon. At maximum power the fuel consumption of this engine was just over 3 gallons per minute.

**Propellers:** Watts four-bladed fixed pitch wooden, 10 ft diameter; Watts four-bladed fixed pitch wooden, 9 ft 9 in diameter; or Hamilton three-bladed two pitch metal airscrew, 10 ft 9 in in diameter.

**Performance:** Maximum speed achieved, 408 mph at 3,000 feet. This is equivalent to about 400 mph at the 200 foot altitude necessary for record breaking runs.

### Author's Comments

Shortly before delivery to the Royal Air Force in November 1940 this aircraft was fitted with standard Merlin XII engine, radiator and oil coolers, pitot system and a three-bladed Rotol constant speed airscrew. Subsequently, while serving with the Photographic Reconnaissance Unit, it was fitted with an F.24 camera in an oblique mounting behind the cockpit facing port, a tail wheel and, later still, a normal type PR windscreen.

# 6.

# HIGH SPEED SPIES—THE MARK I RECONNAISSANCE VARIANTS

The suggestion that the Spitfire might prove suitable as a high speed photographic reconnaissance aircraft came from Flying Officer Maurice 'Shorty' Longbottom. Before the war Longbottom had been involved with the clandestine flights by Sydney Cotton, during which the latter photographed Italian fortifications in Libya for the British Secret Intelligence Service using a modified Lockheed 12 transport aircraft. In August 1939 Longbottom submitted a memorandum to the Air Ministry entitled 'Photographic Reonnaissance of Enemy Territory in War'. His concern was for strategic reconnaissance missions to penetrate deep into enemy territory and he noted: '. . . this type of reconnaissance must be done in such a manner as to avoid the enemy fighters and AA defences as completely as possible. The best method of doing this appears to be the use of a single small machine, relying solely on its speed, climb and ceiling to avoid detection.' Longbottom went on to argue that the ideal aircraft for such work was a single seat fighter, stripped of guns and radio and fitted with extra fuel tanks. 'As most fighters have a very good take-off performance, due to their great reserve of engine power, they could be considerably overloaded with further fuel giving an even greater range.' Since speed and altitude were to be the prime requirements to enable the aircraft to avoid interception over enemy territory, Longbottom considered the Spitfire an obvious choice for such work. Of the all-up weight of 5,935 pounds for the standard fighter version of the Spitfire (fitted with a three-blade two-pitch metal airscrew), Longbottom calculated that for the unarmed reconnaissance role 450 pounds of the service load would not be needed: guns, ammunition, gunsight, flares and the radio set. And since it would not have to dogfight the reconnaissance version could be overloaded by about 15 per cent to give it a gross weight of 6,858 pounds. Longbottom could put the 923 pounds of lifting capacity thus gained to good use. With the inclusion of a couple of aerial cameras, the modified Spitfire could carry 240 gallons of fuel or nearly three times as much as the fighter version. This would be sufficient to give the aircraft a range of 1,500 miles cruising at 300 mph or 1,800 miles at 250 mph, all at altitudes of 30,000 feet and over.

Today Longbottom's concept of a lone unarmed high-speed high-flying reconnaissance aircraft sneaking through the

defences to its target, photographing it and then sneaking away with a minimum of fuss, is so well accepted that it scarcely seems worthy of comment. But in 1939 it was a radical departure from conventional service thinking on reconnaissance. At that time nearly all long range reconnaissance aircraft in all air forces were converted bomber types, which retained their defensive armament so they could if necessary fight their way out of trouble. But the guns and gunners imposed their penalty on performance, and brought the aircraft within reach of the very defences it had to avoid if it was to stand a good chance of accomplishing its mission.

Almost immediately after the outbreak of war, towards the end of September 1939, Sydney Cotton was given the acting rank of Wing Commander and ordered to set up a unit within the Royal Air Force able to fly long range reconnaissance missions into enemy territory. The unit was based at Heston and received the innocuous title of 'Heston Flight'; it came under the operational control of Fighter Command. And one of the pilots summoned to join the unit on its inception was Longbottom himself.

Initially it was planned that the Heston Flight would operate specially modified Blenheim bombers, stripped of armament and all unnecessary equipment, and with a carefully applied high speed finish to reduce drag to a minimum. But even with these improvements the Blenheim was unable to fly fast or high enough to stand much chance of avoiding the enemy defences. The real answer was to modify Spitfires along the lines Longbottom had suggested, and in October Cotton managed to prise a couple of these precious aircraft out of Fighter Command.

Longbottom's original idea had been to install the aerial cameras in the rear fuselage of the Spitfire behind the pilot. But engineers at Farnborough considered that, with the extra fuel tankage, this would push the centre of gravity of the aircraft too far rearwards for safety. As an interim measure pending investigation, Cotton was permitted to install cameras in his two Spitfires in the spaces which had been occupied by the two inboard guns and their ammunition boxes; there were to be no additional fuel tanks on these first reconnaissance Spitfires. The two cameras in each aircraft, F.24s with 5-in focal length lenses, looked almost vertically downwards to cover an oblong-shaped area of ground with slight overlap between their cover. Thus the two Spitfires, serial numbers N 3069 and N 3071, were modified into PR Mark IAs. After the fitting of cameras the two aircraft were 'cleaned up' in the Heston workshops: the gun ports were blocked over with metal plates and all cracks were filled with plaster of Paris then rubbed down. As a further move to make interception more difficult, the aircraft were doped overall in a very pale shade of duck-egg green, or

**83** and **84.** The scene at Seclin near Lille in France on 18 November 1939, as Flight Lieutenant 'Shorty' Longbottom prepared to take off for the first operational photographic reconnaissance sortie by a Spitfire. The aircraft, Type PR IA N 3071, had had its armament removed and was fitted with an F.24 camera in each wing. It was painted in very pale green 'Camotint' overall; the normal fighter-type windscreen with laminated glass front was retained, but the aircraft was fitted with a modified canopy with perspex side blisters. In photograph **84**, on the right, Sidney Cotton is seen adjusting Longbottom's parachute straps. *(Green)*

CAMERA MOTOR

F24 CAMERA

'Camotint' as Cotton called it. He had used this colouring for his Lockheed 12 during the clandestine reconnaissance flights before the war, after noticing that whenever an aircraft was observed from below from a distance it invariably appeared as a dark silhouette against the lighter sky background, unless the sun happened to be glinting off some part of the structure. There was little that could be done about sun glint, but if the silhouette could be made lighter the distance from which it could be seen would be reduced.

After painting, the modified Spitfires were carefully polished up to reduce drag to a minimum; as a result of all these improvements their maximum speed was 10-15 mph greater than the equivalent fighter version.

At the beginning of November 1939 Cotton's unit was renamed No 2 Camouflage unit, a further move to conceal its true function. Later that month one of the modified Spitfires

**85.** Close-up of the installation of the F.24 camera in the wing of a Spitfire PR IA, seen from above.

**86.** The Belgian village of Bulligen (centre, two-thirds of the way up) as photographed during the first successful Spitfire reconnaissance sortie on 22 November 1939. Taken from 33,000 feet with a 5-in focal length camera, the picture gives little ground detail. *(via Brookes)*

**87.** Compare photograph **86** above, with this one of the same village, taken in April 1944 from a Spitfire at approximately the same altitude using a 36-in focal length camera fitted in the rear fuselage. Considerably more ground detail is visible, and the two photographs show well the advances made in equipment during the war years. *(via Brookes)*

**88.** Previously erroneously described as a PR IC, this aircraft lacked underwing blisters and was in fact a PR IB with an 8-in focal length camera in each wing and a 29 gallon extra fuel tank behind the pilot, This particular aircraft, P 9331, operated with No 212 Squadron from Seclin during the spring of 1940; it was left in France following the Dunkirk evacuation and captured intact by the Germans. *(Lukesch)*

was detached to Seclin near Lille in France, as part of the so-called Special Survey Flight. On the 18th Longbottom, now a Flight Lieutenant, took off from Seclin for what was to be the first operational flight by a reconnaissance Spitfire; it was, moreover, the first operational flight by a Spitfire of any type based outside Great Britain. Longbottom's target was the German city of Aachen and the nearby fortifications; but navigation from 33,000 feet proved more difficult than expected and he returned with photographs of the Belgian side of the frontier south of Aachen. The lessons of the failure were soon learned and on the 22nd Longbottom successfully photographed fortifications along the Belgian–German border east of Liège. Further attempts to photograph targets in Belgium and Germany were thwarted by cloud until 29 December when Longbottom, this time operating from Nancy, flew a successful sortie over the Aachen and Cologne areas. During the first week of 1940 Longbottom and the unit's other pilot, Flight Lieutenant Bob Niven, photographed Kaiserslautern, Wiesbaden, Mainz and parts of the Ruhr.

These early Spitfire reconnaissance sorties proved that the concept of this type of operation was sound and such aircraft could penetrate enemy territory without being intercepted by fighters or engaged effectively by anti-aircraft guns. But with the 5-in focal length lenses, at 30,000 feet the cameras produced prints of such a small scale that, even when they were blown up by the photo interpreters' magnifying glasses, there was little indication of troop positions: roads, railways, small villages and major fortifications could be picked out, but anything much smaller than that was likely to be missed.

Having proved the concept of the Spitfire as a reconnaissance aircraft, Cotton was able to obtain others for modification for the new role. In the new aircraft the wing-mounted F.24 cameras were fitted with 8-in focal length lenses which gave a scale improvement on ground photographs one third greater; it

was a major improvement, but it still would not allow military vehicles to be seen from 30,000 feet. The other problem with the PR Mark IA was that on the same 84 gallon fuel tankage as the fighter version, it lacked the range to go far into enemy territory. By playing on the fact that the Spitfires with the three-blade two-pitch metal propellers had to carry 40 pounds of lead ballast in the rear fuselage to balance out the extra weight on the nose, Cotton was able to secure permission to install a 29 gallon fuel tank behind the pilot and dispense with the lead. On 16 January 1940 Longbottom collected the first Spitfire modified in this way from Farnborough. This was the PR Mark IB or 'medium-range' version which had an operational radius of action of 325 miles. On 10 February this would be sufficient for Longbottom, operating from a forward refuelling airfield in East Anglia, to photograph the German naval base at Wilhelmshaven. For high altitude operations the light 'Camot-int' colouring was found to be unsuitable, and the PR IBs were painted in the medium blue scheme which was to be known throughout the war as 'PR Blue'.

Also in January No 2 Camouflage Unit was renamed the Photographic Development Unit; at last its true purpose could be mentioned in its title, though the unit's operations were still shrouded in secrecy.

**89** and **90.** The PR Type IC carried its two 8-in focal length cameras in the flattened blister under the starboard wing, 30 gallons of extra fuel in the rounded blister under the port wing and 29 gallons in a tank behind the pilot. *(Green)*

**91.** R 6903 was a PR IC, seen here with the front-hinged camera blister under the starboard wing open. The LY code-letters were those of the Photographic Reconnaissance Unit. Unusually for a PR IC this aircraft had a deepened engine cowling, indicating that it was fitted with an enlarged oil tank. Pilot Officer Gordon Green flew this aircraft during his first Spitfire reconnaissance mission to St Nazaire on 13 February 1941, and during the mission when he located the *Scharnhorst* and *Gneisenau* in Brest harbour on 28 March. *(Green)*

The next step was to improve range still further with the new PR 1C or 'long-range' version of the Spitfire. This had a 30 gallon fixed blister tank under the port wing, counterbalanced by a similarly shaped blister under the starboard wing which housed a pair of F.24 cameras with 8-in focal length lenses. With the additional tank behind the pilot, this version had 59 gallons of extra fuel. As a result a PR 1C was able to photograph Kiel for the first time, on 7 April 1940.

Early in 1940 the PDU operations in France had been reg-ularised by the formation of No 212 Squadron, equipped initially with a single PR 1B and based at Seclin near Lille. Gradually the unit built up to a strength of eight aircraft; but it was always considered as a detachment from the PDU and there was a continual interchange of men, aircraft and ideas between the two units.

Still more range could be squeezed out of the Spitfire. The obvious place to carry extra fuel, without incurring the penalty of the aircraft's centre of gravity being pushed too far aft, was the hollow leading edge of the wing forward of the main spar—that section of the wing which would have housed the steam condenser, had the aircraft been built with an evapora-tively cooled engine. Early in 1940 work began at Supermarine on modifying a Spitfire on the production line to carry a 57 gallon integral tank in the leading edge of each wing; the cameras were to be fitted in the fuselage behind the pilot. Because of the extent of the modifications and the low priority of the work, however, it would be several months before this version—the PR 1D—would be ready for operations.

In June 1940, following the Dunkirk evacuation and its with-drawal from France, No 212 Squadron was disbanded and its surviving aircraft and personnel rejoined the PDU at Heston.

Thus far the reconnaissance Spitfires had been able to take only vertical photographs, which viewed the target from above from medium or high altitudes. But there was also a require-

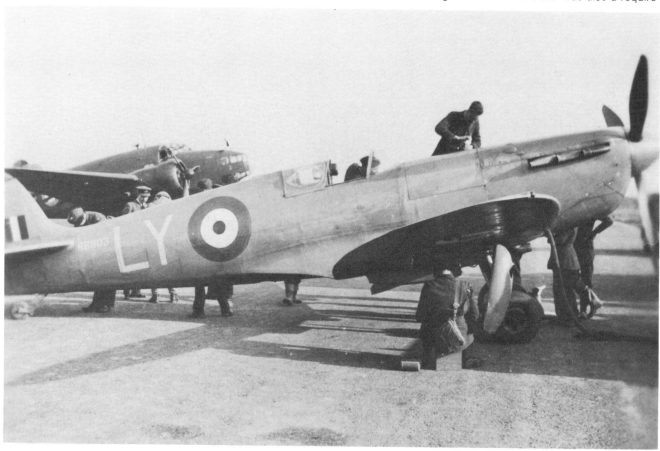

91

ment to be able to take low altitude oblique close-ups of targets and this gave rise to a further version, the PR 1E. It is believed that only one example of the Type E was produced—N 3117—and it carried a single F.24 camera under each wing, in

**92** and **93.** It is believed that only one Spitfire was converted into a PR IE, N 3117. This version was fitted with a single oblique camera under each wing, pointing outwards at right angles to the line of flight and slightly downwards. Flying Officer Alistair Taylor flew this aircraft when he photographed Boulogne harbour from low altitude underneath cloud on 7 July 1940. *(via Duncan, Tuttle)*

**94** and **95.** At first glance the PR IF looked like a PR IC fitted with the enlarged oil tank. But on closer examination it can be seen that both of the underwing blisters were rounded, each containing 30 gallons of fuel; with the extra 29 gallon tank behind the cockpit, this version carried more than twice as much fuel as the Spitfire I fighter. The two vertical (and later sometimes one oblique) cameras were housed in the rear fuselage, which meant there was room for 14-in and later 20-in telephoto lenses. *(Smithsonian, Tuttle)*

a bulged mounting which enabled it to look out at right angles to the line of flight and slightly downwards at about 15 degrees below the horizontal. This version probably carried the 29 gallon fuselage tank. On 3 July 1940 Wing Commander Geoffrey Tuttle, commanding the PDU, flew the first operational sortie in the Type E but was unable to bring back any pictures because of cloud cover at the target. Four days later Flying Officer Alistair Taylor was more successful. He reached the French coast 2 miles south of Boulogne—his target—to find the cloud base at about 700 feet and heavy rain falling. He switched on his starboard camera and photographed the harbour from an altitude of 300 feet as he flew past it. At the end of the run he turned around, and flew a repeat run photographing with his port camera. Taylor encountered no opposition from enemy defences, probably because his runs passed unnoticed in the foul weather. The mission demonstrated the value of low altitude oblique photography from a high speed aircraft and revealed a bonus: using oblique cameras Spitfires could photo-

94

95

graph targets under weather conditions that precluded vertical photography.

During June 1940 the Photographic Development Unit had been transferred to the operational control of Coastal Command, and in the following month it was renamed the Photographic Reconnaissance Unit (PRU). Neither change made any difference to the way it operated, however, and work continued much as before. On 20 July 1940 the unit's complement of Spitfires comprised eight Type Bs, three Type Cs and one Type E.

During the interim period before the PR 1D with the integral wing tanks became available, one further variant appeared: the PR 1F, the so-called 'super-long-range' version. This carried a 30 gallon blister tank under each wing as well as the 29 gallon tank behind the pilot's seat, giving a fuel load of 89 gallons in addition to that carried by the normal fighter version. To provide the extra oil necessary for the extended flights, an enlarged tank was fitted under the nose which gave it a somewhat deeper external line. The cameras in the Type F were carried behind the cockpit and initially comprised two F.24s with 8-in focal length lenses; later 20-in focal length cameras were fitted; and later still some of the Type Fs were fitted with a 14-in focal length oblique camera looking out to port from the rear fuselage behind the cockpit. The Type F began operations at the end of July 1940 and gave a useful increase in the radius of action of 100 miles, compared with the Type C. In due course nearly all of the operational Type Bs and Type Cs would be modified to Type F standard. Operating from forward bases in East Anglia the Type F was just able, under optimum conditions, to reach and photograph Berlin and return.

During the summer of 1940, as the Battle of Britain raged over southern England, the lone Spitfires of the PRU ranged far and wide over north-western Europe and returned with photographs of enemy movements and dispositions. The Spitfire, conceived and built as a short range interceptor fighter, had shown it could be modified into a superb long range reconnaissance aircraft. But still more was demanded from it. The Baltic ports still lay tantalizingly out of sight of the British reconnaissance aircraft, at a time when the Admiralty was making the strongest demands for photographs of that area which would betray any abnormal enemy naval activity leading up to an invasion attempt. The answer to this problem was the long awaited Type D Spitfire, the so-called 'extra-super-long range' version. But whereas the Tyes A, B, C, E and F had all been relatively simple modifications of the standard Spitfire I fighter, the alteration of the leading edge of each wing to enable it to hold 57 gallons of fuel was beyond the limited engineering resources at Heston and Farnborough. The scheme which emerged was to seal off the 'D' shaped torsion box which formed the leading edge of the wings and which was originally to have housed the steam condenser for the evaporatively cooled Merlin. This structure was to hold the fuel. Today such fuel tanks integral with the aircraft structure are commonplace, but in 1940 the idea was a new one. In the summer of 1940 the work of converting wings for the new type of reconnaissance Spitfire led to a conflict of priorities, however, for it clashed with that of hand-building leading edges for the cannon-Spitfires demanded by Fighter Command.

As a result the first PR 1D was not ready until almost the end of October 1940. This type carried 114 gallons of extra fuel in the wing, 29 gallons in the tank behind the pilot and 14 gallons of extra oil in what had been the inboard gun bay in the port wing; behind the rear fuselage fuel tank it could carry two F.24 cameras with 8-in or 20-in focal length lenses, or two F.8s with 20-in lenses.

The Type D Spitfire was so heavily laden with fuel when it took off for a long range mission that it was nicknamed 'the bowser'. And with the rear tank full and the aft mounted cameras, the centre of gravity was so far back that handling was difficult. Wing Commander Tuttle has told the author 'You could not fly it straight and level for the first half hour or hour after take-off. Until you had emptied the rear tank, the aircraft hunted the whole time. The centre of gravity was so far back you couldn't control it. It was the sort of thing that would never have got in during peace-time, but war is another matter.'

Yet in spite of its difficult handling characteristics during the initial stages of each mission, the Type D soon demonstrated that it could achieve great things in the hands of the PRU pilots. On 29 October 1940 Flying Officer S. Millen photographed Stettin during what was by far the longest Spitfire sortie so far, lasting 5 hours and 20 minutes. Other long distance targets were covered by the Type Ds soon afterwards: Marseilles on 2 November, Trondheim on 7 December and Toulon on the 8th.

After the first two hand-built Type Ds—serials P 9551 and P 9552—had proved their worth, the production version which appeared early in 1941 was slightly altered to improve its handling. The wing leading edges were further modified to allow 66½ gallons of fuel to be carried in each and the rear fuselage tank was deleted. In place of the Merlin III engine the production Type D had the more efficient and powerful Merlin 45 as fitted to the Spitfire V. Other modifications included the fitting of a cabin heating system—a great boon for pilots who had to operate for long periods at extreme altitude—and the restoration of the radio which eased the problem of navigation during the return flights. In all a total of 229 Type D Spitfires would be built and this version—later redesignated the PR Mark IV—was to provide the backbone of the Royal Air Force photographic reconnaissance effort during 1941 and 1942.

There was one final reconnaissance variant of the Spitfire I, the Type G. The operations with the single Type E had shown the usefulness of oblique cameras for taking large scale photographs of targets from low altitude, and also for photographing priority targets when the cloud base was low. But by going in low the Spitfire sacrificed the protection that altitude gave and it became vulnerable to enemy fighters attacking from above. So for its low level operations the Type G retained both the normal 8-gun fighter armament and the laminated glass windscreen. This version carried the 29 gallon fuel tank behind the pilot's seat; the camera installation comprised an obliquely mounted F.24 camera with a 14-in length focal lens behind the cockpit looking either port or starboard, and two F.24s looking vertically down, one with a 5-in lens and the other with a 14-in lens. This camera installation gave considerable flexibility, for the Type G was expected to photograph its targets from immediately under the cloud base wherever that happened to be. The oblique camera was used when photographing at altitudes below about 2,000 feet, the F.24 with the 5-in lens when photographing between about 2,000 feet and 10,000 feet, and the F.24 with the 14-in lens was used for photography above 10,000 feet. Most Type Gs were painted in a very pale shade of pink, just off white, which during 1940 had replaced the pale green 'Camotint' originally applied to aircraft engaged in low altitude photography.

The nature of the reconnaissance missions, flying alone either at extreme altitude or low down using cloud cover, endeavouring to sneak out to and from targets and photograph them with a minimum of fuss, was quite unlike any other role assigned to the Spitfire. In the account which follows one of the

**96 and 97.** The PR ID, later re-designated the Spitfire PR IV, entered service after the E and F versions. Apart from the rounded windscreen, bulges on the sides of the canopy, camera ports under the fuselage and absence of armament, this version looked little different from a Mark I or Mark V fighter. But internally the wing structure was considerably altered to accommodate 114, later 133, gallons of fuel in the wing leading edges. The latter gave rise to the unusual spectacle, right (**97**), of a Spitfire being refuelled almost at the wing tip. (*Salwey*)

**98.** View of a pink Spitfire PR IG, R 7059, pictured at St Eval in Cornwall early in 1941 when it was used for low altitude reconnaissance missions over the French ports. Note the unusual positioning of the roundels above the wings, which was fairly common on pink aircraft. This version, which was later re-designated the PR Mark VII, was fitted with a laminated glass windscreen and carried an armament of eight machine guns; one

oblique and two vertical cameras were carried in the rear fuselage, plus a tank for 29 gallons of fuel. *(Salwey)*

**99.** A camouflaged PR IG carrying the DP code letters of No 1416 Flight, a little known army co-operation tactical reconnaissance unit which formed at Hendon in the summer of 1941. *(Green)*

**100.** In September 1941 No 1416 Flight was expanded into No 140 Squadron, code letters ZW, which operated Spitfire PR IGs and Blenheims. The camouflaged PR IG in the foreground (serial number R 7116 just visible under the tailplane) was unusual in that the oblique camera was angled rearwards to reduce the apparent speed of targets passing the side of the aircraft, and therefore picture blur; this change necessitated the fitting of a bulged camera housing. *(Green)*

**101** and **102.** No 140 Squadron operated both pink and camouflaged Spitfire PR IGs. In these photographs X 4784 demonstrates the value of the pale pink scheme against a cloudy background, but they also show that the aircraft was considerably more conspicuous when seen from above against a land or sea background. *(Green)*

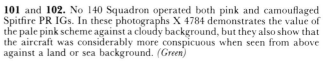

**103.** Pilot Officer Gordon Green, whose account of some of the early Spitfire reconnaissance missions is given on this page. *(Green)*

PRU pilots, Pilot Officer Gordon Green, tells us of some of the missions he flew during 1941.

*   *   *

'I was posted to the Photographic Reconnaissance Unit at Heston in December 1940, initially to fly Hudsons. But at about that time it was decided that the unit would operate only Spitfires and I was given a quick conversion course on to this type at the PRU, which in the meantime had moved to Benson. I had a couple of trips in a Harvard, went solo in a Battle, then I was let loose in a Spitfire. Six weeks and 14 flying hours later, I was pronounced operational as a Spitfire PR pilot.

'The technique of high altitude photography from a single seater like the Spitfire was largely a question of experience, for a great deal depended on being able to judge where the cameras were pointing. One flew alone to the general area of the target, then tipped the aircraft on its side to check one was properly lined up. Once that was done it was a question of holding the aircraft dead straight and level for the photographic run. Until one learned the art it was all too easy—if, for example, one had a bit of bank on—to come back with a lovely line of photographs of the ground a couple of miles to one side of the intended target.

'Early in February 1941 I was one of four pilots of 'A' Flight of the PRU detached to St Eval in Cornwall. We were to keep watch on the French west coast ports: Brest, St Nazaire and Lorient, La Pallice, La Rochelle and Bordeaux. On the 13th I flew my first mission to St Nazaire, at high altitude in a Type C, R 6903, and photographed the target successfully. During the week that followed I flew three other high altitude sorties, only one of which was successful. Cloud was (and still is) a continual problem for the photographic reconnaissance pilot. During my time on the PRU well over half the sorties flown failed to bring back photos of the targets. On 21 February I flew a Type G,

N 3241, to Brest for a low altitude sortie but that was not successful either. Pilots took it in turns to fly high altitude sorties in the blue-painted Type Cs or low altitude ones in the pink Type Gs. By 20 March I had flown five high altitude and two low altitude sorties to the French ports, of which four of the former and none of the latter were successful.

'During those early missions there was no such thing as cockpit heating in our Spitfires. For the high altitude missions we wore thick suits with electrical heating. Trussed up in our Mae West and parachute, one could scarcely move in the narrow cockpit of the Spitfire. While flying over enemy territory one had to be searching the sky the whole time for enemy fighters. On more than one occasion I started violent evasive action to shake off a suspected enemy fighter, only to discover that it was a small speck of dirt on my perspex canopy!

'A big worry over enemy territory was that one might start leaving a condensation trail without knowing it, thus pointing out one's position to the enemy. To avoid that we had small mirrors fitted in the blisters on each side of the canopy, so that one could see the trail as soon as it started to form behind. When that happened one would either climb or descend until the trail ceased. If possible, we liked to climb above the trail's layer because then fighters trying to intercept us had first to climb through the trail's layer themselves and could be seen in good time. But on most occasions the trail's layer extended above the ceiling of the early reconnaissance Spitfires.

'During the final week of March 1941 we had a great panic at St Eval: the German battle cruisers *Scharnhorst* and *Gneisenau* had been out in the Atlantic and it was thought they had put into one of the French ports. Unfortunately, however, at that time the weather was very bad and we were unable to get photographs of the ports to prove or disprove this. Then on the 28th I went out at high altitude in R 6903 to try to photograph Brest. I arrived overhead to find that, as usual, it was covered in cloud. But there were a few clear patches about so I decided to hold off in case one of the gaps drifted over the port. After a wait of about 25 minutes that happened, and I ran over the top and took my photographs. From 30,000 feet all one could see was the town and the sea front, it was impossible to make out any detail

**104.** Green's photograph of Brest on 28 March 1941, taken from PR IC R 6903, was the first to reveal the arrival of the German battle cruisers *Scharnhorst* and *Gneisenau*. *(Green)*

**105.** Gordon Green's photograph of Brest on 7 April 1941, taken from a pink **PR IG** from 1,500 feet, showing one of the German battle cruisers on the right. *(Green)*

or see what if any ships were in port. Only after my return to St Eval, when the photo interpreters had seen my pictures, did I learn that my cameras had observed the two German battle cruisers tied up in the harbour. Afterwards several congratulatory signals arrived, including one from the First Sea Lord: ''We are very grateful for definite information obtained under difficult conditions and after much persistence. Congratulations on your efforts culminating in [sortie number] W 378. Keep it up.'' Very properly, these signals were addressed to the Flight as a whole. We had all put in a lot of flying to find the warships and I just happened to be the man flying the sortie when the sky over the port became clear.

'Now that the Admiralty knew where the battle cruisers were, their big worry was when they would next try to break out into the Atlantic. And when they did, the Admiralty wanted to know immediately. We on 'A' Flight were ordered to drop almost everything else and concentrate on flying regular reconnaissance missions over the port. It had to be covered three times per day—early in the morning, at about mid-day and late in the afternoon, regardless of the weather—and each time we had to produce photographic proof that the two battle cruisers were still in port. In practice this meant that a pair of aircraft had to be sent out each time to ensure the port was covered: a Type C to photograph from high altitude if the skies over Brest were clear; and a Type G at low altitude to photograph underneath cloud if there was a layer over the target. The idea was that unless there was cloud or mist almost to ground level, either one or other of the Spitfires would be able to bring back photographs of the port.

'Sometimes one would set off in a pink Type G for a low altitude sortie, and arrive at the French coast to find a brilliantly sunny day with not a cloud in the sky. Under such conditions it would have been suicidal to try to photograph the heavily defended port at low or medium altitude, so one would turn back and leave it to the high altitude aircraft. Six-tenths cloud was the no-man's-land figure: too much to allow much chance of a successful run from high altitude, too little to shield a Spitfire going in at low altitude.

'The important thing with any photographic mission was to take the photos if one could, and get them back to base. As the ''boss'' of PRU, Wing Commander Geoffrey Tuttle, often used to say ''I want you to get home safely not just because I like your faces, but because if you don't the whole sortie will be a waste of time!'' So it was no use trying to play hide and seek with the Luftwaffe; if one had lost surprise during the approach to a heavily defended target, the best thing was to abandon the mission and go back another time when things might be better.

'After four more sorties against Brest, two at high altitude, one of which was unsuccessful due to too much cloud, and two at low altitude, both of which were unsuccessful because there was not enough, I set out for Brest on 5 April at low altitude in Type G   P 9369. On the way there I was in and out of cloud almost all the way—ideal conditions. The cloud base was down to 300 feet in places. I was approaching the town at 700 feet when, suddenly, there was this bloody great ship right below me! And at that same moment everything opened up at me! It was just like a great firework display with red, green and yellow tracer rounds coming up towards me seemingly very slowly. It was all very pretty—and very dangerous. I stuffed down the nose of the Spitfire and went down close to the ground to the east of the port, to get as much protection as possible from the folds in the ground. There had been no opportunity to line my camera on the target, and it would have been suicidal to go back. But when I returned, even though there were no photographs, I was able to say that without a shadow of doubt one of the German battle cruisers was still in port!

'Two days later, on 7 April, I went out at low altitude in the same aircraft and on that occasion I was able to sneak in and photograph the port from 1,500 feet, without too much trouble from the defences.

'During those early missions to cover Brest we lost about five pilots fairly quickly. After the first couple had failed to return the Flight Commander, Flight Lieutenant Keith Arnold, asked Benson to send some reserve pilots and they duly arrived. They both took off for Brest the evening they arrived, and neither came back. It was a very sobering incident. We had the advantage of knowing just what it could be like over Brest and, most important of all, we knew when things were going wrong and when we had to turn back if we were to survive. Every German in the area knew roughly when we were coming so it needed all the cunning we could muster—approaching from a different direction each time—plus a large share of luck if one was to come through.

'During the remainder of April I flew a total of eleven high and eight low altitude missions to Brest, of which only three of the high altitude missions were successful. Then, early in May, I returned to Benson and for the next three months flew the more normal types of reconnaissance mission at high altitude to the Channel ports and over Germany.

'In August 1941 I was posted to No 1416 Flight, a Spitfire reconnaissance unit based at Hendon, for a rest. This unit operated PR 1Gs in the army co-operation role and, the following month, was re-designated No 140 Squadron.

'Looking back at my time with the PRU, I get a lot of satisfaction from the knowledge that although I played my part in the war I never had to fire a shot in anger. In one sense we in the reconnaissance business had things easy. All the time it was impressed on us: bring back the photographs and, if you can't, bring back the aeroplane. An infantryman taking part in the advance at Alamein could not suddenly decide ''This is ridiculous, I'm going home!'' He just had to go on. But if we thought we had lost the element of surprise we were not only permitted to turn back, we were expected to do so. On the other hand there were times when I knew real fear. When one was 15 minutes out from Brest on a low altitude sortie, one's heart was beating away and as the target got nearer one's mouth got completely dry. Anyone who was not frightened at the thought of going in to photograph one of the most heavily defended targets in Europe, was not human.

'Whenever it was possible to photograph a target flak could engage us: if we could see to photograph they could see to open up at us. But throughout my time as a reconnaissance pilot my luck held. I never once saw an enemy fighter, nor was my aircraft ever hit by flak. Indeed only once during the time we were flying those missions over Brest did one of our aircraft come back with any damage, and that was only minor. It was all rather like a fox hunt—either the fox got away unscathed or else it was caught and killed. There was rarely anything in between.'

# 7.

# MORE PROBLEMS OF PRODUCTION: THE MARK II AND CASTLE BROMWICH

The Spitfire II differed from the final production versions of the Mark I in that it was fitted with the slightly more powerful Merlin XII engine, had pressurised water-glycol cooling and was fitted with a Coffman cartridge starter. Mark I K 9788, the second production aircraft, was fitted with the Merlin XII in the summer of 1939 and, following the success of the trials, it was decided that this engine should power the Mark II. The sole differences in the external shape of the Mark II, compared with the late production Mark Is, were a small blister on the starboard side of the engine cowling just behind the spinner to cover part of the gear train from the cartridge starter, and a slightly blunter spinner.

Early on it was decided that production of the Mark II would be confined to the newly erected factory at Castle Bromwich near Birmingham, managed and equipped by Morris Motors Ltd. Work had begun on the purpose-built plant in the summer of 1938. The motor company had intended to turn out Spitfires in the same way it was turning out cars, using extensive jigging of all components so that they could be produced using relatively unskilled labour. To that end Lord Nuffield had the factory equipped with the most modern machine tools available, far in advance of those in use in the British aircraft industry at that time. But fighter aircraft are quite different from cars and the factory lacked the flexibility to be able to incorporate the changes demanded by the Royal Air Force. Things soon began to go wrong. As the then Vice Chairman of Morris Motors, Miles Thomas (later Lord Thomas of Remenham), told the author:

Lord Nuffield was an idealist, he wanted everything tooled and jigged up to the Nth degree so that each operation could be broken down to a very simple but constituent part. But the Spitfire was continually being modified because the RAF wanted more performance and improvements to this, that and the other. Modifications were coming through at a fantastic rate. This was very serious for a factory being tooled up for mass production because if one had a die made for a component and somebody came along and said it had to be changed, that die had to be scrapped and a new one made. Because there was never any finality in design, production kept being put off. At Castle Bromwich they were producing lots of Spitfire bits, but no completed aircraft. Relations between the Air Ministry and Vickers, on the one hand, and Morris Motors began to fray. To Nuffield, who had made his name as a production engineer, the stream of modifications was becoming a nightmare.

Matters came to a head on 17 May 1940, just three days after Lord Beaverbrook had been appointed to the new post of Minister of Aircraft Production. Beaverbrook rang Nuffield and demanded to know why no Spitfires had yet emerged from the Castle Bromwich factory. By chance I happened to be in Nuffield's office at Cowley when the call came, and he passed me the extension earpiece so that I could hear what was being said. Nuffield opened up with a vociferous defence of the Castle Bromwich operation and said, in effect, that Beaverbrook could have either the Spitfires or the modifications, but not both. Then with a touch of sarcasm, as though he was playing his ace of trumps, Nuffield ended 'Perhaps you would like me to give up control of the Spitfire factory?' And Beaverbrook with his Canadian drawl jumped straight in and replied 'Nuffield, that's very generous of you. I accept!' There was a click in the earpiece and the line went dead.

Nuffield went white as a sheet. He had been out-manoeuvred, and he knew it. From the point of view of Spitfire production, however, it was as well. The Castle Bromwich factory had been financed with government money so Nuffield's 'resignation' gave Beaverbrook a free hand. He immediately handed control of the factory to Vickers, who drafted in management staff and skilled workers from Supermarine to get production moving. Stanley Woodley, one of those sent from Southampton to take charge of the Castle Bromwich plant, later commented:

**106.** Aerial view of the huge aircraft production complex at Castle Bromwich, which produced more Spitfires than all the other plants put together. *(Vickers)*

We were charged with producing ten Spitfires by the end of June 1940. We knew that in the short time available it was impossible to meet that date from the resources at Castle Bromwich alone. But by shipping up from Southampton large numbers of finished components, including some fully equipped fuselages, and working around the clock, the magic 'ten in June' were completed.

The simple fact was that if modifications had to be incorporated, and they had to be in great numbers, production with semi-skilled labour alone was not possible. The answer was to use the expensive jigs and the semi-skilled labourers to produce all those componenents that could be made that way, while the skilled labour forces at Castle Bromwich and Southampton produced those components which could not. With this hybrid process Spitfire production moved ahead rapidly at Castle Bromwich, with 23 aircraft in July, 37 in August and 56 during the month of September.

No 611 Squadron at Digby was the first to receive the Mark II Spitfire, in August 1940. It was followed the next month by Nos 19, 74 and 266 Squadrons and this version went into action during the closing stages of the Battle of Britain.

**107.** Inside one of the assembly halls at Castle Bromwich, showing the mass production of Spitfire fuselages. *(IWM)*

**108.** Alex Henshaw, Chief Test Pilot at Castle Bromwich, discussing his work with Mr Churchill when the latter paid a visit to the plant. During the course of the war Henshaw came to know the Spitfire as few others ever would, for he personally test-flew more than one in ten of the total number built. *(Henshaw)*

**109.** A rare photograph of a Spitfire II taken during the Battle of Britain: P 7375 seen shortly after delivery to No 266 Squadron at Wittering in September 1940. *(via Forder)*

The initial production version, the Mark IIA, retained the same eight .303-in Browning gun armament of the IA; like the Mark IB, the IIB was fitted with two Hispano cannon and four machine guns. Of the 921 Mark IIs built at Castle Bromwich, the first 751 were Mark IIAs, the remainder IIBs. In March 1941 the Mark II began to be phased out of production at Castle Bromwich, in favour of the Mark V.

Some fifty Mark IIAs were each fitted with a fixed 40 gallon fuel tank under the port wing to extend the radius of action of the aircraft, and issued to Nos 66, 118 and 152 Squadrons. An abridged account of the report on the trial of this version is given in Appendix B. Because of the reduction in maximum speed and climbing performance due to the fixed tank, however, this version did not find favour in the operational squadrons.

After they had been replaced in the fighter squadrons, in 1943 some fifty Mark IIs were fitted with the more powerful Merlin XX engine and operated in the air sea rescue role as the Mark IIC. These aircraft carried the Type E sea survival and rescue gear, comprising one large and two small canisters designed to fit into the flare chutes behind the Spitfire's cockpit. The largest of the canisters contained a Type L multi-seater inflatable dinghy; one of the smaller ones contained 75 yards of buoyant rope and the other held rescue equipment. When the pilot pulled the catch to release the gear, the dinghy canister went out first and pulled out the rope from one of the smaller canisters; when it reached the end of the rope the dinghy inflation lever was pulled automatically, then the remaining two canisters followed. The third canister contained canned water, emergency rations, a first aid kit and distress flares and, connected to the dinghy by the length of buoyant rope, served as a drogue to prevent the dinghy being blown away from the survivors. The clever feature of the Type E gear was that the

**110.** Spitfire IIA P 7833 PK-K of No 315 (Polish) Squadron at Northolt in the summer of 1941, bearing the Polish marking on the nose. This aircraft had previously served with No 65 Squadron and still carried that unit's 'East India Squadron' plaque on each side of the fuselage beneath the cockpit. As was usual on No 315 Squadron, the individual aircraft letter K had been made into a Polish girl's name, Krysia. Clearly visible on the side of the engine cowling, just behind the propeller, is the small blister over the cartridge starter gearing which is the only external recognition feature to distinguish a Mark II from a Mark I Spitfire. *(via Tomankiewicz)*

**111.** A cannon-armed Mark IIB, P 8327, pictured immediately before delivery in the spring of 1941. *(via Oughton)*

**112.** A Mark IIA fitted with the fixed 40 gallon fuel tank under the port wing. Aircraft thus modified were issued to Nos 66, 118 and 152 Squadrons for extended range escort and patrol missions. *(Lambermont)*

**113.** P 7378, a Mark IIA operated by No 501 Squadron, seen here fitted with a non-standard canopy with side blisters as used on photographic reconnaissance Spitfires *(IWM)*

113

Spitfire could carry it without requiring special modification or suffering any reduction in its fighting capability. Mark IICs served on the strength of Nos 275, 276, 277, 278, 281 and 282 Squadrons of Fighter Command.

One particularly interesting trial carried out by the Air Fighting Development Unit at Duxford early in 1942 involved the use of K 9830, a Mark I which had been converted into a Mark II. This aircraft was fitted with a periscopic system to enable the pilot to see into the area normally obscured by the top of the engine cowling; such an improvement was particularly valuable when engaging targets at large angles of deflection, when otherwise the pilot had to pull up the nose of the aircraft until it obscured the target then open fire and hope. The periscopic installation fitted to K 9830 comprised a mirror just in front of the gunsight and another inside the top of the windscreen; by looking in the lower mirror, the pilot could see over the engine cowling via the upper mirror. In the event, however, the improvement in visibility thus gained was less than 2 degrees and this and the difficulties of operating with the mirror system led to the idea being dropped.

Spitfire IIs were also involved in trials with the so-called Type 6 Mechanism, a cover name for the gyroscopically corrected gunsight produced by engineers at Farnborough to permit accurate deflection shooting during turns. This device was later known as the Mark I gyro gunsight; the improved Mark II, introduced later in the war, would greatly increase the effectiveness of allied aerial gunnery.

114

The periscopic gunsight, tested on K 9830 in 1942, was intended to provide better vision over the nose for deflection shooting. The dashed line shows the normal line of sight over the nose, the dotted line shows the pilot's line of sight using the periscopic sight. The gain in visibility was not sufficient to offset the difficulties of using the sight, however, and the idea was not taken further.

**114.** The cockpit of Spitfire II K 9830, showing the periscopic gun sighting system tested on this aircraft.

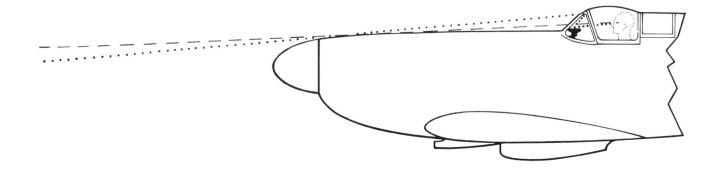

**115.** Groundcrewmen fitting the Type E sea survival and rescue gear into the flare chutes of a Spitfire IIC of No 276 Squadron. The gear fitted into one large and two small canisters and comprised a multi-seater dinghy, canned water, emergency rations, a first aid kit and distress flares. *(IWM)*

**116.** A Spitfire fitted with the 'Type 6 Mechanism', the forerunner of the successful gyro gunsight fitted to British fighters later in the war.

# Appendix A

## SPITFIRE IIA    P 7280

Figures taken from the trials report of this aircraft, the first off the production line at Castle Bromwich, tested at Boscombe Down in September 1940. Compared with the Mark I N 3171 described in Appendix C to Chapter 4, this aircraft was fitted with the IFF equipment and armour carried by Spitfires during the Battle of Britain and its weight is, therefore, almost representative of the late Mark Is which took part in the action.

**Dimensions:** Span 36 ft 10 in, Length 29 ft 11 in
**Weights:** Tare weight 4,783 pounds
    Fully loaded weight 6,172 pounds
    Wing loading when fully loaded, 25.5 pounds per square foot.
**Power plant:** Rolls-Royce Merlin XII
    Maximum power 1,140 BHP at 3,000 rpm at 14,750 ft at +9 lbs boost
**Performance:**

| Height feet | Top Speed mph | Time to Climb mins | Rate of Climb ft/min |
|---|---|---|---|
| Sea level | 290 | — | |
| 2,000 | 294 | 0 m 42 s | 2,925 |
| 5,000 | 306 | 1 m 42 s | 2,955 |
| 10,000 | 326 | 3 m 24 s | 2,995 |
| 15,000 | 345 | 5 m 0 s | 2,770 |
| 17,554 | 354 | | |
| 20,000 | 351 | 7 m 0 s | 2,175 |
| 25,000 | 338 | 9 m 36 s | 1,600 |
| 30,000 | 321 | 13 m 42 s | 995 |

| | |
|---|---|
| Service ceiling (estimated) | 37,600 ft |
| Take-off run | 230 yds |
| Distance to clear 50 ft screen | 400 yds |
| Landing speed | 67 mph |
| Landing run (with brakes) | 350 yds |

**Author's Comments**

The increase in fully loaded weight of 122 pounds, compared with N 3171, was due to the slightly greater weight of the Merlin XII engine and the carriage of an IFF set and armour. Because of the additional weight and the drag of the IFF aerials running from the fuselage to the tips of each tailplane, in spite of the extra power the Mark II had a performance only marginally better than that of N 3171 described earlier, and somewhat worse than the lightly equipped early production Mark Is.

# Appendix B

## SPITFIRE IIA    P 8036

Figures taken from the trials report of this aircraft, fitted with a fixed 40 gallon fuel tank under the port wing, tested at Boscombe Down in September 1941. Figures are given where they are relevant and appeared in the report; where figures are omitted they do not necessarily coincide with those for P 7280.

**Weights:** Tare weight 4,836 pounds
    Fully loaded weight 6,513 pounds
    Wing loading when fully loaded, 26.9 pounds per square foot
**Fuel tankage:** 124 gallons
**Performance:**

| Height feet | Top Speed mph | Time to Climb mins | Rate of Climb ft/min |
|---|---|---|---|
| 2,000 | | 0 m 54 s | 2,240 |
| 5,000 | | 2 m 12 s | 2,240 |
| 10,000 | | 4 m 30 s | 2,240 |
| 15,000 | 321 | 6 m 48 s | 1,990 |
| 16,500 | 328 | | |
| 20,000 | 320 | 9 m 48 s | 1,420 |
| 25,000 | | 14 m 6 s | 1,050 |
| 30,000 | | 20 m 18 s | 545 |

| | |
|---|---|
| Service ceiling (estimated) | 33,900 ft |

The report on this aircraft stated that it handled far better than the similarly fitted Mark I tested earlier with fabric covered ailerons. In the concluding remarks it stated:

On the take-off the control column must be held well over to the right side to keep the aeroplane level, but as the aeroplane accelerates it can be moved nearer the central position . . . . Whilst extra weight on the port wing can be felt, it does not seriously affect the flying qualities of the aeroplane and this particular aeroplane is considered to be pleasant to fly. The metal ailerons have brought about a marked improvement in the lateral control since the report on the Mark I Spitfire with under-wing tank was issued. This aeroplane is considered satisfactory as a fighter.

# 8.

# PHOENIX
# FROM THE ASHES

On 26 September 1940 the Luftwaffe got in its long-expected blow against Spitfire production. On that day, after several unsuccessful attempts to hit the plants both in Southampton and Castle Bromwich, a force of fifty-nine Heinkel 111s of Kampfgeschwader 55 carried out a devastatingly accurate attack on the main Supermarine factory at Woolston and the recently completed plant at Itchen. Both works were wrecked, and it was indeed fortunate that by then the Castle Bromwich plant was in full production and production of many components had been farmed out to other firms.

Yet although the factory buildings themselves had suffered severe damage, most of the all-important machine tools and production jigs inside had survived. Moreover, the final assembly hangars at Eastleigh were untouched. Almost immediately after the attack Lord Beaverbrook visited the scene and ordered the two factories to be abandoned and dispersal of the entire production operation from there into the surrounding area. Never again was the Luftwaffe to be offered so inviting a target.

Beaverbrook's Ministry requisitioned a floor of the Polygon Hotel in Southampton and installed the Supermarine works manager, Commander James Bird, and his staff to begin work on planning the dispersal of production. Much of the credit for the rapid dispersal of Spitfire production which now followed must go to the energetic Len Gooch, who later commented:

My first action was to obtain large scale Ordnance Survey maps of the counties of Wiltshire, Hampshire and Berkshire, and from calculations made of existing areas of factories already in use and scaled up to meet the increased output, we prepared a plan whereby 25 per cent of the output was selected to be made in towns with aerodromes, namely the Southampton area using Eastleigh Airport, Salisbury using High Post and Chattis Hill aerodromes, Trowbridge using Keevil aerodrome and Reading using initially Henley followed later by Aldermaston aerodromes. In each of these towns we planned to put in wing and fuselage jigs which then completely assembled these major assemblies ready for marrying together at the aerodromes, so we were now planning for four production lines not one.

The detail and sub-assembly manufacture was again sub-divided and transferred to a large number of requisitioned

**117.** The Supermarine factory at Woolston, pictured before the war. A Walrus amphibian can be seen on the slipway. *(Payn)*

117

**118.** The mass production of Spitfire wings at Woolston. *(via Scrope)*

**119.** The gutted and abandoned Woolston plant, after the German attack in September 1940. *(via Scrope)*

**120.** Spitfire fuselages at Itchen, a new plant which began production in 1939. In the background can be seen new Walrus amphibians, and Stranraer flying boats undergoing overhaul. *(Vickers)*

**121.** The same assembly hall at Itchen, abandoned after the attack in September 1940. *(via Scrope)*

premises in Southampton, Winchester, Newbury, Reading and Trowbridge, including large garages, laundries, bus stations and a steam roller works.

In each place in which Gooch and his staff had located what appeared to be suitable premises, he visited the site with a member of the police who presented a letter of introduction from the Chief Constable without mentioning either Gooch by name or the reason for the visit. If the premises were required Gooch reported this to the local Government Requisition Officer, who then served requisition papers on the not-always-delighted owner.

As soon as the sites had been taken over, jigs and machine tools were brought in from the shattered factories at Southampton. During the six weeks that followed the attack a total of thirty-five separate premises were taken over for Spitfire production; by the end of that period sixteen were already in production and the remainder were about to begin. The main production sites are listed in Appendix A.

The attacks on Woolston and Itchen did have an effect on Spitfire production, though it is not easy to assess exactly by how much. Certainly output from Supermarine sagged dramatically: from 126 aircraft delivered in August 1940, there were 100 in September, 61 in October, 73 in November and only 42 in December; during January 1941 there were 67 and a steady rise reaching 97 in April and back to 130 in August. During the period of the dispersal, however, a very large number of parts and components, particularly from sub-contractors, were diverted to Castle Bromwich and used to swell production there. So rather than solely that from Supermarine, it is more appropriate to consider overall Spitfire production during the final months of 1940: 163 in August, 156 in September, 149 in October, 139 in November and 117 in December. This would suggest that as a result of the bombing and the dispersal about 90 Spitfires were lost to the end of the year, or about three weeks' production from Supermarine prior to the attack. But the Supermarine phoenix that arose from the ashes of Woolston and Itchen was a far less vulnerable bird than that which had existed before.

**122** and **123.** The camouflaged drawing office re-located at Hursley Park near Southampton, inside and out. *(via Scrope)*

122

123

**124** and **125** The experimental aircraft assembly hangar at Hursley Park, inside and out. *(via Scrope)*

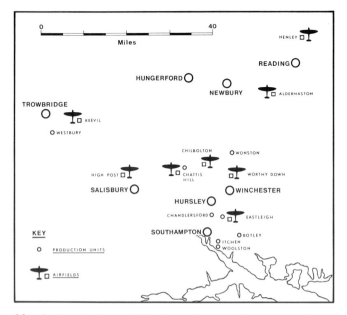

Map showing the dispersal of Spitfire production by Supermarine, following the destruction of the factories at Woolston and Itchen.

Garages requisitioned for Spitfire production: **126** and **127**) Seward's Garage, Southampton, building fuselages and production jigs. (**128** and **129**) Vincent's Garage, Reading, building fuselages. (**130** and **131**) Anna Valley Motors, Salisbury, building wing leading edges and other components. *(via Scrope)*

126

127

128

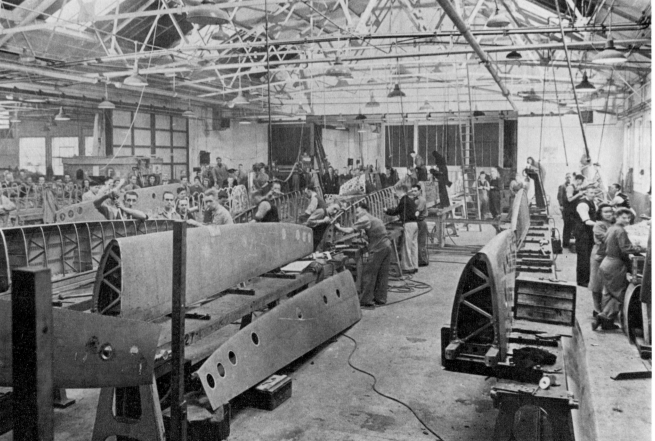

# Appendix A

## DISPERSAL PRODUCTION, MAIN SITES

**Southampton Area**

| | |
|---|---|
| Eastleigh Airport | final erection and test flying |
| Hants & Dorset Garage | wing assembly |
| Hendy's Garage | fuselage assembly |
| Hursley Park House | administration |
| Hursley Park | experimental production workshops |
| Seward's Garage | jigs, tools and templates |
| Sunlight Laundry | detail fitting and assembly |
| Lother's Garage | toolroom |
| Weston Rolling Mills | coppersmiths |
| Newtown Works | woodwork and metal assemblies |
| Short's Garage | machine shop |
| Chisnell's Garage | press shop and sheet metal parts |

**Trowbridge Area**

| | |
|---|---|
| Keevil Aerodrome | final erection and test flying |
| Bradley Road Works | fuselage manufacture, wing assembly |
| Southwick Works | wing leading edge manufacture |

| | |
|---|---|
| Rutland Garage | coppersmiths |
| Hilperton Works | detail fitting and assembly |

**Salisbury Area**

| | |
|---|---|
| High Post Aerodrome | experimental flying |
| Chattis Hill Aerodrome | final erection and test flying |
| Wilts & Dorset Garage | wing assembly |
| Wessex Motors | fuselage manufacture |
| Anna Valley Motors | production of sub-assemblies |
| Castle Road Works | wing and fuselage assembly |

**Reading Area**

| | |
|---|---|
| Henley Aerodrome | final erection and test flying |
| Great Western Garage | wing assembly |
| Vincent's Garage | fuselage manufacture |
| Caversham Works | fuselage assembly |

**Newbury Area**

| | |
|---|---|
| Shaw Works | machine shop and press shop |
| Hungerford Garage | machine shop |
| Mill Lane Works | detail fitting and assembly |
| Pass's Garage | process department |

**132.** Spitfires awaiting flight testing at Chattis Hill aerodrome near Winchester. *(via Scrope)*

**133** and **134.** Final assembly and flight preparation of Spitfire PR IVs at
Henley aerodrome. *(via Scrope)*

# 9.

# THE MARK III—SQUEEZED OUT OF PRODUCTION

The Mark III was the first major attempt to improve the design of the Spitfire since the aircraft went into production in 1938. The new version had a retractable tail wheel, a strengthened main undercarriage with the wheels raked forwards by 2 inches to increase ground stability, and re-introduced the flaps to cover the wheels fully when the undercarriage was retracted. It was powered by the Merlin XX engine which developed 1,390 horsepower for take off and was fitted with a two-speed supercharger to provide improved performance at all altitudes. The wing span was shortened to 30 ft 6 in and the wing area reduced to 220 square feet; the length was increased to 30 ft 4 in. The aircraft carried slightly more armour than the Mark II and had the laminated glass 'bullet-proof' panel built inside the windscreen rather than fixed on the outside.

Only one true Mark III was built, N 3297, and Jeffrey Quill flew it for the first time on 16 March 1940. The intention was that this version would replace the earlier marks in production, but almost from the start circumstances mitigated against the Spitfire III. In August 1940 the Secretary of State for Air, Sir Archibald Sinclair, informed Lord Beaverbrook that only limited numbers of Merlin XXs were available and until production improved the Hurricane II was to take priority because it had to have the more powerful engine if it was to remain effective as a first-line fighter.

Rolls-Royce made strenuous efforts to increase production of the Merlin XX and by the early autumn it seemed there would be sufficient to allow the Spitfire III to go into production. As a result, in October 1940 Supermarine received an order to build 1,000 examples of this version. Almost immediately, however, this was overtaken by the development of the Merlin 45 which was in effect a Merlin XX without the low altitude blower and which could be placed in production without detriment to that of the latter engine. In December 1940 the decision was taken to push ahead with installing a Merlin 45 in a Spitfire; the combination was to result in the Spitfire V, described in the next chapter.

During February 1941 the Mark V was tested successfully at Boscombe Down. On 6 March, at a meeting of the Joint Development and Production Committee the Chief of the Air Staff, Air Chief Marshal Sir Charles Portal, sounded the death knell of the Mark III. The minutes recorded:

CAS has decided that the Spitfire V with Merlin 45 engines with single speed blowers shall be put into production instead of Spitfire IIIs. The Spitfire V with improved Merlin 45 (a slightly larger blower impeller) will give better performance at altitude and ceiling. This will meet the needs of Fighter Command for high altitude fighters. Its ceiling will be higher

than a pilot can stand without a pressure cabin, but its improved rate of climb and manoeuvrability at high altitudes is a distinct operational advantage. If the type is a success the Air Staff will want as many as can be produced.

The next stage will be a Spitfire with the even more improved Merlin 45 (single speed supercharger) and a pressure cabin.

The succeeding stage is a Spitfire with the Merlin RM6SM with the 2 stage supercharger. As the engine is several inches longer the Spitfire III airframe will require modification. There will be a pressure cabin.

As well as establishing that the Spitfire V was to go into production as the successor to the Marks I and II, the minutes give a useful pointer on how development of the fighter was expected to go during the rest of 1941 and the first half of 1942. The 'next stage' Spitfire after the stop-gap Mark V was to have an 'even more improved Merlin 45 . . . and a pressure cabin'; this would become the Spitfire VI, powered by the Merlin 47 engine. The 'Merlin RM6SM with 2 stage supercharger' was to become the Merlin 60 series engine; the Spitfire with this engine and a pressure cabin was to become the Mark VII, which was expected to succeed the Mark VI in large scale production. These new versions of the Spitfire would be the first to allow RAF pilots to fight at altitudes much above 30,000 feet, of which there was almost no previous experience. Looking back, it is now clear that the requirement for pressurised cabins for the high altitude fighters was overstated. Once the Spitfire V entered service pilots would operate it to the very limits of its altitude capability, accepting where necessary the discomfort resulting from the lack of a pressure cabin.

But all of that was in the future, and we must return to the career of N 3297. Now the Spitfire III was no longer being considered for production, the prototype was to be used as a development machine. It was fitted with normal-span wings and early in April it was delivered to Rolls-Royce at Hucknall for the installation of the new RM6SM engine.

When N 3297 next flew, in September 1941, she was a rather different animal. The Merlin 61, as the fighter version of the Merlin 60 was now known, had a two-stage supercharger with an intercooler to cool the charge before it entered the second stage of supercharging. The intercooler required its own radiator so N 3297 was given two oblong section radiators of similar external shape, one under each wing. The port one contained the re-shaped oil cooler and half of the main coolant radiator, the starboard one contained the intercooler radiator and the other half of the main coolant radiator. To absorb the extra power the aircraft was fitted with a large four-bladed

Rotol propeller, and the engine was fitted with the new multi-ejector exhausts. All of these features would become commonplace on later marks of Spitfires, but when N 3297 emerged after modification she looked markedly different from her predecessors.

From the start the new Merlin 61 engined Spitfire showed great promise, but initially there were intercooler problems and in November 1941 the engine had to be changed. Fitted with a new Merlin 61, N 3297 went to Boscombe Down in January 1942 where she demonstrated a considerable improvement in performance over previous versions of the Spitfire: maximum level speed 391 mph at 15,900 feet, 414 mph at 27,200 feet and 354 mph at 40,000 feet; there were similar improvements in the rate of climb and the service ceiling was estimated at 41,800 feet. Performance and other details of this aircraft are given in Appendix A.

This sparkling speed and altitude performance is all the more remarkable when one considers that at the time of these trials N 3297 was beginning to show her age. The official report on the trials stated:

> The airframe was in very poor condition and deteriorated appreciably during the progress of the tests. In several places the paint had flaked away from the skin; this was particularly noticeable in the case of the ailerons, where large patches had broken off leaving an unevenness in the surface of about 1/16'' or more. The panels of the engine cowling too were badly fitting, there being gaps of 1/8'' to 1/4'' in some of the joints. In addition there are two 'bumps' on top of the engine cowling which house the corners of the intercooler. These became badly dented and were straightened out as much as possible near the end of the tests.

In spite of the poor state of her airframe, which was to get even worse, N 3297 continued in use in the Merlin 61 test programme until September 1942. Although her breed never went into production, the improvements tested on her were to keep the Spitfire abreast of world fighter development during the mid-war years.

**135** and **136.** N 3297, the sole Spitfire III to be built as such, pictured at about the time of her maiden flight in March 1940. This aircraft featured clipped wings, a retractable tail wheel, a redesigned windscreen, flaps on the bottom of the undercarriage fairings plus other smaller changes, and was powered by a Merlin XX engine. Although this version did not go into production, many of its features were incorporated in later marks of Spitfire. *(MOD)*

**137.** N 3297 pictured at Boscombe Down during the winter of 1941-1942, fitted with the Merlin 61 engine and normal span wings.

137

# Appendix A

## SPITFIRE III N 3297, WITH MERLIN 61 ENGINE

Figures taken from the trials report of this aircraft, fitted with its second Merlin 61 and tested at Boscombe Down between January and April 1942. By the time of these tests the aircraft was a unique hybrid, with a Mark III fuselage with retractable tailwheel, Mark IA wings and a Merlin 61 engine. The armament had been removed and the guns ports sealed over, but ballast had been fitted to represent eight machine guns and their ammunition. The aircraft carried the normal VHF radio but no IFF equipment. As mentioned previously, the airframe of N 3297 was in a poor state by the time of these tests.

**Weight:** Fully loaded weight 7,225 pounds
   Wing loading when fully loaded, 29.8 pounds per square foot
**Power plant:** Rolls-Royce Merlin 61 with two stage, two speed supercharger
   1,390 BHP at 3,000 rpm at 15,500 ft at +12 pounds boost
   1,190 BHP at 3,000 rpm at 27,000 ft at +12 pounds boost
**Propeller:** Rotol hydraulically operated four-bladed constant speed, duralamin blades 10 ft 9 in diameter

**Performance:**

| Height feet | Top Speed mph | Time to Climb mins | Rate of Climb ft/min |
|---|---|---|---|
| 4,000 | 345 | 1 m 18 s | 2,900 |
| 8,000 | 360½ | 2 m 45 s | 2,620 |
| 12,000 | 376 | 4 m 23 s | 2,330 |
| 16,000 | 391 | 6 m 12 s | 2,040 |
| 22,000 | 393 | 9 m 39 s | 1,480 |
| 26,000 | 409 | 12 m 37 s | 1,200 |
| 27,200 | 414 | | |
| 30,000 | 411 | 16 m 39 s | 820 |
| 36,000 | 388 | 25 m 43 s | 730 |
| 40,000 | 354 | 33 m 57 s | 300 |

Service ceiling (estimated)      41,800 feet

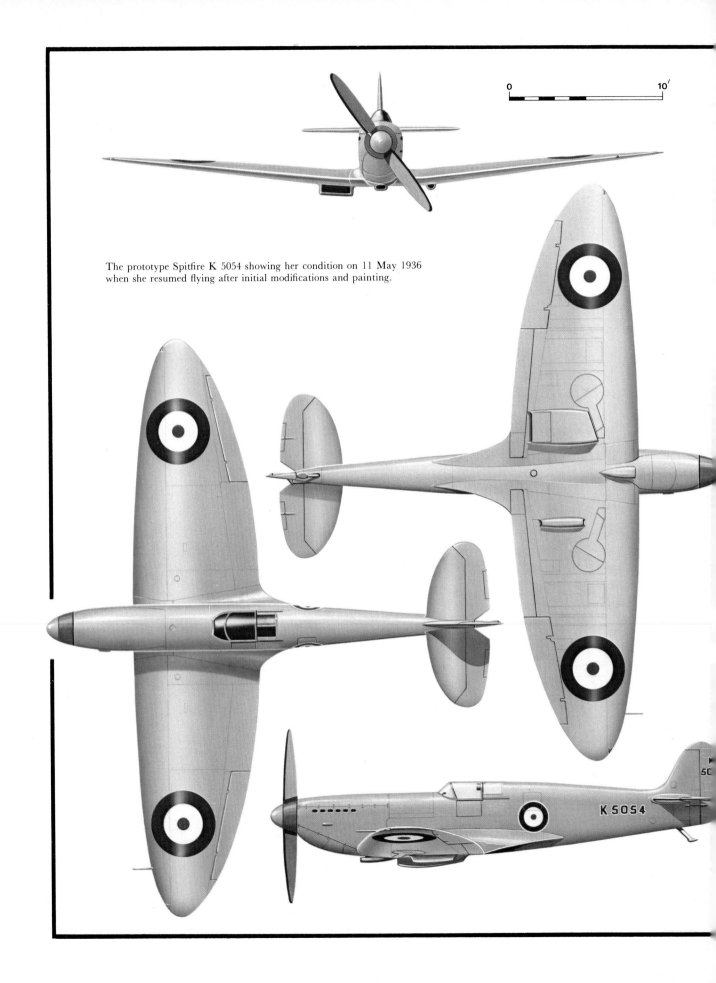

The prototype Spitfire K 5054 showing her condition on 11 May 1936 when she resumed flying after initial modifications and painting.

0         10′

K 5054

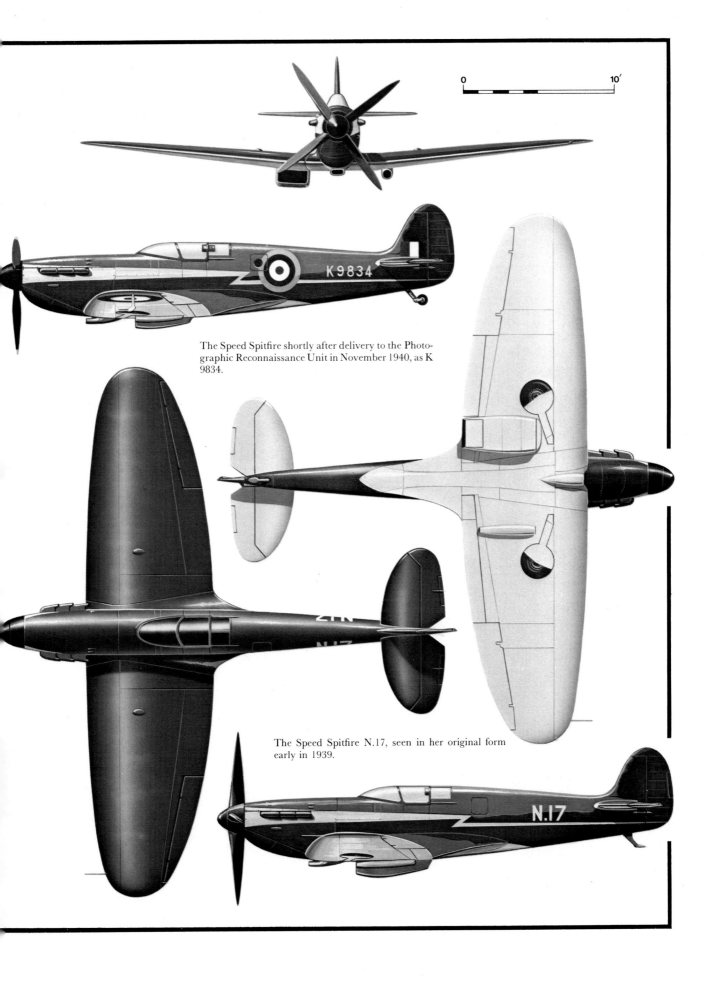

The Speed Spitfire shortly after delivery to the Photographic Reconnaissance Unit in November 1940, as K
9834.

The Speed Spitfire N.17, seen in her original form
early in 1939.

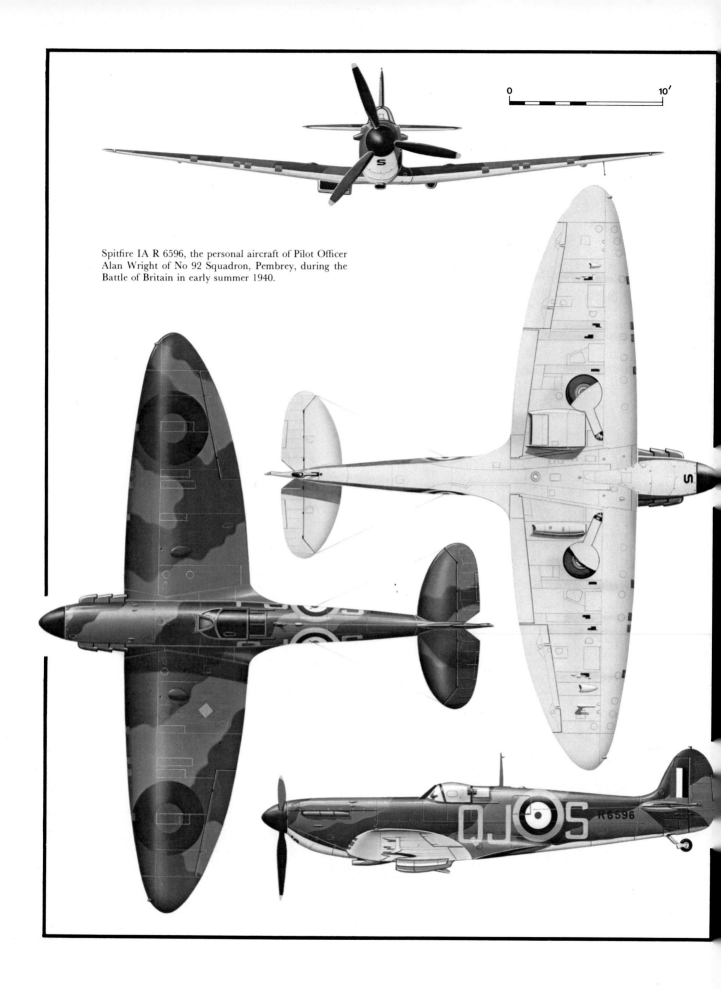

Spitfire IA R 6596, the personal aircraft of Pilot Officer
Alan Wright of No 92 Squadron, Pembrey, during the
Battle of Britain in early summer 1940.

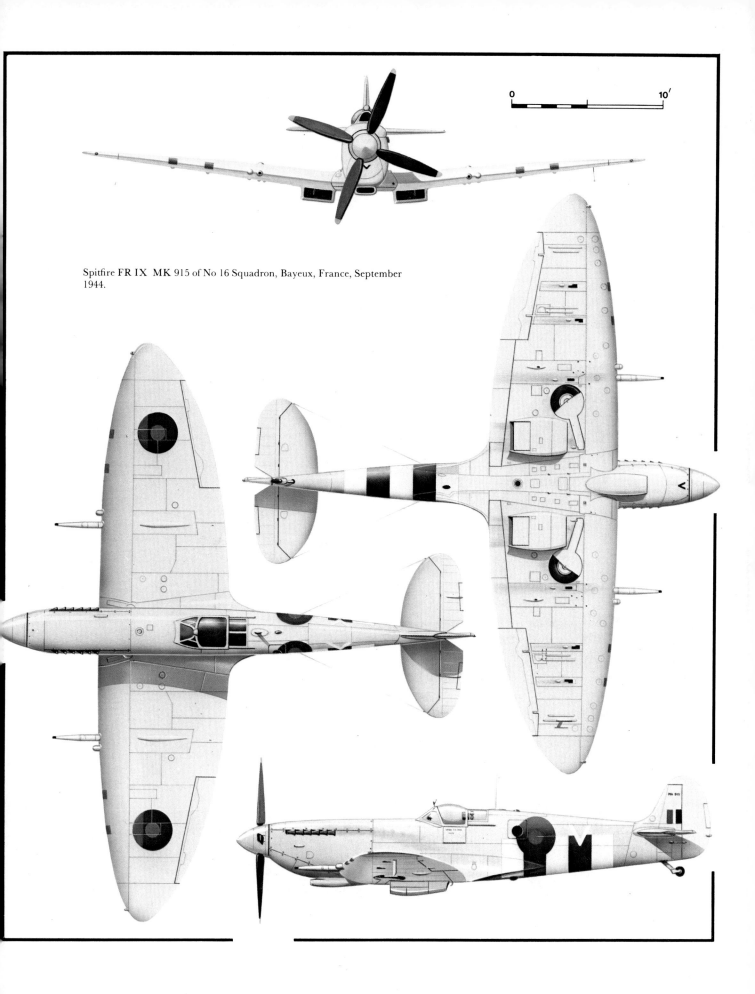

Spitfire FR IX MK 915 of No 16 Squadron, Bayeux, France, September 1944.

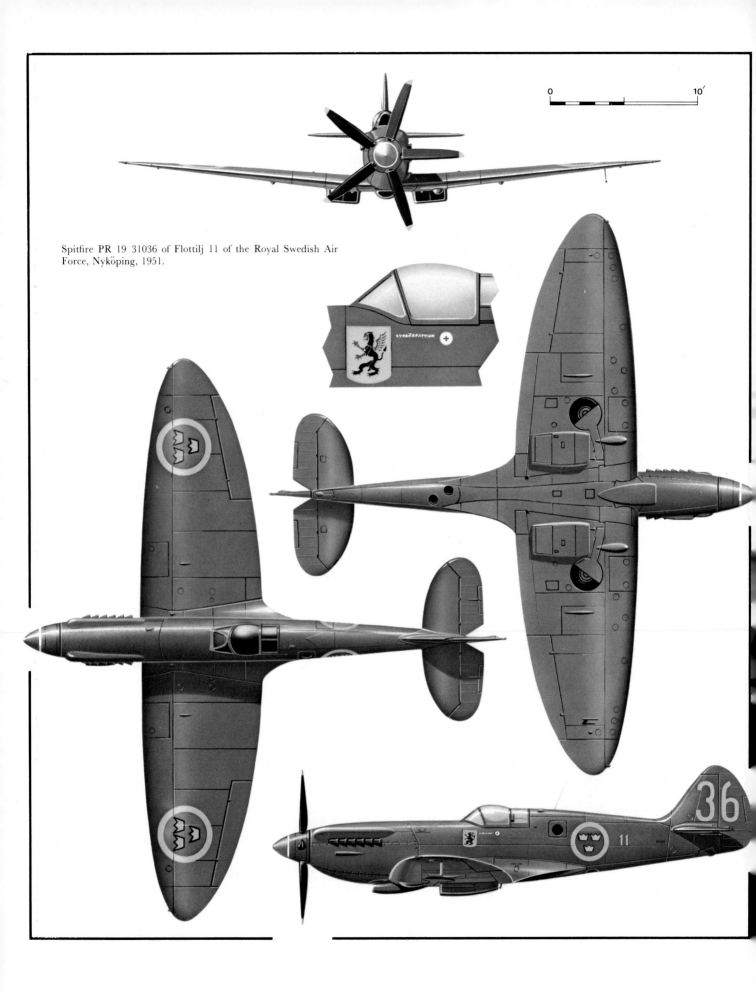

Spitfire PR 19 31036 of Flottilj 11 of the Royal Swedish Air Force, Nyköping, 1951.

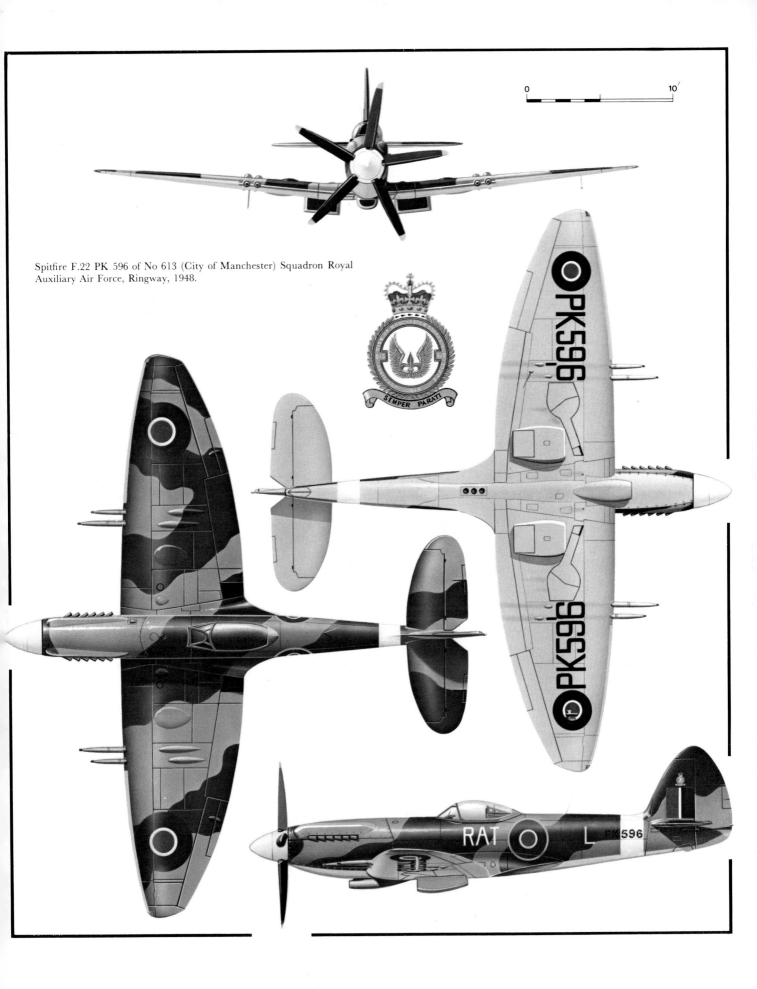

Spitfire F.22 PK 596 of No 613 (City of Manchester) Squadron Royal
Auxiliary Air Force, Ringway, 1948.

# 10.

# VARIANT MUCH VARIED: THE MARK V

At the end of 1940 Fighter Command's main worry was that it would have to re-fight the Battle of Britain again in the spring and summer of 1941, possibly against German fighters and bombers with improved performance at high altitude; already the diesel engined Junkers 86P reconnaissance aircraft had demonstrated that it could operate with impunity over Britain at altitudes above 38,000 feet. Early in 1941 the Air Staff decided to put the Spitfire V in production in small numbers in place of the Mark III (the Mark IV was a purely experimental version which will be described later). Initially the Mark V was seen only as a stop-gap, to provide a fighter with an improved high altitude performance pending production of the eagerly awaited Mark VI, a specially designed high altitude version with a pressurised cabin.

The Mark V was simply a Mark I or II airframe with the engine mounting strengthened to take the heavier and more powerful Merlin 45. Apart from the slightly blunter nose shape, which is not easy to discern, the main recognition feature of the Mark V compared with the Marks I and II was that the former had a larger diameter oil cooler with a circular, instead of a semi-circular, intake.

The initial Mark Vs were converted from Mark Is and IIs. Jeffrey Quill flew one of these, X 4922, for the first time on 20 February 1941. Also during that month another modified Mark I, K 9788 the second production Spitfire, was tested with the Merlin 45 at Boscombe Down; an account of this aircraft's performance is given in Appendix A.

When it first went into production the Mark V was built in two versions: the VA, with an eight machine gun armament like that of the IA and IIA; and the VB with two cannon and four machine guns as in the case of the IB and IIB. But after 94 examples of the Mark VA had been built at the Supermarine factories production of this version ceased in favour of the Mark VB. The Supermarine, Castle Bromwich and Westland facilities all went into mass production of the Mark VB version of the Spitfire during 1941. The performance of W 3134, an early Mark VB built by Supermarine, is given in Appendix B.

The first squadron to receive the Spitfire V was No 92 at Biggin Hill, in February 1941. Others followed in rapid succession: No 91 in March, Nos 54 and 603 in April, Nos 74, 111, 609 and 611 in May. By the end of 1941 almost every day fighter squadron in Fighter Command had re-equipped with this version of the Spitfire.

The introduction of the Mark V into service coincided with the transition of Fighter Command from the defensive to the offensive, and this variant was used increasingly over France and Belgium during the fighter sweeps and bomber escort missions. With this change the operational radius of action of the

Spitfire was found to be inadequate, so work began on producing jettisonable 30- and 45-gallon 'slipper' tanks to fit under the fuselage.

In October 1941 the Mark VC appeared, which bore an external resemblance to the VB but whose wing was internally much stronger and incorporated many features of the Mark III. The Mark VC was fitted with the so-called 'universal' wing, which could house an armament of eight machine guns, or two cannon and four machine guns, or four cannon. When cannon were fitted, the re-designed magazine and feed system allowed 120 rounds per gun to be fitted compared with only 60 per gun in the case of the Mark VB. A further change with the Mark VC was that the undercarriage wheels were raked forwards 2 inches to improve ground stability, as in the case of the Mark III.

Following the German invasion of Russia in June 1941 the feared renewal of the daylight bombardment of Britain, possibly high altitude, did not materialise. As a result the pressurised Mark VI variant of the Spitfire did not go into large scale production. The Mark V, which had been built as a stop-gap measure pending the Mark VI, was better able to cope with Fighter Command's requirements as they now emerged and it continued as the main production version.

As has been said, by the end of 1941 the Spitfire V equipped almost every day fighter squadron in Fighter Command. But none of these fighters had yet been deployed to the Mediterranean theatre, where the hardest-fought battles involving British forces were taking place. Before the Spitfire could operate for any length of time in the dusty conditions of Egypt, Libya or Malta, however, it had to be fitted with an effective carburettor air intake filter system; otherwise dust ingested into the cylinders would greatly increase the rate of engine wear. The initial solution was to install the filters in a large beard-like fairing under the engine cowling. The additional drag caused by this fairing, and the reduction in ram air pressure to the carburettor, combined to cause a reduction in the maximum speed by about 8 mph and reduced the rate of climb by about 550 feet per minute lower down; the performance of X 4922, one of the first Mark Vs to be fitted with the tropical modifications, is given in Appendix C.

At the close of 1941 a larger, 90 gallon 'slipper' tank was developed for the Spitfire to extend its range still further. This was used operationally for the first time on 7 March 1942 during Operation Spotter: the delivery of 15 tropicalised Spitfire VBs to Malta, off the deck of the aircraft carrier HMS *Eagle* from a position off the coast of Algeria. For this, the first overseas deployment of a Spitfire fighter squadron, the aircraft had to fly a distance of 660 miles—about as far as from London to Prague. *Eagle* returned to Gibraltar to pick up more Spitfires,

**138.** One of the early Spitfire VBs, R 6923 was a converted Mark IB which was issued to No 92 Squadron early in 1941. The main recognition feature of the Mark V, compared with the Marks I and II, was the circular section oil cooler under the starboard wing. *(Charles Brown, copyright RAF Museum)*

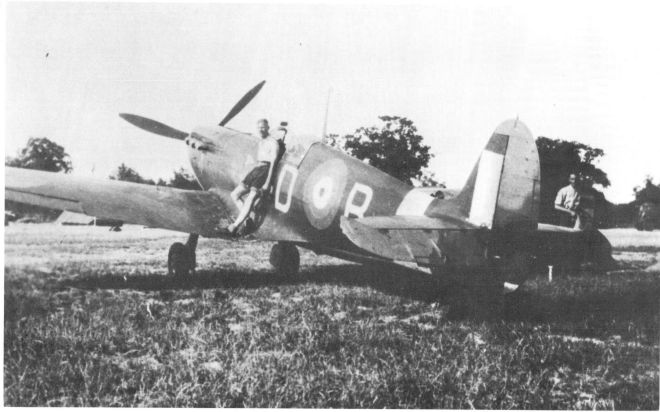

**139.** D-B, the personal aircraft of Wing Commander Douglas Bader who commanded the Tangmere Fighter Wing during the spring and summer of 1941. The absence of cannon barrels and magazine bulges identifies this aircraft as one of the few Mark VAs built; Bader preferred to engage from short range using machine guns, and for a long time resisted having to fly a cannon-fitted aircraft. *(via Goulding)*

**140.** Spitfire VBs undergoing final assembly at Castle Bromwich early in 1942. *(Vickers)*

and carried out two more delivery operations before the end of the month which put an additional 16 Spitfires into Malta. But the delivery of Spitfires to the beleagured island in such small numbers had little effect on the powerful bombardment being launched by the Luftwaffe: there simply were not enough British fighters to provide a proper defence. So, following representations to President Roosevelt by Mr Churchill, the large American carrier USS *Wasp* was made available for the delivery operations. During the first of these, Operation Calendar on 20 April, 47 Spitfire VCs were flown off. During the next, Operation Bowery on 9 May, *Wasp* and *Eagle* combined to fly off 64 Spitfires for Malta. The arrival of these powerful reinforcements to the island turned the tide of battle and, with later smaller deliveries, achieved a degree of air superiority over Malta which would never again be seriously challenged.

Throughout the war years there was a constant stream of improvements to the Spitfire to increase its operational effectiveness. By the close of 1941 the end was in sight for one of the long-standing faults of the Spitfire: the cutting out of the engine if the pilot made any manoeuvre which imposed negative-G on the aircraft. After trying several schemes to overcome the problem, Rolls-Royce came up with a clever new type of carburettor which used a diaphragm mechanism to meter the fuel flow. An example of the new negative-G carburettor was fitted to Spitfire VB W 3228 and received enthusiastic acclaim during the flight trials at Boscombe Down in December 1941. The report on the trial concluded:

The diaphragm operated carburettor transforms the Spitfire V into a much better fighting machine, as any manoeuvres used in air combat involving the application of negative acceleration forces to the carburettor can be made without loss of power. This feature is also most noticeable when performing aerobatics and the aeroplane can be flown around in manoeuvres which would be impossible with the normal float controlled carburettor.

High or sustained values of negative G result in a loss of engine oil pressure which may result in engine failure if such flight is unduly prolonged, e.g. inverted flying. While this feature is not considered serious from a normal operational viewpoint, it should be brought to the notice of pilots to obviate the possibility of an outbreak of engine failures during stunt flying with the diaphragm operated carburettor.

During April and May 1942 the American aircraft carrier USS *Wasp* despatched 111 Spitfire VCs to Malta, flying them off from a position north of Algiers, during two reinforcement operations. (**141** and **142**). The Spitfires, armed with four 20 mm cannon, fitted with tropical filters and 90-gallon slipper tanks, painted in 'sand and spinach' camouflage and with their wing tips removed and placed in the cockpits, are seen being hoisted on board *Wasp* as she lay alongside the dock at Glasgow. (**143**). A Spitfire begins its take-off from *Wasp*, during the second reinforcement operation on 9 May. In the course of this operation the aircraft flown by Pilot Officer Smith, a Canadian, suffered a failure of the slipper tank fuel feed; Smith waited for the remainder of the Spitfires to get airborne then landed back on *Wasp*, the first man to put an un-hooked Spitfire down on a carrier. (**144**). Smith pictured back on *Wasp*, his hand touching the US Navy pilots' wings awarded to him to commemorate his feat. *(USN)*

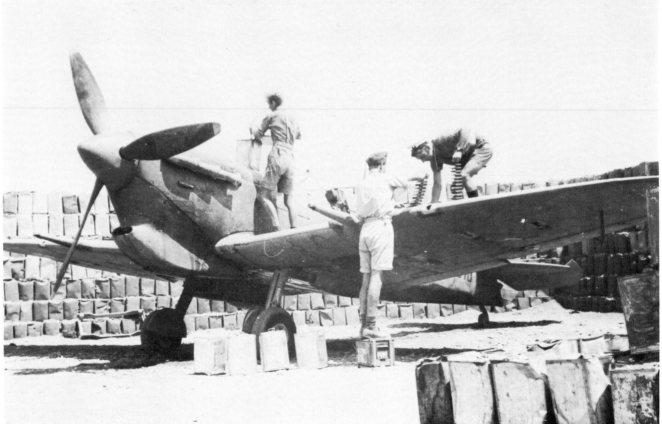

The diaphragm-type carburettor was fitted in the Merlin 50 series of engines, which powered later production versions of the Spitfire V.

While the Spitfire was being improved in various ways, the Germans were also introducing improved fighters. During the early months of 1942 it gradually became clear that the Spitfire V was in many respects outclassed by the Focke-Wulf 190 fighter which had just entered service in the Luftwaffe. In June 1942 an example of the FW 190 landed in Britain in error, thus presenting the RAF with the chance to conduct comparative trials between it and various Allied fighter types. The report of the comparative trial of the FW 190 and the Spitfire V is given in Appendix D and reveals the degree of superiority of the former: the FW 190 could out-run, out-climb, out-dive and out-roll the Spitfire V. Fortunately for RAF Fighter Command, however, the Luftwaffe remained largely on the defensive in the west throughout 1942 and failed to exploit the superiority of its new fighter.

The real answer to the FW 190 would be the Spitfire with the two-stage-supercharged Merlin 61 engine, which was then being hastened into production; this will be described in a later chapter. But there were things that could be done to improve

**145.** A soldier, a sailor and an airman working to refuel and rearm a Spitfire VC of No 603 Squadron at Takali in April 1942. Because of the shortage of 20 mm ammunition on the island, the Spitfire VCs delivered with four cannon had two removed and machine guns fitted instead. The aircraft in this picture has had the two inner cannon removed and the holes covered with wooden bungs, and carries only two machine guns. The improvised blast pen has been constructed from empty petrol tins filled with sand. *(Westmacott)*

**146.** The Focke-Wulf 190 fighter, which entered service in the Luftwaffe in mid-1941, rapidly asserted its superiority over the Spitfire V. The aircraft in this photograph inadvertently landed at Pembrey in South Wales and was captured intact in June 1942. It was later test flown against various marks of Spitfire.

the ability of the Spitfire V against the FW 190 particularly at low altitudes. One such move was to 'clip' the wings of the Spitfire by removing the detachable tips, thereby reducing the span to 32 ft 6 in and the wing area by 11 square feet to 231 square feet. This change reduced the aircraft's inertia moment in the rolling plane and made a noticeable improvement to rolling performance; it also gave a slight improvement to acceleration, diving performance and speed below 10,000 feet. Part of the report of the Air Fighting Development Unit trial, which compared a clipped-winged Spitfire V with a standard aircraft, is given in Appendix E.

A further improvement in low altitude performance could be gained by fitting the Merlin 50M engine; this was similar to the Mark 45 but, as well as the negative-G carburettor, it had a smaller diameter 'cropped' supercharger impeller which allowed a maximum of +18 pounds boost to be applied at only 5,900 feet and gave a maximum speed of 350 mph at this altitude, about the same as that of the FW 190. The performance of the Spitfire V with this engine is given in Appendix F. The combination of clipped wings and the low altitude rated engines resulted in the Spitfire LF V which became known as the 'clipped and cropped' Spitfire. Less reverently, it was known in some squadrons as the 'clipped, cropped and clapped Spitty' because the airframes to which these modifications were applied had in many cases seen better days.

Also during 1942, bombs were reinstated under the wings of the Spitfire, for the first time since their removal from specification F.37/34 seven years erlier. In August of that year No 126 Squadron based on Malta began operating over Sicily with its Spitfire VCs modified to carry a 250 pound bomb under each wing. From then on the Mark VC and succeeding variants of the Spitfire saw increasing use in the fighter-bomber role.

Initially all Spitfires delivered to Malta were flown off the decks of aircraft carriers and this method, though it worked well

**147.** A clip-winged Spitfire VB of No 401 (Canadian) Squadron pictured at Redhill in July 1943. The inscription above the badge on the fuselage reads 'Corps of Imperial Frontiersmen'. *(Public Archives of Canada)*

**148.** With a giant 170 gallon tank under the fuselage, 29 gallons of extra fuel in the rear fuselage tank and a deepened nose section to accommodate an enlarged oil tank, this Spitfire VB is seen running up on the ground at North Front, Gibraltar. The aircraft is about to take-off for the 1,100 mile hop to Malta, a distance equivalent to that from London to Leningrad. Altogether 17 Spitfires set out for the island from Gibraltar during the final three months of 1942, and all but one arrived there. By the end of the year the siege of Malta had been lifted, and fighters could be delivered by more conventional means. *(RAF Museum)*

enough, had the disadvantage that it meant diverting these scarce and valuable ships from their normal tasks. To overcome this a modification kit was developed to enable the Spitfire VC to fly from Gibraltar to Malta in one hop—a distance of just over 1,100 miles or roughly equivalent to that from London to Leningrad. The modifications involved fitting a 29 gallon fuel tank in the rear fuselage behind the pilot's seat, an enlarged oil tank in the nose below the engine, and a 170 gallon jettisonable fuel tank underneath the fuselage. During these delivery flights, which began in October 1942, the Spitfires carried a token armament of two .303-in machine guns. On arrival in Malta the extra fuel and oil tanks were removed and the tropical filters and the rest of the armament fitted. An account based on the Boscombe Down report on the long range flying trials of the Spitfire VC with the full 284 gallon fuel tankage is given in Appendix G.

As well as being fitted with three different types of wing, the Type A, B and C, with or without clipping, in its time the Spitfire V was powered by nine different versions of the Merlin engine: the Mark 45, 45M, 46, 50, 50A, 50M, 55, 55M and the 56. The M series engines had cropped supercharger blowers for optimum performance at low altitude; the Mark 46 was a higher altitude version of the Mark 45; the 50 series and subsequent engines were fitted with diaphragm-type negative-G carburettors; the Mark 50A and the Mark 56 were high altitude versions similar to the Mark 46; and the Mark 55 and Mark 56 incorporated a two-piece block. Thus performance varied greatly between the different variants of the Spitfire V. And these differences could be further emphasised by the loading of the aircraft, whether or not it was tropicalised and what detailed changes had been made to the exterior of the aircraft. In order to determine the difference that could be made to performance by the last of these, in 1943 Farnborough engineers carried out a series of trials with Spitfire VB EN 946. This aircraft underwent a series of minor modifications to improve performance, and after each the increase in maximum speed at full throttle height was carefully measured. Initially the maximum speed of the aircraft was found to be 357 mph. The fitting of multi-ejector exhausts in place of the previous 'fishtail' type gave a speed increase of 7 mph; the removal of the carburettor ice guard gave 8 mph; the fitting of a different

**149.** A Mark V of No 225 Squadron in Italy in 1943, locally modified to carry an oblique camera for fighter reconnaissance missions.

**150.** Preparing the oblique camera for fitting into an aircraft of No 225 Squadron. Note that this Mark V is fitted with individual ejector exhausts, a feature of late production aircraft.

**151.** A Spitfire V of No 1435 Squadron which operated from Luqa, Malta, from the summer of 1942 until the autumn of 1943. This aircraft was used as a target tug and had been fitted with a towing bracket behind the tail wheel.

**152.** A Spitfire VB belonging to the operational conversion unit at Fayid, Egypt, fitted with the simplified tropical filter developed at the RAF Maintenance Unit at Aboukir and known as the 'Aboukir Filter'.

rear-view mirror with a fairing gave 3 mph; the installation of a whip aerial in place of the early mast type gave ½ mph; cutting the cartridge case and link ejector chutes flush with the wing gave 1 mph; sealing all cracks, rubbing down, painting and polishing the leading edge of the wing gave 6 mph; and polishing the remainder of the aircraft using wax added a further 3 mph. Together, these individually small changes increased the speed of the Spitfire VB from 357 to 385½ mph. Of course, similarly small deteriorations in the airframe could combine to reduce performance by similar amounts: oil leaked on to the outside of the airframe which then picked up dust or sand; dents to or scratches on the aircraft (particularly to the leading edge of the wing); repaired battle damage, etc; these could reduce the maximum speed of an aircraft to well below that of a standard machine.

Altogether some 6,500 Spitfire Vs of all versions were built (the exact number is not clear from the official records) at the Castle Bromwich works, the various dispersed Supermarine factories and the Westland Company. In addition, about 180 Mark Is and IIs were converted into Mark Vs by the installation of Merlin 45 engines.

Spitfire Vs were supplied to several foreign air forces, including those of the USA, Turkey, Portugal, Italy, Yugoslavia, Egypt and the USSR. In the case of the last named, it received 143 Spitfire VBs early in 1943 via the Iranian port of Abadan. The account which follows, published for the first time in the west, provides some idea of how these fighters were received by the Red Air Force and how they were used.

\* \* \*

Until now little information has appeared in the west on how the Soviet Air Force used the Spitfire VBs it received at the beginning of 1943. The account which follows is based on the memoirs of the fighter pilot Senior Lieutenant (later Colonel) Anatoli Ivanov; some of his phrases might ring a little strangely in western ears, but are included to give the flavour of what he wrote. Ivanov's unit, the 36th Fighter Aviation Regiment, had been in action on the Caucasian front with Polikarpov I-16 fighters until near the end of 1942 when it was pulled back to an airfield near Baku on the Caspian Sea to reform and re-equip. In February 1943 the Regiment received its first Spitfires:

We studied the new aircraft carefully, but because there were no manuals we could not find out what it would be like in the air. Neither our instructors nor the technicians had any figures on its performance. We knew that at the time the English had a better fighter, the Spitfire IX, and the word was that it was good. The aircraft our allies had presented to us, however, were of a much older version. Ours had fought against the Germans over the Channel during 1941 and 1942, and these Spitfires had taken some knocks before they were repaired and transferred to us.

**153.** Spitfire VBs pictured at Abadan, Iran, early in 1943 prior to delivery to the Soviet Air Force. Ivanov's comment that the aircraft received by his unit had previously taken some knocks is borne out by examination of the records of some of these aircraft. For example BM 185, nearest the camera, had previously seen action with Nos 403 and 111 Squadrons. The next in line, AD 236, had previously served with Nos 602, 485, 81 and 132 Squadrons, and had undergone repairs following serious damage. *(IWM)*

The comments on the condition of the Spitfire VBs passed to the Soviet Air Force are justified. Most were elderly machines which had previously seen action with the RAF, some had served with several different squadrons and undergone major repairs before their transfer.

Ivanov tried out the British fighter and the remarks he penned were hardly flattering. In reading them, however, it should be borne in mind that they are in keeping with the general trend of reporting in the Soviet open press, that foreign items should never be shown to be significantly better than the home-built product:

> Its speed was not much greater than that of the I-16. Its ceiling was not greater than 9,000 metres [29,500 feet] and it was armed with 2 cannon and 4 machine guns . . . . The Spitfire was simple to fly and tolerant of mistakes, but it wasn't anything special. The I-16 had been much more demanding. Still the Spitfire did have a radio, albeit a poor one.* The Soviet fighters designed by Lavochkin and Yakovlev had a significantly better performance. The sole advantage of the Spitfire was the fact that it was very light and, with its powerful engine, it climbed well; this would give us the advantage of height. Its worst feature was that the guns were mounted in the wings; the distance between the cannon was nearly 4 metres, so when attacking the enemy from close range the concentration of fire power was low.

Ivanov described the Spitfire as 'a kaftan for someone else's shoulders', ie 'someone else's jacket', but acknowledged that the Soviet Air Force was short of fighters and had to make use of anything it could get.

Near Baku the 36th Fighter Aviation Regiment, and a sister unit nearby, received their complement of Spitfires and the task of conversion training proceeded. During February the 36th was honoured with the award of Guards status and re-designated the 57th Guards Fighter Regiment. By the third week in April the unit was ready again for operations, and began moving to the Kuban area on the southern front to join the heavy fighting around the German bridgehead based on the port of Novorossiysk on the Black Sea. Ivanov's Regiment arrived at its base, a forward airfield situated near the village of Popovicheskoy, to find that the air war had changed a great deal since it had left the front. Both sides now regularly put up forces of over a hundred aircraft, and when these clashed large scale battles would ensue with losses on both sides. During these actions the main German fighter opposition came from the Messerschmitt 109s of Jagdgeschwader 52, though from time to time FW 190s were also seen in the area.

Initially the Spitfires were not used properly on the Kuban front, and suffered accordingly. As Ivanov explained:

> Usually we were given a specific area, bounded by three or four points on the ground, over which we were to provide cover for our ground forces. Specific altitudes and times for these patrols were laid down. But because the points defining the patrol areas were close together, we had to decrease speed to remain in the area and so found ourselves at a disadvantage compared with the enemy. If we tried to comb the area at high speed, we risked running short of fuel and could not cover it for the required period. The enemy fighters quickly took the measure of these poorly thought-out tactics and made attacks which cost us dearly. During our first encounter with escorted Fascist bombers, on 28 April, the Spitfires paid not a small price. Patrolling a designated area at low speed and being tied to points on the ground, the force of

Spitfires was unable to manoeuvre freely and co-ordinate the action of its pairs and fours. The enemy fighters, using their altitude advantage, attacked us without hindrance.

Another problem the Soviet Spitfire pilots soon discovered was that their aircraft looked quite unlike Russian-built fighters and were often taken for those of the enemy by ground gunners and the pilots of other units. Several times Spitfires came under attack from 'friendly' forces and some were shot down or damaged, including Ivanov's:

> I was attacking a Fascist Junkers 87 bomber and, having got myself into an advantageous position, would probably have shot him down. But then our Yaks appeared. 'Yaks!' I shouted over the radio, 'Yaks, don't hinder my attack. Give me cover—I'm on your side!' But one of the pilots obviously did not understand, he swung round on to my tail and opened up with everything. My wings were holed and glycol vapour started to trail from the engine cowling. I wanted to bale out but by then I was too low. I reduced speed and somehow managed to level out the Spitfire, I barely made it home.

Following this and other incidents, the Spitfires made demonstration flights over gun sites in the area and paid visits to neighbouring fighter units to familiarise everyone with the lines of the British fighter. Initially the Spitfires carried the Regiment's emblem, a large yellow arrow painted across the fuselage. But it was felt that it confused rather than aided identification and the design was hastily removed.

Ivanov's Regiment quickly established itself at the front and developed effective tactics. The pace of action was severe:

> Over the Kuban large numbers of aircraft took part in the combats. Things started at dawn. As soon as our reporting posts detected that the Fascist air force was up, Soviet fighters took off to engage. Then it would begin.
>
> Fighters of all types gathered in the sky at all altitudes, from ground level to 8 or even 10 thousand metres. The battle was joined. Enemy aircraft burned, ours too. Damaged ones strove to regain their own territory, trailing smoke or glycol vapour. Everywhere, parachutes descended. A multicoloured canopy, that would be a Fascist; a white canopy, a Soviet pilot.
>
> Each day we had to fly five or even seven missions. It demanded considerable effort to maintain this pace of combat and not go under physically. We were tired as Hell, but morally we felt superior. April ended and then the real heat began. That really hit people, they just did not want to eat. Each dusk you went to bed and fell asleep immediately. And at 4 o'clock the next morning we had to be up again for the next mission . . . .

Ivanov had a most successful day on 3 May 1943, during a couple of interception missions near the German bridgehead:

> Chernetsov noticed nine Heinkel 111s and nine Junkers 88s heading for the front, covered by a dozen Messerschmitts or Focke-Wulfs. He attacked one of the Heinkels and immediately a pair of Messerschmitts from the covering force latched on to him 'Vitya! There's one on your tail!', I shouted over the radio. Chernetsov turned steeply and the Messerschmitt's wing man ended up right in front of me. I lined him up in my sight, opened fire, and the Fascist fighter hurtled towards the ground spewing flames.
>
> That evening, led by the regimental commander, we again flew cover for our ground troops. It was dusk as we approached the front. 'Attention Spitfires', came the voice of our ground controller, '18 Heinkels followed by 10 Mes-

---

*Before delivery to the Soviet Air Force the Spitfire VBs had had their VHF sets removed and TR 9 high frequency sets installed.

**154.** This Spitfire VB, one of those delivered to the Soviet Air Force early in 1943, was used for catapult trials from the cruiser *Molotov* in 1946. *(via Geust)*

serschmitts coming in from the west, the sea.'

'Shikalov, Ivanov, attack the bombers, I'm going after the fighters!', commanded Osipov [Major Alexander Osipov, the Regimental commander].

We increased speed and headed west, Osipov with his two fours climbing to engage the Messerschmitts. The Fascist bombers were flying tight three-aircraft flights.

'Volodya I'm attacking the leader. You take the second lot!', I shouted to Shikalov. At the same time I noticed a couple of Messerschmitts coming down almost vertically on me. I ordered my second pair to attack the next flight of bombers, then I began a steep climb; but the Messerschmitts continued on down.

By this time the leader of Mironenko's second pair had set one of the Heinkels on fire. The Fascist bomber, going down steeply, tried to regain its own territory.

Now I had plenty of altitude, the leader of the Heinkels seemed to have seen neither my aircraft nor that of my wing man, and the covering Messerschmitts were battling with Osipov's force. With my wing man I went down steeply and sneaked in behind the leading Heinkel. 'Cover me, I'm going in to attack!', I commanded Ragozin my wing man. 'OK!' came the reply. The nose of my Spitfire was pointing at the belly of the Fascist. I opened fire, turned away just in time and saw an explosion. The Heinkel began to tilt and two parachutes fell clear. I felt great, I had knocked down my second enemy aircraft that day.

I turned and slowed down, so that Mironenko's approaching pair could close in to bring our four together again.

'How did you get on?' Osipov asked. 'OK'.

'Let's get some height, they can bounce us down here!' We increased speed to maximum, peeled off to the side and then tried to gain altitude as quickly as possible so that we could have a go at the Messerschmitts. We glanced over at the Heinkels. Our Yaks were tearing into them and they, having dropped their bombs on their own forces, headed west in disorder.

The battle over the Kuban continued through May and into June 1943, with the Spitfires flying bomber escort as well as interception missions. Then, at the end of June, the 57th Guards Fighter Aviation Regiment began a withdrawal to re-equip with Russian-built fighters.

# Appendix A

## SPITFIRE VA   K 9788

Figures taken from the trials report of this aircraft, the first Mark V tested at Boscombe Down, in February 1941. This aircraft was the second production Mark I, re-engined with the Merlin 45. The report gave no power rating for the engine, but stated that the maximum settings used were +9 pounds boost at 3,000 rpm. Nor did the report mention whether armament was carried or ballast in lieu; however, the aircraft was fitted with the early 'Type A' wing.

**Dimensions:** Span 36 ft 10 in, Length 29 ft 11 in
**Weight:** Fully loaded 6,070 pounds
Wing loading when fully loaded, 25.7 pounds per square foot
**Performance:**

| Height feet | Top Speed mph | Time to Climb mins | Rate of Climb ft/min |
|---|---|---|---|
| 2,000 | | 0 m 42 s | 3,170 |
| 5,000 | | 1 m 36 s | 3,240 |
| 10,000 | 331 | 3 m 06 s | 3,360 |
| 15,000 | 351 | 4 m 36 s | 3,380 |
| 20,000 | 368.5 | 6 m 12 s | 2,620 |
| 25,000 | 358 | 8 m 24 s | 2,030 |
| 30,000 | 335 | 11 m 24 s | 1,340 |

Service ceiling (estimated)                   38,000 ft

**Author's Comments**

During this trial K 9788 fitted with a Merlin 45 engine demonstrated that she was about 14 mph faster than the Mark II, and climbing and altitude performance was also improved. It must however be pointed out that at the time of the trial K 9788 did not carry full operational equipment.

# Appendix B

## SPITFIRE VB   W 3134

Figures taken from the trials report of this aircraft, the first Mark VB built as such and with full operational equipment, tested at Boscombe Down in May 1941.

**Weight:** fully loaded 6,525 pounds
Wing loading when fully loaded 27 pounds per square foot
**Armament:** two 20 mm Hispano cannon with 60 rpg
Four .303-in Browning machine guns with 350 rpg
**Performance:**

| Height feet | Top Speed mph | Time to Climb mins | Rate of Climb ft/min |
|---|---|---|---|
| 2,000 | | 0 m 36 s | 3,240 |
| 5,000 | | 1 m 30 s | 3,240 |
| 10,000 | 331 | 3 m 06 s | 3,250 |
| 15,000 | 351 | 4 m 36 s | 3,250 |
| 20,000 | 371 | 6 m 24 s | 2,440 |
| 25,000 | 359 | 8 m 24 s | 1,750 |
| 30,000 | | 12 m 12 s | 1,170 |

Service ceiling (estimated)                   37,500 ft

**Author's Comments**

The speed figures given above were recorded with the carburettor snow guard removed. With the guard fitted the speeds at 20,000 feet and above were reduced by about 6 mph; this would bring these figures in to line with those of K 9788 given in Appendix A, which was flown with the snow guard fitted.

# Appendix C

## SPITFIRE VA (TROPICALISED) X 4922

Figures taken from the trials report of this aircraft, the first Mark V fitted with tropical modifications, tested at Boscombe Down early in 1942. This aircraft was a Mark VA and somewhat lighter than W 3134 described in Appendix B; its service ceiling was slightly higher than that of the latter aircraft in spite of the tropical modifications. On this aircraft the guns had been removed and ballast fitted in lieu, and the gun ports had been sealed over. This aircraft was fitted with the Merlin 46 engine, similar to the Merlin 45 fitted to W 3134 but with a slightly higher rated altitude.

**Weight:** fully loaded 6,440 pounds

Wing loading when fully loaded, 26.6 pounds per square foot

**Performance:**

| Height feet | Top Speed mph | Time to Climb mins | Rate of Climb ft/min |
|---|---|---|---|
| 2,000 | | 0 m 45 s | 2,680 |
| 5,000 | | 1 m 53 s | 2,680 |
| 10,000 | | 3 m 45 s | 2,680 |
| 16,000 | 343½ | 6 m 00 s | 2,490 |
| 20,000 | 360 | 7 m 48 s | 1,860 |
| 20,800 | 363 | | |
| 26,000 | 353 | 11 m 03 s | 1,740 |
| 30,000 | | 13 m 51 s | 1,200 |
| 35,000 | | 19 m 48 s | 550 |

Service ceiling (estimated)　　　　　　　　38,500 ft

**Author's Comments**

This same aircraft, fitted with a mock-up of the 90 gallon jettisonable fuel tank and ballasted to a representative weight of 7,420 pounds (wing loading 30.7 pounds per square foot), had a maximum speed of 355½ mph at 20,800 feet, a maximum rate of climb of 2,050 feet per minute at 14,600 feet, and a service ceiling of 35,000 feet.

# Appendix D

## SPITFIRE VB VERSUS FW 190

The account below is taken from the comparative trial of the Spitfire VB with the Focke-Wulf 190, flown by the Air Fighting Development Unit at Duxford in July 1942

\*　　\*　　\*

The FW 190 was compared with a Spitfire VB from an operational squadron for speed and all-round manoeuvrability at heights up to 25,000 feet. The FW 190 is superior in speed at all heights, and the approximate differences are as follows:

At 1,000 ft the FW 190 is 25-30 mph faster than the Spitfire VB

At 3,000 ft the FW 190 is 30-35 mph faster than the Spitfire VB

At 5,000 ft the FW 190 is 25 mph faster than the Spitfire VB

At 9,000 ft the FW 190 is 25-30 mph faster than the Spitfire VB

At 15,000 ft the FW 190 is 20 mph faster than the Spitfire VB

At 18,000 ft the FW 190 is 20 mph faster than the Spitfire VB

At 21,000 ft the FW 190 is 20-25 mph faster than the Spitfire VB

**Climb:** The climb of the FW 190 is superior to that of the Spitfire VB at all heights. The best speeds for climbing are approximately the same, but the angle of the FW 190 is considerably steeper. Under maximum continuous climbing conditions the climb of the FW 190 is about 450 ft/min better up to 25,000 feet.

With both aircraft flying at high cruising speed and then pulling up into a climb, the superior climb of the FW 190 is even more marked. When both aircraft are pulled up into a climb from a dive, the FW 190 draws away very rapidly and the pilot of the Spitfire has no hope of catching it.

**Dive:** Comparative dives between the two aircraft have shown that the FW 190 can leave the Spitfire with ease, particularly during the initial stages.

**Manoeuvrability.** The manoeuvrability of the FW 190 is better than that of the Spitfire VB except in turning circles, when the Spitfire can quite easily out-turn it. The FW 190 has better acceleration under all conditions of flight and this must obviously be most useful during combat.

When the FW 190 was in a turn and was attacked by the Spitfire, the superior rate of roll enabled it to flick into a diving turn in the opposite direction. The pilot of the Spitfire found great difficulty in following this manoeuvre and even when prepared for it, was seldom able to allow the correct deflection. A dive from this manoeuvre enabled the FW 190 to draw away from the Spitfire which was then forced to break off the attack.

Several flights were carried out to ascertain the best evasive manoeuvres to adopt if 'bounced'. It was found that if the Spitfire was cruising at low speed and was 'bounced' by the FW 190, it was easily caught even if the FW 190 was sighted when well out of range, and the Spitfire was then forced to take avoiding action by using its superiority in turning circles. If on the other hand the Spitfire was flying at maximum continuous cruising and was 'bounced' under the same conditions, it had a reasonable chance of avoiding being caught by opening the throttle and going into a *shallow* dive, providing the FW 190 was seen in time. This forced the FW 190 into a stern chase and although it eventually caught the Spitfire, it took some time and as a result was drawn a considerable distance away from its base. This is a particularly useful method of evasion for the Spitfire if it is 'bounced' when returning from a sweep. This manoeuvre has been carried out during recent operations and has been successful on several occasions.

If the Spitfire VB is 'bounced' it is thought unwise to evade by diving steeply, as the FW 190 will have little difficulty in catching up owing to its superiority in the dive.

The above trials have shown that the Spitfire VB must cruise at high speed when in an area where enemy fighters can be expected. It will then, in addition to lessening the chances of being successfully 'bounced', have a better chance of catching the FW 190, particularly if it has the advantage of surprise.

# Appendix E

## SPITFIRE VB: CLIPPED WING VERSUS STANDARD VERSION

The account below is taken from the report on the comparative trial of clipped wing and standard wing Spitfire VBs, flown by the Air Fighting Development Unit at Duxford towards the end of 1942. The sole difference in the case of the former was that the wing tips had been removed and thin streamlined fairings fitted in their place. Thus wing span was reduced from 36 ft 10 in to 32 ft 6 ins, and wing area from the normal 242 square feet to 231. The removal of the wing tips reduced the fully loaded weight by 30 pounds; wing loading was increased by about one pound per square foot.

\*   \*   \*

### Method of Test

Two Spitfire VB aircraft were selected with a performance which was almost identical, the loading and equipment carried were standard in each, and the propeller, engine and finish of each aircraft were similar. A test flight was made under maximum cruising conditions and no differences could be determined. The wing tips were then removed from one aircraft and trials were carried out, each trial being performed twice to enable the pilots to be changed. The wing tips were then replaced on one aircraft and removed on the other and similar tests carried out. Differences in speed were taken as relative increases or decreases owing to possible instrument inaccuracies, and position error differences with and without tips. Readings for level speeds were taken at 10,000, 15,000, 20,000 and 25,000 feet; zoom climbs were made 10,000-15,000 ft and 20,000-25,000 ft; dives were made with similar engine settings.

### Results of Comparative Tests
#### Level Speed
10,000 feet. In each case the clipped wing Spitfire proved the faster by a small margin estimated in the nature of 5 mph.

15,000 and 20,000 feet. The average results at these two heights showed that the difference in speed is not measurable.

25,000 feet. The standard Spitfire is very slightly faster than the clipped wing Spitfire.

In all level speed runs the clipped wing Spitfire accelerated rather better than the standard Spitfire.
#### Climb
The average difference in time during zoom climbs from 20,000 to 25,000 feet was 15 seconds in favour of the standard Spitfire.

From 10,000 to 15,000 feet no differences were indicated.
#### Dive
In all diving tests the clipped wing Spitfire drew away from the standard Spitfire.

### Manoeuvrability
At all heights to 25,000 feet the rate of roll is considerably improved by removal of the wing tips. The response to aileron movements is very quick and very crisp. Four dog-fights were carried out, starting with the standard Spitfire on the tail of the clipped wing Spitfire. On two occasions the clipped wing Spitfire evaded so rapidly in the rolling plane that it was able to lose the standard Spitfire and reverse the positions in about 20 seconds. On the third occasion the clipped wing Spitfire was also able to lose the standard Spitfire. The fourth occasion was at 25,000 feet and the standard Spitfire was able to keep the clipped wing Spitfire in sight.

The minimum turning circle of the clipped wing Spitfire at 20,000 ft has been increased by 55 feet at 1,025 feet compared with the FW 190 turning circle of 1,450 feet (RAE Farnborough figures). This slight increase does not therefore detract from the fighting qualities of the aeroplane in any way, since the clipped wing version is unlikely to be in combat with the standard Spitfire.
### Take-off
The take-off run must theoretically be slightly longer, but in taking off with the clipped wing Spitfire in close formation behind the standard Spitfire, no difference was detected.
### Landing
No difference detected.
### General
The view downwards over the wing tips, for what it is worth, is improved by a not inconsiderable amount. The strengthening of the wing by removal of the wing tips may permit higher maximum IAS to be used.

### Conclusions
The trials have shown that:

| | Below 1,000 ft | 15,000-20,000 ft | Above 20,000 ft |
|---|---|---|---|
| Speed | Clipped wings give an increase | No difference | Standard wings are slightly faster |
| Climb | Differences hardly measurable | | In zoom climb from 20,000-25,000 ft from level flight at full throttle, standard wings about 15 seconds faster |
| Rate of roll | Clipped wings superior | Clipped wings superior | Clipped wings superior |
| Acceleration | ditto | ditto | ditto |
| Dive | ditto | ditto | ditto |
| Turning circle | Slight increase for clipped wings, amounting to 55 feet at 20,000 feet. | | |

# Appendix F

## SPITFIRE LF VB   W 3228, MERLIN 50M
## (CROPPED SUPERCHARGER)

These figures refer to the aircraft fitted with the Merlin 50M engine, with the diameter of the supercharger impeller 'cropped' to 9½ inches for optimum performance at low altitude. At the time of the trial, flown at Boscombe Down early in 1943, the state of the aircraft was as follows:

Standard Mark VB armament fitted, two 20 mm cannon and
    4 machine guns
Muzzles of all guns sealed, ejection chutes open
Standard wing tips
No IFF aerial
Balloon type hood
External laminated glass windscreen
External rectangular rear view mirror without fairing
Temperate type carburettor air intake, without ice guard
Individual ejector exhaust stubs
Rotol three-bladed propeller, 10 ft 10 in in diameter

**Weight:** fully loaded 6,450 pounds
Wing loading when fully loaded, 26.6 pounds per square foot
**Power plant:** Rolls-Royce Merlin 50M, with negative-G carburettor
1,585 BHP at 3,000 rpm at 3,800 ft at +18 pounds boost

**Performance:**

| Height feet | Top Speed mph | Time to Climb mins | Rate of Climb ft/min |
|---|---|---|---|
| 2,000 | 333½ | 0 m 24 s | 4,720 |
| 5,900 | 350½ | | |
| 8,000 | 348½ | 1 m 45 s | 4,100 |
| 12,000 | 345½ | 2 m 48 s | 3,500 |
| 18,000 | 339½ | 4 m 48 s | 2,610 |
| 24,000 | 327½ | 7 m 36 s | 1,740 |

Service ceiling                          35,700 ft
**Author's Comments**

The low altitude speed and climb performance figures were considerably better than that of aircraft fitted with uncropped superchargers, but performance fell away rapidly above 12,000 feet. Although LF (low altitude fighter) versions of the Spitfire used by operational squadrons usually had clipped wings, it should be noted that this designation referred to the type of engine fitted and not to the absence of wing tips.

# 11.

# SPITFIRE UNDER PRESSURE: THE MARK VI

As we have seen, when the Spitfire V was placed in production early in 1941 it was regarded as stop-gap, pending development of the Mark VI with a better high altitude performance and a pressurised cabin. At the time it was feared the Germans were about to put into large-scale production very high flying bombers like the Junkers 86P, and a version of the Spitfire was required with the performance to catch these. At a meeting of the Ministry of Aircraft Production held in London on 16 June 1941, the minutes recorded with respect to the Mark VI: 'The firm have already been informed that the Air Ministry require 350 of these in all, with a trickle to follow to make up wastage. A very definite requirement is for two squadrons (60 aircraft) before the end of 1941.' Joe Smith, the Chief Designer of Supermarine who was present at the meeting, commented that the prototype aircraft with a pressurised cabin modified by the company was nearly finished and was expected to fly shortly.

Jeffrey Quill flew the Supermarine prototype of the pressurised Spitfire, X 4942, on its maiden flight on 5 July. He reported favourably on the pressure cabin for very high altitude flying, it made life at such altitudes much more comfortable for the pilot. He did, however, point out several snags with the pressurised cabin in its initial form: Oil mist from the compressor leaked into the cockpit causing an unpleasant smell; the control cables passed through rubber seals at the pressurised bulkheads, which caused friction in the elevator and aileron controls and seriously affected longitudinal and lateral stability especially at high altitude; he found the cabin temperature uncomfortably high at low altitudes; and he regarded the 'Clamped-on' canopy, which could be opened in flight only by jettisoning, as acceptable only as an interim measure and pressed for the development of a sliding canopy. In view of the urgency of the RAF requirement for a pressurised version of the Spitfire he gave it as his view that the installation, though far from perfect, was acceptable.

Such was the urgency to develop a pressurised cabin for the Spitfire that a separate system was designed at the Royal Aircraft Establishment at Farnborough and incorporated in a

**155.** X 4942, a Mark V converted by Supermarine by the addition of a pressurised cabin, first flew in its new guise in July 1941 and was regarded as the prototype Spitfire VI. The intake for the cabin blower can be seen just under the ejector exhausts. The pressurised canopy could only be lifted on and off, not slid back; note the absence of rails behind the canopy.

**156.** In parallel with X 4942 another Spitfire V, R 7120 seen here, was fitted with a pressurised cabin at Farnborough. In this installation the pressurised air was ducted to the cabin from the blower along the outside of the fuselage. The production Mark VI incorporated the best features of both the Supermarine and the Farnborough designs for the pressurised cabin.

Mark V, R 7120. Both types of pressurised cabin were tested at high altitude and the best features of each were used in the production version.

The partially pressurised cabin fitted to the Spitfire VI cannot be likened to the fully pressurised cabin of a modern airliner. The pressure differential achieved in the Spitfire was only 2 pounds per square inch, which meant in practice that at 37,000 feet with pressurisation the cabin environment was the same as that at 28,000 feet without. Thus, while the pilot still had to wear his oxygen mask at high altitude, he was protected from the difficult physiological problems incurred during flight at extreme altitudes. It was found that the normal Spitfire cabin was quite strong enough to take the additional pressure, but leakage continued to be a problem even after the most likely sources had been eliminated. One unexpected source of leakage, which took a lot of tracking down, was through the cores of electrical cables passing into the pressurised cabin.

As well as the pressurised cabin and high altitude rated engine, the Spitfire VI differed from the Mark V in several respects. To assist in cabin sealing, the high altitude fighter had no side door. After the canopy was clamped into place by the ground crew it was sealed with an inflatable rubber gland. To absorb the additional power at high altitude, the Mark VI was fitted with a four-bladed propeller. And for greater efficiency at high altitude the wing tips were extended, increasing the span to 40 feet 2 inches and the area to 248.5 square feet.

The first production Spitfire VI emerged from the Supermarine factories in December 1941. In February 1942 the second production aircraft, AB 200, was tested at Boscombe Down; the performance figures recorded are given at Appendix A. The first squadron to receive this version was No 616, based at Kings Cliffe, which was issued with the type in April 1942.

In May 1942 a Mark VI from the middle of the production run, BR 289, was tested by the Air Fighting Development Unit at Duxford. The trial revealed the advantages and the disadvantages of the pressurised cabin as fitted to the Mark VI; the report is given at Appendix B.

Later in 1942 a Mark VI was fitted with a system of liquid oxygen injection for the Merlin, developed at Farnborough. The additional oxygen greatly increased the efficiency of combustion at high altitude, and at extreme altitude raised the ceiling by 2,000 feet and increased the maximum speed by 40 to 50 mph.

By the time the Spitfire VI did get into service in any numbers, however, the performance of the German Junkers 86 high altitude bomber had improved to the point where the Mark VI was unable to catch it. It would be left to the later Spitfire IX to counter this menace. Production of the Mark VI ceased in October 1942, after 100 had been built.

eiifl157

**157.** BR 579, Spitfire VI operated by No 124 Squadron, was a standard production aircraft with four-bladed propeller, extended span wings and a cabin blower intake on the starboard side of the nose. *(IWM)*

**158, 159, 160** and **161.** Close ups of the 'Lobelle' sliding canopy, tested on Mark VI AB 528 late in 1942 and fitted to later pressurised versions of the

Spitfire. The canopy was normally held in place by runners fitted to the outside of the fuselage. When the canopy jettison handle was pulled a powerful spring situated behind the pilot's seat forced the runners to snap open and the airflow lifted the canopy off. **161**, the spring is seen being tensioned using the special crank handle. *(via Vanags–Baginskis)*

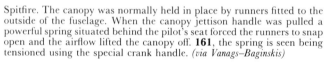

158, 159

EMERGENCY
PULL TO
RELEASE HOOD

# Appendix A

## SPITFIRE VI  AB 200

Figures taken from the trials report of this aircraft, the second production Mark VI, tested at Boscombe Down in February 1942. The state of this aircraft at the time of the trial was:

Merlin 47 engine with intake duct on starboard side of cowling for blower to pressurise cabin

Rotol four-bladed propeller, diameter 10 ft 9 in

Pressurised cabin

Extended wing tips; total wing area 248.5 sq ft

Two 20 mm cannon and four .303 in machine guns, gun ports sealed over, ejection chutes open

Rectangular rear view mirror, no fairing

Wire IFF aerials to tips of tailplane

Aerial mast for VHF

Metal ailerons

**Dimensions:** span 40 ft 2 in, length 29 ft 11 in

**Weight:** Fully loaded weight, 6,740 pounds

Wing loading when fully loaded, 27 pounds per square foot

**Performance:**

| Height feet | Top Speed mph | Time to Climb mins | Rate of Climb ft/min |
|---|---|---|---|
| 4,000 | 292 | 1 m 34 s | 2,555 |
| 12,000 | 320 | 4 m 41 s | 2,600 |
| 20,000 | 349 | 7 m 50 s | 2,390 |
| 21,800 | 356 | | |
| 28,000 | 343 | 12 m 15 s | 1,350 |
| 34,000 | 317 | 18 m 25 s | 680 |
| 38,000 | 264 | 27 m 54 s | 240 |

Service ceiling                                           39,200 feet

# Appendix B

## TACTICAL TRIAL: SPITFIRE VI  BR 289

The account below is taken from the tactical trial of Spitfire VI BR 289, flown by the Air Fighting Development Unit at Duxford in May 1942.

*   *   *

### Introduction

In accordance with arrangements with Headquarters, Fighter Command, a Spitfire VI aircraft, No BR 289, was delivered to this Unit on 23rd May 1942 for tactical trials.

The all-up weight of the aircraft with full war load is approximately 6,738 lbs, which is 180 lbs more than the Spitfire VB, and it was flown throughout the trials in this condition. The aircraft had fittings for a jettisonable fuel tank holding 30 gallons but this was not available during the trials.

### Brief Description of the Aircraft

The Spitfire VI is similar to the Spitfire VB but is fitted with a Merlin 47 engine, a 4-bladed Rotol propeller, a pressure cabin and extended wing tips giving an extra wing span of 3 ft 7 in.

The fuel tanks were not pressurised and immersed fuel pumps were not fitted.

### Pressure Cabin

The normal hinged panel on the port side of the cockpit is omitted and for sealing the cabin there are two bulkheads, one in front just aft of the fuel tanks and the other behind the pilot's seat.

The cockpit hood, which is jettisonable, cannot be opened in flight and is clamped in place by 4 toggles, two on each side, which are interconnected by a wire for quick release. It is difficult for the pilot to tighten the rear toggles before take-off as they are not easy to reach, being positioned behind him.

There is a hinged clear view panel on the port side of the windscreen and a cold air ventilator on the starboard side of the cockpit, both of which have to be closed when the cockpit is under pressure. Pressurised air is injected into the cabin from numerous pipes. The air, which is warm, can be directed on to the bullet-proof windscreen to keep the screen free from mist. In addition, there are two detachable rubber pipes which fit on to the cockpit hood to eject warm air on to the perspex and these are attached by the pilot before take-off. These rubber tubes are not very secure and are liable to become detached during flight. It is understood, however, that a modification is being incorporated which will have a bayonet attachment and a weak spot in the tube to allow the hood to be jettisoned.

The cabin is pressurised to a maximum of 2 lbs differential pressure by means of a lever on the port side of the cockpit, level with the pilot's elbow. This is badly positioned and is often accidentally moved by the pilot. The pilot generally pressurises the cockpit at around 10,000 feet by pulling the lever back slowly. It is understood that in later Spitfire VIs the pressurising will be fully automatic.

The only extra instruments in the pressure cabin are (a) two red warning lights which illuminate when the difference of pressure inside the cabin from that outside is less than 1 lb, and (b) an internal altimeter by which the pilot adjusts his oxygen. The oxygen equipment is standard.

During trials the pressure in the cockpit often dropped below 1 lb difference from the pressure outside, and the red warning lights came on denoting a leak in the cockpit. Cracks in the perspex behind the hood appeared after the second flight and were sealed with Bostick which was not altogether satisfactory, and 'Tenasco' if available would be more suitable.

After some hours' flying, deposits of oil which came through the pressurised air tubes were left on the perpex inside the aircraft. It was found that oil had leaked from the engine and had entered the air system through a rubber joint just aft of the air pump.

### Cockpit Heating

As soon as the engine is started, hot air enters the cockpit from the cabin blower. This arrangement is beneficial in cold weather and at high altitudes, but in hot weather makes the cockpit uncomfortably warm and at altitudes below 15,000 feet pilots felt muzzy and sleepy, although both the ventilator and the clear view panel were open. On one occasion on a particularly hot day, the temperature at low altitude inside the cockpit was almost unbearable, being +37°C [98°F] inside and +28°C [82°F] outside. This heat persisted in the cockpit during the climb to 12,000 feet and prevented any continuous flying at lower altitudes under these conditions.

## Tactical Trials
### Flying Characteristics
The Spitfire VI is similar to the Spitfire VB for take-off, but for landing a slightly faster approach is necessary due to the higher stalling speed.

The aileron controls are considerably heavier than the Spitfire VB—this appears to be partly due to the air-tight seals attached to the control cables passing through the cockpit. As a result the manoeuvrability is much slower in the rolling plane and the 'going in' and 'coming out' of steep turns is slowed down.

The longer wing tips on the Spitfire VI add to the lateral stability especially above 25,000 feet, but the elevator control is unstable at altitudes over 30,000 feet.

The balloon hood distorts the pilot's vision near the forward frame, and sometimes gives a double image. This has a slight adverse effect on landing and formation flying, but the hood is excellent for search and general flying.

### Taxying
The greater wing span makes taxying slightly more difficult than in the normal Spitfire. This is especially noticeable in a high wind when the wing tips come perilously near the ground.

### Performance
Comparative performances were carried out with a Spitfire VC as a VB was not available. Both aircraft took off with a full war load. Below 20,000 feet the Spitfire VI was slightly slower but by 22,000 feet (its rated altitude) it was about 6 mph faster.

### Climb
Comparative climbs were carried out with a Spitfire VB and up to 20,000 feet there is little to choose between the two aircraft. The Spitfire VB is faster up to 10,000 feet and climbs at a steeper angle, but from 10,000 feet to 20,000 feet the Spitfire VI is slightly faster. From 20,000 to 30,000 feet the Spitfire VI is about 1 minute faster than the Spitfire VB. Above 30,000 feet the superiority of the Spitfire VI is even more marked and it climbs from 30,000 to 35,000 feet in half the time of the Spitfire VB.

The highest altitude reached was 37,500 feet Indicated. At this height excessive hunting and intermittent cutting out of the engine was experienced due to the petrol vapourising in the feed line due to insufficient fuel pressure. On a very hot day (28°C [82°F] on the ground) it was impossible to climb above 28,500 feet due to this trouble.

The rate of climb falls off to 1,000 feet per minute at about 34,000 feet and this is considered to be the operational ceiling for a squadron, but sections of two could operate up to 37,000 feet.

### Manoeuvrability
Although the aileron controls are heavier than the Spitfire VB, the rate of turn is as good up to 25,000 feet and above this height is appreciably better. At 32,000 feet the Spitfire VI got on the tail of the Spitfire VB after 1½ turns. At these heights and above the increased wing area and higher rated altitude of the engine gave the Spitfire VI a great advantage over the Spitfire VB.

The Spitfire VI was fitted with a 6½ lb inertia device and below 25,000 feet there was no tendency to tighten-up in the turn if the elevators were trimmed correctly. If incorrectly trimmed the aircraft tended to tighten the rate of turn. During dog-fights, above 30,000 feet there was a definite tightening of the turn.

Evasive action of half rolling the aircraft and doing aileron turns was slowed down considerably by the heavy aileron control. A better method of evasion is considered to be diving steeply, as the engine only cuts out momentarily when negative 'G' is applied due to the restrictor fitted in the fuel supply pipe.

### High Flying
Numerous flights have been carried out between 30,000 and 37,500 feet and the pilot has greatly benefited by the pressure cabin. There have been no complaints of ill-effects from being at altitude, even for long periods, and pilots have nothing but praise for the comfort of the cockpit. At 37,500 feet the pressure inside the cockpit was equal to 28,500 feet. The cockpit was warmed by the air so that at −42°C [−49°F] outside the cockpit it was +8°C [+46°F] inside. For comfort above 30,000 feet, only flying boots and light overalls are needed by the pilot.

No serious icing-up of the cockpit was experienced and during rapid descents from high altitude the cockpit was almost free from internal misting-up, while the Spitfire VB misted up badly.

The elevator control above 30,000 feet is most sensitive and at 36,000 feet the aircraft often loses as much as 1,000 feet while the pilot is searching or looking at his instruments.

Freezing-up of the elevator and rudder trimmers was experienced during the first two flights above 30,000 feet, but after treatment with anti-freeze oil it was possible to trim the aircraft correctly at all heights.

Vapour trails, non persistent, were generally experienced around 30,000 feet (−36°C [−33°F]), but disappeared above 36,000 feet. On one occasion vapour trails were made at 25,000 feet (−42°C [−43°F]) and disappeared at 30,000 feet (−54°C [−65°F]).

### Endurance
The Spitfire VI consumes approximately the same amount of petrol as the Spitfire VB. During the climb to 30,000 feet starting at +2 boost, 2,600 rpm, and 45 minutes spent at this height, the Spitfire VI used 48 gallons of petrol and the Spitfire VB, formating at a distance, used 50 gallons.

### Armament
No firing trials were carried out as the gun installations are identical with those of the Spitfire VB.

## Conclusions
The pressure cabin adds greatly to the pilot's comfort at high altitude. He is kept warmer and needs less oxygen, but on a hot day below 15,000 feet the cabin is unbearably hot. The cabin showed no signs of misting up.

The rated altitude of the Spitfire VI is 22,000 feet and above this height the performance is better than the Spitfire VB. This difference becomes more marked above 30,000 feet, its climb from there to 35,000 feet being twice as fast as that of the Spitfire VB. The operational ceiling for a squadron is considered to be about 34,000 feet, although sections of two could operate up to 37,000 feet.

The Spitfire VI is more manoeuvrable than the Spitfire VB above 30,000 feet and below this height has an equally good rate of turn, although it is slow in the rolling plane.

Owing to the slow rate of roll the best method of evasion is to dive steeply.

The cockpit is uncomfortably hot for low altitude flying in summer conditions.

# 12.

# SUCCESSFUL STOP-GAP: THE MARKS IX AND XVI

Following the huge increase in performance revealed during the trials of Spitfire III N 3297 fitted with the Merlin 61 engine, and the realisation that the Spitfire V was no match for the new German Focke-Wulf 190 fighter, there was considerable pressure to get Spitfires powered by the new engine into production as rapidly as possible. The Spitfire VII was to be a high altitude pressurised variant with the Merlin 61, with the additional refinements of a somewhat stronger airframe than the Mark V, additional fuel in two small wing tanks and a retractable tail wheel. The Spitfire VIII was to be a medium altitude version of the Mark VII, without the pressurised cabin but with the other airframe refinements. But a certain amount of re-tooling was necessary to produce these versions. During the early months of 1942 it was imperative to get the Merlin 61 Spitfire into the operational squadrons as quickly as possible and with an absolute minimum of refinement. To that end a couple of Mark VCs, AB 196 and AB 197, were sent to the Rolls-Royce works at Hucknall and, after strengthening the fuselage longerons to take the heavier and more powerful engine, they were fitted with Merlin 61s. The new combination became the Spitfire IX. It was considered to be insufficiently stressed but, until the stronger Mark VIII airframe was ready to go into production, the Ministry of Aircraft Production placed orders for Spitfire IXs to be converted or built as rapidly as possible.

In April 1942 one of the converted Spitfire VCs, AB 505, was delivered to the Air Fighting Development Unit at Duxford. Its trials made a profound impression and the performance figures and trials report on this aircraft are given in Appendices A and B. The report concluded: 'The performance of the Spitfire IX is outstandingly better than the Spitfire V, especially at heights above 20,000 feet. On the level the Spitfire IX is considerably faster and its climb is exceptionally good . . . . Its manoeuvrability is as good as the Spitfire V up to 30,000 feet, and above that it is very much better. At 38,000 feet it is capable of a true speed of 368 mph, and is still able to manoeuvre well for fighting.'

A few months later a Spitfire IX was pitted against the captured Focke-Wulf 190. The report on the comparative trial is given in Appendix C and revealed that the two aircraft were closely matched as regards performance; in combat victory would probably go to the side which gained and held the initiative.

**162.** AB 196 started life as a Spitfire VC and was the first such aircraft to be converted into a Mark IX by the installation of a Merlin 61 engine. It is seen here fitted with four 20 mm cannon, one of the few Mark IXs to be so armed. *(via Oughton)*

**163.** BS 306, a Mark IXC of No 402 (Canadian) Squadron the fourth unit to re-equip with this version, seen on the ground at Kenley in November 1942. *(Public Archives of Canada)*

Production Mark IXs started to emerge from the Supermarine plants in June 1942 and before the end of the month 18 were delivered. No 64 Squadron at Hornchurch was the first to receive the new variant, in June; it was followed by No 611 in July, Nos 401 and 402 (Canadian) Squadrons in August and No 133 (US Eagle) Squadron in September. Production of the Mark IX built up rapidly, with 38 delivered in August and 58 in September.

Towards the end of August 1942 the Luftwaffe began a new phase of its bombing offensive against Britain, using the Junkers 86R high altitude bomber. This aircraft, with its two-man crew in a pressurised cabin, was able to attack from altitudes above 40,000 feet; at this time, however, only two Ju 86Rs were available. During the initial attacks Spitfire VIs of No 124 Squadron attempted to intercept the high-flying German bombers, but proved quite unable to reach the prey.

The answer to the problem was the Spitfire IX which, though it lacked a pressurised cabin, had a high altitude performance considerably better than the Mark VI. Accordingly a new unit, the Special Service Flight, was formed at Northolt to operate a couple of modified Spitfire IXs against the Ju 86Rs. These aircraft were stripped of everything not strictly necessary for the high altitude interception role: all armour and four machine guns were removed, leaving an armament of two 20 mm cannon; the aircraft were fitted with lighter weight propellers driven through a slightly lower reduction gear, to optimise performance in the climb and at high altitude, and given a lightweight blue finish similar to that carried by photographic reconnaissance aircraft. Thus modified the Spitfire IX had a fully laden weight of 6,954 pounds, 450 pounds less than normal for this mark. On 12 September 1942 Pilot Officer Prince Emanuel Galitzine in one of the modified Spitfire IXs successfully intercepted a Junkers 86R near Southampton at 41,000 feet and chased it to above 43,000 feet. After the initial attack, however, his port cannon jammed; thereafter, each time he manoeuvred into a firing position and opened fire, the Spitfire slewed to starboard and fell out of the sky. The German bomber escaped with just a single hit on its port wing; but with this action it was clear that the Ju 86R was no longer immune from fighter attack over England, and no further high altitude attacks were mounted with these aircraft.* The action on 12 September 1942 was the highest air battle of the Second World War.

Like the Mark V before it, the Spitfire IX was produced with versions of the Merlin engine optimised for low altitude and

*A full account of the action on 12 September 1942, with accounts from both Galitzine and the German pilot involved, is given in *Spitfire: a Documentary History* by Alfred Price, Jane's.

**164.** EN 149, one of the fifteen Mark IX fighters converted into PR IXs late in 1942. These aircraft had their armament removed and cameras fitted in the rear fuselage but lacked the wing leading edge fuel tanks which were to be a feature of the Mark XI, the definitive photographic reconnaissance version of the Spitfire IX. *(via Oughton)*

high altitude fighting. The low altitude LF IX was powered by the Merlin 66; the performance of an example of this version running on 150 octane fuel is given in Appendix D. As in the case of the LF V, many LF IXs were operated with clipped wings; the effect on performance of this change was about the same as it had been with the Mark V. The high altitude HF IX was powered by the Merlin 70; the performance of an example of this version is given in Appendix E.

Pending production of the specialised photographic reconnaissance version of the Spitfire with the Merlin 61, the Mark XI, fifteen Mark IX fighters were modified at Benson for this role. The armament was removed from these aircraft and the gun ports were faired over; a pair of vertical cameras was installed in the rear fuselage and a larger oil tank was fitted under the nose. It is believed that the Spitfire PR IX, as it became known, carried no additional internal fuel; for extended range flights the aircraft carried a slipper tank under the fuselage. The PR IX was first used operationally in November 1942, by No 541 Squadron. In May 1943 it was a PR IX of No 542 Squadron, piloted by Flying Officer F. D. Fray, that brought back the famous photographs of the breached Moehne and Eder Dams after the attack by No 617 Squadron.

A small number of Spitfire IXs were also modified for the fighter reconnaissance role, by the addition of a single oblique camera fitted in the rear fuselage and facing port; in this version the normal cannon and machine gun armament was retained.

One of the units which operated the Spitfire FR IX was No 16 Squadron, a 2nd Tactical Air Force unit which operated in support of the army during the campaigns in France, Holland, Belgium and into Germany in 1944 and 1945. No 16 Squadron operated both FR IX and PR XI Spitfires; the former were used for low and medium altitude photography below cloud and were painted pink.

Production of the Spitfire IX ceased at the Supermarine factories in June 1943, but was to continue at the Castle Bromwich plant until after the end of the war in Europe. Late production Mark IXs differed considerably from those in the early batches, after a cumulative series of changes and improvements to the airframe. The first change to the fighter's external appearance was the fitting of the broad-chord and pointed rudder, in place of the rounded one which had characterised previous versions of the Spitfire. Next came the 'E Type' wing which provided for the fitting of four 20 mm cannon or, as was almost invariably the case, two 20 mm cannon and two .5-in Browning machine guns; for the latter the cannon were fitted in the outboard cannon mountings, and the .5-in machine guns immediately inboard of the cannon. Later production Mark IXs were fitted with two additional fuel tanks in the rear fuselage, with a total capacity of 75 gallons. And finally the rear fuselage was cut back and a 'tear drop' type canopy was fitted which greatly improved rearwards visibility (if the 'tear drop' canopy was fitted, the rear fuselage tankage was reduced to 66 gallons); the 'tear drop' canopy had been proposed by Jeffrey Quill after his attachment to an operational squadron during the Battle of Britain. It was first tried out on a Spitfire VIII and will be described in the next chapter.

Starting in September 1944, an increasingly large proportion of the Spitfire IX airframes on the Castle Bromwich production line were fitted with the Merlin 266, a low altitude Merlin 66 built under licence by the Packard Motor Company in the USA. The Packard Merlin 266 differed from its Rolls-Royce counterpart only in detail, but a new mark number was issued for those versions of the Spitfire fitted with it: it became the Mark XVI. There was no difference in external shape between the Marks IX and XVI, and the two versions were built side-by-side on the production line. The Mark XVIs incorporated the same airframe changes as Mark IXs built at the same time and the former had the same enlarged rudder, 'C-' or 'E-Type' wing, clipped wings, rear fuselage fuel tanks and 'tear drop' canopies.

Altogether some 5,710 Spitfire IXs were built by the Supermarine plants and at Castle Bromwich. The Castle Bromwich factory turned out some 1,055 Mark XVIs; and 280 Mark Vs were converted into Mark IXs during the initial rush to get this version into service. Thus the total number of Mark IXs or XVIs built or converted ran to more than seven thousand and this was the most numerous variant of the Spitfire.

**165.** One of the most famous reconnaissance photographs of the war, showing the breached Moehne Dam on the morning of 17 May 1943 after the attack by No 617 Squadron, taken by Flying Officer F. D. Fray in a Spitfire PR IX of No 542 Squadron. *(IWM)*

165

**166, 167** and **168.** Spitfire FR IXs of No 16 Squadron seen at airfield A 12 near Bayeux, Normandy, in September 1944. These aircraft were painted pale pink overall but carried invasion stripes under the rear fuselage; they retained their full armament and carried a single oblique camera in the rear fuselage, facing to port. Aircraft 'X' was MK 716; 'V' was MK 915. *(Horsefall)*

**169.** Clipped winged Spitfire LF IX fighter bombers of No 601 Squadron seen taking off from Fano, Italy, in November 1944. The rear aircraft, UF-Q MJ 250, was painted silver overall. *(Public Archives of Canada)*

**170** and **171.** No 74 Squadron of the 2nd Tactical Air Force operated Spitfire IXEs, later Mark XVIEs, during the closing stages of the war in Europe. It is believed this was the only RAF Spitfire unit to fire rockets operationally during the Second World War. The photographs show one of the unit's aircraft with two single-rocket launchers under the wings and a 500 pound bomb under the fuselage. They also show the ·5-in machine gun muzzle inboard of the 20 mm cannon on each wing, which identifies the E-Type wing. *(Murland)*

172

**172.** Cockpit of a Mark IX, with the pilot's helmet draped over the control column in readiness for a scramble take-off. Above the instrument panel can be seen the Mark II Gyro gunsight. *(Murland)*

**173.** This Mark IX, MN 477, was tested with the American M 10 three-tube cluster rocket installation. The weapon was not used in action by British forces.

173

**174.** Mark IXC MA 587 differed considerably from the standard aircraft, being fitted with a Merlin 77 engine driving a Rotol contra-rotating propeller and a Mark XIV-type tail with retractable wheel. *(Greensted)*

**175.** Close-up of the contra-rotating propeller installation on a Mark IX; at least five Spitfires of this version were fitted with this type of propeller.

**176.** Mark IXC MK 210 pictured at Wright Field, Ohio, USA in May 1944 where it had been fitted with a 43 gallon fuel tank in the rear fuselage, 16½ gallon flexible tanks in the leading edge of each wing and Mustang-type 62 gallon tanks under each wing, to bring the total fuel load to 285 gallons. Note the small venturies at the base of each drop tank, for the wind-driven fuel pumps. The fuel load carried by this aircraft was one gallon more than the 284 gallons carried by the Spitfire Vs flown to Malta direct from Gibraltar nearly two years earlier, and the Wright-modified aircraft was able to carry its full armament as well as the additional fuel (the Spitfires flown to Malta could not). During the early summer of 1944 MK 210 was flown across the Atlantic via Iceland, and underwent further trials at Boscombe Down.

**177.** This somewhat blurred shot, taken during the cine film of the tank dropping trials of MK 210 from Boscombe Down in July 1944, shows clearly the loop aerial for the radio direction finder fitted to the aircraft for its transatlantic flight.

**180.** Late production Spitfire LF XVIEs with clipped wings, cut back rear fuselages and 'tear-drop' canopies, photographed undergoing final assembly at Castle Bromwich in the spring of 1945. *(Vickers)*

**178.** A late production Mark IX, RR 228, pictured in February 1945 fitted with extra tanks for 75 gallons of fuel in the rear fuselage. The upper tank and filler pipe are visible under the rear cockpit glazing. *(via Oughton)*

**179.** Apart from the serial number, there was no external feature to distinguish the Rolls-Royce Merlin engined Mark IX from the Packard Merlin engined Mark XVI. This aircraft was a clipped winged LF XVIE with a 45 gallon slipper tank, belonging to No 403 (Canadian) Squadron, seen taking off from Soltau in Germany in July 1945. *(Public Archives of Canada)*

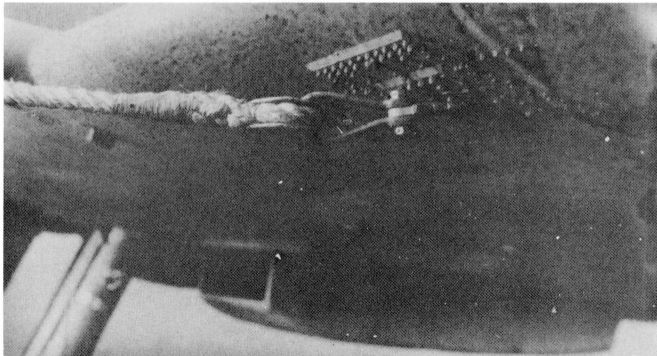

**181, 182, 183** and **184.** Towards the end of 1943 the Flight Refuelling Company tested a system of towing a Spitfire to extend its ferry range, using a Wellington as tug. The towing line consisted of a 'Y' shaped bridle, whose ends were attached to quick-release catches under the Spitfire's wings mid-way along the span. For take-off the apex of the bridle was fitted to a quick release catch on the underside of the Spitfire's rear fuselage; this prevented the rope getting entangled with the undercarriage or propeller when the fighter took off under its own power in formation with the tug. When the two aircraft were at cruising altitude the Spitfire pilot released the apex of the bridle and the rest of the 700 foot long towline was paid out from the tug. The fighter was then gradually slowed until the towline was taught, then its engine could be shut down and re-started just before the cast-off. Flight trials revealed problems with the system, however. If the fighter's engine was shut down for long it was liable to oil up; but if the engine was kept running and the throttle opened sufficiently to prevent this, the Spitfire began to overtake the tug! To overcome this problem the Spitfire was fitted with a fully feathering propeller — the only time this fighter was fitted with one. Flying the Spitfire in the tow required continuous concentration on the part of the pilot, however, and the system was considered unsuitable for long ferry flights. (**181**) The Spitfire with the bridle in place for towing. (**182**) Close-up of the strengthened attachment point on the Spitfire's wing. (**183**) The apex of the bridle attached under the Spitfire's fuselage, for take-off. (**184**) BF 274, the Spitfire IX used during the towing trials, seen with the bridle held clear of the runway and attached to the inspection cover at the rear of the fuselage, for flights prior to attachment to the tug.

183

184

185

**185.** One of the 1,188 Spitfire IXs, in this case an LF IXE, despatched to the Soviet Air Force during 1944 and 1945. *(via Geust)*

**186.** Pilots of the 26th Guards Fighter Regiment of the Soviet Air Force lined up in front of their Spitfire LF IXEs, April 1945. The unit operated as part of the Leningrad Air Defence Force. Behind the cockpit of each aircraft can be seen the red-star-in-laurel-leaves emblem, carried by guards units' aircraft. *(via Geust)*

186

# Appendix A

## SPITFIRE IX AB 505

Figures taken from the trials report of this aircraft, tested by the Air Fighting Development Unit at Duxford in April 1942. Converted from a Mark VC by the installation of a Merlin 61 engine, for the trial the aircraft carried full internal fuel, guns, ammunition, radio and IFF. Further details of this aircraft are contained in the trials report given at Appendix B.

**Dimensions:** span 36 ft 11 in, length 30 ft 0 in
**Weight:** Fully loaded weight 7,400 pounds
Wing loading when fully loaded, 30.6 pounds per square foot
**Performance:**

| Height feet | Top Speed mph | Time to Climb mins |
|---|---|---|
| 4,000 | 326 | 1 m 10 s |
| 8,000 | 344 | 2 m 20 s |
| 12,000 | 363 | 3 m 30 s |
| 16,000 | 383 | 4 m 40 s |
| 20,000 | 378 | 6 m 0 s |
| 24,000 | 390 | 8 m 0 s |
| 28,000 | 409 | 10 m 20 s |
| 32,000 | 395 | 13 m 15 s |
| 36,000 | 377 | 17 m 0 s |

### Author's comment
The AFDU was not equipped to carry out accurate performance checks, and its figures should not be considered as authoritative as those produced by Boscombe Down.

# Appendix B

## SPITFIRE IX AB 505

The account below is taken from the report on the service trial of this aircraft, flown by the Air Fighting Development Unit at Duxford at the end of April 1942. For this trial the aircraft carried the full war load of guns, ammunition, radio, IFF and full internal fuel.

*     *     *

### Brief Description of the Aircraft
#### General
The Spitfire IX is a Spitfire VC modified to incorporate a Merlin 61 engine fitted with the latest negative-G carburettor. The main differences between the two aircraft are the slightly longer nose due to the larger engine, a 4-bladed Rotol constant speed propeller, two thermostatically controlled radiators and two-speed superchargers which are automatically controlled. The fuel capacity is increased by approximately 10 gallons and the tanks are pressurised.

#### Pilot's Cockpit
The cockpit is similar to that of the Spitfire VC but has additional controls for ground testing the full supercharger gear and radiators, and for pressurising the fuel tanks. There is only one fuel cock.

The supercharger gear is fully automatic, so that MS gear only is in operation below about 22,000 feet and FS gear above that height. For ground testing there is a push button to bring the FS gear into operation. A red light illuminates when the button is pressed and also in the event of the aneroid failing to change down to MS on descent so as to warn the pilot that there will be a loss of power should he have his landing baulked and have to go round again. If the aneroid is functioning correctly FS is not available below 22,000 feet, nor is MS available above this height.

The radiator is thermostatically controlled so that the pilot does not have to operate it manually. For ground testing there is a push button which will open the radiator while the button is held down, otherwise the shutters open when the coolant temperature reaches 115°C. This press button and the button for testing FS gear are situated on a plate aft of the throttle box and are in the way of the pilot's arm.

A cock is provided for pressurising the fuel tanks and must always be kept on above 20,000 feet to avoid engine failure due to vapour locks. In the event of a tank being holed by enemy action it is essential to turn off the pressure to avoid excessive loss of fuel. The cock is on the starboard side of the cockpit and is liable to be fouled by the pilot's elbow. A red fuel pressure warning light is fitted instead of a pressure gauge on the dash-board and lights when the pressure falls to 3 lbs.

There is a gauge mounted on the port side of the dash-board showing the temperature of the mixture charge, which should read about 40°C in MS gear and 60-80°C in FS.

There is an efficient system of heating the cockpit which can be regulated by the pilot.

The constant speed control for the airscrew is in the usual position and controls between 1,700 and 3,000 rpm. The travel of the lever is, however, very short indeed and the selection of desired rpm far too critical.

#### Sighting View
The Spitfire IX is fitted with the GM 2 pilot's reflector sight and although the aircraft is longer in the nose than the Spitfire VC the 100 mph ring of the sight is still just clear of the nose.

#### Oxygen Equipment
The oxygen supply is obtained from two bottles provided with an economiser and is the same as that used in the standard Spitfire.

### Tactical Trials
The Spitfire IX was compared with a Spitfire VC with similar armament and a Typhoon I, for performance and manoeuvrability; all aircraft were carrying full war load.

#### Flying Characteristics
The Spitfire IX is similar to the Spitfire VC for take-off and landing, although the landing speed is slightly higher. The extra weight and length of the aircraft has made the elevators a little heavier and as a result controls are better harmonised. It was noticed that during dives there was less tendency for the aircraft to yaw and this was thought to be due to the extra radiator fitted on the port wing. Tight turns were made up to

5G and there was no sign of 'tightening up', the aircraft recovering normally when the control column was released.

## Performance

The speed of the Spitfire IX was compared with a Spitfire VC and a Typhoon I at various heights. Its maximum true speed in MS gear is developed at a height of 16,300 feet and is approximately 386 mph, and in FS gear at 28,000 feet and is approximately 409 mph. These figures are slightly less than those obtained by Messrs Rolls-Royce, but it is understood that the aircraft they used was not fitted with cannons and did not carry a full war load. The speed of the Spitfire IX at all heights was vastly superior to that of the Spitfire VC.

Two speed runs were made against a Typhoon I from an operational squadron. At 15,000 feet the Spitfire IX was approximately 10 mph faster, and at 18,000 feet approximately 2 mph faster.

## Climb

Comparative climbs were carried out and it was found that the Spitfire IX was superior to the Spitfire VC and Typhoon I at all heights. This superiority becomes even more marked as height increases. The Spitfire IX was climbed under maximum continuous climbing conditions, to an indicated height of 39,500 feet where the rate of climb was about 700 feet per minute. It was particularly noticed that the oil and glycol temperatures were normal throughout. The operational ceiling is considered to be about 38,000 feet where the rate of climb is 1,000 feet per minute. This height can be reached by a single aircraft in 18½ minutes.

## Manoeuvrability

The Spitfire IX was compared with a Spitfire VC for turning circles and dog-fighting at heights between 15,000 and 30,000 feet. At 15,000 feet there was little to choose between the two aircraft although the superior speed and climb of the Spitfire IX enabled it to break off its attack by climbing away and then attacking again in a dive. This manoeuvre was assisted by the negative G carburettor, as it was possible to change rapidly from climb to dive without the engine cutting. At 30,000 feet there is still little to choose between the two aircraft in manoeuvrability, but the superiority in speed and climb of the Spitfire IX becomes outstanding. The pilot of the Spitfire VC found it difficult to maintain a steep turn without losing height, whereas the pilot of the Spitfire IX found that he had a large reserve of power which enabled him to maintain height without trouble. The all-round performance of the Spitfire IX at 30,000 feet is most impressive.

Short trials were carried out against a Typhoon I and the Spitfire IX was found to be more manoeuvrable and superior in climb but inferior in dive. During a dog-fight at 18,000 feet the Spitfire out-turned the Typhoon and got on its tail after 1½ turns.

## High Flying

Several climbs were made to heights between 39,000 and 40,000 feet and the pilot felt that the aircraft was capable of going even higher. Although the operational ceiling is considered to be 38,000 feet, it is thought that Sections of two could operate up to 39,000 feet and probably higher. The aircraft is easy to fly at high altitudes, but freezing up of the trimming tabs occurred. It was therefore difficult to keep the aircraft level as it was still trimmed for climb. During manoeuvres there is otherwise little tendency to lose height even at 38,000 feet. At this height the aircraft was dived for 1,500 feet and zoomed up to 39,000 feet. Steep turns were carried out at 38,000 feet where it was necessary to maintain an indicated airspeed of at least 110 mph to prevent stalling. The cockpit heating kept the pilot warm at all heights and flying clothing was unnecessary.

Slight icing up of the cockpit was experienced during turns but this dispersed as soon as the aircraft was flown straight. The cold air spray to the windscreen was turned on during descents and no misting up was experienced.

During the high flying trials vapour trails were formed between 30,000 and 36,000 feet, but above this height trails were not visible. All flights took place under conditions of no cloud and extremely low temperatures, −64°C [−83°F] being reported on one occasion.

## Endurance

The fuel capacity of the Spitfire IX is 92 gallons, 57 in the top tank and 35 in the bottom tank. This is 8 gallons more than the Spitfire VC. There are fittings under the fuselage for a jettisonable tank holding 30 gallons. Petrol consumption during the trials was high and during a comparative flight of 75 minutes the Spitfire IX used 76 gallons and the Spitfire VC 54 gallons. In a flight of one hour, three speed runs of 4 minutes each and a maximum continuous climb to 39,000 feet were carried out and the Spitfire IX used 76 gallons. On investigation of engine trouble experienced at the latter stage of the trials it was found that the aircraft had been delivered with the mixture control locked in the 'rich' position instead of 'weak'.

## Armament Characteristics

The Spitfire IX, like the VC, is fitted with the universal wing and for the trials 2 × 20 mm cannon and 4 × .303" Brownings were carried. When fitting the 20 mm cannons it was found that the inboard rib on the gun panel housing fouled the feed mechanism and the gun panel had to be eased by filing. Time did not permit firing trials to be carried out but this installation has already been reported on by this unit.

## Cine Camera Gun

It was impossible to fit a G 45 cine camera gun as ducts for the radiator system obstructed the camera mounting.

### Conclusions

The performance of the Spitfire IX is outstandingly better than the Spitfire V, especially at heights above 20,000 feet. On the level the Spitfire IX is considerably faster and its climb is exceptionally good. It will climb easily to 38,000 feet and when levelled off there, can be made to climb in stages to above 40,000 feet by building up speed on the level and a slight zoom. Its manoeuvrability is as good as the Spitfire V up to 30,000 feet, and above that is very much better. At 38,000 feet it is capable of a true speed of 368 mph, and is still able to manoeuvre well for fighting.

\* \* \*

## Author's Comments

It should be noted that there were considerable differences in detail between initially modified Spitfire IXs, and some of the features of AB 505 mentioned in the report were not present on other examples of this variant. This is so regarding the enlarged main fuel tank and the cockpit heating system.

# Appendix C

## SPITFIRE IX VERSUS FOCKE-WULF 190

The account below is taken from the comparative trial of the Spitfire IX with the Focke-Wulf 190, flown by the Air Fighting Development Unit at Duxford in July 1942.

\* \* \*

The FW 190 was compared with a fully operational Spitfire IX for speed and manoeuvrability at heights up to 25,000 feet. The Spitfire IX at most heights is slightly superior in speed to the FW 190 and the approximate differences in speeds at various heights are as follows:

At 2,000 ft the FW 190 is 7-8 mph faster than the Spitfire IX

At 5,000 ft the FW 190 and Spitfire IX are approximately the same

At 8,000 ft the Spitfire IX is 8 mph faster than the FW 190

At 15,000 ft the Spitfire IX is 5 mph faster than the FW 190

At 18,000 ft the FW 190 is 3 mph faster than the Spitfire IX

At 21,000 ft the FW 190 and Spitfire IX are approximately the same

At 25,000 ft the Spitfire IX is 5-7 mph faster than the FW 190

### Climb

During comparative climbs at various heights up to 23,000 feet, with both aircraft flying under maximum continuous climbing conditions, little difference was found between the two aircraft although on the whole the Spitfire IX was slightly better. Above 22,000 feet the climb of the FW 190 is falling off rapidly, whereas the climb of the Spitfire IX is increasing. When both aircraft were flying at high cruising speed and were pulled up into a climb from level flight, the FW 190 had a slight advantage in the initial stages of the climb due to its better acceleration. This superiority was slightly increased when both aircraft were pulled up into the climb from a dive.

It must be appreciated that the differences between the two aircraft are only slight and that in actual combat the advantage in climb will be with the aircraft that has the initiative.

### Dive

The FW 190 is faster than the Spitfire IX in a dive, particularly during the initial stage. This superiority is not as marked as with a Spitfire VB.

### Manoeuvrability

The FW 190 is more manoeuvrable than the Spitfire IX except in turning circles, when it is out-turned without difficulty.

The superior rate of roll of the FW 190 enabled it to avoid the Spitfire IX if attacked when in a turn, by flicking over into a diving turn in the opposite direction and, as with the Spitfire VB, the Spitfire IX had great difficulty in following this manoeuvre. It would have been easier for the Spitfire IX to follow the FW 190 in the diving turn if its engine had been fitted with a negative G carburettor, as this type of engine with ordinary carburettor cuts out very easily.\*

The Spitfire IX's worst heights for fighting the FW 190 were between 18,000 and 22,000 feet and below 3,000 feet. At these heights the FW 190 is a little faster.

Both aircraft 'bounced' one another in order to ascertain the best evasive tactics to adopt. The Spitfire IX could not be caught when 'bounced' if it was cruising at high speed and saw the FW 190 when well out of range. When the Spitfire IX was cruising at low speed its inferiority in acceleration gave the FW 190 a reasonable chance of catching it up and the same applied if the position is reversed and the FW 190 was 'bounced' by the Spitfire IX, except that overtaking took a little longer.

The initial acceleration of the FW 190 is better than the Spitfire IX under all conditions of flight, except in level flight at such altitudes where the Spitfire has a speed advantage and then, provided the Spitfire is cruising at high speed, there is little to choose between the acceleration of the two aircraft.

The general impression gained by the pilots taking part in the trials is that the Spitfire IX compares favourably with the FW 190 and that provided the Spitfire has the initiative, it has undoubtedly a good chance of shooting it down.

\*The great majority of Spitfire IXs were fitted with negative G carburettors. The aircraft in the trial would appear to be one of the early conversions, with an old-type float carburettor.

# Appendix D

## SPITFIRE LF IX   JL 165,
## RUNNING AT +25 POUNDS BOOST
## USING 150 OCTANE FUEL

Figures taken from the trials report of this aircraft, tested at Boscombe Down early in 1944. The aircraft was fitted with a Merlin 66 engine with a Stromberg pressure carburettor, using 150 octane fuel which allowed it to run at +25 pounds boost for periods not exceeding 5 minutes. The aircraft was optimised for low altitude operations, with its full throttle altitudes at 2,800 feet in MS gear and 13,800 feet in FS gear; its state was as follows:

Standard wing tips
Two 20 mm guns with sealed muzzles
Two 20 mm gun stubs with hemispherical fairings
Four .303" Browning guns, ports and ejection chutes sealed
Internal laminated glass windscreen
Circular rear view mirror with hemispherical fairing
Multi-ejector exhaust mainfolds
Aerial mast
Tropical pattern air intake without gauze, but with blanking plate installed; no ice guard fitted to intake
Four-bladed Rotol propeller, 10 ft 9 in diameter

**Weight:** Fully loaded weight, 7,400 pounds
Wing loading when fully loaded, 30.6 pounds per square foot

**Performance:**

| Height feet | Top Speed mph | Time to Climb mins | Rate of Climb ft/min |
|---|---|---|---|
| 2,000 | 360 | 0 m 25 s | 4,725 |
| 4,000 | 364 | 0 m 50 s | 4,730 |
| 6,000 | 364 | 1 m 15 s | 4,735 |
| 10,000 | 370 | 2 m 6 s | 4,745 |
| 13,800 | 389 | | 4,350 |
| 20,000 | 388 | 4 m 30 s | 3,450 |
| 30,000 | 380 | 8 m 17 s | 1,950 |

### Author's Comments

Using 150 octane fuel and +25 pounds boost, the Spitfire LF IX was about 30 mph faster and had a rate of climb about 950 ft/min better, than a similar aircraft using 100 octane fuel and +18 pounds boost, at low altitudes. When running at full power at the higher boost rating, however, fuel consumption was almost one quarter greater.

The improvement in low altitude performance conferred by the 150 octane fuel would be put to good use in the summer of 1944, when it would enable Spitfire LF IXs to intercept V.1 flying bombs coming in at low altitude.

# Appendix E

## SPITFIRE HF IX   BS 310

Figures taken from the trials report of this aircraft, tested at Boscombe Down early in 1944. This aircraft was fitted with a Merlin 70 engine optimised for high altitude operations, with its full throttle altitudes at 14,600 feet in MS gear and 25,400 feet in FS gear; its state was as follows:
Standard wing tips
Two 20 mm guns with sealed muzzles, ejection chutes open
Two 20 mm gun stubs with hemispherical fairings
Four .303" Browning guns, muzzles sealed, ejection chutes open
Rectangular rear view mirror without fairing
Balloon type hood
Multi-ejector exhaust manifolds
Aerial mast
Temperate air intake
Rudder with enlarged area
**Weight:** Fully loaded weight 7,320 pounds
Wing loading when fully loaded, 30 pounds per square foot

**Performance:**

| Height feet | Top Speed mph | Time to Climb mins | Rate of Climb ft/min |
|---|---|---|---|
| 6,000 | 353 | 1 m 24 s | 4,400 |
| 12,000 | 378 | | 4,470 |
| 14,600 | 388 | | |
| 18,000 | 388 | 4 m 18 s | 3,430 |
| 22,700 | | 5 m 33 s | 3,400 |
| 25,400 | 405 | | |
| 30,000 | 399 | 8 m 18 s | 2,240 |
| 36,000 | | 11 m 48 s | 1,270 |
| 40,000 | | 16 m 15 s | 610 |

Service ceiling (estimated)                              43,100 feet

# 13.

# VARIATIONS ON A THEME: THE MARKS VII AND VIII

Like the Mark VI, the Spitfire VII featured a pressurised cabin and initial production versions were fitted with extended span wings. But in many respects the Mark VII differed from its predecessor. It was fitted with the Merlin 61, or later variants of it, and had rectangular section radiators under each wing. Moreover the airframe of the Mark VII was considerably strengthened compared with that of previous variants and was fully stressed to take the more powerful engine. A 14 gallon fuel tank was fitted in the leading edge of each wing, the tail wheel was made retractable, and on later production aircraft the 'Lobelle' type hood was fitted which slid open and closed like that of the non-pressurised versions of the Spitfire (a great improvement over the 'clamp on' hood fitted to the Mark VI). On the Mark VII and later versions featuring its strengthened wing, the ailerons were reduced in span by 8½ inches, to 6 ft 3 in. This was to reduce the length of aileron outboard of the outer hinges, to make aileron flutter less likely (there had been a few cases of Mark Is, IIs and Vs breaking up in the air during high speed dives, and aileron flutter was considered a possible cause).

The first Spitfire VII left the Supermarine production line in August 1942, but initially the rate of production was low and it was April 1943 before the monthly rate exceeded four aircraft. As late as May 1943 No 124 Squadron, the sole unit then operating the Mark VII, had available only seven Spitfires of this type. Moreover the performance of the Spitfire VII was found to be disappointing compared with that of the specially lightened Mark IXs used for high altitude interceptions, described in the previous chapter. To improve performance No 124 Squadron's Mark VIIs were operated with the armour and cannon removed, and an armament of only four machine guns.

During the summer of 1942 a limited trial was flown at Boscombe Down using Mark VII AB 450; the results of this trial are given in Appendix A.

Altogether some 140 Spitfire VIIs were built by the Supermarine factories before this variant was phased out of production early in 1944. One the last to be built, MD 176, was tested with a Merlin 71 engine in the summer of 1944 and demonstrated a superb high altitude performance; the figures are given in Appendix B. But by the time the Mark VII had shown what it could really do, the threat of the German high altitude attacks had ended and the need for a special version of the Spitfire to combat them had passed. Only six RAF squadrons received the Spitfire VII, and for the most part it was operated as a normal fighter providing top cover for other units (in this role the fighter carried its full armour and armament).

The Spitfire VIII was an adaptation of the Mark VII, with the same stronger airframe, retractable tail wheel and wing leading edge tanks of the latter, but without the pressurised cabin. The Mark VIII was to have been the main production version with the Merlin 61 series of engines, but it was November 1942 before the first Spitfires of this type emerged from the Supermarine factories. The Mark VIII eventually replaced the Mark IX in production at Supermarine, though it was June 1943 before monthly production of the former exceeded 50 and that of the latter was phased out.

Some early production Mark VIIIs were delivered with extended-span wings, but the majority of aircraft of this version had normal-span wings. The Mark VIII was fitted with the Type C wing and armament, and later production aircraft were fitted with the broad-chord and pointed rudder as fitted to later versions of the Mark IX. Like the Mark IX, the Mark VIII appeared in low altitude and high altitude versions, powered respectively by the Merlin 66 and Merlin 70 engines; in each case performance was approximately the same as that of the Mark IXs with these engines.

The Spitfire VIII was a beautiful aircraft to fly, and many pilots remember this version with affection. Jeffrey Quill commented:

When I am asked which mark of Spitfire I consider the best from the pure flying point of view, I usually reply 'The Mark VIII with standard wing tips.' I *hated* the extended wing tips on the Mark VIII and did everything I could to get rid of them. Originally all Mark VIIIs had the long wing tips until I succeeded in getting them reverted to standard. They were of no practical value to the Mark VIII and simply reduced the aileron response and the rate of roll. On the Marks VI and VII, being essentially for high altitude operations, the extended tips were of value.

In the summer of 1943 a Mark VIII, JF 299, was the first Spitfire to be fitted with a cut-back rear fuselage and 'tear-drop' canopy. The Air Fighting Development Unit was enthusiastic about the new type of canopy, though it also gave some suggestions for improving it further; the report on their trial is given in Appendix C.

Another interesting modification considered for the Mark VIII was to fit a Malinowski trailer to enable it to carry additional fuel to extend its range for delivery flights. This scheme never passed beyond the initial proposal stage, however.

Altogether 1,658 Spitfire VIIIs were built, all of them at the Supermarine plants. Thirty squadrons received this version and it was used in large numbers in the Mediterranean and Far Eastern theatres of operation.

**187.** The Spitfire VII was a pressurised version, externally similar to the Mark VI but with a Merlin 61 engine and radiators similar to the Mark IX and a retractable tail wheel. *(Smithsonian)*

**188.** Internal view of the cockpit of an early production Mark VII, fitted with a non-sliding canopy and clear vision panel fitted to the windscreen. Note the ducting along the top of the instrument panel, which carried in the pressurised air. *(Smithsonian)*

**189.** Spitfire HF VIII of No 417 (Canadian) Squadron, based at Canne in Italy in January 1944. This aircraft was fitted with extended span wing tips and the revised tropical filter. *(Public Archives of Canada)*

**190.** A Mark VIII of No 548 Squadron based at Darwin, Australia in the summer of 1945, fitted with standard wing tips. *(Glaser)*

**191** and **192.** JF 299, a Spitfire VIII, was the first aircraft of this type to have a cut back rear fuselage and 'tear-drop' hood fitted. Air Fighting Development Unit pilots reported enthusiastically on this innovation and, with some improvements, it was fitted to most Spitfires built after the early spring of 1945.

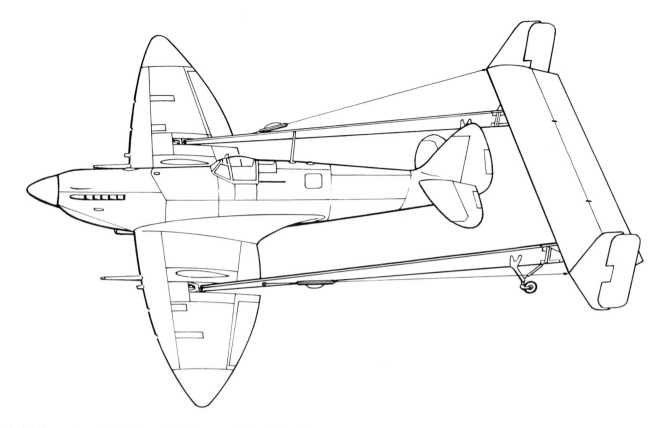

Artist's impression of the Malinowski Trailer towed fuel tank fitted to a
Spitfire VIII. This method was considered at one time as a means of
increasing the fighter's ferry range.

# Appendix A

## SPITFIRE VII   AB 450

Figures taken from the trials report of this aircraft, the first prototype Mark VII modified from a Mark V, tested at Boscombe Down in August 1942. This aircraft was fitted with a Merlin 61 engine, with full throttle altitudes of 16,000 feet in MS gear and 27,500 feet in FS gear. Unfortunately the aircraft was required by Rolls-Royce for further work before the full trial could be completed and this aircraft was tested only in MS gear; had the full FS gear trial been completed it would certainly have revealed a better performance at high altitude. At the time of the trial the state of the aircraft was as follows:

Universal wings with extended tips
Two 20 mm cannon and four .303-in machine guns; muzzles
    sealed, ejection chutes open
Two 20 mm gun stubs with hemispherical fairings
Aerial mast for VHF
No IFF
Retractable tail wheel
Pressurised cabin, internal laminated glass windscreen
Normal span ailerons
Non-sliding canopy, as fitted to Mark VI
Lead ballast in wings to represent leading edge fuel tanks
    which were not fitted
Four bladed propeller, 10 ft 9 in in diameter

**Dimensions:** span 40 ft 2 in, length 30 ft 0 in
**Weights:** Fully loaded weight, 8,000 pounds
Wing loading when fully loaded, 32 pounds per square foot

**Performance:**

| Height feet | Top Speed mph (true) | Time to Climb mins | Rate of Climb ft/min |
|---|---|---|---|
| 4,000 | 340 | 1 m 26 s | 2,710 |
| 10,000 | 362 | 3 m 43 s | 2,500 |
| 14,000 | 379 | 5 m 22 s | 2,350 |
| 16,200 | 390 | | |
| 20,000 | 388 | 8 m 14 s | 1,930 |
| 26,000 | 376 | 11 m 30 s | 1,660 |
| 32,000 | | 15 m 52 s | 1,430 |
| 38,000 | | 22 m 4 s | 520 |

Service ceiling                                    39,600 feet

**Author's Comments**

As has been said, the trial of this aircraft was not completed; had it been the performance above 20,000 feet would have been shown to be considerably better. When used for operations at extreme altitudes by the RAF, Mark VIIs had their cannon, wing tanks and armour removed, thereby bringing down the take-off weight to 7,062 pounds or 938 pounds less than that of AB 450; in this loading configuration Mark VIIs were flown up to 44,000 feet and reached speeds of around 400 mph at 40,000 feet.

# Appendix B

## SPITFIRE VII   MD 176

Figures taken from the trials report of this aircraft, tested at Boscombe Down in the summer of 1944. This aircraft was fitted experimentally with a Merlin 71 engine which gave it an improved high altitude performance compared with normal production Mark VIIs. At the time of the trial the state of the aircraft was as follows:

Two 20 mm cannon and four .303-in machine guns; muzzles
    sealed, ejector chutes open
Two 20 mm gun stubs with hemispherical fairings
Lobelle sliding hood
Broad chord and pointed rudder
Pressurised cabin, blower intake on starboard side of nose
Internal laminated glass windscreen
Circular rear view mirror, hemispherical fairing
Aerial mast for VHF
IFF aerial under starboard wing
Beam approach aerial under fuselage
Retractable tail wheel
No snow guards fitted to intakes
Four bladed propeller, 10 ft 9 in diameter
**Weights:** Fully loaded weight 7,990 pounds

**Performance:**

| Height feet | Top Speed mph (true) | Time to Climb mins | Rate of Climb ft/min |
|---|---|---|---|
| 10,000 | 373 | 2 m 30 s | 3,930 |
| 16,200 | 400 | | |
| 20,000 | 400 | 5 m 24 s | 2,920 |
| 26,000 | 412 | 7 m 24 s | 2,900 |
| 29,400 | 424 | | |
| 34,000 | 420 | 10 m 54 s | 1,760 |
| 40,000 | 409 | 15 m 30 s | 930 |
| 44,000 | 376 | 22 m 12 s | 300 |

Service ceiling                                    45,100 feet

**Author's Comments**

Although the report on this trial went into considerable detail, it omitted to state whether this aircraft was fitted with normal span or extended span wings.

# Appendix C

## SPITFIRE VIII   JF 299 WITH TEAR-DROP CANOPY

The account below is taken from the report of the trial of Spitfire VIII JF 299 fitted with a cut-back rear fuselage and a tear-drop canopy, flown by the Air Fighting Development Unit at Wittering in August 1943.

\*   \*   \*

### Description

#### Windscreen

This is made up of a sheet of bullet-proof glass set behind a curved windscreen of perspex. The side panels which are smaller than standard are of bullet-proof glass and the aft frames of these panels are raked further forward than on the standard Spitfire.

#### Sliding Hood

This is an entirely new design and consists of a long moulded perspex hood giving direct vision to the rear. It is a trifle wider than the old type flat hood but not so wide as a balloon hood. The hood is manipulated in a similar fashion to the standard hoods. Armour protection is provided as before.

### Flying Trials

#### General

The aircraft was flown by pilots of this Unit and the Naval Air Fighting Development Unit, also by four pilots from other Fighter Command Units, whose comments and criticisms are summarised below.

#### Rearward View

This is an enormous improvement over the standard Spitfire rear view. The pilot can see quite easily round to his fin and past it, almost to the further edge of the tailplane, ie if he looks over his left shoulder he can practically see to the starboard tip of the tail. By banking the aircraft slightly during weaving action, the downward view to the rear is opened up well. The whole field of search is increased very appreciably.

#### Forward View

In general, this is now better than on the standard Spitfire, since the original small panel at the top to which the rear view mirror was mounted has been removed and a longer piece of bullet proof glass runs right up to the top of the hood. There are, however, the following criticisms:

a. Slight reflections are picked up by the curved windscreen in a similar fashion to those described in Report No 78 [on the curved windscreen fitted to a Spitfire V], but now that the cowlings have been treated with a matt black dope forward of the windscreen and between the curved screen and the bullet proof screen, these have been cut down to a minimum and are considered acceptable. Slight distortion is found when looking through this screen.

b. The bullet proof side panels are now smaller than those on previous Spitfires with the result that the pilot has to be leaning well forward to make full use of them and the landing view is not as good as normal.

c. The frames supporting the rear part of the bullet-proof side panels are thought to be unnecessarily wide; together with frames of the sliding hood when closed they form quite a large obstruction. The pilot can see round them by moving his head, but he is always conscious of them since they are more in his line of vision than previously.

#### Reflections

Besides those mentioned in the previous paragraph, reflections off the top of the front bullet proof glass and off the hood catches and handle appear in the top of the sliding hood at its front end. Matt black paint on the frame of the bullet proof glass causes this almost to disappear.

#### Misting and Icing-up

Weather during the trials was such that very little opportunity for trials of misting-up were possible. On one occasion after a flight of about ½ hour at 35,000 feet, the aircraft was dived quickly with the result that both side panels froze on passing through a thin layer of cloud and remained covered with frost for approximately 15 minutes. The centre panel and front perspex, however, remained free of misting or icing. It is feared that in winter conditions the front screen will also suffer from misting and that some kind of heating and/or drying installation will be necessary.

#### Reflector Sight

The sight has been raised almost 3 inches to improve the view for deflection shooting. This is considered a great benefit and full use of it can be made with the new hood and screen. The view over the nose cowling is almost equal to that from the Spitfire XII's cockpit. The reflector glass was removed from the GM 2 sight by this Unit and an excellent image was thrown direct on to to the bullet proof glass.

#### Operation of the Hood

This is far from satisfactory, both hands are usually necessary either for opening or closing and at most speeds the hood jams about 5 inches from the closed position, when use of both elbows has to be resorted to for opening. At speeds above 200 mph the hood tends to stick solid when it had been opened about 5 inches and could not be forced open without great difficulty. Below 170 mph the same sticking occurred but it could be freed more easily. It is thought that manipulation by a handle on the port side of the cockpit will be required in service.

#### Draught

With the hood opened there is considerably more draught than in the standard Spitfire.

#### Rear View Mirror

Owing to the very great improvement in all-round search view, particularly to the rear, the omission of the rear view mirror is not considered to be of any disadvantage to pilots flying with this new hood.

#### Armour Plate

This is at present the same as fitted to the standard Spitfire, and there is room for improvement. The armour is a little too far behind the pilot's head when he is in the normal sitting position, but it has been found that if it is moved forward and is retained the same size, some of the newly acquired view is lost. It is considered that the armour plating could profitably be made higher because pilots look round the armour plating not over it, and also the possibility of fitting full width armour glass behind the pilot's head could be investigated.

#### Comparison with the Tempest

An opportunity was taken of comparing this new installation with that now fitted to the Tempest and the following points were noted:

(i) Rear view. The Tempest hood is ballooned and this gives much better rear vision than the narrow hood on the Spitfire. There is considerably more head freedom in the Tempest, whereas in the Spitfire the pilot has to hold his chin well in when turning round to look behind, to avoid catching his oxygen mask on the side of the hood.

Furthermore, goggles worn lifted up on the head are bound to touch the hood when looking aft and this has already caused serious scratches to the particular hood under trial within the few days of flying. The Tempest armour plate is further away from the pilot's head than in the Spitfire, but is a slightly better shape as it goes as high as possible.

(ii) Forward View. The Tempest is again preferable as the frames to hold the centre bullet proof glass are slightly inclined inwards and therefore the smallest possible obstruction is presented to the pilot's view. There is no curved front windscreen and the front bullet proof panel is fairly narrow, with the result that the side panels are set at a wider angle than in the Spitfire, making them of more use to the pilot for search and landing. The aft frames of the side windows are set at a better angle and are narrower than those of the Spitfire.

## Maintenance

All pilots have commented on the difficulty that will be experienced in getting the average pilot and ground crew to keep the front of the bullet proof glass clean, as this can only be done with a rag on the end of a stick and in service is likely to be overlooked.

## Conclusions

### Sliding Hood

The all-round rearward view has been enormously improved. This type of hood should be made standard, but the following suggested modifications will effect still greater improvement:

(i) The hood needs to be ballooned—the cockpit is now too cramped, and the hood is easily scratched by the pilot's head gear.

(ii) A handle is needed for easy manipulation.

(iii) The armour plate should be increased in height or possibly replaced by bullet proof glass.

### Windscreen

The general forward view is also improved over the standard Spitfire, but attention to the following points is thought necessary:

(i) The side panels are too small to be really useful. They might also be set at a wider angle—at the expense of narrowing the centre panel—with good effect.

(ii) The curved screen in front of the centre bullet proof glass should be removed. It is viewed with suspicion as it may easily mist up in winter conditions and certainly makes cleaning the front of the bullet proof glass difficult. In spite of a matt black finish to the top cowlings, slight reflections are still found.

(iii) The frames between the centre panel and the side panels need to be inclined inwards to present the pilot with the least possible obstruction.

(iv) The frames on the aft sides of the side panels must be made smaller and preferably set more upright so as to increase the size of the side panels and cause less of an obstruction to the view.

(v) The side panels freeze up seriously.

### Reflector Sight

This has been raised 3 inches and can be reflected direct on to the screen. The shooting view is comparable to that of the Spitfire XII.

# 14.

# SECOND GENERATION SPIES: THE MARKS X, XI AND XIII

Following the huge improvement in performance conferred on the fighter versions of the Spitfire by the installation of the Merlin 61 series of engines, it was only a matter of time before specialised reconnaissance versions were produced with this engine also. As has been said, such was the haste to get these into operation that fifteen Mark IX fighters were converted into PR IXs at Benson by the removal of the armament and the installation of two vertical cameras behind the pilot.

The Mark XI, the first reconnaissance version of the Spitfire to go into production with the Merlin 61, was unarmed and modified to carry 66½ gallons of fuel in the leading edge of each wing as in the case of the PR Mark IV (alias PR D), and it had the enlarged oil tank under the nose which characterised the PR Type F. The Mark XI also had a retractable tail wheel as in the case of the Marks VII and VIII, but reverted to the normal span ailerons as fitted to the Mark IX; the camera installation, comprising two vertical cameras and sometimes an oblique as well, was installed in the rear fuselage behind the cockpit.

The first Mark XIs came off the Supermarine production line in November 1942 and this version soon replaced the Mark IV in the photographic reconnaissance squadrons. In the summer of 1943 a Spitfire XI, MB 789, underwent performance testing at Boscombe Down and the figures are given at Appendix A.

When used for photographing battlefield targets, the tactical reconnaissance squadrons working for the army found their long focal length cameras ineffective if cloud forced them to photograph targets at medium altitudes; the 'footprint' photographed on the ground was so small that targets were likely to be missed altogether. So tactical reconnaissance Mark XIs were fitted with a pair of additional F.8 cameras with 5-in focal length lenses, one under each wing in a small blister fairing. These wing cameras pointed downwards played out at an angle of 10° and were used to photograph targets from medium and low altitudes.

Because the Spitfire had the highest limiting Mach No of any aircraft during the mid-war period, and airframes of the reconnaissance versions were cleaner than those of fighters, a Mark XI was chosen for the series of high speed diving trials conducted at Farnborough in the spring of 1944 to explore handling as aircraft dived at speeds close to the sound barrier. During one of these dives, in EN 409 on 27 April, Squadron Leader 'Marty' Martindale reached a true airspeed of 606 mph and .89 Mach; then he came close to disaster. His report on the incident was a matter-of-fact account of cool thinking in the face of death that can have few equals. He had taken the Spitfire up to 40,500 feet and 340 mph, then bunted gently over into his 45° dive. Once he was established in the dive the speed built up rapidly:

I glanced at the altimeter when I was down to 32,000 feet and saw it spinning merrily. The dive by this time was very steep and I was pulling back on the stick in the usual way due to the change of trim at the shock stall.

I glanced at the altimeter again and saw it drop from 28,000 to 27,000 and knew I was past the highest speed. I began to think of easing out of the dive when there was a fearful explosion and the aircraft became enveloped in white smoke. I incorrectly assumed that a structural failure had occurred as I knew this to be a danger. The aircraft shook from end to end. I knew I could not bail out at such speed so I sat still. The aircraft was doing nothing startling. The screen and hood were now quite black and I could see nothing. Automatically I eased the stick back. After a time I discovered by looking backwards through a chink in the oil film that I was climbing. The airspeed was obviously falling as the noises were dying down. I realised instantly that I could now bail out and opened the hood. It had not jammed.

I then realised that the aircraft was under partial control at least and so switched off the camera [the recording camera photographing the instruments] which had been winking away all this time. I began to think I might be able to get the aircraft down and so save the film and all the special apparatus. I still did not know what had happened as I could not see through the windscreen.

I pointed the aircraft towards base and called up on the radio. It was working. I tried to look round the screen but my goggles were whipped away. After a time the screen cleared a little. The engine clearly was not going and I could see no propeller. Bits of engine were sticking out and the engine seemed to have shifted sideways . . . .

With considerable skill Martindale glided the 20 miles back to Farnborough and made a wheels down landing. Only when he was out of the aircraft did he see the full extent of the damage: the entire propeller and reduction gear had broken away due to a failure of the reduction gear, one of the connecting rods had pushed its way out of the crank case and a main engine bearer had buckled.

193. A Spitfire PR XI rolls on to its back to show the two slightly offset windows cut in the rear fuselage for the split-pair of vertical cameras. The bulges in front of the radiators were fairings over the pumps which forced fuel from the wing tanks up to the engine. *(IWM)*

194. A PR XI of the US 7th Photo Group, based at Mount Farm near Oxford as part of the 8th Air Force, seen retracting its undercarriage immediately after take-off. *(USAF)*

The following month, whilst flying a replacement Spitfire XI on the same project, Martindale was almost at 600 mph when the supercharger burst and the engine caught fire. Again he tried to land the aircraft, but this time luck was against him. The airfield at Farnborough was shrouded in cloud and he was forced to attempt a dead-stick landing in open fields nearby. Too late he saw a line of high tension cables in his path, and as he swerved to avoid them the Spitfire crashed into a wood. Martindale managed to scramble out of the burning aircraft then, in spite of spinal injuries, he returned and retrieved the precious recording camera. For his bravery Martindale was later awarded the Air Force Cross.

Altogether 471 Spitfire XIs were built or converted on the Supermarine production line from Mark IX fighters. Production continued well into 1944, before this version was phased out in favour of the Mark 19.

**195.** Squadron Leader 'Marty' Martindale's Spitfire XI pictured on the ground at Farnborough following his epic flight on 27 April 1944, when the propeller came adrift when the aircraft was diving at a true airspeed of around 600 mph. *(Crown Copyright)*

The system of allocating mark numbers to the Spitfires was anything but methodical, and the PR Mark X followed the Mark XI into production. The two versions were essentially similar, except that the former was fitted with a pressurised cabin and had a Lobelle sliding hood; the two versions had a similar performance. In the event only sixteen Spitfire Xs were built by Supermarine, and this version saw limited operational use as a high altitude reconnaissance aircraft from May 1944, by Nos 541 and 542 Squadrons.

The third of the new photographic reconnaissance Spitfire variants was the Mark XIII, an improvement on the PR Type G with the same camera fit, but powered by the special low-altitude-rated Merlin 32 engine. The PR XIII carried a deterrent armament of four .303-in Browning guns. The first prototype Mark XIII was tested at Boscombe Down in March 1943, and the performance figures are given at Appendix B.

A total of 26 Spitfire XIIIs were converted, from Mark II, V and PR Type G versions, and these saw service with Nos 4, 400, 541 and 542 Squadrons. This type was used during the low level reconnaissance effort to photograph the French beaches, during the preparations for the Normandy invasion.

195

**196.** After the war the Royal Norwegian Air Force bought three PR XIs, which were operated by No 1 Photographic Reconnaissance Wing based at Gardermoen. Under the wing of the aircraft on the left can be seen the bulge and window for the short focal length F.8 camera used for medium altitude photography. *(USAF)*

**197.** This Spitfire XI was purchased in 1947 for aerial survey and mapping work in Argentina and received the civil registration LV-NMZ. In addition to the normal fuselage and wing tanks, plus a 170 gallon ferry tank, this aircraft was specially fitted with two further 20 gallon tanks in the wings; its total fuel load was thus 428 gallons, the greatest amount ever carried by a Spitfire. In the spring of that year Captain Jamie Storey took the aircraft to Argentina in several stages the longest of which, across the South Atlantic from Dakar in Senegal to Natal in Brazil, about 1,850 miles (a distance equivalent to that from London to well beyond Moscow), he made on 5 May. The eight-hour flight was the longest ever achieved in a Spitfire. *(via Oughton)*

198

**198.** Externally similar to the Spitfire PR XI, the PR X which entered service in the spring of 1944 was fitted with a pressurised cabin — betrayed by the cabin air intake on the starboard side of the engine cowling and the thicker runners holding down the 'Lobelle' sliding canopy. *(IWM)*

**199.** The Spitfire PR XIII was essentially similar to the earlier PR VII (ex PR Type 'G'), but was fitted with the Merlin 32 engine which developed greater power at low altitude and it carried an armament of only four machine guns.

199

# Appendix A

## SPITFIRE PR XI   MB 789

Figures taken from the trials report of this aircraft, one of the early production Mark XIs, tested at Boscombe Down in August 1943. This aircraft was powered by the Merlin 63 engine, a slightly strengthened version of the Merlin 61. Since this aircraft was to be used for long range photographic reconnaissance rather than air fighting, the trial concentrated on measuring the maximum speed and maximum cruising speeds and did not measure the maximum rates of climb. The maximum speed was measured at 3,000 rpm and at +18 pounds boost up to full throttle altitude, and could be used for a maximum of 5 minutes; maximum cruising speed was measured at 2,650 rpm at +7 pounds boost up to full throttle altitude and could be held indefinitely. At the time of the trial the state of the aircraft was as follows:

Standard span wing
Leading edge fuel tanks, no armament
Total fuel load 216 gallons
Enlarged oil tank under nose
Temperate carburettor air intake, no ice guard
Rounded windscreen, no laminated glass panel
Balloon type hood with internal rear view mirror on each side
Aerial mast for VHF
Retractable tail wheel
Early type curved rudder

Two holes cut in the underside of the fuselage behind the cockpit, and windows fitted, for cameras; two F.24 cameras fitted

**Dimensions:** span 36 ft 10 in, length 30 ft 0 in
**Weight:** fully loaded 8,040 pounds
Wing loading when fully loaded, 33 pounds per square foot
**Performance:**

| Height feet | Top Speed mph (5 mins max) | Max. Continuous Cruising Speed mph |
|---|---|---|
| 24,000 | 417 | 369 |
| 28,000 | 412 | 385 |
| 32,000 | 405 | 395 |
| 38,000 | 387 | 378 |

### Author's Comments

The report made no mention of a maximum operating altitude for the Mark XI. During operational sorties, however, the aircraft was often taken in slow cruise climbs to altitudes above 40,000 feet, which was beyond the physiological limits of the pilot for any length of time without a pressurised cabin.

# Appendix B

## SPITFIRE PR XIII   L 1004

Figures taken from the trials report of the first prototype of this version, which had begun life as a Mark I, been converted into a Mark V, then into a Mark XIII, tested at Boscombe Down in March 1943. The aircraft was fitted with a Merlin 32 engine optimised for low altitude operation, with a full throttle height of 5,400 feet. At the time of the trial the state of the aircraft was as follows:

Standard type wing
Four .303-in Browning guns, with muzzles and ejection chutes sealed
Balloon type hood with external laminated glass windscreen
Triple ejector exhausts
Same fuel tankage as the Mark I fighter
Aerial mast for VHF
No IFF aerials
External rear view mirror with hemispherical fairing
Three-bladed propeller, 10 ft 9 in diameter
Two holes cut in the underside of the fuselage behind the cockpit and one on the port side behind the cockpit, and

windows fitted, for cameras. Two F.24 vertical cameras, and one F.24 oblique camera, fitted

**Dimensions:** span 36 ft 10 in, length 29 ft 11 in
**Weight:** fully loaded 6,355 pounds
Wing loading when fully loaded, 26 pounds per square foot
**Performance:**

| Height feet | Top Speed mph | Time to Climb mins | Rate of Climb ft-min |
|---|---|---|---|
| 2,000 | 332 | 0 m 24 s | 4,920 |
| 5,400 | 349 | | |
| 10,000 | 345½ | 2 m 15 s | 3,690 |
| 18,000 | 338 | 4 m 54 s | 2,430 |
| 24,000 | 327 | 7 m 57 s | 1,610 |
| 34,000 | | 19 m 12 s | 430 |

Service ceiling (estimated)                    37,000 feet

# 15.

# THE FIRST GRIFFON SPITFIRES: THE MARKS IV, XII AND 20

Although the Merlin engine had been a considerable success, and proved able to accept considerable development, the designers at Rolls-Royce knew well that there were limits to the amount of power that could be squeezed out of a 27 litre engine. Accordingly, shortly after the outbreak of war, work had begun on the development of a new engine based on the Merlin, also with 12 cylinders but with a capacity of 36.7 litres: the Griffon. Though initially the Griffon gave an output of 1,700 horsepower, by some clever juggling the designers managed to keep its frontal area within 6 per cent, its length within 3 inches and its weight within 600 pounds of those of the Merlin. So, with a stronger engine mounting and the repositioning of the oil tank, the Spitfire could accept the new and more powerful engine.

**200.** DP 845, the prototype Griffon Spitfire, seen in its early form as a Mark IV with a mock-up six 20 mm cannon armament installation and guides for the slotted flaps. *(Vickers)*

**201.** DP 845 in the spring or summer of 1942, after re-designation as a Mark XII. *(Vickers)*

**202.** DP 845 pictured in the autumn of 1942 during trials at Boscombe Down. For some reason, by that time the retractable tail wheel and doors had been removed and a fixed tailwheel substituted.

Early in 1941 an order was placed for two Griffon powered Spitfires, initially designated Mark IVs. To take the heavier engine a stronger main longeron was needed, running along the fuselage on either side back from the engine mounting. Jack Davis remembered the problems involved with this:

A dural longeron could not be made strong enough within the space allowed, so we had to make one out of steel. And what a game that was! To make the first we had to use about 50 small vices bolted along a bench one beside the next, to hold the steel while it was hammered from a channel section to a top-hat section in the complex double curvature required to conform with the shape of the fuselage. Later, for production Griffon Spitfires, we had a special hydraulic press to form the steel longerons; but those first hand-built ones were very difficult to make.

The first of the Griffon-powered Spitfire IVs, serial DP 845, made its maiden flight with Jeffrey Quill at the controls on 27 November 1941. The aircraft was powered by a single-stage supercharged Griffon IIB driving a four-bladed propeller, and the longer engine increased overall length to 30 feet 6 inches; it had normal span wings and, like the Mark III, a retractable tail wheel.

203

Although the Griffon would never run as smoothly as the Merlin, and initially there were some reliability problems, the extra power was greatly appreciated by pilots. Jeffrey Quill remembers the first Griffon Spitfire with affection: 'DP 845 was my favourite Spitfire. It had a wonderful performance at low altitude; it had a low full throttle height, and a lot of power on the deck.'

Initially it was intended that if the Mark IV went into production it would be able to carry an alternative armament of six 20 mm cannon, four 20 mm cannon, or two 20 mm cannon and four .303-in machine guns; and for a short time this version was fitted with a mock-up of the six-cannon installation. But DP 845 was soon converted back to the more conventional armament of two cannon and four machine guns.

**203.** A beautiful Charles Brown photograph of MB 882, a late production Mark XII, in her element low down. *(Charles Brown, copyright RAF Museum)*

**204.** Underneath view of MB 882, now carrying the markings of No 41 Squadron, showing off her clipped wings. The Mark XII was the only Griffon-powered Spitfire version with single-stage supercharging, and it retained the early-type oil cooler under the port wing. *(IWM)*

Not long after its maiden flight DP 845 was re-designated from a Mark IV to a Mark XX (the Mark IV designation was taken over by the PR Type D). Then this aircraft became the prototype Mark XII low altitude fighter; Jeffrey Quill noted his first flight in DP 845 redesignated as a Mark XII on 10 April 1942.

The second Griffon Spitfire, DP 851, flew for the first time on 8 August 1942 and Jeffrey Quill's logbook recorded it as a 'Mark 20'. Although the external shape of its wing was the same as that of previous Spitfires, internally its structure had been considerably revised to make it far stronger even than that of the Mark VII. Before the end of the year, however, this aircraft was converted to take the two-stage supercharged Griffon 61 engine and thus became the first prototype of the Mark 21; it will, therefore, be dealt with in a later chapter.

In its element, low down, DP 845 was one of the fastest fighters in the world in July 1942. Jeffrey Quill had great pleasure in demonstrating this fact, during a comparative speed trial with a Typhoon and a captured Focke-Wulf 190; as he later told the author:

In mid-1942 there was a lot of flap about the FW 190. Supermarine were told to take a Spitfire to Farnborough for a

low level speed trial against a Typhoon and the captured FW 190. Nobody had specified what sort of Spitfire was wanted but, having some idea of what was going on, I took DP 845. On 20 July we all took off from Farnborough and flew to a point near Odiham, where we moved into line abreast formation. On the command 'Go!' we all opened our throttles and accelerated towards Farnborough where an assortment of dignitaries had assembled to see which aircraft was the fastest. It was generally expected that the FW 190 would come in first, the Typhoon second, and the poor old Spitfire would come limping in some way behind the other two. Well, I won the race easily in DP 845, the Typhoon came second and the Focke-Wulf was third, which was absolutely the wrong result!

A few months later DP 845 was tested at Boscombe Down and the figures are given at Appendix A. At the time of this trial the aircraft still had normal span wings and, for some reason, the retractable tail wheel had been removed and a fixed one fitted in its place.

The Spitfire XII was built in limited numbers at Supermarine and the first production aircraft, essentially a Mark VC airframe with revised and strengthened engine bearers to take the Griffon, appeared in October 1942. In December the third production aircraft, EN 223, underwent tactical trials with the Air Fighting Development Unit at Duxford; the report on these trials is given at Appendix B. Apart from the initial production aircraft, EN 221, Spitfire XIIs were delivered with clipped wings; and the later production aircraft were fitted with Mark VIII type tail units with retractable tailwheels.

The first squadron to receive the Mark XII was No 41 at High Ercall in February 1943, followed shortly afterwards by No 91. No other squadrons equipped fully with this version and production ceased in September 1943, after 100 had been built.

Despite its superb low altitude performance, the Spitfire XII did not prove very successful in service. During fighter sweeps over occupied Europe its low altitude performance could be exploited only if enemy aircraft could be drawn down to fight, and the German pilots showed a marked reluctance to do this; higher up the Spitfire IX was a much better all round fighter. For a time Spitfire XIIs were used in an attempt to counter the occasional 'tip-and-run' attacks by FW 190 fighter-bombers on coastal targets in southern England but, in the absence of adequate radar warning of the approach of these high speed low flyers, successes were few and far between. Only at the very end of its service career, when it was used to counter the V.1 flying bombs launched against London in June, July and August 1944, did the Spitfire XII have the chance to shine and this version shot down a large number of flying bombs before it passed out of front-line service in September.

# Appendix A

## SPITFIRE XII   DP 845

Figures taken from the trials report of this aircraft, the prototype Mark XII, tested at Boscombe Down in September and October 1942. At the time of the trial the state of the aircraft was as follows:

Standard span wing
Griffon IIB engine, with individual ejector exhausts
Two 20 mm guns with sealed muzzles, ejector chutes open
Four .303-in Browning guns, muzzles and ejector chutes sealed
Two 20 mm gun stubs with hemispherical fairings
Internal laminated glass windscreen
Circular rear view mirror with hemispherical fairing
Fixed tail wheel
Aerial mast for VHF
Temperate carburettor air intake, no ice guard
Pointed-topped rudder
Four bladed propeller, 10 ft 5 in diameter
Special attention had been paid to the finish of this aircraft. It was flush rivetted throughout and filling had been applied at joints and edges of overlapping panels. The whole surface had been polished to give a smooth finish.

**Dimensions:** span 36 ft 10 in, length 30 ft 9 in
**Weight:** Fully loaded weight 7,415 pounds
Wing loading when fully loaded, 30.6 pounds per square foot

**Performance:**

| Height feet | Top Speed mph | Time to Climb mins | Rate of Climb ft/min |
|---|---|---|---|
| 2,000 | 355 | 0 m 33 s | 3,760 |
| 5,700 | 372 | | |
| 8,000 | 372 | 2 m 15 s | 3,130 |
| 14,000 | 379½ | 4 m 35 s | 2,760 |
| 17,800 | 397 | | |
| 24,000 | 392 | 8 m 45 s | 1,780 |

Service ceiling                                        38,200 feet

# Appendix B

## TACTICAL TRIAL: SPITFIRE XII   EN 223

The account below is taken from the report of the tactical trial of the third production Spitfire XII, EN 223, flown by the Air Fighting Development Unit at Duxford in December 1942.

\* \* \*

### Description

This aircraft is a standard Spitfire VC airframe modified to take a Griffon III engine in order to produce a high performance low altitude fighter. It differs otherwise from the VC in that the wing tips have been removed to improve manoeuvrability, the bulge over the cannon feed on the mainplane is much smaller, the rudder and trimming tabs are larger, and the engine cowlings and spinner differ considerably. It is fitted with facilities for beam approach and about the first seven, including the aircraft on trial, have the oil tank behind the pilot. This is not acceptable operationally and subsequent aircraft will have the oil tank mounted immediately aft of the fireproof bulkhead. The fuel capacity is retained at 85 gallons, and jettisonable tanks can be used if required. The first six aircraft, again including EN 223, have dural propellers, the remainder will have wooden ones. The external finish of EN 223 was far better than has been seen on standard production Spitfire Vs and IXs.

The Griffon III engine has a two speed manually operated supercharger, giving full throttle heights at 6,000 feet and 18,000 feet. It is fitted with a standard Claude Hobson carburettor and cuts fairly easily under negative acceleration forces. In the early models .45 reduction gear is fitted; later aircraft will have .511 reduction gear which will improve the rate of climb, especially at low altitude. The Coffman [cartridge] method of starting is employed. No automatic radiator shutter is at present fitted.

### Tactical

### General

The aircraft was flown throughout the trials with wings clipped and full armament, ie 2 × 20 mm cannon and 4 × .303 in Browning guns. All guns were loaded with full ammunition. IFF was carried and one oxygen bottle. The all-up weight for the trials was about 7,400 lbs. With wooden propeller and certain other equipment such as IFF removed, the rate of climb and handling can be further improved.

### Flying Characteristics

This aircraft has the normal Spitfire feel about it, but the take-off needs care as the large amount of torque causes it to swing away to the right, not to the left as usual, and if the pilot is slow in reacting the swing is so strong that he will not be able to correct even with full left rudder. This is being considerably improved by fining off the fine pitch stop on the propeller and so enabling full rpm to be obtained at lower boost values. In the air the handling of both EN 223, and another production Spitfire XII which was made available by Supermarine for one day, were felt to be far superior to the normal Spitfire IX or VB, being exceptionally good in the lateral control which is crisper and lighter due to the clipped wings. The longitudinal stability is much better than that of the Spitfire V, and in the dive it was particularly noticed that when trimmed for cruising flight, it stays in easily at 400 mph IAS and does not recover fiercely. In turns the stick load is always positive and the control very comfortable. The rudder, however, is most sensitive to changes in engine settings and needs re-trimming for most alterations of flight as it is too heavy to be held by the feet for long periods. The Spitfire XII has the usual Spitfire stall characteristics. The engine runs noticeably more roughly than a Merlin.

## Performance

The Spitfire XII is capable of high speed at low altitude and is considerably faster than the Spitfire V. It is faster than the Spitfire IX with the dropped blower peak [Merlin 65, 66] by about 14 mph at sea level, and 8 mph at 10,000 feet; above 20,000 feet it is slower than the Spitfire IX. The figures produced by A & AEE [Armament and Aircraft Experimental Establishment—Boscombe Down] for the prototype XII with special finish including high polish, flush rivetting and wing tips on at a weight of 7,415 lbs [given at Appendix A] show maximum speeds are 372 mph at 5,700 feet and 397 mph at 18,000 feet. Checks were made with EN 223 and the speeds were found to be almost identical with those quoted. the absence of wing tips probably making up for the special finish of the prototype.

## Climb

The climb at full combat rating is not as good as that of the Spitfire IX with the dropped blower peak. Comparative zoom climbs were carried out with a Spitfire IX of this type which had the standard wing tips, with the following results:

Zero to 10,000 feet—Spitfire XII slower by about 30 seconds

10,000 to 20,000 feet—Spitfire XII slower by about 45 seconds

When compared in the climb below 10,000 feet with the Spitfire V using +16 pounds boost, it was found there was little to choose between them during a full throttle climb away from take-off.

On the production aircraft with clipped wings the operational ceiling of 1,000 ft/min is reached at 28,500 feet, and the rate of climb for the earlier aircraft is slightly slower. The time taken for a section climbing easily to reach 28,500 feet is about 25 minutes.

## Dive

In comparative dives with the Spitfire IX when both aircraft maintained the engine settings they had had in formation, the XII pulled away slightly as being the cleaner design, but at full throttle there was nothing to choose between the two aircraft.

## Manoeuvrability

The manoeuvrability of the Spitfire XII is considered to be excellent. It was compared with the Spitfire IX [Merlin 65 or 66], also designed as a high performance low-altitude fighter, over which it has an advantage in speed but not in climb, and found to be much better in rate of roll. Above 20,000 feet, however, the Spitfire IX with standard wing tips has a better all-round performance and was able to out-manoeuvre the XII. It was unfortunate that in the trials the Spitfire IX was only an average aircraft on controls and was inferior to both Mk XIIs flown. It is considered that when used below 20,000 feet it will be able to out-pace, out-turn the FW 190 and roll as well. The general manoeuvrability for dogfighting is slightly limited by the fact that the engine cuts under negative acceleration forces.

## Endurance

Accurate consumption figures are not yet available. One practice operation carried out in company with a VB gave a consumption 5 gallons higher for 1 hr 30 mins. Further consumption tests are being carried out.

## Sighting View

Owing to the engine having been set lower than the Merlin in the V or IX, the sighting view over the centre of the cowlings is increased from 100 mph standard to 120 mph [equivalent deflection angle of an aircraft in the gunsight], which gives a total of four degrees downward view.

## Low Flying

Owing to the slightly improved forward view and to the benefit obtained when looking sideways over the clipped wing tips, pilots have felt very confident in low flying in the Spitfire XII. The aircraft handles very well in all turns but when throttle alterations are made during turns close to the ground, pilots must be careful to guard against the alterations in trim, particularly in a right-hand turn when the nose is pulled down.

## Night Flying

No night flying was carried out as the exhausts fitted to the engine at present are the open type without flame dampers, but it is thought that the aircraft will have no different characteristics from other Spitfires once the take-off has been accomplished.

## Other Points

### Cine Camera Gun

No cine camera gun can be carried in the aircraft at present as the oil pressure filter and air charging valve are in the wing root at the normal place for mounting the G 45 camera.

### Maintenance

Throughout the trial the standard of maintenance of aircraft and engine was high, except for one or two accessories which were not peculiar to the aircraft. In particular, the crews commented upon the accessibility of the engine especially for the scavenge filters and ignition. Oil and coolant consumptions appear normal and the propeller gave no trouble throughout the trial. The priming pump is much larger than usual and starting needs a maximum of 6 dopes in cold weather.

## Conclusions

The Spitfire XII handles in general better than the previous marks of Spitfire. Its longitudinal stability has been improved, but the rudder control is not at present completely satisfactory as it needs constant re-trimming and is rather heavy.

The aircraft fills the category of a low-altitude fighter extremely well, being capable of speeds of 372 mph at 5,700 feet, and 397 mph at 18,000 feet.

The climb is not as good as the rest of the performance in general, being inferior to that of the Spitfire IX [Merlin 65 or 66] and similar to the Spitfire V at 16 lb boost up to 10,000 feet. The operational ceiling (with clipped wings) is about 28,500 feet. Modifications already in hand should improve the rate of climb, especially at low altitudes.

The aircraft dives well and benefits from having its wing tips clipped.

Manoeuvrability is excellent, particularly the rate of roll.

The sighting view over the nose has been slightly increased to give a total deflection allowance of 120 mph.

The similarity of design to the Spitfires V and IX will make its identification by the enemy difficult.

# 16.

# SPITFIRES ON

# FLOATS

Immediately after the opening of the German attack on Norway in April 1940, and the subsequent campaign during which the Royal Air Force suffered greatly from the lack of airfields from which to operate its fighters, discussions began at the Air Ministry regarding the possibility of converting Spitfires and Hurricanes into floatplane fighters. On 24 April a conference was held at Farnborough to consider the possibilities, chaired by Mr N. Rowe, an assistant director at the Joint Directorate of Research and Development at the Air Ministry; amongst those who attended were Alan Clifton from Supermarine and Sydney Camm from Hawker. The minutes of the meeting recorded:

Spitfire III fitted with Roc-type floats and an enlarged fin and rudder, considered for production in the late spring of 1940.

The chairman stated that the object of the meeting was to discuss the conversion of Hurricane and Spitfire aircraft for operation as floatplanes; the Air Staff regard this matter as a most urgent requirement, which must be treated on the highest priority . . . .

The meeting learned that fifty complete floatplane undercarriages were immediately available, which had been designed for the Blackburn Roc two-seat turret fighter; the complete sets of floats with supports each weighed 1,274 pounds, of which the floats themselves weighed 912 pounds. The Roc floatplane fighter weighed 8,660 pounds fully loaded and it was estimated that the Spitfire or Hurricane on floats would weigh between 7,000 and 7,300 pounds. Thus the floats were somewhat larger than necessary for the Spitfire or Hurricane; it was

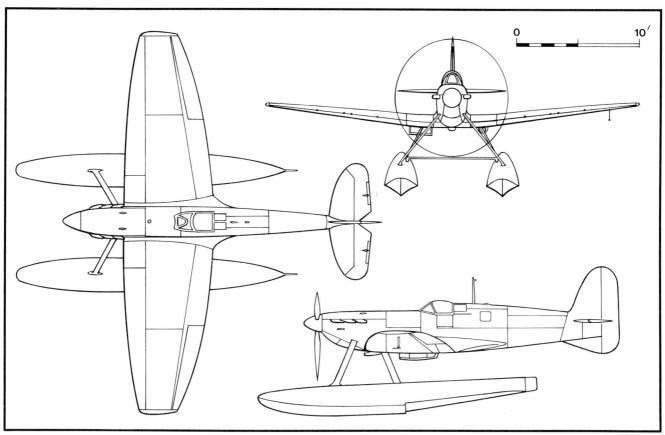

thought that this would not adversely affect the handling of the fighters on the water, but in the air their maximum speed would be 5 to 10 mph less than if floats of the optimum size were fitted. It was agreed that new floats should not be designed and built unless those of the Roc proved unsatisfactory; but those present considered it quite practicable to fit Roc floats on the Spitfire and Hurricane. The minutes of the meeting concluded with the statement that:

No precise estimate of the time to make a trial installation and get it flown can be made at this stage. If no major difficulties are encountered and the flight trials are satisfactory without alterations, it should be possible to clear the trial installation in two or three months by putting the work on the highest priority and arranging for night and day working.

Shortly after the meeting work began at Woolston on the conversion of a Spitfire I, R 6722, to take the Roc floats. And in May tank tests were carried out at Farnborough using a 1/7th scale model to investigate the likelihood of the aircraft porpoising on the water and whether spray thrown up by the floats might cause problems. The Spitfire was found to be reasonably stable and free from any tendency to porpoise on the water. On the question of seaworthiness the report on the tank trials noted:

The Spitfire is remarkably clean, the radiator and the air intake are clear of spray, though they would be splashed in deeper waves. During the take-off the airscrew is clear in calm water, and lightly splashed in waves between speeds of 9 and 22 knots [10-25 mph)], though not severely enough to damage it. On landing with flaps down, the flaps are splashed between speeds of 40 to 15 knots [46-17 mph] though only heavily in the inner two feet at 22 knots [25 mph]. It is understood that these portions of the flaps will be omitted from the seaplane version if necessary. The tailplane is satisfactorily clear.

At this time the Spitfire III was considered to be about to go into production, and tests carried out simultaneously in the Farnborough wind tunnel of the Spitfire floatplane used a 1/10th scale model of a Mark III with reduced span wings. These trials showed that a 20 per cent increase in fin area was needed to give the floatplane the required degree of stability in the yawing plane, and a revised fin design was proposed with additions above and below the fuselage.

Although the work of converting R 6722 to take Roc floats progressed rapidly, before it could make its first flight from water the Norwegian campaign had ended and the requirement passed. Moreover, with the Battle of Britain about to begin, the Royal Air Force was desperately short of normal landplane versions of the Spitfire. R 6722 was hastily de-converted and sent to war.

In 1942, following the entry of Japan into the war, the idea of the Spitfire floatplane was revived. This time the aircraft converted was a Mark V, W 3760, fitted with a pair of floats 25 feet 7 inches long on cantilever legs specially designed by Arthur Shirvall of Supermarine who had been responsible for the floats on the Schneider Trophy racers, and built by Folland Aircraft Ltd. The Spitfire V floatplane was powered by a Merlin 45 engine driving a four-bladed propeller, and fitted with external lifting points on the sides of the fuselage in front of and behind the cockpit. In its initial form the floatplane had its armament removed and was fitted with a beard-type tropical filter on the carburettor air intake, a spin recovery parachute and rudder horn balance guard, a normal-type fin above the fuselage with a fin extension below. Jeffrey Quill flew the floatplane for the first time on 12 October 1942, from Southampton Water.

Quill flew the floatplane seven more times in October, then Lieutenant Commander Don Robertson joined in the testing. During one of his flights Robertson flew over Poole Harbour and came under disconcertingly fierce anti-aircraft fire; from then on the two pilots were very careful where they took the odd-looking Spitfire.

After initial testing the aircraft was fitted with a revised fin with a straight leading edge and increased area, to improve directional stability; also the early type tropical filter was replaced by a later type fitted to the Spitfire IX and the lip was extended forwards to take it clear of spray, and the guns were installed.

In mid-January 1943 the floatplane prototype was dismantled and taken by road to the Marine Aircraft Experimental Establishment at Helensburgh near Glasgow, for its service trials; delivery by air was ruled out because of the lack of suitable slipway facilities along the route, if it had to put down in an emergency. After reassembly Quill test flew it on 27 January, then it was handed over to the RAF. The resultant performance figures are given at Appendix A, the handling trials report at Appendix B.

Also in the spring of 1943 Folland Aircraft converted two more Spitfire Vs to floatplanes, EP 751 and EP 754, and these were sent to Helensburgh to join the prototype.

By the end of August the testing of the Spitfire floatplane was complete and the aircraft were pronounced fit to go to war. They were crated and loaded on board the freighter SS *Penrith Castle,* which carried them to Egypt in October. An operational role had been found for the floatplanes. At this time the German outposts on the Dodecanese Islands in the eastern Mediterranean depended heavily on resupply by transport aircraft. An ambitious plan was hatched to operate the Spitfire floatplanes from a concealed base on one of the unoccupied islands in the chain, to cut this aerial lifeline. Supporting these operations was to be a submarine fitted with search radar and VHF radio, to guide the Spitfires to their prey.

In the event, however, the scheme came to nothing. In October 1943, even before the Spitfire floatplanes arrived in Egypt, German troops with powerful Luftwaffe backing re-entered the Dodecanese in force and by mid-November had ejected the British forces from the islands of Kos and Leros. As a result the planned operation of the floatplanes from a concealed base was no longer feasible and had to be dropped. The three Spitfires were re-assembled and flew for a time off the Great Bitter Lake, but no further operational use could be found for them.

In the spring of 1944 a Spitfire IX, MJ 982, was converted into a floatplane with a view to using this version in the Pacific theatre. Jeffrey Quill flew it for the first time on 18 June 1944, from the Saunders Roe slipway at Beaumaris on Anglesey. He later recalled: 'The Spitfire IX on floats was faster than the standard Hurricane. Its handling on the water was extremely good and its only unusual feature was a tendency to "tramp" from side to side on the floats, or to "waddle" a bit when at high speed in the plane.' Soon after testing began, however, the idea of using such aircraft in the Pacific area was dropped and MJ 982 was re-converted into a landplane.

Altogether five Spitfires were converted into floatplanes, of which one never flew and none ever went into action. Nevertheless, the story of the Spitfire floatplane illustrates once again the vast range of uses to which this fighter could be put.

**205, 206.** W 3760, the first Spitfire V modified into a floatplane, pictured during her early flight trials on Southampton Water in October 1942. The armament had been removed from the aircraft and, in addition to the floats, she had been fitted with a four-bladed propeller, a tropical filter, spin recovery parachute and rudder horn balance guard, and an extension fin under the fuselage. *(Vickers, Quill)*

**207.** Jeffrey Quill seated in the cockpit of W 3760 during the trials from Southampton Water. Visible on the fuselage sides, in front of and behind the cockpit, are the starboard slinging points to enable the aircraft to be lifted by crane. *(Quill)*

**208.** W 3760 early in 1943, after completion of initial modifications. The early-type tropical filter had been replaced with the later version with the intake lip extended forwards; the armament had been fitted and the fin area increased by fitting a straight-fronted fin. *(Vickers)*

**209.** W 3760 with beaching wheels fitted, during her service trials at Helensborough in the spring of 1943.

210

**210, 211, 212, 213** and **214.** The three Spitfire V floatplane conversions,
W 3760, EP 751 and EP 754, pictured during training flights off the Great
Bitter Lake in Egypt following the cancellation of their planned operation
against German transport aircraft over the Dodecanese late in 1943. *(via
Sissons)*

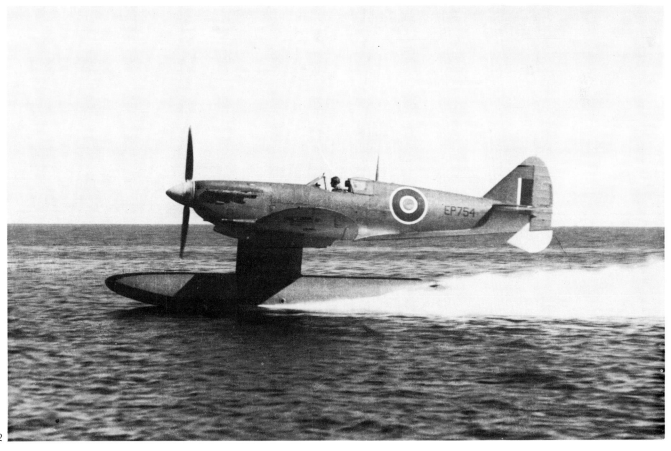

**215.** MJ 892, the sole Spitfire IX floatplane conversion, pictured during flight trials in the Summer of 1944. No further Mark IXs were converted, and after the trials MJ 892 was de-converted back into a landplane. *(Vickers)*

# Appendix A

## SPITFIRE VB FLOATPLANE   W 3760

Figures taken from the trials report of this aircraft, the first Spitfire floatplane to fly, tested at the Marine Aircraft Experimental Establishment at Helensburgh near Glasgow in the spring of 1943. At the time of the trial the condition of the aircraft was as follows:

Standard span wing, undercarriage removed and wheel wells faired over

Merlin 45 engine

Two 20 mm cannon and four .303-in Browning guns, muzzles and ejector chutes sealed

Internal laminated glass windscreen

Rectangular rear view mirror with no fairing

Aerial mast for VHF

Spitfire IX-type filter on carburettor air intake, with lip extended forwards to avoid spray ingestion

Floats mounted on streamlined fairings, with pneumatically operated water rudders at the rear of each

Fin and rudder of increased area, with fin extension below fuselage

External lifting points on each side of fuselage.

Spin recovery parachute housed in container in rear fuselage immediately in front of fin; rudder horn balance guard fitted at top of fin

Four bladed propeller, 11 ft 3 in diameter

**Dimensions:**

Span and length of airframe, as Mark V

Length overall (from nose of floats to rear of aircraft rudder, when tail down on beaching wheels)     35 ft 4 in

Length of floats (including water rudders)     25 ft 7 in

Maximum beam of floats     3 ft 4 in

**Weights:**

Tare weight     6,014 pounds

Fully loaded weight     7,580 pounds

Wing loading when fully loaded

31.3 pounds per square foot

**Performance:**

| Height feet | Top Speed mph | Time to Climb mins | Rate of Climb ft/min |
|---|---|---|---|
| Sea level | 251 | — | 2,240 |
| 2,000 | 257 | 0 m 54 s | 2,260 |
| 5,000 | 267 | 2 m 12 s | 2,300 |
| 10,000 | 285 | 4 m 06 s | 2,380 |
| 15,500 | 306 | 6 m 48 s | 2,450 |
| 19,500 | 324 | 8 m 48 s | 1,800 |
| 25,000 | 306 | 12 m 06 s | 1,260 |
| 30,000 | 283 | 17 m 0 s | 570 |

Service ceiling (estimated)     33,400 feet

Optimum alighting speed (flaps down)     71 mph (Indicated)

Take-off speed     115 mph (Indicated)

# Appendix B

## HANDLING TRIAL:   SPITFIRE VB FLOATPLANE   W 3760

The account below is taken from the report on this aircraft, whose performance figures are given in Appendix A.

\*   \*   \*

### Handling

#### Water Handling

The water handling of this aircraft, including behaviour during take-off and landing, is very good. Taxying tests were made in winds up to 20 mph and water rudder control was found to be effective. Turns to port could be made more easily than turns to starboard and similarly it was more difficult to taxi on a steady course at slow speeds with the wind on the port side than on the starboard side. The aircraft has been taxied across winds up to 12 mph to the slipway without difficulty, but in beam winds above 15 mph it would be advisable to tow the aircraft in. In calm conditions or light winds it is only necessary to use the water rudders when turning in a confined space.

At normal taxying speeds in winds up to 20 mph only a fine spray is thrown into the propeller. At higher taxying speeds across wind the spray becomes heavier but this condition can be avoided as it is not necessary to use much engine when turning across wind if the water rudders are used. Prolonged taxying with the wind on the starboard beam results in high coolant temperatures owing to the blanking effect of the streamlined starboard float strut on the radiator.

Beaching and launching present no difficulty; the beaching gear is of the normal type.

The towing pennant provided consists of two cables spliced to a ring for attachment to moorings by means of a shackle. To the end of each cable is fitted a metal plate for attachment to the nose bollards of the floats. A locking device is provided to retain these plates on the bollards. It is considered that if the aircraft is to be used as a fighter a quick release mechanism operated by the pilot would be essential for a quick get-away from the moorings.

#### Take-Off

On opening the throttle the control column should be held central. The nose rises at first and then falls as the speed increases. When on the step the control column should be eased back to overcome a slight tendency to nose down further. This tendency is by no means pronounced, and any correction made on the control column should be only slight because the elevator control is light and sensitive. A slight pull on the control column is required for take-off at a speed of 81 to 83 mph IAS in moderate or calm sea conditions. Full right rudder bias should be used. About one third to one half rudder is required to check swing to port during the take-off.

In choppy sea conditions a lateral rocking motion sometimes takes place when on the step, but this is not dangerous and can be controlled by the use of aileron.

## Landing

Flaps should be lowered at about 1,000 ft at a speed not exceeding 140 mph. The nose drops sharply when the flaps are lowered.

The best speed for approach is 115 mph IAS with about ¼ inch of throttle and the elevator trim set to 2 graduations up. This method of approach gives a good forward view and enables the pilot to judge his height better than when approaching at a slower speed with more engine.

A slower approach with more engine can be made at 100 mph IAS and this method should be adopted in very glassy sea conditions, the engine being throttled back on touch down. It is emphasised that the forward view during this slow approach is very bad and a turn should be made early in the approach to ensure a landing clear of obstructions. Also, on holding off, the forward view is obscured still further and may cause the pilot to hold off too high.

Care should be exercised during an approach over hangars, trees, etc, because the rate of descent with the engine throttled back is about 2,000 ft/min, a fact which is not apparent at first since the gliding attitude of the aircraft is rather flat.

The aircraft has been landed tail well down in calm conditions without bouncing, but the best landing is made at about 70 mph IAS, slightly tail down. One landing at 80 mph IAS resulted in a gentle bounce, but no difficulty was experienced in landing immediately afterwards using a little engine.

When making the normal landing the pilot may either keep the engine on until touch down, or throttle back when sure of his height. As the aircraft holds off very well the latter method is recommended.

Cross wind landings and take-offs have been made in light winds without difficulty. There was no tendency to yaw under these conditions.

## Air Handling

Air handling is good except for an appreciable change of elevator trim in the dive. The aircraft is very manoeuvrable in the air and little or no rudder is required when turning at the higher level speeds. At lower speeds a little rudder is required for turns.

After take-off some rudder bias should be removed to trim for straight flight in the climb.

Elevator trim is very good. The change in elevator trim when diving up to 350 mph IAS, however, is considerable and correction for tail heaviness is essential at this speed, otherwise when the control column is eased back when coming out of the dive a high speed stall will result, followed by a flick roll. Also, when throttling back and diving, a considerable yaw occurs unless corrected by use of rudder.

Stalls have been made with the aircraft loaded to 7,300 lb with and without flap. The stalling speed was found to be 69 to 70 mph IAS with full flap and 82 mph IAS without flap. In both conditions the stall occurred with the control column almost central with the nose rather high and there was no increased load on the stick. At the stall in each case there was a fluttering noise and the port wing dropped about 20 or 30°. Elevator control was lost on both occasions. Except for the nose up attitude there was no preliminary warning of the stall. Recovery was effected by easing the control column forward and was more rapid without flap than with flap.

\*     \*     \*

## Author's Comments

In this report indicated airspeed (IAS) was recorded. At altitudes close to sea level, indicated airspeed and true airspeed are approximately the same.

During a later trial the same Spitfire floatplane was tested for its spinning characteristics with its centre of gravity at 5.54 inches aft of the datum point (representing typical service loading) and 6.05 inches aft of the datum point (representing the extended aft limit of loading). The ending of the report on this trial is given below.

\*     \*     \*

C.G. 5.54'' aft of Datum

The aircraft goes into a spin easily in either direction.

After two turns to the right, recovery can be effected in about 1½ turns with a height loss of 2,800 ft.

In spins to the left, full opposite rudder must be held longer for recovery. The rudder must be centralised and the control column eased forward immediately the spin ceases, otherwise the aircraft will flick into a spin in the opposite direction.

After two turns to the left, recovery can be effected in 2¼ to 2¾ turns with a height loss of 3,000 ft.

C.G. 6.05'' aft of Datum

To spin to the right, the aircraft first drops a wing, then the nose drops smartly but rises again, and the aircraft remains for about ¼ turn in a very flat attitude. The nose then drops and a normal spin develops.

After two turns to the right, recovery can be effected in 1¼ turns, with a height loss of 2,000 ft.

In spins to the left, the initial flat attitude obtained in spins to the right does not occur.

After two turns to the left, recovery can be effected in 1¼ to 1¾ turns, the height loss being 2,300 to 2,500 ft.

In general, the spins are steady, and in both C.G. positions tested one turn is made in about 2¾ to 3 seconds.

## Conclusions

The spinning characteristics of this aircraft are similar to those on the landplane and are satisfactory.

In all cases tested, recovery after two turns was effected in a maximum of 2¾ turns, with a corresponding height loss of 3,000 ft.

# 17.

# SECOND GENERATION GRIFFON SPITFIRES: MARKS XIV, 18 AND 19

The Spitfire XII, the first Griffon-powered variant to go into service, had been a hasty improvisation using the single-stage supercharged version of this engine initially available. As a result, although the Mark XII had an excellent performance at low and medium altitudes, higher up its performance was inferior to that of the Spitfire IX. The answer was, of course, to fit two-stage supercharging to the Griffon. Rolls-Royce engineers had been working on this, but it was the spring of 1943 before the first production engines with this feature—the Griffon 61 series—became available.

Early in 1943 six Spitfire VIII airframes were converted on the Supermarine production line to take the Griffon 61. These became the prototypes for the Mark XIV: the first five, JF 316 to JF 320, were all fitted with five-bladed propellers while the sixth, JF 321, was fitted with a Griffon 85 engine driving a six-bladed contra-rotating propeller. Initially these aircraft flew with the early type fin and broad chord, pointed topped rudder, as fitted to the late production Mark VIIIs. But early on it became clear that a fin and rudder of greater area was necessary so a revised fin with a straight leading edge and an even wider rudder were fitted to these aircraft. Thus modified, three of the prototype Mark XIVs were tested at Boscombe Down in the late spring and summer of 1943; the performance figures for one of these, JF 319, are given at Appendix A and reveal that the Spitfire XIV was as great an improvement over the Mark IX as the Mark IX had been over the Mark V.

The first production Spitfire XIVs appeared in October 1943, differing externally from the modified prototypes in having fins and rudders of slightly smaller area and with a much more graceful curved outline. Early on in the production run the Griffon 61 engine was replaced with the slightly different Griffon 65 and one of the first aircraft thus fitted, RB 179, was put through tactical trials by the Air Fighting Development Unit in February and March 1944; the report on this trial is given at Appendix B. After re-reading this report recently, Jeffrey Quill commented:

The tactical trial report of the Spitfire XIV by the AFDU is interesting and it is clear that they fully appreciated its excellent performance and general 'fightability'. They also noted

**216.** JF 318, one of the original five Mark VIII airframes converted into Spitfire XIVs by the fitting of two-stage supercharged Griffon engines. At the time this photograph was taken, late in the spring of 1943, the aircraft was still fitted with the original Mark VIII fin and a Mark IX-type pointed-topped rudder.

**217.** JF 319, another of the initial Mark VIII conversions into Spitfire XIVs, seen fitted with the interim-type fin and rudder of increased area, in the summer of 1943. *(IWM)*

that the Mark XIV, with its tremendous power, increased propeller solidity and increased all-up weight and moments of inertia, was a good deal more of a handful for the pilot and so required more attention to 'flying' than its predecessors. Direction stability was a problem and the aircraft was apt to shear about a lot with coarse use of the throttle; large changes in speed required prompt attention to rudder trim. We at Supermarine tried all manner of expedients to improve the directional characteristics of the Mark XIV. But the only real answer was to fit a much larger fin and rudder; work was begun on this, but it was a major design change and the Spitfire 22 was the first production version to be fitted with it.

So far as the Mark XIV was concerned, I took the view that performance was paramount; and if the pilots had to work a bit harder and concentrate a bit more on their flying, that was better than sending them to war in an aircraft of inferior performance.

The first squadron to receive the Mark XIV was No 610 based at Exeter, which re-equipped in January and February 1944. During March Nos 91 and 322 (Dutch) Squadrons also began to re-equip with this version.

All three squadrons of Spitfire XIVs were fully operational by June, when the Germans opened the bombardment of London using V1 flying bombs. Together with No 41 Squadron flying Mark XIIs, these became by far the most successful Spitfire units engaging the low-flying robot aircraft.

To further increase the maximum speed of the Spitfire XIV at low altitude for anti-V1 operations, several were modified to operate at +25 pounds boost using 150 octane fuel. This increased speed by about 30 mph low down, giving a maximum of about 400 mph at 2,000 feet.

The main V1 bombardment ended early in September 1944, as Allied ground forces over-ran the launching sites in northern France. By the end of the month four more Spitfire XIV units were either operational or about to become operational: Nos 41, 130, 350 (Belgian) and No 402 (Canadian) Squadrons. From then until the end of the war the Spitfire XIV was the main high altitude air superiority fighter operated by the 2nd Tactical Air Force in northern Europe.

Also in the autumn of 1944 the Spitfire FR XIV appeared, fitted with a single F.24 oblique camera in the rear fuselage pointing port or starboard and a rear fuselage tank carrying 33 gallons of fuel. The first of these fighter reconnaissance aircraft were delivered to Nos 2 and 430 Squadrons of the 2nd Tactical Air Force, in November 1944.

The airframes of the initial production Spitfire XIVs were basically the same as the Mark VIII, but improvements were

218

**218.** A standard Spitfire XIV of the mid-production series, RN 119, bearing the markings of No 402 (Canadian) Squadron of the 2nd Tactical Air Force. This aircraft was fitted with the curved fin and rudder standard on production Mark XIVs. *(Public Archives of Canada)*

**219.** JF 317, one of the original Spitfire XIVs converted from Mark VIIIs, seen here after later fitting of a Griffon 85 engine and Rotol six-bladed contra-rotating propeller. *(Greensted)*

219

**220.** Close-up of the curved windscreen and revised canopy tested on Spitfire XIV RM 689 in August 1944. Although it reduced drag compared with the earlier type, the curved windscreen was not popular and did not go into production. *(via Oughton)*

incorporated in later aircraft in much the same way as with the late production Mark IXs and XVIs being built at Castle Bromwich: Mark XIVs were fitted with the 'E-Type' wing, with an armament of two 20 mm cannon and two .5-in machine guns; and from the end of 1944 Spitfire XIVs were delivered with cut-back rear fuselages and 'tear-drop' canopies.

In June 1945 the first Spitfire XIVs were delivered to No 11 Squadron in India, but the war ended before this version could go into operation in the Far East.

After the war one interesting trial involving a Spitfire XIV, TZ 138, was the cold weather testing at Churchill in Manitoba, Canada, in the winter of 1946-1947. During a stop for refuelling at The Pass airfield, the Spitfire broke through the packed-snow runway and shattered its propeller. The propeller was replaced then, to enable it to take-off from the snow, a pair of Tiger Moth skis were adapted for the Spitfire. On the top of the skis a small wooden cradle was built up into which the fighter's wheels fitted; the skis were not attached, however, and were to fall clear of the fighter once it was airborne. The subsequent report on the taxying and take-off of the 'Ski-Spitfire' stated:

Taxying-trials were carried out and it was found that more than normal engine power was required to maintain taxying speed. It was not necessary to lock the brakes to the skis, and control of the aircraft by the rudder alone was excellent due to the use of the extra engine power. It was intended to hold the aircraft down until a speed of 120-130 mph had been attained and then pull it well up, in order to clear the skis

which would drop immediately the wheels were off the ground. This was found to be impractical due to the fact that bouncing occurred, and it was considered advisable to pull the aircraft off as soon as possible. Take-off was accomplished at a little below 100 mph, this being near the stalling point since a 90 gallon drop tank was being carried in addition to the normal fuel load.

In view of the above experiences, it is not recommended that single engine fighter aircraft operate from snow packed runways. It is, however, considered that ski-assisted take-offs, with the necessary development, are practical for emergency purposes . . . .

Altogether 957 fighter and fighter reconnaissance versions of the Spitfire XIV were built, before production ceased at the end of 1945. After the war 132 examples were bought for the Royal Belgian Air Force, 70 were handed over to the Royal Indian Air Force and 30 FR XIVs were bought for the Royal Thai Air Force. In each case the exported aircraft were second hand machines previously used by the RAF.

Externally the Spitfire 18 was exactly like the late production Mark XIV with the 'tear-drop' canopy and 'E-Type' wing. Internally, however, the wing structure had been revised to make it stronger with solid spar booms instead of laminated square tubular booms; the fighter version of the Mark 18 was fitted with two 31 gallon fuel tanks in the rear fuselage; the fighter reconnaissance version was fitted with only one 31 gallon tank plus two vertical cameras and one oblique camera in the rear fuselage. The Spitfire 18 used the same Griffon 65 engine as the Mark XIV and its performance was almost exactly the same as that of the earlier mark; this was probably why there was no performance testing of the Mark 18 by either Boscombe Down or the Air Fighting Development Unit.

221

222

**221** and **222.** Late production Spitfire FR XIVs with E-Type wings, cut-down rear fuselages and 'tear-drop' canopies, belonging to No 2 Squadron based at Gatow, Berlin, in 1946. The single oblique camera in the rear fuselage could be mounted to face either port or starboard. *(Clifton)*

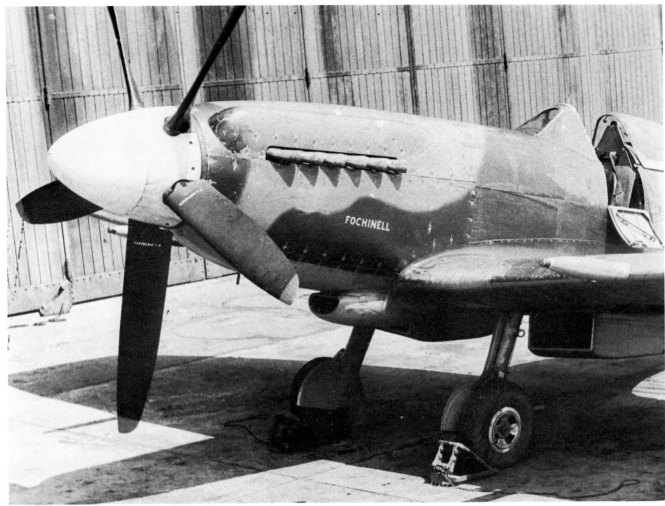

**223.** Close-up of the nose of an **FR XIVE** of No 2 Squadron, NM 821, bearing the ancient Scottish battle cry. *(Clifton)*

**224.** Some of the 132 Spitfire F and **FR XIVs** purchased for the Royal Belgian Air Force in 1947. These were operated by the 2nd Escadrille of No 2 Figher Bomber wing, based at Florennes. *(via Oughton)*

**225, 226** and **227.** Tiger Moth type skis adapted to fit on the main wheel of Spitfire FR XIVE TZ 138, during cold weather trials in Manitoba, Canada, in the winter of 1946-1947. The skis were to assist the aircraft only during taxying and take-off and were designed to fall away from the aircraft as it left the ground. *(via Arnold)*

The first Spitfire F 18, NH 872, made its maiden flight in June 1945 and this version entered service too late for the Second World War. The first unit to re-equip with this version was No 60 Squadron operating from Seletar, Singapore, in January 1947. Later Nos 11, 28 and 81 Squadrons in the Far East received fighter and fighter reconnaissance versions of the Spitfire 18, as did Nos 32 and 208 Squadrons in the Middle East. Operated by Nos 28 and 60 Squadrons, the Spitfire 18 saw some action against guerrillas during the Malayan emergency; and Nos 32 and 208 Squadrons unwittingly became involved in the armed clashes between Jews and Arabs at the time of the establishment of the state of Israel.

Altogether 300 Spitfire F 18s and FR 18s were built, before production of this version ended early in 1946. Some twenty ex-RAF Spitfire 18s went into service with the Royal Indian Air Force in 1947 and were operated by that service.

The Spitfire 19 was the final photographic reconnaissance variant of this aircraft, and combined the wing tankage and camera installation of the Mark XI with the Griffon power of the Mark XIV; the combination produced an outstanding reconnaissance aircraft, with the range of the former and the performance of the latter. After the initial 25 production aircraft, the Spitfire 19 was fitted with a pressurised cabin similar to that of the Mark X and the capacity of the wing leading edge tanks was increased to 86 gallons each to give an internal fuel capacity of 256 gallons—three and a half times as much as that of the prototype Spitfire!

The first Spitfire 19s were delivered to No 542 Squadron in May 1944, and by the end of the war it had virtually replaced the Mark XI in the RAF photographic reconnaissance squadrons. The Mark 19 had a maximum speed performance closely akin to that of the Mark XIV, though with a full load of fuel its performance in the climb was somewhat worse; it would appear that the Mark 19 did not undergo a full performance test at Boscombe Down. In service this aircraft demonstrated that it could cruise at 370 mph at 40,000 feet, which was sufficient to place it beyond the effective engagement reach of the German wartime jet fighters. During exercises after the war Spitfire 19s sometimes climbed to 49,000 feet during their approach flights to targets; not until the introduction into service of the first swept-wing jet fighters, the F-86 Sabre and the MiG-15 in 1949, did fighters exist which were able to intercept the Spitfire 19 with any prospect of success.

Altogether 225 Spitfire 19s were built, and with the Mosquito this type equipped the backbone of the RAF photographic reconnaissance force until the advent of reconnaissance versions of the Meteor and Canberra. Fifty Spitfire 19s were exported to Sweden in 1948, and in 1951 the Indian Air Force (it had dropped the 'Royal' prefix in 1950) received sufficient to form one squadron.

**228** and **229.** Spitfire FR 18s of No 208 Squadron, which operated from
Fayid in the Suez Canal Zone from 1948 until early in 1950.

**230.** A well-worn Spitfire FR 18 of No 28 Squadron, pictured at Kai Tak airfield, Hong Kong, late in 1950. The aircraft carried Korean War black and white identification bands on the rear fuselage and above and below the wings.

**231.** The prototype Spitfire PR 19, SW 777, pictured in May 1944 at about the time of its first flight. The first 25 aircraft of this version lacked pressurised cabins, but these were fitted to subsequent aircraft. The aircraft is seen fitted with a 90-gallon slipper tank. *(Vickers)*

231

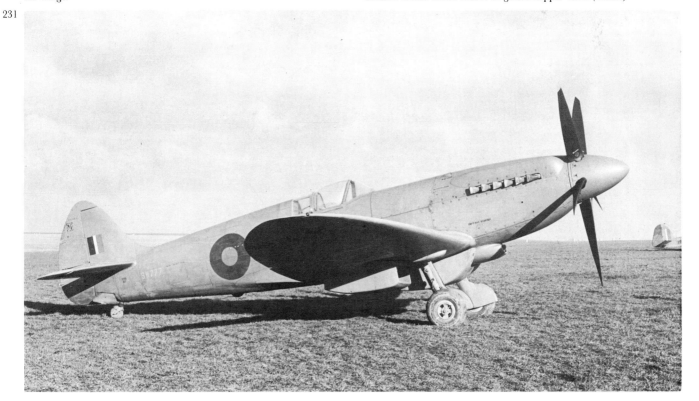

**232.** PM 660, a Spitfire 19 of No 2 Squadron, preparing to take off from Furstenfeldbruch in southern Germany in 1946. The intake for the cabin blower was fitted on the port side of the engine cowling on this version. *(Clifton)*

**233.** PS 925, a late production Mark 19, pictured after the war wearing the markings of the Photographic Reconnaissance Development Unit. *(RAF Museum)*

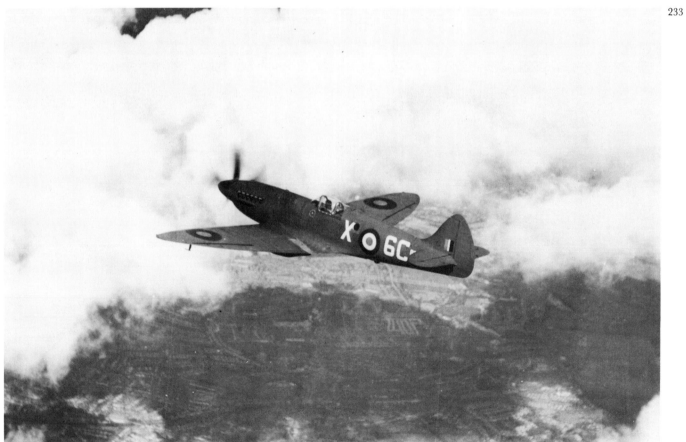

**234.** The initial batch of six Spitfire PR 19s for the Royal Swedish Air Force, being prepared at Chilbolton for delivery in October 1948. *(Vickers)*

**235.** PS 915, one of three Mark 19s which operated with the Meteorological Flight at Woodvale in Lancashire and flew regular sorties until the unit was disbanded in June 1957. These were the last Spitfires to see normal use in the RAF.

236

**236.** Spitfire PR 19 PS 853 had originally been delivered to the Central Fighter Establishment at West Raynham in 1958 as a 'gate guardian', but was maintained by the unit in a flyable condition. In 1963, following the unit's move to Binbrook, this Spitfire became the last of its type to perform an operational act: a battle trial against the jet-propelled Lightning which was its successor by three generations. At that time the Indonesian confrontation was in progress and the RAF needed to know how its Lightnings should best engage the P-51 Mustangs they might have to fight; PS 853 was used to represent a Mustang during the battle trial. Provided the Lightning did not drop its speed too much and let itself be drawn into a turning fight with its more agile opponent, a piston-engined fighter stood little chance in such an encounter. The most effective attack by the Lightning was in a high speed climb from below its opponent, where there was a good chance it could get into a missile-firing position without being seen.

# Appendix A

## SPITFIRE XIV    JF 319

Figures taken from the trials report of this aircraft, one of the initial six Mark XIVs converted from Mark VIIIs, tested at Boscombe Down in September 1943. At the time of the test the aircraft was fitted with the Griffon 61 engine, which differed slightly from the Griffon 65 fitted to production aircraft; the figures below are however representative of those for a production aircraft.

At the time of the trial the condition of the aircraft was as follows:

Standard 'C-Type' wing
Two 20 mm cannon and four .303-in Browning guns; gun ports and muzzles sealed, relevant ejection chutes open
Two 20 mm gun stubs with hemispherical fairings
Griffon 61 engine with individual ejector exhausts
Radiator installation deeper than that on the standard Mark VIII, with coolant radiator and oil cooler in the duct beneath the port wing and a further coolant radiator, and intercooler coolant radiator, in a duct beneath the starboard wing
Small span ailerons
Circular rear view mirror with hemispherical fairing
Balloon type cockpit hood
Whip aerial for VHF
No IFF aerials
Modified fin of increased area, with straight leading edge; rudder of increased area
Retractable tail wheel
This aircraft had been highly polished to give a glossy finish

**Dimensions:** span 36 ft 10 in, length 32 ft 8 in
**Weight:** Fully loaded weight 8,400 pounds
Wing loading when fully loaded, 34.7 pounds per square foot

**Performance:**

| Height feet | Top Speed mph | Time to Climb mins | Rate of Climb ft/min |
|---|---|---|---|
| Sea level | 363 | — | 5,110 |
| 4,000 | 385 | 0 m 48 s | 4,640 |
| 5,050 | 391 | | |
| 8,000 | 389 | 1 m 45 s | 3,830 |
| 12,000 | 388 | 2 m 51 s | 3,600 |
| 16,000 | 405 | 3 m 57 s | 3,600 |
| 20,000 | 423 | 5 m 06 s | 3,600 |
| 25,400 | 446 | | |
| 30,000 | 443 | 8 m 21 s | 2,390 |
| 34,000 | 436 | 10 m 15 s | 1,800 |
| 39,000 | 421 | | |
| 42,000 | | 18 m 15 s | 460 |

Service ceiling (estimated)                    44,000 feet

# Appendix B

## TACTICAL TRIAL: SPITFIRE XIV    RB 179

The account below is taken from the report of the tactical trial of an early production Mark XIV, RB 179, flown by the Air Fighting Development Unit at Wittering in February and March 1944.

\*    \*    \*

### Introduction

Aircraft RB 141 was delivered to this Unit on 28.1.44 for comparative trials with a Tempest V. It was discovered that this aircraft was not representative of production aircraft for squadrons and Spitfire XIV No RB 179 was therefore made available and delivered on 25.2.44. The operational weight with full fuel and ammunition is 8,400 lbs. To give a clear picture to the greatest number, the Spitfire IX (maximum engine settings +18 lbs boost, 3,000 revs) has been chosen for full comparison, and not the Spitfire XII which is a low-altitude aircraft built only in small numbers. Tactical comparisons have been made with the Tempest V and Mustang III, and combat trials have been carried out against the FW 190 (BMW 801D) and Me 109G.

### Brief Description

The Spitfire XIV is a short-range medium-high altitude fighter, armed with 2 × 20 mm cannon and 4 × .303 Browning guns in the wings. It is fitted with a Griffon 65 engine of approximately 2,000 hp. Pick-up points are provided for carrying of 30 gallon, 45 gallon or 90 gallon drop tanks. At present there are no bomb racks. In appearance it is very similar to the Spitfire XII with normal wings, except that it has a five-bladed propeller. The fin and rudder have been further modified.

### The Cockpit

The pilot's cockpit is generally similar in layout to all Spitfire cockpits, but has been considerably improved in some respects.

(a) A larger throttle quadrant has been fitted, incorporating a greatly improved friction damper for throttle and pitch levers. For normal conditions the throttle and pitch may be used together as one. If this is done, the boost and rpm obtained should be as follows:

| Boost | rpm |
|---|---|
| −4 | 2,000 |
| 0 | 2,200 |
| +4 | 2,400 |
| +8 | 2,500 |
| +12 | 2,650 |
| +18 | 2,750 |

(b) The electric master switch is now on the left-hand side of the dashboard, and is interconnected by means of a sliding bar with the main engine switches, which cannot be switched on when the master switch is off.

(c) An additional green light has been introduced under the undercarriage indicator, which goes out when the tail-wheel is retracted.

(d) The engine is started up by means of a Coffman Cartridge Starter, which has given considerable trouble both on this aircraft and RB 141.

(e) The normal position of the compass was very bad, only a portion of the instrument being visible to the pilot without unlocking the Sutton Harness and bending right down in the cockpit. A modification was introduced on aircraft RB 179, lowering the bracket holding the compass to enable the pilot to obtain a better view. The instrument can now be seen and reached by the pilot with the greatest ease without unlocking the Sutton Harness or bending down.

(f) As the Griffon engine revolves in the opposite direction to the Merlin, likewise propeller, the trail trim, if not left central, should be wound *back* for take-off and not forward.

### Flying Characteristics

In most respects this aircraft is similar to the Spitfire IX, except for some very marked changes in trim with alteration of throttle setting below 0 boost. This applies principally to the rudder, despite the incorporation of the servo-operated trimming tab. This is the one bad characteristic of the aircraft. The elevators also require more frequent trimming than in a Spitfire IX.

### Taxying

The aircraft is nose-heavy and considerable care must be exercised in taxying, particularly in a strong wind

### Take-off

During take-off the aircraft tends to swing to the right and to drag the right wing; full power should therefore not be used immediately on opening the throttle, but only when the aircraft is almost airborne, ie +6 lbs boost is quite sufficient. The nose must not be allowed to fall lower than the horizon as the propeller clearance is very slight.

### Turning Stall

The Spitfire XIV gives less warning of a stall in a tight turn than a Spitfire IX, though the same pre-stall characteristic ('Shuddering') occurs. This is a good point as it allows sighting to be maintained nearer the stall. The aircraft tends to come out of a dive in a similar manner to other Spitfires.

### Landing

The landing run is slightly longer and the aircraft sinks rather more rapidly than a Spitfire IX on landing. In all other respects the landing is quite normal and very easy. There is no tendency to swing.

### Formation Flying

Quite straightforward, similar to the Spitfire IX.

### Low Flying

The view from the cockpit is as good as from the Spitfire IX, the longer nose making no appreciable difference. Engine handling is a little more inconvenient because of the recurring trimming changes to elevators and rudder. The aircraft does not therefore handle quite so well as the Spitfire IX near the ground.

### Night Flying

Night flying was carried out with and without blinkers, under conditions of half moon, 9/10th cloud. Cockpit lighting is satisfactory except that there is no compass light. The exhaust glow is rather a brilliant blue, being brighter than the Spitfire IX. Without blinkers this causes no inconvenience in the air, providing the pilot does not sit too high in the cockpit. When taking off the throttle must be opened very slowly to prevent swing; at the same time the tail must be raised as soon as possible so that the flarepath can be seen. When landing an approach speed of 120 mph is recommended, engine-assisted, in order that the flarepath may be seen over the nose. The aircraft is then levelled off before the flarepath is reached, so that a landing may be made reasonably near the beginning of the flarepath. When the lighting conditions are less than the equivalent of half moon, blinkers are recommended. Blinkers cause some interference with view during day flying and make taxying at night very difficult. The

pilot's view at touch-down is also further restricted. They are not therefore recommended except when taking-off or landing on a dark night. From the ground the exhaust flames can easily be seen when the aircraft is flying at 1,000 feet.

### Tactical Comparison with Spitfire IX

The tactical differences are caused chiefly by the fact that the Spitfire XIV has an engine of greater capacity and is the heavier aircraft (weighing 8,400 lbs against 7,480 lbs of Spitfire IX).

### Range and Endurance

The Spitfire XIV, without a long-range tank, carries 110 gallons of fuel and 9 gallons of oil. When handled similarly, the Spitfire XIV uses fuel at about 1¼ times the rate of the Spitfire IX. Its endurance is therefore slightly less. Owing to its higher speed for corresponding engine settings, its range is about equal. For the same reasons, extra fuel carried in a long-range tank keeps its range about equal to that of the Spitfire IX, its endurance being slightly less.

### Speeds

At all heights the Spitfire XIV is approximately 30-35 mph faster in level flight. The best performance heights are similar, being just below 15,000 ft, and between 25,000 and 32,000 ft.

### Climb

The Spitfire XIV has a slightly better maximum climb than the Spitfire IX, having the best maximum rate of climb yet seen at this Unit. In the zoom climb the Spitfire XIV gains slightly all the way, especially if full throttle is used in the climb.

### Dive

The Spitfire XIV will pull away from the Spitfire IX in a dive.

### Turning Circle

The turning circles of both aircraft are identical. The Spitfire XIV appears to turn slightly better to port than it does to starboard. The warning of an approaching high speed stall is less pronounced in the case of the Spitfire XIV.

### Rate of Roll

The rate of roll of both aircraft is also very much the same.

### Search View and Rear View

The all-round view from the pilot's cockpit is good; the longer nose of the aircraft interferes with the all-round visibility, which remains the same as that of the Spitfire IX. Rear view is similar.

### Sighting View and Fire Power

The sighting view is slightly better, being 4° (140 mph) as against 3⅓°. The two bulges at the side cause little restriction. The fire power is identical with the Spitfire IX.

### Armour

As for the Spitfire IX.

### Conclusions

The all-round performance of the Spitfire XIV is better than the Spitfire IX at all heights. In level flight it is 25-35 mph faster and has a correspondingly greater rate of climb. Its manoeuvrability is as good as a Spitfire IX. It is easy to fly but should be handled with care when taxying and taking off.

### Brief Tactical Comparison With Tempest V

#### Range and Endurance

Rough comparisons have been made at the maximum cruising conditions of both aircraft. It is interesting that the indicated airspeed of each is about 280 mph and the range of each is about identical, both with full fuel load (including long-range tanks) and without (also no nose-tank—Tempest).

#### Maximum Speed

From 0-10,000 feet the Tempest V is 20 mph faster than the Spitfire XIV. There is then little to choose until 22,000 feet, when the Spitfire XIV becomes 30-40 mph faster, the

Tempest's operational ceiling being about 30,000 feet as opposed to the Spitfire XIV's 40,000 feet.

**Maximum Climb**

The Tempest is not in the same class as the Spitfire XIV. The Tempest V, however, has a considerably better zoom climb, holding a higher speed throughout the manoeuvre. If the climb is prolonged until climbing speed is reached then, of course, the Spitfire XIV will begin to catch up and pull ahead.

**Dive**

The Tempest V gains on the Spitfire XIV.

**Turning Circle**

The Spitfire XIV easily out-turns the Tempest.

**Rate of Roll**

The Spitfire XIV rolls faster at speeds below 300 mph, but definitely more slowly at speeds greater than 350 mph.

**Conclusions**

The tactical attributes of the two aircraft being completely different, they require a separate handling technique in combat. For this reason Typhoon squadrons should convert to Tempests, and Spitfire squadrons to Spitfire XIVs and definitely never vice-versa, or each aircraft's particular advantages would not be appreciated. Regarding performance, if correctly handled the Tempest is the better below about 20,000 feet and the Spitfire XIV the better above that height.

### Tactical Comparison with Mustang III

**Radius of Action**

Without a long-range tank, the Spitfire XIV has no endurance. With a 90 gallon long-range tank it has about half the range of the Mustang III fitted with 2 × 62½ gallon long-range tanks.

**Maximum Speed**

The maximum speeds are practically identical.

**Maximum Climb**

The Spitfire XIV is very much better.

**Dive**

As for the Spitfire IX. The Mustang pulls away, but less markedly.

**Turning Circle**

The Spitfire XIV is better.

**Rate of Roll**

The advantage tends to be with the Spitfire XIV.

**Conclusion**

With the exception of endurance no conclusions can be drawn, as these two aircraft should never be enemies. The choice is a matter of taste.

### Combat Trial Against FW 190 (BMW 801D)

**Maximum Speeds**

From 0-5,000 ft and 15,000-20,000 feet, the Spitfire XIV is only 20 mph faster; at all other heights it is up to 60 mph faster than the FW 190 (BMW 801D). It is estimated to have about the same maximum speed as the new FW 190 (DB 603) at all heights.

**Maximum Climb**

The Spitfire XIV has a considerably greater rate of climb than the FW 190 (BMW 801D) or (estimated) the new FW 190 (DB 603) at all heights.

**Dive**

After the initial part of the dive, during which the FW 190 gains slightly, the Spitfire XIV has a slight advantage.

**Turning Circle**

The Spitfire XIV can easily turn inside the FW 190. Though in the case of a right-hand turn this difference is not quite so pronounced.

**Rate of Roll**

The FW 190 is very much better.

**Conclusions**

In defence, the Spitfire XIV should use its remarkable maximum climb and turning circle against any enemy aircraft. In the attack it can afford to 'mix it' but should beware of the quick roll and dive. If this manoeuvre is used by an FW 190 and the Spitfire XIV follows, it will probably not be able to close the range until the FW 190 has pulled out of its dive.

### Combat Trial Against Me 109G

**Maximum Speed**

The Spitfire XIV is 40 mph faster at all heights except near 16,000 ft, where it is only 10 mph faster.

**Maximum Climb**

Same results. At 16,000 ft identical, otherwise the Spitfire XIV out-climbs the Me 109G. The zoom climb is practically identical when the climb is made without opening throttle. Climbing at full throttle, the Spitfire XIV draws away from the Me 109G quite easily.

**Dive**

During the initial part of the dive, the Me 109G pulls away slightly, but when a speed of 380 mph is reached the Spitfire XIV begins to gain on the Me 109G.

**Turning Circle**

The Spitfire XIV easily out-turns the Me 109G in either direction.

**Rate of Roll**

The Spitfire XIV rolls much more quickly.

**Conclusion**

The Spitfire XIV is superior to the Me 109G in every respect.

### Combat Performance with 90 Gallon Long-Range Tank

As the Spitfire XIV has a very short range it has been assumed that when a long-range tank is to be carried, it is most likely to be the 90 gallon tank rather than the 30 gallon or 45 gallon. Pending further instructions, no drops or trials have been carried out with the 30 gallon or 45 gallon tanks. The aircraft's performance with either can be estimated from the results given below of trials with the 90 gallon long-range tank.

**Drops**

The aircraft was fitted with assistor springs as for the Spitfire IX. Two drops were made with empty tanks at 50 ft and 25,000 ft, ASI 250 mph, with no trouble. Cine photographs were taken and show the tank dropping quite clear of the aircraft. Further trials would be necessary to check these results thoroughly.

**Speeds**

About 20 mph is knocked off the maximum speed and correspondingly off the speed at intermediate throttle settings. The aircraft is then still faster than the FW 190 (BMW 801D) and the Me 109G above 20,000 feet.

**Climb**

Climb is most affected. With a half-full tank its maximum climb becomes identical with the Spitfire IX without the tank. Even with a full tank it can therefore climb as fast as the FW 190 or Me 109G. Its zoom climb is hardly affected.

**Dive**

So long as the tank is more than 1/3 full, the dive acceleration is similar.

**Turning Circle**

The Spitfire XIV now has a definitely wider turning circle than before, but is still within those of the FW 190 (BMW 801D) and Me 109G.

**Rate of Roll**

Similar.

## Conclusions

Even with the 90 gallon long-range tank, the Spitfire XIV can equal or outclass the FW 190 (BMW 801D) and Me 109G in every respect. Its main advantages remain the right turn and maximum climb.

## Technical

### Gun Harmonisation
As for Spitfire IX.

### Gun Firing
Trials were carried out without any troubles or difficulties.

### Re-arming
As for Spitfire IX.

### Cine-gun Installation and Harmonisation
There is no difference in installation, but in the Spitfire XIV the camera is fitted on the port side.

### Radio
One VHF set is fitted as in the Spitfire IX.

### Oxygen
Normal British type oxygen system, as in all Spitfires.

### Engine Temperatures
The glycol radiator shutters are automatically controlled. There was no overheating at any time, except during sustained climbs at maximum boost and rpm when the glycol temperature once exceeded 105°C.

## Starting Hints

The aircraft is generally more difficult to start than the Spitfire IX. Care should be taken not to over-dope it and one third of a pump full is usually quite sufficient when the engine is warm.

## Servicing Hints

Careful watch should be maintained on the Rolls-Royce Auxiliary Gear Box oil contents level. The aircraft under test (RB 179) suffered from a bad oil leakage, all oil being consumed or lost in a 30-minute flight. This was cured by a careful check and tightening of all connections and plugs, when the consumption was decreased to approximately ½ pint per hour.

Trouble has also been experienced with the Coffman Starter Breech sticking. A daily shot with a grease gun on the grease nipple provided helped to eliminate this stickiness. Normal Spitfire equipment was used throughout the trials.

## General Conclusions

The Spitfire XIV is superior to the Spitfire IX in all respects. It has the best all-round performance of any present-day fighter, apart from range.

Modification to the compass bracket, to enable the pilot to obtain an unrestricted view of the compass, should be incorporated.

## Author's Comments

Regarding the captured FW 190A and the Me 109G against which the Spitfire XIV was tested, it should be borne in mind that these were in each case relatively early versions with performances somewhat lower than the latest sub-types the Luftwaffe had in service early in 1944. The Spitfire XIV was superior to these latest sub-types too, though not by so great a margin as that shown in the report. The FW 190D did not become operational until the summer of 1944, and when it did it was powered by the Junkers Jumo 213 and not the Daimler Benz 603 engine expected by the Allied intelligence services.

# 18.

# SPITFIRES MADE FOR TWO

The idea of adding a second seat to the Spitfire to make it into a conversion trainer had originally been put forward by Supermarine in 1941, but at the time the shortage of fighters was such that the Air Ministry turned the idea down. Moreover there was little requirement for such an aircraft: pilots were proving able to convert to the Spitfire from the normal advanced training types, the Harvard and Master, with little difficulty.

So far as is known the first two-seat Spitfire to fly was a locally modified Mark V, ES 127, operated by No 261 Squadron in the Middle East in 1944. This aircraft had the normal fuel tanks in front of the cockpit removed, and a seat fitted in front of the normal cockpit with a windscreen but no canopy. This aircraft probably carried its fuel in wing tanks. There was no second set of controls, the aircraft could be used only as a run-about.

In the event the Russians were to be the first to modify the Spitfire as an operational conversion trainer. The Red Air Force operated two-seat trainer versions or conversions of almost every fighter type it placed into large scale service, and the Spitfire was no exception. In the case of the Spitfire IX UTI (UTI = Uchebno Trenirovochnii Istrebityel = fighter trainer) the second seat was submerged in the rear fuselage behind the first and was topped with a normal Spitfire canopy. The existence of this trainer version was unknown in the west until recently; it is not known how many were modified in this way, but at least two were and there might have been as many as one for each 36-aircraft regiment operating the Spitfire IX.

In Britain the first Spitfire trainer was a Mark VIII converted into a two-seater by Supermarine, as a private venture in 1946. This conversion was more ambitious than the earlier ones and involved fitting a single, smaller, main fuel tank of 39 gallon capacity which allowed the front cockpit to be moved forwards by 13½ inches; the second seat, with a separate windscreen and 'tear-drop' canopy, was fitted behind and above the first. Instruments and controls were duplicated in the rear cockpit. In addition to a fuel tank in each wing leading edge, capacity 12¾ gallons, a 14-gallon tank was fitted into the cannon bay in each wing. This version of the Spitfire had provision for only four .303-in Browning guns, in the outer wing positions. Fully loaded, carrying two pilots, the aircraft weighed 7,400 pounds.

Early in 1947 the Spitfire VIII trainer, formerly MT 818, bearing the civil registration G-AIDN, underwent brief handling trials with the RAF at Boscombe Down. In the air the aircraft handled well and the report on the trial stated:

Aerobatics, including loops, rolls, upward rolls and half rolls

off the top of loops, were carried out, there being sufficient power to execute all normal aerobatic manoeuvres at climbing power. The aerobatic behaviour of the aircraft, when piloted from either cockpit, was considered similar to that of a standard Spitfire at comparable weight.

Concerning the suitability of the aircraft as a trainer, however, the report had some criticisms:

### Instructor in the Rear Cockpit

The instructor's view from the rear cockpit was bad at take-off until the tail was raised, and also bad in the final stages of landing. It was considered an experienced pilot should have no difficulty in giving flying instruction from the rear cockpit, and there was sufficient view for him to 'save' a bad landing providing the intercom was working. For gunnery instruction the aircraft was considered unsuitable for air-to-ground training owing to the difficulty of judging heights at low altitude whilst diving, and owing to the absence of gun sights it would be unsuitable for air-to-air training.

When the aircraft was flown from the rear cockpit there was a tendency for the tail to be raised too high at take-off and care had to be taken otherwise there was a danger of the propeller hitting the ground.

### Layout of Cockpits

The following adverse criticisms were made in respect of the front and rear cockpits:

Both cockpits were cramped, particularly the rear cockpit, which was considered too narrow even for a pilot of average build.

In the front cockpit the undercarriage control lever was set too close to the fuselage and this made selection difficult with gloves on.

In the rear cockpit the undercarriage control lever, together with the trimmer wheel, was almost out of reach. The compass was very difficult to see and the engine revolution counter was half hidden and difficult to see.

Provision for opening the hoods was merely by handgrips and it was considered winding mechanisms for both hoods were desirable. The rear windscreen gives a very distorted view and this was embarrassing when landing with the rear hood closed. The rear hood cannot be opened or kept open whilst the front hood is closed [in the air].

Difficulty was experienced in entering the rear cockpit and it is desirable a step should be incorporated.

**237, 238.** Spitfire IX UTI fighter trainer conversions, by the Soviet Air Force late in 1944 or early 1945. The aircraft above (**237**) had its armament removed and has full span wings; that below (**238**) has clipped wings and a rear view mirror. Those by the Soviet Air Force were the first dual control Spitfire conversions; it is not known how many were turned out, but there may have been one for each 40-aircraft Regiment operating Spitfires. *(via Geust)*.

**239.** The all-yellow Spitfire VIII two-seat dual control conversion, here bearing the identification code N 32, first flew in 1946. Later it received the civil registration G-AIDN. *(Vickers)*

No RAF order was placed for the Spitfire trainer. On the Boscombe Down report, Jeffrey Quill later commented:

Really the Spitfire trainer came too late. Had it been produced earlier it might have saved a lot of prangs at the RAF conversion units. On the other hand it would have used up productive capacity needed to build fighters, so a difficult decision had to be made. Some of Boscombe Down's comments on the trainer seem a bit nit-picking—symptomatic of the immediate post-war era when there was no urgency and not much to do except pick holes in everything. Probably the Spitfire was never cut out to be a comfortable 2-seater. If it had been it would have been too large in the first place—and Mitchell's masterpiece would not have been a masterpiece.

No other Spitfire VIIIs were converted into trainers. But the company also offered similarly converted Mark IXs and drew orders for 20 from foreign air forces: 10 for the Royal Indian Air Force, 6 for the Irish Air Corps, 3 for the Royal Dutch Air Force and one for the Royal Egyptian Air Force. Apart from the normal differences between the Mark VIII and the Mark IX, the trainers differed in that the latter version had both fuel tanks in each wing positioned behind the main spar, and they were of 13 and 14½ gallon capacity.

**240.** One of the ten Spitfire IX two-seat conversions purchased for the
Royal Indian Air Force. *(Vickers)*

# 19.

# END OF THE LINE:
# THE MARKS 21, 22, 23 AND 24

As the two-stage supercharged Griffon 61 series of engines came in prospect early in 1942, it became clear that a major re-design of the Spitfire airframe, with considerably stiffer wings, was necessary if the additional power was to be exploited to the full. The new version was designated the Spitfire 21 though, such were the changes proposed, for a time it was considered the aircraft should be given the entirely new name of 'Victor'.

The second Spitfire 20, DP 851, had, as has already been mentioned, made its first flight with a Griffon II in August 1942. During the autumn of that year it was re-engined with a Griffon 61 and when it resumed flight trials in December it was re-designated as a Mark 21. In this 'interim Mark 21' form DP 851 was fitted with a wing of normal Spitfire shape with pointed tips, but with a revised internal structure and thicker gauge light alloy covering to make it considerably stronger. The aircraft was fitted with a modified, curved-fronted windscreen and revised canopy to match, and a broad-chord pointed rudder on an early-type fin. Initially the aircraft had a four-bladed propeller, though later this was replaced by one with five blades. Tests carried out by the company established that at an all-up weight of 9,000 pounds and a combat rating of 2,750 rpm and +18 pounds boost, the aircraft had a maximum level speed of 455 mph at 25,600 feet, a maximum rate of climb of 4,800 feet per minute at 7,700 feet; it took 7 minutes 51 seconds to climb to 30,000 feet and the service ceiling was 42,800 feet.

DP 851 was written off in May 1943 but shortly afterwards, on 24 July, Jeffrey Quill flew the first fully modified Spitfire 21, PP 139. This aircraft differed from previous Spitfires in several respects. To improve rolling performance the ailerons were 5 per cent larger than those on early-type Spitfires. Instead of being of the Frise balanced type, the new ailerons were attached using continuous piano-type hinges pivoting on the upper surface; balance was achieved by means of balance tabs. The extensions added some 8 inches to the outer end of each aileron, caused a straightening of the trailing edge of the wings, added slightly to their area and caused the first change in the outline of the basic wing since the first prototype. Like DP 851, PP 139 was flown initially with pointed wing tips. The wing fuel tankage was increased to 34 gallons and armament was standardised at four 20 mm cannon with no machine guns. To improve ground handling, the main undercarriage legs were placed 7¾ inches further apart than on previous versions. And to allow ground clearance for a propeller larger than any previously fitted to a landplane version of the Spitfire, the oleo legs were lengthened by 4½ inches. Two doors fitted to the main-plane covered the wheels completely when the undercarriage was retracted. The longer undercarriage legs allowed the Spit-

fire 21 to take a five-bladed Rotol propeller eleven feet in diameter, 7 inches greater than that fitted to the Mark XIV. The widening of the undercarriage track and the lengthening of the main wheel legs gave rise to a retraction problem which had to be solved. Jack Davis explained the problem and its solution:

We had a longer main wheel leg and there was no space into which to retract the wheel without encroaching on the gun bays on either side. So a system of levers was designed to compress the oleo legs by about 8 inches as the undercarriage was raised, to get it to fit into the space available. When the undercarriage was lowered, the oleos extended to their full length. It was rather clever really.

Initially PP 139 had the revised windscreen and canopy as fitted to DP 851, and a straight-leading-edge fin and enlarged rudder as fitted to the prototype Mark XIVs; but later in its career both of these features were altered to make them the same as those on the production Mark XIV. PP 139 underwent performance testing at Boscombe Down in the autumn of 1943 but, due to troubles with engines, the time-to-climb trials were not completed. The level speeds of this aircraft, measured during the tests, are given at Appendix A.

The first production Spitfire 21, LA 187, made its maiden flight on 15 March 1944. Still it had the pointed wing tips, but the cockpit canopy and fin and rudder were like those fitted to the Mark XIV. The changes made to the airframe and controls had combined to bring about a marked deterioration in handling characteristics, however. In November 1944 this aircraft underwent a brief trial at Boscombe Down and the report on these commented:

The rudder trimmer tab was very sensitive and required a very delicate touch to trim the aircraft for flight without yawing. This latter characteristic was accentuated by the large change of directional trim with speed, power and applied acceleration, rendering it necessary for the pilot to retrim the aircraft frequently during manoeuvres in order to avoid what appeared to be dangerous angles of sideslip.

The directional qualities of the aircraft deteriorated markedly with altitude and also noticeably with aft movement of the c.g. The bad directional qualities linked up with their effect on the longitudinal control, gave rise to very peculiar corkscrew behaviour of the aircraft, particularly at high Mach numbers, and at none of the loadings tested did the pilot feel comfortable when carrying out combat manoeuvres in the region of the aircraft's optimum performance altitude (25,000 ft).

**241.** DP 851, the second Griffon Spitfire built, was originally designated a Mark 20 when powered by the Griffon II. It was then re-engined with a Griffon 61 and became the first prototype Spitfire 21 in December 1942, as seen here. This aircraft was fitted with a wing with revised internal structure and pointed tips, and a curved windscreen; the early-type undercarriage, without wheel covering doors, was retained. *(RJ Mitchell Museum)*

**242.** The first true prototype of the Mark 21 was PP 139, which made its maiden flight in July 1943. Like DP 851 it featured the strengthened wing with pointed tips, but this aircraft was fitted with the revised ailerons with balance tabs, revised undercarriage with fairing doors to cover the main wheels, a straight leading edge fin and a curved windscreen as fitted to DP 851. Later in its career PP 139 was fitted with windscreen, canopy and tail unit as fitted to production Mark XIVs. *(Vickers)*

**243.** LA 187, the first production Mark 21, made its maiden flight in July 1944 fitted with Mark XIV-type windscreen, canopy and tail, but it retained the extended span wing of the previous Mark 21s. The poor handling of this aircraft drew unfavourable reports from RAF test pilots at Boscombe Down in November 1944. *(IWM)*

Moreover, the performance of LA 187 was found to be disappointing compared with that of PP 139 when the former underwent speed and climbing trials at Boscombe Down early in 1945; the figures recorded are given at Appendix B and revealed an aircraft 15 to 20 mph slower than the earlier one at optimum altitudes.

Also in November 1944 the fifteenth production Spitfire 21, LA 201, was tested at the Air Fighting Development Unit at Wittering and drew a highly critical report which pulled no punches. The report is given at Appendix C and ended with the statement:

> It is recommended that the Spitfire 21 be withdrawn from operations until the instability in the yawing plane has been removed and that it be replaced by the Spitfire XIV or Tempest V until this can be done.
>
> If this is not possible then it must be emphasised that, although the Spitfire 21 is not a dangerous aircraft to fly, pilots must be warned of its handling qualities and in its present state it is not likely to prove a satisfactory fighter.
>
> No further attempts should be made to perpetuate the Spitfire family.

As might be expected, these highly critical reports from service pilots caused a considerable stir, especially as tooling up was already well advanced at the Castle Bromwich plant to meet orders placed for more than three thousand Spitfire 21s. And with each day that passed yet more of the initial production batch were coming off the line, all with the same poor handling characteristics as their predecessors.

On the stability problems of the Mark 21, and the work to cure them, Jeffrey Quill has told the author:

From the time I first flew the Spitfire 21 it was clear that we had a hot potato. There was too much power for the aeroplane and what was needed were much larger tail surfaces, both horizontal and vertical. The work to design and build these was already in hand, but would take several months to complete. In the meantime the great production 'sausage machine' was already rolling. So the immediate problem was to make the handling of the Mark 21 in the air reasonably tolerable, so that the aeroplane would be operationally viable pending the happy day when the much larger tail did become available.

We tried all sorts of expedients: different sorts of tabs, anti-balance tabs, changes to horn-balance areas, etc. Throughout these trials very few detailed reports were written. Modifications were decided upon overnight at meetings and incorporated. I would test their effect and report on them verbally to Joe Smith and his staff, then they were adopted or discarded. This was Joe Smith's method of operation and also mine.

The AFDU were quite right to criticise the handling of the Mark 21, although in my opinion their report overdid it a bit. Where they went terribly wrong was to recommend that all further development of the Spitfire family should cease. They were quite unqualified to make such a judgement, and later events would prove them totally wrong.

The task of isolating the faults of the Mark 21 aircraft, and curing each one in turn, went forward at the highest priority both at the company and the service trials establishments. The root cause of the problems was over-control, and in each case modifications to the controls provided the cure. The rudder over-control was cured by removing the balance action of the rudder trim tab. The elevator over-control was cured by reducing the gearing to the elevator trim tab by half and by fitting metal-covered elevators with rounded-off horn balances of slightly reduced area.

These modifications were incorporated on aircraft LA 215,

**244.** LA 188, the second production Spitfire 21, showing the revised wing planform, without pointed tips, which became standard on this version. Casting a shadow across the starboard wing, from a position behind the inboard cannon, was the re-positioned IFF post aerial.

228

**245.** Though initially the Spitfire 21 was found to suffer from over-sensitive controls, once the causes had been isolated relatively small changes provided the cure. The sole external changes can be seen here: LA 281, on the left, is seen with the original elevator horn balance; LA 125, on the right, is seen with the rounded elevator horn balance which, with other internal control changes, gave a considerable improvement in handling. *(via Oughton)*

which then showed an immediate improvement during the second series of Air Fighting Development Unit trials in March 1945. The report on the trials stated:

> The critical trimming characteristics reported on the production Spitfire 21 have been largely eliminated by the modifications carried out to this aircraft. Its handling qualities have benefited to a corresponding extent and it is now considered suitable both for instrument flying and low flying.

The text of this report is given at Appendix D.

During January 1945 No 91 Squadron at Manston became the first service unit to receive the Spitfire 21. Initially its aircraft were unmodified, but at the end of March these were all replaced with modified machines. In April the squadron moved to Ludham in Norfolk with its full complement of eighteen Spitfire 21s and on the morning of the 10th began operations by flying armed reconnaissance sorties over the area near The Hague from which V2 rockets were being launched against England.

That afternoon a section of four Spitfire 21s, led by Flight Lieutenant H. Johnson, ran into trouble during a strafing attack on ships off the Dutch coast and two of their number were shot down but the pilots were rescued. Following this inauspicious start, the squadron settled down to flying armed reconnaissance missions over Holland and patrols off the coast looking for German midget submarines. At mid-day on April 26 Spitfire 21s scored a rare success when two of them, piloted by Flight Lieutenants W. Marshal and J. Draper, shot up and claimed sunk a midget submarine caught on the surface as it was putting out of The Hook. Thereafter, however, the Spitfire 21s had little opportunity to engage the enemy before the war in Europe ended in May.

A few Spitfire 21s were fitted with Griffon 85 engines driving contra-rotating propellers and shortly after the end of the war in Europe, on 23 May 1945, LA 218 thus fitted underwent brief testing at Tangmere, by pilots of the Air Fighting Development Unit. The report on the trial, included at Appendix E, was most enthusiastic and stated:

The elimination of the need for rudder trim during ground attack reduces the possibility of skid at the moment of firing. This factor has always been one of the major sources of aiming error in the past. The fitting of a contra-rotating airscrew has now turned the aircraft into a very reasonable gun platform and without any apparent loss in performance.

Air-to-air combat is similarly enhanced and it was found that no change of trim was necessary with change of throttle setting. A considerable improvement in sighting accuracy may be expected.

What a difference of opinion on the Spitfire 21, compared with that given by the same unit just four months earlier!

Despite the enthusiastic report on the contra-rotating propeller, however, the device was not yet ready for general service use. Jeffrey Quill recounted some of the reasons why:

> The contra-prop was a rather expensive and weighty item, and at first it tended to be unreliable. Mechanically it was quite a box of tricks, with the six blades and two great big hubs. The hydraulic cylinder which changed the pitch was fitted to the front propeller, and the pitch change was transmitted to the rear propeller—which was rotating in the opposite direction—via the translation bearing. Initially the translation bearings gave quite a lot of trouble. If it failed there was no pitch control over the rear propeller, which usually put itself straight into fine pitch. The front propeller would continue operating normally, but the overall efficiency of the two propellers fell drastically. I had it happen, and it was a disconcerting experience flying on full power and doing only about 120 mph. Later the bugs were ironed out and it worked well on the Seafire 47, but it was not fitted to many Spitfires delivered to the RAF.

Although by the end of the war the Spitfire 21 was fully effective as an operational fighter, with the end of the conflict the bulk of the huge orders for it were either cancelled or else amended to cover the construction of other versions of the Spitfire or Seafire. Only 120 examples were completed and they served with Nos 1, 41, 91 and 122 Squadrons for a short time before these units were re-equipped or disbanded. The Spitfire 21s were then transferred to the Auxiliary Air Force and flown by Nos 600, 602 and 615 Squadrons until the last of these received its Mark 22s in 1948.

The Spitfire 22 differed from the Mark 21 in the fitting of a

**246** and **247.** Only one unit, No 91 Squadron based at Ludham in Norfolk, went into action with Spitfire 21s before the war ended. These are amongst the few photographs showing the unit's Mark 21s in squadron markings. *(via Arnold, Horsefall)*

**248.** LA 218, the Spitfire 21 fitted with contra-rotating propellers which drew enthusiastic comments from Air Fighting Development Unit pilots following the flight trials in May 1945. *(via Oughton)*

**249.** PK 312, the prototype Spitfire 22, seen early in 1945 with her original tail as fitted to the Mark 21. *(via Oughton)*

**250.** PK 312 seen later in 1945, with the enlarged tail surfaces which would be fitted to all Mark 22s and 24s delivered for service use. *(Vickers)*

cut-back rear fuselage and a 'tear-drop' canopy, changes which had not in the past resulted in the introduction of a new mark number. The first Mark 22 completed, PK 312, was delivered in March 1945 and had a performance essentially similar to that of production Mark 21s. Towards the end of the year this aircraft was fitted with the long-awaited enlarged tail, which increased the length overall to 31 ft 11 in. During a weigh-in at Boscombe Down in December 1945, fitted with the larger tail surfaces, PK 312 was found to have a normal loaded weight of 9,309 pounds or just 4 pounds more than the first production Mark 21. As expected the enlarged fin and tailplane improved handling and they became a feature of all Spitfire 22s delivered to RAF squadrons.

Only one regular Royal Air Force unit, No 73 Squadron in the Middle East, operated with Spitfire 22s and it did so for less than a year before it re-equipped with jet fighters in October 1948. The main user of the Spitfire 22 was the Auxiliary Air Force, twelve of whose squadrons operated this version until the last of them received jets in March 1951.

Only 278 Spitfire 22s were built. After service in the Royal Air Force 52 of these were exported: 22 went to what was then the Southern Rhodesian Air Force, 20 to the Royal Egyptian Air Force and 10 to the Syrian Air Force.

The Spitfire 23 was to have been externally similar to the Mark 22, but with a wing of revised cross-section with the leading edge raised by about an inch and many of the characteristics of the laminar flow wing designed for the Spiteful fighter. The revised wing was fitted to a Spitfire VIII, JG 204, which also had a re-designed wing root to reduce interference drag at the wing-fuselage joint. Jeffrey Quill flew the modified aircraft for the first time in January 1944. The advantages of the revised wing section were outweighed by its less pleasant handling characteristics, however, and the Mark 23 was never built.

The final Spitfire variant, the Mark 24, was in its initial form externally no different from the Mark 22; the main changes were the incorporation of two 33 gallon fuel tanks in the rear fuselage which when full increased the normal fully loaded weight of this aircraft by about 600 pounds compared with its predecessor. It also had wing fittings to carry rocket projectiles. Late production Spitfire 24s were distinguished by the fitting of the shorter-barrel Mark V Hispano cannon.

Fifty-four Spitfire 24s were built by Supermarine, and a further 27 were converted from Mark 22s, before the last of this version, VN 496, was delivered from the South Marston works in February 1948. Only one Royal Air Force Squadron, No 80, received the Spitfire 24. It re-equipped with the type in January 1948 while based at Guetersloh in Germany. In July 1949 it moved to Kai Tak, Hong Kong, and operated from there until January 1952 when it re-equipped with Hornet twin-engined fighters. Later some of the ex-80 Squadron Spitfire 24s were taken over by the Hong Kong Auxiliary Air Force, which operated them until April 1955.

**251.** PK 312 showing off the enlarged tailplane which went with the enlarged fin and rudder. *(Vickers)*

**252.** PK 664, one of the few Mark 22s fitted with contra-rotating propellers. *(via Oughton)*

**253.** A Spitfire 22 in standard service camouflage, operated by No 613 (City of Manchester) Squadron of the Royal Auxiliary Air Force, pictured in 1948 or early 1949. *(via Cain)*

**254.** The Spitfire 23 was to have been similar to the Mark 22, but with a wing of revised cross-section with many of the characteristics of the laminar flow wing designed for the Spiteful. The revised-section wing was fitted to a Mark VIII, JG 204 (above, with a standard wing seen below for comparison), and flight tested early in 1944. On the revised-section wing the leading edge was about 1 inch higher than on the standard wing to give a more symmetrical section; and at the root the section was further altered to reduce interference drag at the wing-fuselage joint. The revised-section wing did not produce a worthwhile improvement in the high speed handling characteristics of the Spitfire, however, and the Mark 23 was never built.

**255.** PK 570, a Mark 22 belonging to No 603 (City of Edinburgh) Squadron, Royal Auxiliary Air Force, painted silver over-all and bearing the unit's checker-board markings. *(via Batchelor)*

**256.** Spitfire 24s undergoing final assembly at the South Marston factory in 1947. Visible in the background, with contra-rotating propellers, are a couple of late model Seafire Mark 46 or 47s. *(Vickers)*

**257.** This late production Mark 24, VN 324, differs externally from the Mark 22 only in the shorter barrels of its Mark V Hispano cannon. *(Vickers)*

**258.** Believed to be the only Spitfire 24 to be fitted with contra-rotating propellers, PK 684 is seen at Brussels in 1946 after being flown there by Jeffrey Quill for a demonstration to the Royal Belgian Air Force. *(Vickers)*

259

**259.** Groundcrewmen working on a Spitfire 24 of No 80 Squadron at Kai Tak, Hong Kong, where the unit flew this version from July 1949 to January 1952.

**260, 261.** After No 80 Squadron re-equipped with Hornets early in 1952, some of its Spitfire 24s were taken over and flown by the Hong Kong Auxiliary Air Force which also operated from Kai Tak. These photographs show the fighters about to take off for their final flying past with the Hong Kong Auxiliary Air Force, in April 1955. *(Cairns)*

260

261

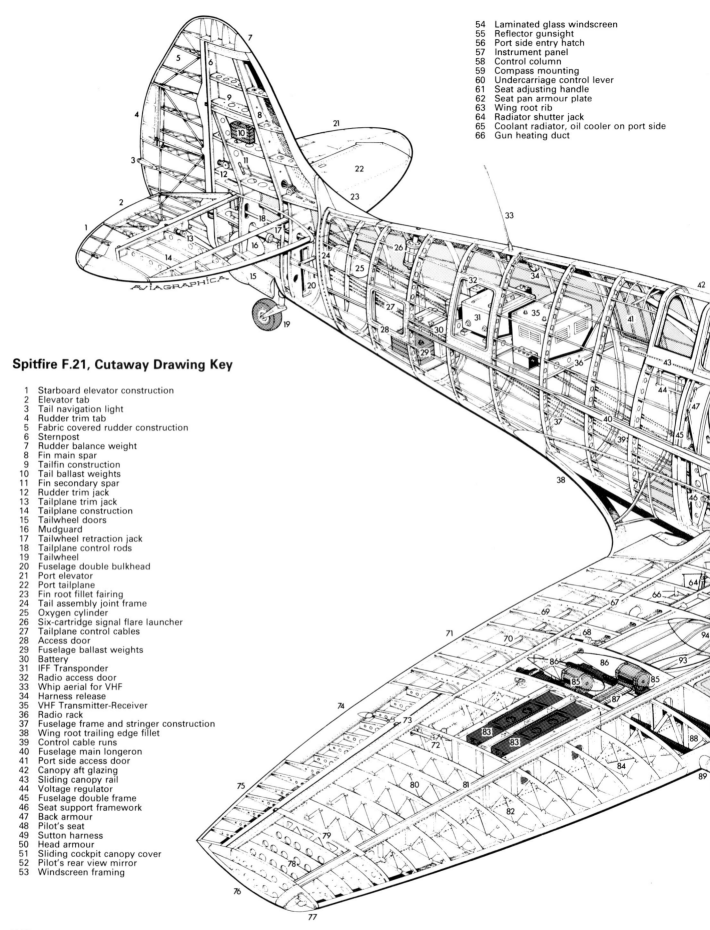

54 Laminated glass windscreen
55 Reflector gunsight
56 Port side entry hatch
57 Instrument panel
58 Control column
59 Compass mounting
60 Undercarriage control lever
61 Seat adjusting handle
62 Seat pan armour plate
63 Wing root rib
64 Radiator shutter jack
65 Coolant radiator, oil cooler on port side
66 Gun heating duct

## Spitfire F.21, Cutaway Drawing Key

1 Starboard elevator construction
2 Elevator tab
3 Tail navigation light
4 Rudder trim tab
5 Fabric covered rudder construction
6 Sternpost
7 Rudder balance weight
8 Fin main spar
9 Tailfin construction
10 Tail ballast weights
11 Fin secondary spar
12 Rudder trim jack
13 Tailplane trim jack
14 Tailplane construction
15 Tailwheel doors
16 Mudguard
17 Tailwheel retraction jack
18 Tailplane control rods
19 Tailwheel
20 Fuselage double bulkhead
21 Port elevator
22 Port tailplane
23 Fin root fillet fairing
24 Tail assembly joint frame
25 Oxygen cylinder
26 Six-cartridge signal flare launcher
27 Tailplane control cables
28 Access door
29 Fuselage ballast weights
30 Battery
31 IFF Transponder
32 Radio access door
33 Whip aerial for VHF
34 Harness release
35 VHF Transmitter-Receiver
36 Radio rack
37 Fuselage frame and stringer construction
38 Wing root trailing edge fillet
39 Control cable runs
40 Fuselage main longeron
41 Port side access door
42 Canopy aft glazing
43 Sliding canopy rail
44 Voltage regulator
45 Fuselage double frame
46 Seat support framework
47 Back armour
48 Pilot's seat
49 Sutton harness
50 Head armour
51 Sliding cockpit canopy cover
52 Pilot's rear view mirror
53 Windscreen framing

67 Wing rear spar
68 Flap hydraulic jack
69 Flap shroud ribs
70 Tubular flap spar
71 Starboard split trailing edge flap
72 Aileron control bellcrank
73 Aileron hinge
74 Aileron tab
75 Aluminium skinned aileron construction
76 Wing tip fairing
77 Starboard navigation light
78 Wing tip construction
79 Aileron outer hinge rib
80 Wing rib construction
81 Main spar
82 Leading edge nose ribs
83 Ammunition boxes, 150-rounds per gun
84 Mainwheel fairing door
85 Ammunition feed drums
86 Blister fairings
87 Ammunition belt feed
88 Hispano, 20-mm cannon barrels
89 Cannon barrel support fairing
90 Recoil springs
91 Fuel filler cap
92 Leading edge fuel tank, 17-Gal
93 Main undercarriage wheel well
94 Mainwheel blister fairing

95 Undercarriage retraction link
96 Undercarriage leg pivot
97 Shock absorber leg strut
98 Hydraulic brake pipe
99 Starboard mainwheel
100 Mainwheel leg fairing door
101 Undercarriage torque scissors
102 Fuel pipe runs
103 Main spar stub attachment
104 Lower main fuel tank, 48-Gal
105 Upper main fuel tank, 36-Gal
106 Fuel filler cap
107 Oil tank vent
108 Oil tank, 9-Gal
109 Oil tank access door
110 Engine compartment fireproof bulkhead
111 Port split trailing edge flap
112 Flap hydraulic jack
113 Flap synchronising jack
114 Port twin 20-mm Hispano cannon
115 Spent cartridge case ejector chute

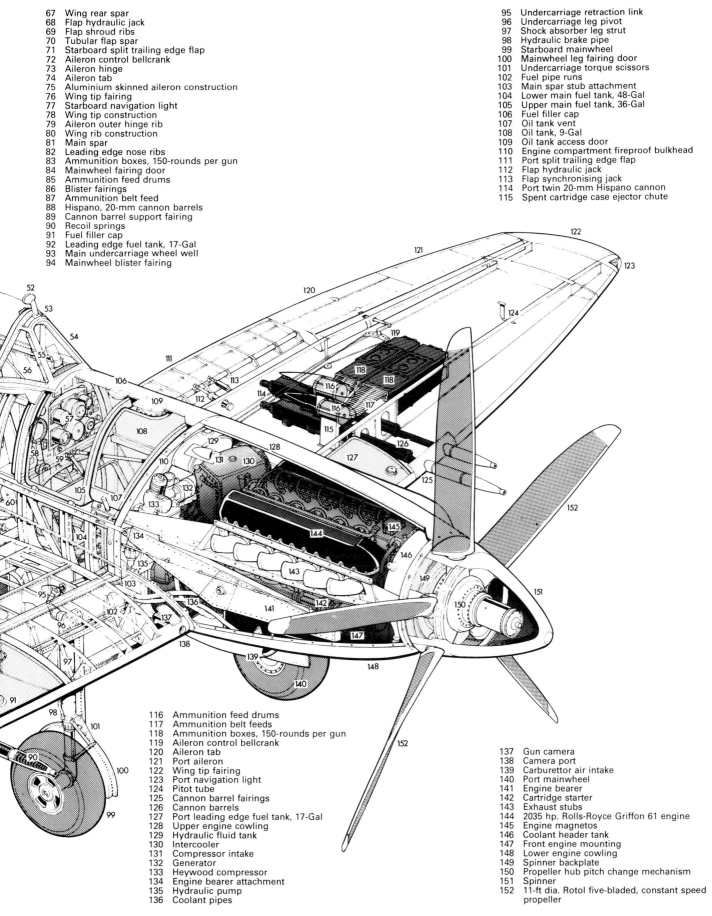

116 Ammunition feed drums
117 Ammunition belt feeds
118 Ammunition boxes, 150-rounds per gun
119 Aileron control bellcrank
120 Aileron tab
121 Port aileron
122 Wing tip fairing
123 Port navigation light
124 Pitot tube
125 Cannon barrel fairings
126 Cannon barrels
127 Port leading edge fuel tank, 17-Gal
128 Upper engine cowling
129 Hydraulic fluid tank
130 Intercooler
131 Compressor intake
132 Generator
133 Heywood compressor
134 Engine bearer attachment
135 Hydraulic pump
136 Coolant pipes

137 Gun camera
138 Camera port
139 Carburettor air intake
140 Port mainwheel
141 Engine bearer
142 Cartridge starter
143 Exhaust stubs
144 2035 hp. Rolls-Royce Griffon 61 engine
145 Engine magnetos
146 Coolant header tank
147 Front engine mounting
148 Lower engine cowling
149 Spinner backplate
150 Propeller hub pitch change mechanism
151 Spinner
152 11-ft dia. Rotol five-bladed, constant speed
    propeller

# Appendix A

## SPITFIRE F.21   PP 139

Figures taken from the trials report of this aircraft, the first to include the major airframe design alterations of the Mark 21, tested at Boscombe Down during the period September to November 1943. This machine differed from later production Mark 21s in that it was fitted with the Griffon 61 instead of the Griffon 65 engine which had slightly lower reduction gearing. Due to engine problems the full speed and climb measurements could not be completed and the performance report gave only the level speed measurements. At the time of the trial the condition of the aircraft was as follows:

Revised, Mark 21, wing with extended tips of thinner section
Metal covered ailerons with inset balance tabs
Four 20 mm cannon with muzzles sealed, ejection chutes open
Individual bulges on the top surface of the wing above each gun
Bulge above each undercarriage wheel well
Two fuel tanks in the leading edge of each wing, total capacity 36 gallons
Doors under each wing, to enclose the wheels completely when undercarriage retracted
Retractable tail wheel
Aircraft flush riveted overall
Air intake in a more forward position under the nose, compared with earlier Spitfires. No ice guard or air cleaner
Six single ejector exhausts on each side with fishtails

Modified windscreen with a curved front, forward of the normal windscreen. Sliding hood built up at front to match with revised windscreen
No rear view mirror
Whip aerial for VHF; no IFF aerials
Revised fin of increased area, with straight leading edge; rudder of increased area
Five-bladed Rotol propeller, 11 ft diameter

**Dimensions:** span 40 ft 4 in, length 32 ft 8 in
**Weights:** Tare weight 6,853 pounds
Fully loaded weight 9,124 pounds
**Performance:**

| Height feet | Top Speed mph |
|---|---|
| 4,000 | 390 |
| 8,000 | 412 |
| 12,000 | 434 |
| 20,000 | 431 |
| 25,800 | 457 |
| 30,000 | 451 |
| 34,000 | 444 |
| 38,000 | 434 |

# Appendix B

## SPITFIRE F.21    LA 187

Figures taken from the trials reports on this aircraft, the first production Mark 21, tested at Boscombe Down from November 1944 to July 1945. Like its predecessor PP 139, however, this aircraft was powered by a Griffon 61 (later production aircraft would have the Griffon 65). When it initially flew, LA 187 had pointed wing tips as fitted to PP 139. By the time of these trials, however, the pointed tips had been removed and the aircraft had the normal Mark 21-type wing. At the time of the trial LA 187 differed from PP 139 in the following respects:

Revised, Mark 21-type wing, without extended tips
Standard-type windscreen and canopy, as fitted to earlier versions of the Spitfire
Fin and rudder as fitted to production Mark XIVs
Rear view mirror

**Dimensions:** span 36 ft 11 in, length 32 ft 8 in
**Weights:** tare weight 6,985 pounds
Fully loaded weight 9,305 pounds
Wing loading when fully loaded, 38 pounds per square foot

**Performance:**

| Height feet | Top Speed mph | Time to Climb min | Rate of Climb ft/min |
|---|---|---|---|
| 4,000 | 389 | 0 m 54 s | 4,440 |
| 8,000 | 407 | 1 m 51 s | 4,000 |
| 12,000 | 411 | 2 m 54 s | 3,570 |
| 21,800 | 442 | | 3,200 |
| 26,000 | 439 | 7 m 06 s | 2,610 |
| 30,000 | 436 | 8 m 51 s | 2,030 |
| 34,000 | 432 | 11 m 09 s | 1,445 |
| 40,000 | 407 | 17 m 27 s | 575 |

Service ceiling (estimated)                42,400 feet

The report drew attention to the fact that the maximum speed of LA 187 was 15 to 20 mph slower than PP 139, its predecessor:

Part of this difference may be attributed to the fact that LA 187 was fitted with a flat windscreen, as opposed to the curved type on PP 139, and the former aircraft also had an external rear-view mirror, which was not fitted to PP 139. Tests on a Spitfire aircraft at the RAE indicated that the difference in performance attributable to these two items was on 3 mph TAS. The remaining speed loss of the production aircraft would be attributed to differences of surface finish, engine powers and propeller efficiencies.

Certainly LA 187 was not in a good external condition at the time of the speed trials:

As the aircraft had been engaged on a long programme of tests, both at this Establishment and at the Contractor's works, the external condition had deteriorated considerably when the performance trials were made. The paintwork was chipped and some of the filler had worked out of the joints in the wing leading edge.

# Appendix C

## TACTICAL TRIAL: SPITFIRE F.21    LA 201

The account below is taken from the report of the tactical trial of an early production Mark 21, LA 201, flown by the Air Fighting Development Unit at Wittering in November and December 1944. The report is probably the most critical ever written on the Spitfire.

\*   \*   \*

### Introduction

Aircraft No LA 201 was allotted for these trials and was fully representative of the aircraft now being delivered to squadrons. It was flown throughout completely equipped and fully armed. Eight pilots from this Establishment and two outside pilots have flown the aircraft.

### Description

#### Role

The Spitfire 21 is a short-range, medium-high altitude single seat fighter, designed to replace the Spitfire XIV.

#### Airframe

Compared with the Spitfire XIV the mainplanes of the Spitfire 21 have been strengthened and have tips of thinner section. The ailerons are of all metal construction and are fitted with inset balance tabs. The rudder and elevator are of metal construction, fabric covered, and are provided with trimming tabs, the elevator having the normal Supermarine enlarged area horn balance. Split flaps are fitted between the inboard ends of the ailerons and the mainplane root ends.

The undercarriage consists of two separate cantilever main wheel units and a tail wheel unit, all of which are retractable. When retracted all the units are completely faired in, the main units by fairings on the struts and doors on the mainplanes, and the tail unit by doors in the fuselage. The undercarriage is 7¾'' wider than on previous marks of the Spitfire, and the oleo legs have been lengthened approximately 4½'' to accommodate the extra length of the propeller blades.

The operational weight with full fuel and ammunition is given as 9,182 pounds. Supermarine state the wing loading of the aircraft is 38 pounds per square foot. The corresponding figures for the Spitfire XIV are 8,490 pounds and 35 pounds per square foot.

#### Engine

The power plant is a Rolls-Royce Griffon 61 which develops 2,015 hp at 7,500 ft in MS gear, and 1,810 hp at 22,000 ft in FS gear. The Spitfire XIV is fitted with a Griffon 65 which develops the same power but has a reduction gear of .51 to 1 as against .45 to 1. The propeller is a Rotol five bladed propeller of 11 ft diameter, which is 7'' greater in diameter than that fitted to the Spitfire XIV. The Spitfire 21 is equipped for operation in any part of the world.

#### Fuel Capacity

Compared with the Spitfire XIV, the Spitfire 21 has two additional fuel tanks each of 5½ gallons inboard of the mainplane tanks, giving a total fuel capacity of 120 gallons as against 109 gallons.

#### Armament

The armament consists of four Mk II 20 mm Hispano guns, mounted two in each mainplane outboard of the airscrew. Two ammunition boxes, one for each gun, are housed outboard of the guns and aft of the main spar. The forward box is for the inboard gun and the aft box for the outboard gun and hold 175 rounds and 150 rounds respectively. The cannon are fired pneumatically by means of a selective push button on the control column spade grip. Pressing the top of the button fires the inboard cannon, pressing the bottom fires the outboard cannon, and all four cannon are fired simultaneously if the centre of the button is pressed. The aircraft on trial was fitted with the standard Mark II* sight. A bomb carrier for either a 250 pound or 500 pound bomb can be fixed underneath the fuselage on the drop tank fittings.

#### Armour

The armour protection is designed to give protection against 20 mm AP Mauser ammunition within a 20° cone to the rear and against 13 mm AP ammunition within a 20° cone from ahead.

#### Cockpit Layout

The flying controls are conventional, with a spade grip type control column and a rudder bar. The controls for the throttle and propeller are interconnected and it is understood from Supermarine that all later production models will incorporate this modification. The flaps are lowered pneumatically and are controllable by a 3 position butterfly lever marked 'Up', 'Air Off', and 'Down'. To lower the flaps the lever is turned to the 'Down' position, and to raise them, through the 'Air Off' position to the 'Up' position. When the flaps are fully up the lever must be turned to the 'Air Off' position to prevent loss of pressure.

### Flying Limitations

The maximum speed of this aircraft is restricted to 450 mph Indicated at all altitudes, pending the completion of further diving trials at A & AEE Boscombe Down. Intentional spinning is prohibited.

When carrying long range fuel tanks (30, 45 or 90 gallon), the following limitations must be observed:

- (a) None of the tanks is to be jettisoned at speeds exceeding 300 mph Indicated.
- (b) When the 90 gallon tank is carried the aircraft is limited to gentle manoeuvres.

When carrying drop tanks or stores, the maximum permissible take-off weight is 10,000 pounds. The maximum permissible weight for landing, except in an emergency, is 9,250 pounds.

### Handling in the Air

#### Take-off

Full port rudder trim, ie control wound right back, is used for take-off and the throttle should be opened slowly as the aircraft swings to starboard, although not so badly as the Spitfire XIV. This swing can be held easily on the rudder. Except on very short runways it should not be necessary to exceed +18 pounds boost at maximum revs (2,750) as the take-off run is short, being approximately 500 yards at this throttle setting and 400 yards at +12 pounds boost (take-off) setting. Immediately after take-off the retrimming necessary in yaw and the extreme sensitiveness of the elevator control make it difficult to hold the aircraft in a steady climb until a speed of 180 mph Indicated is reached, and careful flying and attention to trim is necessary.

#### Landing

Landing is perfectly straightforward and the actual touchdown is more easy than with previous marks of Spitfire as the wider undercarriage and greater weight help to keep the aircraft on the ground.

## Flying Controls

The aircraft is unstable in the yawing plane, especially at altitude and at high speeds. The rudder is extremely sensitive to small movements and very careful flying is necessary to avoid skidding and slipping.

Aileron control is light and positive at all heights and at all speeds up to 350 mph indicated. Above this speed the ailerons tend to stiffen, the deterioration being more rapid above 400 mph indicated but nevertheless they are the best yet encountered on any mark of Spitfire.

Although the elevator control is positive in action and the aircraft is stable in pitch, constant correction is necessary, particularly at low speed and at high altitude at all speeds.

Trimming tabs are provided for rudder and elevators. Trimming is at all times extremely critical, and harsh use of the trimming tabs is to be avoided. Reaction to acceleration in the dive, deceleration in the climb and change of throttle, is marked.

## General Handling

Whilst this aircraft is not unstable in pitch, above 25,000 feet the instability in yaw makes it behave as if it were unstable about all three axes. Because of its higher wing loading the high speed stall comes in earlier than with other marks of Spitfire and in a steep turn the general feeling of instability, combined with its critical trimming qualities, is unpleasant. The control characteristics are such that this aircraft is most difficult to fly accurately and compares most unfavourably with other modern fighters.

## Search and Sighting View

The all-round search view from the pilot's cockpit is good although, as with the Spitfire XIV, the view straight ahead is poor due to the longer nose of the aircraft. No trouble was experienced with misting-up of the front panel. The sighting view is similar to the Spitfire XIV and gives 4° view over the nose as against 3½° on the Spitfire IX.

## Low Flying

At low altitude in conditions of bad visibility, the comparatively poor view from the cockpit and the feeling of instability makes this aircraft almost dangerous to fly. It is far too sensitive on the elevator and the slightest twitch by the pilot is sufficient to cause a loss or gain in height. In conditions of good visibility the accurate flying which is at all times necessary still limits the pilot's ability to search.

## Aerobatics

The aerobatic qualities of this aircraft may seem good on the first impression because of the excellent aileron control, but in fact the instability and constant trimming required more than outweigh this advantage and make the aircraft less easy for aerobatics than previous Spitfires.

## Formation Flying

This aircraft is less easy to fly in formation than any other modern fighter; formation becomes increasingly difficult at altitude.

## Operational Ceiling

The height at which the rate of climb fell below 1,000 feet per minute was 36,500 feet.

## Night Flying

The aircraft was flown in moonlight conditions only and without blinkers fitted. The exhaust glare did not interfere with taxying, but for landing it was necessary to keep the engine running fairly fast as the exhaust glow and stream of sparks was pronounced with the engine throttled right back. The exhaust glow could be easily seen from the ground at a range of 1,000 feet and for dark conditions it would be necessary to fit blinkers. Apart from the stability and trimming qualities already mentioned, the aircraft was comparatively easy to fly and land.

## Instrument Flying

Owing to the pronounced sensitivity of the elevator control the aircraft is difficult to fly on instruments; this difficulty would be exaggerated to outside members of a formation, who would also be upset by the considerable alterations in the yawing plane caused by sudden movements of the throttle.

## Sighting Platform

The good aileron control of the Spitfire 21 enables the pilot to anticipate the manoeuvres of any other fighter, but due to lack of stability it is difficult to hold the sight on the target especially when changes of direction are rapid. The effects of instability on the aircraft as a sighting platform will be more pronounced when it is fitted with a gyro gun sight.

It can be flown accurately enough for ground attack purposes in the hands of an experienced pilot and under trial conditions but the elimination of skid is more difficult with this aircraft than with any other modern fighter and makes it unsuitable for the ground attack role.

## Pilot's Comfort

The sliding hood is the normal Spitfire balloon hood, which has never been comfortable for a large pilot to operate; in particular the forward spring catch remains a latent danger to the pilot, as it strikes his head whenever the hood is pulled back with the seat in the up position. The hood on aircraft LA 201 was not a good fit and allowed a stream of air to flow onto the right cheek of the pilot.

The position of the cine-gun switch at the bottom right hand side of the spade grip is unsatisfactory and requires adjustment so that the button can be operated without altering the position of the hand.

## Tactical Comparison with Spitfire XIV using +18 Pounds Boost

### Range and Endurance

As the consumption of the Griffon 61 is similar to that of the Griffon 65 the Spitfire 21 has greater range and endurance than the Spitfire XIV, measured by the extra 11 gallons of fuel. This has been calculated to represent a difference of 15 miles in radius of action and 10 minutes in endurance.

### Speeds

As a result of checks carried out by this Establishment on figures from Supermarine, it appears that the Spitfire 21 is approximately 10-12 mph faster than the Spitfire XIV at all altitudes.

### Acceleration in straight and level flight

The Spitfire 21 and the Spitfire XIV have approximately the same acceleration in straight and level flight. After opening to full power from maximum cruise settings (2,400 revs +7 pounds boost on both aircraft) each aircraft takes about 2½ minutes to reach maximum speed.

### Climbs

In the climb at maximum power (2,750 revs +18 pounds boost on both aircraft) there was very little to choose between the two at all altitudes. Up to 15,000 feet the Spitfire XIV had a slight advantage, above 15,000 feet the Spitfire 21 was slightly the better.

### Zoom Climbs

The Spitfire 21 has a slightly better zoom climb than the Spitfire XIV.

### Dive

Initially the Spitfire 21 out-dives the Spitfire XIV, but after reaching a speed of 350 mph Indicated there is little difference between the two aircraft.

### Turning Circles

The Spitfire 21 is definitely out-turned by the Spitfire XIV at all speeds. As previously stated, the Spitfire 21 is not pleasant in the turn and the high speed stall comes on early.

## Rate of Roll

At speeds below 300 mph Indicated there is little to choose between the two aircraft, but above this speed the Spitfire 21 becomes increasingly superior due to its lighter ailerons.

## Conclusions

The Spitfire 21 posseses the following advantages over the Spitfire XIV:

(i)  It has a slightly greater range
(ii)  It is faster at all heights by some 10 to 12 mph
(iii)  It has slightly better acceleration in the dive
(iv)  It has better aileron control at speeds above 300 mph
(v)  It has the greater fire power

The instability in the yawing plane and the critical trimming characteristics of this aircraft make it difficult to fly accurately under the easiest conditions and as a sighting platform it is unsatisfactory both for air-to-air gunnery and ground attack. Its handling qualities compare unfavourably with all earlier marks of Spitfire and with other modern fighters and more than nullify its advantages in performance and fire power.

The Spitfire XIV is a better all round fighter than the Spitfire 21. The handling qualities of successive marks of the basic Spitfire design have gradually deteriorated until, as exemplified in the Spitfire 21, they prejudice the pilot's ability to exploit the increased performance.

## Recommendations

It is recommended that the Spitfire 21 be withdrawn from operations until the instability in the yawing plane has been removed and that it be replaced by the Spitfire XIV or Tempest V until this can be done.

If it is not possible then it must be emphasised that, although the Spitfire 21 is not a dangerous aircraft to fly, pilots must be warned of its handling qualities and in its present state it is not likely to prove a satisfactory fighter.

No further attempts should be made to perpetuate the Spitfire family.

# Appendix D

## TACTICAL TRIAL: MODIFIED SPITFIRE
## F.21   LA 215

The account below is taken from the report of the tactical trial of the modified early production Mark 21, LA 215, flown by the Air Fighting Development Unit at Wittering in March 1945, to discover whether the alterations made had overcome the handling problems previously encountered with the Mark 21.

*   *   *

### Introduction

Aircraft No LA 215 was delivered from the A & AEE Boscombe Down and was flown by six pilots from this Establishment who had taken part in the previous trials, and by Wing Commander Oxspring of RAF Manston.

### Description

Spitfire 21 No LA 215 was loaded by the Contractor to represent a typical full service load, ie an all up weight of 9,160 pounds with the centre of gravity 4.5'' aft, and incorporating the following modifications:

(i) Deletion of the balance action of the rudder tab.

(ii) Reduction in gearing of the elevator trimming control to render it less sensitive.

(iii) Fitting of a metal elevator with slightly reduced area horn which has its inboard edge rounded off.

### Results of Trials

#### Take-off

Take-off is similar to that in the production Spitfire Mark 21 but once airborne there is a marked improvement in the handling of the modified aircraft. The hunting which was previously experienced as a result of the extreme sensitiveness of the elevator control is no longer apparent and it is possible to put the aircraft into a quick turn in either direction without unpleasantness. Very much less trimming is required and altogether the elevator and the rudder control are more steady.

#### Landing

The approach to landing is improved owing to the more steady elevator control, while the actual touch-down remains straightforward.

#### Flying Controls

The reduced gearing of the elevator trimmer control makes smooth and accurate flying possible, but the rudder trimmer control is still very sensitive to small movements and careful flying is necessary if skid is to be avoided. It is understood that the makers have a modification in hand to reduce the sensitivity of the rudder trimmer tab control. Aileron control is not affected by these modifications.

#### General Handling

The modifications carried out to this aircraft have resulted in an improvement of the general handling characteristics at all heights. The high speed stall comes in earlier than with other marks of Spitfire, but the usual warning is given to the pilot in the form of heavy shuddering.

#### Low Flying

As a result of the modifications the aircraft is much more satisfactory for low flying than the production version and even in conditions of bad visibility when the pilot has to weave, the control is good.

#### Aerobatics

The aircraft compares favourably with other marks of Spitfire for aerobatics at all heights up to 30,000 feet, although the sensitiveness of the rudder trimmer control requires careful watching.

#### Formation Flying

It is considered that the average pilot should have no difficulty now in maintaining formation for all accepted manoeuvres at all altitudes.

#### Instrument Flying

Here again the reduction in sensitivity of the elevator control allows the pilot to fly on his instruments smoothly and it is considered that the aircraft is now acceptable for cloud flying by formations of aircraft. The pilot can maintain a steady rate of climb with hands off the controls. It is recommended, however, that sudden movements of the throttle be avoided to obviate inducing a strong yawing moment.

#### Sighting Platform

There has been considerable improvement in the qualities of the aircraft as a sighting platform and it is considered that the average pilot should be able to hold his sight on the target throughout all combat manoeuvres. The rudder was noticeably heavier than on the production aircraft and reduces the amount of unintentional side-slip, except at speeds in excess of 400 mph Indicated when the pilot is liable to over-correct.

### Conclusions

The critical trimming characteristics reported on the production Spitfire 21 have been largely eliminated by the modifications carried out to this aircraft. Its handling qualities have benfited to a corresponding extent and it is now considered suitable both for instrument flying and low flying.

It is considered that the modifications to the Spitfire 21 make it a satisfactory combat aircraft for the average pilot.

### Recommendations

It is recommended that the modifications carried out on the Spitfire 21 tested be incorporated immediately in all production models, including the present Squadron equipped, and that the aircraft is then cleared for operational flying.

# Appendix E

## TRIAL OF SPITFIRE F.21 WITH CONTRA-ROTATING PROPELLER, LA 218

The account below is taken from the report of the trial of Spitfire F.21 LA 218, fitted with a contra-rotating propeller, flown from Tangmere by pilots of the Air Fighting Development Squadron on 23 May 1945.

\* \* \*

### Introduction

Spitfire F.21 No LA 218 was delivered from Messrs Vickers Supermarines at High Post on 23 May 1945 for brief handling trials and was flown by nine experienced pilots from this Establishment.

This aircraft was fitted with a Rotol contra-rotating propeller and had a slight modification to the rudder. Otherwise it was representative of the production model.

As the aircraft was available for only one afternoon it was not possible to carry out a full and comprehensive trial, and it must be borne in mind that the opinions expressed are based on one flight only by each pilot. However, it was felt that the opinions were so unanimous that it was worth while putting them on paper to make them available for wider distribution.

### Handling on the Ground

Taxi-ing is quite straightforward and exactly similar to the normal Spitfire.

### Handling in the Air

#### Take-off

Although the take-off run appears to be longer than on the normal Spitfire 21, the actual handling is much improved. Provided the rudder has been trimmed there is no tendency to swing whatever and it is possible to climb the aircraft immediately, with hands and feet free from the controls and without skid or slip. If correct trim has not been applied there is a decided swing once the aircraft becomes airborne.

#### Flight

Handling in the air is remarkably pleasant and all manoeuvres, including aerobatics, can be carried out without attention to rudder trim and irrespective of throttle setting and/or the speed. It is possible to loop and slow roll with feet free from the rudder.

#### Throttle Response

Violent opening of the throttle produced surging, but there is no indication of this if the throttle is opened smoothly. The engine of the aircraft tested appeared to run excessively rough at most throttle settings and at high rpm there appeared to be a phase of vibration which could not be attributed to the engine rough running.

#### Ground Attack

In dives up to 60 degrees and at all speeds and throttle settings the sight can be held on the ground target without the slightest tendency to skid or slip. The aircraft becomes tail heavy at about 280 mph and a large forward trimming movement is necessary in order to fly 'hands off', especially above 400 mph Indicated; but once trimmed the dive is absolutely straight. With hands and feet off the controls, recovery from the dive was carried out by means of tail trimming and the ensuing climb was found to be without tendency to turn, skid, or slip. Moreover, the light aileron control and excellent manoeuvrability of this aircraft at high speed make it eminently suitable for straffing where a quick turn on to the target and violent evasive action are frequently required.

#### Combat

The throttle can be opened and closed without any noticeable change of aim in azimuth but the absence of need for rudder trimming emphasises the importance of correct elevator trim, which previously might have passed unnoticed. The aircraft handles pleasantly in steep turns and shows no tendency to tighten up.

#### Landing

Landing is straightforward with a very marked braking effect with the propeller in the fully fine position. There is no tendency to swing but the landing run appeared to be considerably longer on the aircraft tested than on other marks of Spitfire. This may have been due to the fact that the engine was idling too fast as throttling back on the engine in question was liable to cause a complete cut-out. When the throttle is opened near stalling speed, for example to correct a bad landing, the lack of torque greatly improves the stability of the aircraft and reduces the risk of accident.

### Conclusions

The Spitfire 21 with the contra-rotating propeller shows a considerable improvement in handling over the normal aircraft, and allows all manoeuvres to be carried out without attention to rudder trim.

The elimination of the need for rudder trim during ground attack reduces the possibility of skid at the moment of firing. This factor has always been one of the major sources of aiming error in the past. The fitting of a contra-rotating airscrew has now turned the aircraft into a very reasonable gun platform and without any apparent loss in performance.

Air-to-air combat is similarly enhanced and it was found that no change of trim was necessary with change of throttle setting. A considerable improvement in sighting accuracy may be expected.

### Recommendations

From the limited amount of flying carried out by the Central Fighter Establishment on the Spitfire F.21 fitted with the contra-rotating propeller it would appear that skid, the major source of error in accuracy for ground attack, is largely eliminated by the introduction of the contra-rotating propeller. This innovation promises such advantage for conventional airscrew fighters that it is strongly recommended that another aircraft with a contra-rotating propeller be attached to the Central Fighter Establishment as soon as possible for intensive and exhaustive tactical trials.

# 20.

# THE SPITFIRE
# SUMMED UP

From the time the first metal of the prototype was cut at Woolston in the spring of 1935, until the final production Spitfire 24 was rolled out of the South Marston works in February 1948, a total of some 20,400 Spitfires of 22 different versions were built (there are some discrepancies in the official records concerning the exact number). This figure excludes the Seafire, which remained in production until March 1949. During that period Reginald Mitchell's basic design was developed out of almost all recognition. Jeffrey Quill summed up this part of the Spitfire story as follows:

It was a case of having the right man at the right time: Mitchell, the very clever designer and innovator; Smith, the hard pragmatic engineer who oversaw the development and made it all work. And overshadowing all else was the intense urgency to produce the aircraft in the numbers required and get them tested, without relaxing standards, while at the same time being involved in a neck-and-neck technical race with the enemy. This gave rise to an immense drive for improvement and performance. The result of it all was a train of development utterly unique in the history of aviation. It could never happen now—modern combat aircraft simply do not have that potential for development.

Probably the story of the Spitfire would have been quite different had Mitchell lived to see the end of the war. He was an innovator rather than a developer and almost certainly he would have preferred to produce a series of new designs—as his rival Sidney Camm did with the Hurricane, Typhoon, Tempest and Fury series of fighters—rather than try to squeeze everything possible out of the design he had. Be that as it may, the Spitfire saw the Royal Air Force through the entire era of the piston-engined monoplane fighter; and at its end the Mark 24 was a match for the best piston-engined fighters being built anywhere else.

Certainly the Spitfire was developed to a prodigious extent. Compared with the prototype in its initial form, the Mark 24 was more than one-third faster, had its rate of climb almost doubled and its fire-power increased by a factor of five. At its maximum permissible take-off weight the Mark 24 tipped the scales at just over 6,790 pounds more than the prototype; this is a weight equivalent to 30 passengers each with 40 pounds of baggage on board a modern airliner, and it shows just how far the design had been pushed (the final Seafire 47 had a maximum permissible take-off weight slightly higher still).

As we have observed, the story of the development and production of the Spitfire did not run quite so smoothly as

previous accounts on this aircraft have suggested. Initially the fighter proved very difficult to produce in quantity and there were considerable delays in getting it into service. But the problems were solved and by the summer of 1940 the Royal Air Force had just enough Spitfires to enable it to win the Battle of Britain.

Nor, as has usually been implied, was every version of the Spitfire an excellent fighting machine. The Mark VI, the first pressurised version, handled poorly at high altitude and was not popular with the operational squadrons. The Mark 21 in its initial form was considered by service test pilots to be 'unsatisfactory both for air-to-air gunnery and ground attack'; later, however, its control problems were sorted out and it became a first-class fighting aircraft. Yet such relative failures are the exceptions and for the most part the derivatives from Reginald Mitchell's design, at the time of their construction, were numbered amongst the best fighters and reconnaissance aircraft in the world.

On the evolution and testing of the Spitfire, and the procedure under which successive versions were accepted by the RAF, Jeffrey Quill made some interesting remarks which put matters into perspective:

In general it is true to say that almost every major change made to the Spitfire, in the course of its remarkable development history, tended to be in some way or other detrimental to its handling qualities in the air. These effects had wherever possible to be counter-acted as we went along, by means which did not result in large increases in weight, interruptions in production or other undesirable side effects.

The main factors which caused a deterioration in handling were:
(1) Longer and longer noses (caused by larger and more powerful engines).
(2) Progressive increases in propeller solidity (total blade area), to absorb the increases in power.
(3) Increased moments of inertia due to increases in, and re-distribution of, mass.
(4) Extended flight envelopes in both speed and altitude.
(5) The carriage of greatly increased fuel and armament loads, both internally and externally.

It was the task of the firm to keep the handling of the Spitfire within manageable limits as all of this went on, without recourse to unnecessarily large changes to the basic design.

Every major design change or major modification to the Spitfire was initiated, and every new variant conceived, either in response to an official requirement or as a result of official or unofficial contacts with RAF officers at all levels. All of this was done in the continual search for improvement, to keep ahead of the enemy.

It was my job as Chief Test Pilot at Supermarine, helped by my colleague pilots, to test each major change of the aircraft. Apart from establishing the performance of each version in the air, we had to ensure that its handling qualities were acceptable. If they were not, we had to test it with various modifications until in my opinion the version was acceptable. So I had to exercise my judgement and recommend to the Chief Designer whether or not a modified aircraft was likely to be acceptable to Boscombe Down. In making this judgement several factors had to be considered, not least of them the urgency of the RAF requirement (for example, given the position Fighter Command found itself in early in 1942 with the Focke-Wulf 190, almost anything was acceptable to get the Spitfire IX into service).

Every major modification or change, especially those affecting performance or handling qualities, was exhaustively tested by the firm before submission to the Aircraft and Armament Experimental Establishment at Boscombe Down for official approval (this was a contractual requirement, but we should have done it anyway). Establishing the accurate performance of any variant involved a lot of flying and a great deal of full power bashing of the engine and systems. As time went on Boscombe Down came increasingly to accept the firm's figures, making only spot checks themselves, in order to save wear and tear on prototypes. In other words Boscombe Down provided the official seal of approval, though many of the performance figures quoted in their reports were in fact measured by Supermarine's experimental flight test unit at Worthy Down, later at High Post.

The A and AEE made its own judgements on the aircraft's handling and other qualities. However, if there was disagreement between them and the firm about what was acceptable, this was usually resolved during meetings between the two sides.

The Air Fighting Development Unit represented Fighter Command, and thus the main users of the Spitfire. They did a most useful job in relating the various British fighters to those of the enemy and in developing tactics on behalf of the Command. They were fully entitled to express their opinions about the handling of aircraft and they certainly did so. But the people at Boscombe Down were the final arbiters of what was fit for service use and what was not, and whether or not an aircraft met its specifications and contractual conditions. This was a principle which had to be firmly upheld, when occasionally too many people started to shout the odds.

No assessment of the story of the development of the Spitfire can be complete without mention of the parallel development of the Rolls-Royce engines which powered it, the Merlin and the Griffon. Engine power rose from 990 hp from the 27 litre Merlin Type C of the prototype, to 1,580 hp from the Mark 66 of the same volume fitted to the Spitfire IX; but with the one-third increase in power went a weight increase of only one-seventh. With modifications the basic Spitfire airframe was able to accommodate the 36.7 litre Griffon engine which developed 2,220 horsepower—more than double the power of the original Merlin for only one-third more weight; and all of this, within an acceptably small increase in size over the earlier engine.

So much for the technical side of the Spitfire story. But the Spitfire was more than a piece of machinery, albeit a clever one: it became a symbol of defiance and hope for Britain and her allies in the dark days of 1940, of victory in the air during the years of conflict that followed, and today of nostalgia amongst those who lived through those hectic times. It is almost eighty years since Orville Wright became the first man to make a sustained flight in a heavier-than-air machine, and about seventy since aeroplanes first began to extend the horizons of armies and navies. In the turbulent history of military aviation that followed these first tentative steps no aircraft type has carved a deeper niche than Reginald Mitchell's little fighter, which someone else chose to call 'Spitfire'.

# LIST OF SOURCES

*Aeroplane Spotter* magazine: 'Spitfire Notebook' series of articles, June 1946 to October 1947

Cross, Roy and Scarborough Gerald: *Spitfire,* Patrick Stephens Ltd

Flying Logbooks: G. Pickering, J. Quill

Geust, Carl-Fredrik, Kalevi Keskinen, Klaus Niska and Kari Stenman: *Red Stars in the Sky,* Tietoteos, Finland

Ivanov, Colonel A. L.: *War Memoires*

Hooton, Ted: *Spitfire Special,* Ian Allan
  *Supermarine Spitfire Mk 1-XVI,* Osprey
  *Supermarine Spitfire Mk XII-24,* Osprey

Mansbridge, Ernie: Unpublished memoranda concerning the testing of the prototype Spitfire

Moss, Peter: *Spitfire,* Ducimus

Official Handbook: *The Spitfire V Manual,* Arms and Armour Press

Price, Alfred: *Spitfire at War,* Ian Allan
  *FW 190 at War,* Ian Allan
  *Blitz on Britain,* Ian Allan
  *Spitfire, a Documentary History,* Jane's
  *World War II Fighter Conflict,* Jane's
  *Battle of Britain: the Hardest Day,* Jane's

Profile Publications: No 39 *Supermarine S4-S6B,* Andrews and Cox
  No 42 *Spitfire I and II,* Moyes
  No 166 *Spitfire V,* Hooton
  No 206 *Spitfire IX,* Moss and Batchelor
  No 246 *Spitfire XIV and XVIII,* Batchelor

Public Record Office, Kew
  Air 2/2824 and 2825 cover general development of Spitfire
  Air 6/26 et seq, minutes of meetings of S of S for Air
  Avia 18/636 and /682 Spitfire trials reports, A & AEE

Robertson, Bruce: *Spitfire — the Story of a Famous Fighter,* Harleyford

Royal Aeronautical Society, Southampton: *Forty Years of the Spitfire*

Royal Air Force Museum, Hendon: Supermarine company papers

Taylor, John and Maurice Allward: *Spitfire,* Harborough Ltd

# INDEX